THE YEAR OF THE LASH

Early American Places is a collaborative project of the University of Georgia Press, New York University Press, and Northern Illinois University Press. The series is supported by the Andrew W. Mellon Foundation. For more information, please visit www.earlyamericanplaces.org.

The Year of the Lash

Free People of Color in Cuba and the Nineteenth-Century Atlantic World

MICHELE REID-VAZQUEZ

The University of Georgia Press
ATHENS AND LONDON

Athens, Georgia 30602
www.ugapress.org

The paper in this book meets the guidelines for permanence and durability of the Committee on Production Guidelines for Book Longevity of the Council on Library Resources.

Printed in the United States of America

15 14 13 12 11 P 5 4 3 2 1

LIBRARY OF CONGRESS CATALOGING-IN-PUBLICATION DATA

Reid-Vazquez, Michele.

The year of the lash : free people of color in Cuba and the nineteenth-century Atlantic world / Michele Reid-Vazquez.

p. cm. — (Early American places)

Includes bibliographical references and index.

ISBN-13: 978-0-8203-3575-9 (hardcover : alk. paper)

ISBN-10: 0-8203-3575-4 (hardcover : alk. paper)

ISBN-13: 978-0-8203-4068-5 (pbk. : alk. paper)

ISBN-10: 0-8203-4068-5 (pbk. : alk. paper)

1. Cuba—History—Negro Conspiracy, 1844. 2. Cuba—History—Negro Conspiracy, 1844—Influence. 3. Blacks—Cuba—History—19th century. 4. Social conflict—Cuba—History—19th century. 5. Cuba—Race relations—History—19th century. 6. Blacks—Atlantic Ocean Region—History—19th century. I. Title.

F1783.R35 2011

972.91'05—dc22

2011010448

British Library Cataloging-in-Publication Data available

To the next generation: Reid Alejandro, Maliq, Desmond, Simone, and Evan

Contents

Acknowledgments

The development and completion of *The Year of the Lash* has been a shared journey. This project would not have come to fruition without the initial support of several faculty at the University of Texas at Austin. I owe a special thanks to Aline Helg and Toyin Falola, who shepherded the dissertation phase of this study and continued to make suggestions as I converted the work into a book manuscript. I would also like to thank Jonathan Brown, Ginny Burnett, Susan Deans-Smith, Myron Gutmann, James Sidbury, and Pauline Strong for their guidance and support.

Critical financial assistance from the following institutions and organizations facilitated research in Cuba and Spain: the University of Texas at Austin's Department of History, Institute of Latin American Studies, College of Liberal Arts, and Study Abroad Office; the Fulbright Commission, the Conference on Latin American History, and the Program for Cultural Cooperation at the Spanish Ministry of Education, Culture, and Sports in United States Universities. The knowledgeable staff at the Archivo General de Indias in Seville, the Archivo Histórico Nacional in Madrid, and the Archivo Nacional de Cuba, the Biblioteca Nacional José Martí, and the Instituto de Literatura y Lingüística in Havana, as well as the insights of Asmaa Bourhass, Tomás Fernández Robaina, Fé Iglesias García, and Pedro Pablo Rodríguez enriched this study.

Numerous institutions provided financial support for revising the manuscript. A postdoctoral fellowship from the Center for the Americas at Wesleyan University enabled me to initiate changes and conduct additional research. I especially thank Ann Wightman, who provided early comments on converting the dissertation to book form, as well as Demetrius Eudell, Patricia Hill, Kēhaulani Kauanui, Claire Potter, Lorelle Semley, Anthony Webster, and Carol Wright for creating a collegial atmosphere in which to nurture this project. I also thank Adriana Naveda Chavez-Hita for her guidance and Irina Córdoba for her research assistance in Mexico. Scholarships from the Newberry Library and the University of Florida allowed me to explore their rich collections, and funding from my home institution, Georgia State University, facilitated indexing and the presentation of chapters-in-progress at conferences. I would also like to thank Jeff Needell and Richard Phillips for their assistance and hospitality in Gainesville.

A postdoctoral fellowship at Emory University's Fox Center for Humanistic Inquiry and a summer scholarship from the John Carter Brown Library enabled me to complete manuscript revisions. My interdisciplinary reading group with Regine Jackson, Esther Jones, and Yael Simpson Fletcher was phenomenal, and Yael's editorial and indexing skills have been invaluable. Lively discussions with staff and scholars in both settings, particularly Keith Anthony, Colette Barlow, Martine Brownley, Amy Erbil, Hazel Gold, Philip Misevich, Mark Sanders, and Rivka Swenson in Atlanta, and Nicholas Dew, Elizabeth Maddock Dillon, Evelina Guzauskye, Javier Villa-Flores, Ted Widmer, and Ken Ward in Providence, helped enhance this work, as well as my developing project on race, freedom, and migration in the age of revolution.

Several scholars took time from their busy schedules to review individual chapters and offer insightful suggestions. Toyin Falola, Aline Helg, and Jane Landers provided important commentary on the opening sections. Caroline Cook, Mark Fleszar, Frank Guridy, and Jeffrey Lesser shared unique perspectives on analyzing black mobility and Rachel O'Toole offered thoughtful questions regarding urban labor and black resistance. Amanda Lewis, Ben Narvaez, and Christine Skwiot's expertise on the Chinese in the Caribbean and Spanish America and labor migration, respectively, aided the formulation of the final chapter. Sandra Frink read multiple versions of the conclusion with patience and a critical eye toward illuminating the humanity of free people of color until the last word.

I received additional intellectual support from scholars and friends at Georgia State University (GSU) and across the country. At GSU, my thanks go out to Mohammed Hassen Ali, Robert Baker, Carolyn Biltoft, Kimberly Cleveland, Ian Fletcher, Jonathan Gayles, Amira Jamarkani,

Kelly Lewis, Jared Poley, Jake Selwood, Shelley Stevens, Cassandra White, and Kate Wilson for their intellectual exchange and friendship. I bounced professional and personal issues off of *mi hermano*, Charles Beaty-Medina, and *mis hermanas* Beauty Bragg, Jenifer Bratter, Margo Kelly, and Anju Reejhsinghani. Adventures and conversations with Abou Bamba, Denise Blum, Sherwin Bryant, David and Sasha Cook, Duane Corpis, Michal Friedman, Kristin Huffine, Russ Lohse, Gillian McGillivray, Marc McLeod, Kym Morrison, Melina Pappademos, Lauren Ristvet, and David Sartorius also informed this project.

I am indebted to the editorial staff at the University of Georgia Press and the Early American Places series. My heartfelt thanks to Derek Krissoff, John McLeod, Beth Snead, and Tim Roberts for overseeing this project's publication. The detailed commentaries by Peter Blanchard, Matt Childs, Ben Vinson, III, and anonymous reviewers enabled me to refine the final manuscript.

My family has steadfastly encouraged my goals, even when they wondered what I was up to when research carried me far from home. I thank my parents, Rebecca Farris Reid and Herman E. Reid, Jr., my siblings, Michael, Maurice, and Mabel, and sister-in-law, Sherri, for fostering my personal and professional creativity. I am especially grateful for my grandparents, Mabel Peasant Farris, Bernard Young Farris, Beatrice New, Herman E. Reid, Sr., and Emma Dean Reid; although you did not witness the completion of this book, your lifetime of nurturing flows through every page.

Jose Vazquez, *mi amor*, swept into my life during my travels and transformed it. The thousands of miles we have logged together since then—by car, plane, and train—reveal his enduring encouragement of my professional and personal development. 'Ihe curiosity and energy of my stepson, Evan, and my niece and nephews, Simone, Desmond, and Maliq, continue to inspire me. Finally, the newest edition to our family, Reid Alejandro, arrived a few hours after I submitted the final manuscript for *The Year of the Lash* from my hospital bed. He has set the stage for new adventures to come. *Muchísimas gracias a todos*!

The Year of the Lash

Introduction

At dawn on June 29, 1844, a firing squad in Havana executed ten accused ringleaders of the Conspiracy of La Escalera, an alleged plot among free people of African descent (*libres de color*), slaves, creoles, and British abolitionists to end slavery and colonial rule in Cuba. The group of condemned men represented some of the most prominent artisans, property owners, and militia officers within the colony's free community of color, including the acclaimed poet "Plácido" (Gabriel de la Concepción Valdés).[1] Convinced that recent rebellions involving slaves and free blacks formed part of a larger conspiracy, officials sought out its leaders and collaborators through a spectacle of arrests, tortured confessions, and public executions. In addition, Spanish colonial authorities in Cuba coerced hundreds of *libres de color* into exile, prohibited all free blacks from disembarking in local ports, banned native-born men and women of color from select areas of employment, and dismantled the *pardo* and *moreno* militia units.[2] In the process, local officials redrew social and economic lines by extending race-based occupational restrictions and promoting immigration from Spain, the Canary Islands, and China to supplement or replace black laborers and reverse the "Africanization" of Cuba. The unprecedented wave of violence that engulfed Cuba in 1844 became known as the "Year of the Lash." The violence and restrictive polices that accompanied it, however, persisted into the 1860s, in an attempt to silence and resubordinate the free population of African descent by stripping away decades of moderate political, economic, and social gains.

This book explores the lives of free blacks and their strategies of negotiating nineteenth-century Cuban society in the aftermath of the Conspiracy of La Escalera. It examines the impact of the Escalera era (1844–1868) on *libres de color*, their resistance to colonial policies of terror, and their pursuit of justice. As both a circum- and cis-Atlantic study, this work situates Cuba within its political, social, and economic relationship with Spain and within the late Spanish empire. It also features the transnational linkages sparked by migrations to and from Cuba involving free blacks, Spanish colonists, and Asian indentured workers. Petitions from exiles on the Gulf coast of Mexico and prisoners in Ceuta, Spanish Morocco, and Seville and Valladolid, Spain; exemption requests from conscripted militiamen in Havana; and clandestine networks forged by compatriots and African Americans in New York City demonstrate both formal and extralegal methods of adaptation and resilience. These responses provide a critical window into understanding free black agency within the shifting and intertwined boundaries of race, freedom, and politics in colonial Cuba.

Although debates persist over whether or not a "vast conspiracy" actually existed, this work focuses on the very real repression experienced by *libres de color*.[3] In doing so, it unearths the voices of those who "trembled," but persevered, under the targeted violence and the Military Commission rulings of execution, banishment, and imprisonment.[4] Using the Military Commission sentencing records as evidence of the repression, rather than as proof of a conspiracy, I unmask the impact of the violence on free people of color, reveal tensions over freedom and slavery, and shed light on how the Escalera era transformed colonial Cuban race relations. Moreover, exploring how *libres de color* responded to the repression creates a model for investigating the meanings and makings of Afro-diasporic identities that simultaneously overlapped, converged, and conflicted with Cuban notions of political and social order in the nineteenth century. Within the broader contexts of colonial Cuban society, Spanish imperial structures, and circum-Atlantic politics, I analyze how *libres de color* endured an intense era through the use of resistance and strategic accommodation.

* * *

The expansion of slavery, rebellion, and independence movements in the Caribbean and Latin America during the early nineteenth century facilitated colonial Cuba's transformation into a slave society and the Antillean jewel of sugar production in the Spanish empire. From the 1810s through the early 1840s, the colony struggled to balance rising imports of enslaved Africans and the steady growth of its local free black population with the arrival of Spanish immigrants. Many officials and planters claimed that maintaining whites as the majority of the population and limiting alliances between slaves and *libres de color* would avert a Haitian-style rebellion. In the process, the free population of color came under persistent scrutiny. Their diverse origins as freedmen and women and free-born, both in Cuba and as emigrants from other territories in the Americas, fostered an intricate social web that linked them to both slaves and creoles. Spanish authorities in Cuba wrestled with the obvious contradictions of having a substantial free black population within a slave society, but could not ignore the critical contributions *libres de color* made toward military defense, health care, and skilled labor, or as proprietors and writers, in one of Spain's few remaining American colonies.

As the tensions of slavery, abolition, colonialism, and independence took hold in the Atlantic World, free blacks' collaboration in slave insurgencies and dissident creole uprisings challenged racial hierarchies throughout the Americas. The Cuban government addressed these persistent threats to the colonial and slave systems with increasingly repressive measures. In November 1843, officials responded with unparalleled brutality to a series of slave revolts in western Cuba. The collective rebellions, which officials deemed a conspiratorial plot, became known as the Conspiracy of La Escalera (the Ladder). The ladder, to which officials tied and whipped the accused until they confessed or died, symbolized the violence of the 1844 repression both literally and figuratively.

Of the accused, free people of color suffered in unusually high numbers compared to their actual proportion in the population. They represented 15 percent of the colony's inhabitants, but comprised over 67 percent of those sentenced.[5] Moreover, prominent free blacks, particularly artisans, militiamen, and their families, became prime targets. They included two of Cuba's most important nineteenth-century black literary figures: Plácido (Gabriel de la Concepción Valdés), a renowned poet, and Juan Francisco Manzano, the author of Cuba's first and only published slave narrative. Plácido's execution, Manzano's letters from prison, and countless documents from the era underscore why the Escalera repression is considered one of the most controversial events in colonial Cuban history. However, despite contemporaneous and scholarly proclamations that this episode hardened racial lines, intensified debates over slavery and labor, and eroded Cuba's already fragmented colonial perceptions and policies, we know surprisingly little about the experiences and struggles of *libres de color* in the wake of the repression.

Thus, my primary questions deal with African diasporic agency within the free sector of color before and after the repression. What was the sociopolitical status of *libres de color* between 1800 and 1844, and how did it change in the ensuing decades? How did free *pardos* and *morenos* counter the government's immediate efforts to suppress the rebellions? How did they react, on and off the island, when the colonial state adopted a conscious policy of limiting free blacks' influence and demographic growth over the course of two decades? This book seeks answers to these questions by examining how free people of African descent maneuvered through the aftermath of the dramatic repression in 1844 and beyond.

In pursuing this line of inquiry, I also trace how the turbulent political conditions taking place within Cuba, the Spanish empire, and the circum-Atlantic world impacted social relations from the late eighteenth to the early nineteenth century. Atlantic warfare in the Caribbean theater during the Seven Years' War (1756–1763) brought Havana (and Manila in the Pacific) under British control and ushered in unprecedented levels of commercial activity and international trade. The eleven-month occupation of Cuba (and the Philippines) culminated in Spain's cession of Florida.[6] In rapid succession, struggles over human rights and political sovereignty produced revolutionary turmoil in France and Europe, Saint-Domingue insurgents wrestled for and won sovereignty, and continental Spanish America gave birth to independent republics. Situating free people of color within these dramatic contexts brings into focus the complexities of their colonial relationships and multifaceted experiences, which have been simplified or marginalized in much of the scholarship on race and politics during this era.

My research does offer some evidence in support of scholarly assertions that colonial corporate identities, such as military service, often trumped modern notions of racial solidarity. For instance, during much of the colonial period, Spain broadened the role of free men of color, as well as that of creoles and slaves, in the military. By the late eighteenth century, *pardos* and *morenos* represented an average of approximately 40 percent of all militiamen in Cuba, Venezuela, and Mexico, and 30 percent of all Spanish forces in these territories.[7] The changes in imperial policy, which afforded free men of color and their families access to military benefits, effectively stimulated black economic growth and upward social mobility throughout these regions, particularly in Cuba.[8] In other words, Spain's reforms to aid the defense of its American colonies also fostered new personal opportunities and professional alliances among *pardos*, *morenos*, creoles, and Spaniards, although these remained in constant flux.

I underscore, however, that such spaces of accommodation represented only one aspect of individual or group identity for colonial subjects, particularly for *libres de color*. Free blacks in Cuba and throughout the Americas combined multiple arenas—defense, skilled occupations, property and business ownership, social organizations, and notions of honor—to define themselves and their families. They mobilized one or more of these areas to adjust to the changing conditions. For example, officers in the militias of color supplemented their modest pay with income as artisans, and extended their networks in the community with leadership positions in *cabildos de nación* (ethnic-based sociocultural mutual aid associations). These combined activities enabled some to accumulate significant levels of property and savings that they redistributed to family and friends in both the free and enslaved communities. Nevertheless, these decades of relative black prosperity were riddled with tensions of the era. Despite Cuba's label as the "Ever-Faithful Isle," conflicts over Spanish absolutism, creole political autonomy, slavery, and hierarchies of freedom produced volatile conflicts that would erode preexisting arenas of accommodation.

Pardos' and *morenos'* exalted positions within the military and their occupational niches created constant social clashes. Militiamen regularly had their loyalty challenged. In 1823, twenty-four militia officers of color resorted to publishing a manifesto reiterating their long-standing loyalty to the Spanish crown after creoles accused *pardo* militiamen of conspiring to foment a revolution akin to Haiti's.[9] Meanwhile, a string of captain generals, planter advocates, creole thinkers, and foreign visitors, including Francisco Dionisio Vives, Francisco Arango y Parreño, José Antonio Saco, and Abiel Abbot, noted the ubiquitous presence of free people of color in general, and black artisans in particular, as detrimental to the morale, honor, and economic vitality of the colony's white population. Over time, these tensions produced new and evolving expressions of identity for Cubans of all hues. In the wake of the Escalera rebellions, however, *libres de color* would suffer an almost irreversible blow to their economic stability, military standing, and social status. Past patterns of accommodation faded as the Escalera era took hold.

The slave revolts in March, May, June, July, and November 1843 provided the impetus for escalating state violence to suppress them, especially on *ingenios* (the complex of sugarcane plantation fields and sugar mills) in western and central Cuba.[10] The powder keg finally exploded with the November uprisings in Sabanilla, Matanzas, Cuba's rich sugar district. Local sugar planter Esteban Santa Cruz de Oviedo uncovered information linking the slaves to a plan for widespread insurrection. In response, Antonio García Oña, governor of the Matanzas province, gained approval from Captain General Leopoldo O'Donnell to send troops into the region, quell further uprisings, and determine the origins and instigators of the plot.[11] In January 1844, authorities extracted slave testimonies that implicated free people of color in the uprisings.[12] Using this mounting "evidence," secured under duress, authorities accused *libres de color* of leading a conspiracy to overthrow slavery and Spanish rule on the island through an alliance of slave men and women, creole dissidents, and British abolitionists.

Scholars of the Conspiracy of La Escalera agree the brutal suppression, labeled one of the most famous, violent, and controversial episodes in Cuba's history, had disastrous social, economic, and political consequences for Cuba's free population of African descent.[13] Nevertheless, there are no studies that address its impact on *libres de color*.[14] By examining the decades following the repression of the Conspiracy of La Escalera, I seek to unveil the spaces within which free people of color negotiated the complex interplay, constraints, and contradictions among race, freedom, and empire in nineteenth-century Cuba, the Caribbean, and the Atlantic World.

The conspiracy itself has garnered tremendous scholarly attention to determine the plot's origins and authenticity. Cuban historians dominated the research until the 1960s, when specialists in the United States and Britain began turning their attention to Cuba to explore the comparative history of slavery and rebellion. These investigations produced two competing theories. One group of historians posited that the colonial state invented machinations in order to justify the repression. Cuban scholars Vidal Morales y Morales, Francisco González del Valle, and José Luciano Franco crystallized this interpretation of the Conspiracy of La Escalera. Cuban historian Pedro Deschamps Chapeaux agreed, adding that scholars should also consider the impact of the repression on *libres de color* as an integral part of their analysis of the rebellions.[15] They, as well as U.S.-based scholars Herbert Klein and Franklin Knight, concurred that the colonial government fabricated the conspiracy and used it as a means to destroy the free community of color's influence and growth.[16]

Studies by Cubans José Manuel de Ximeno, Daisy Cué Fernández, Rodolfo Sarracino, and later by Jorge Castellanos and Enildo García, have countered the predominant view. They argued that Cuba's history of slave rebellion, examples of collaborative dissidence among slaves, free blacks, and whites, and the massive number of trial testimonies recorded by the Military Commission confirmed the possible existence of a plot to topple slavery and end colonial rule. Walterio Carbonell joined this group, but denied any leadership by free people of color.[17] British historian Hugh Thomas, as well as North American historians Arthur Corwin, Gwendolyn Midlo Hall, and David Murray concurred on the existence of a plot.[18] Philip Foner leaned toward the possibility of a joint plan, but stopped short of claiming it outright, preferring to examine aspects of Cuban slavery, Spanish immigration, and Cuban-U.S. relations in greater detail.[19] In the 1980s, Robert Paquette asserted that there was not one, but rather numerous conspiracies that converged between 1841 and 1843.[20] In her 2007 dissertation, Aisha Finch confirmed the reality of the conspiracy as she explored the culture of resistance through testimonies from enslaved witnesses in 1843 and 1844.[21] To date, these compelling and contradictory findings have yet to be resolved. Critically investigating the nature of race and freedom in the transformative context of slavery and rebellion, however, unites these competing perspectives. By detailing reactionary and often contradictory imperial modes of control, I also emphasize the ways in which free black agency circumvented and undermined colonial authority before and after 1844.

Despite debates surrounding the plot's veracity, Cuban, U.S., and British scholars agree that the repression virtually destroyed the free black community and reconfigured nineteenth-century social relations. Very few, however, have delved into its impact on this sector. As noted above, only Deschamps Chapeaux raised the issue. Indeed, his extensive writings on free people of color between 1800 and 1843 established the context for the government backlash targeting *libres de color* and traced the economic, social, and political decline of numerous individuals subsequent to 1844.[22] Furthermore, according to Aline Helg, the repression collapsed previous racial categories separating blacks and mulattoes, merging them into the *raza o clase de color* (race or class of color), making everyone of African descent "of color" or black.[23] Escalera-era legislation, which restricted local gatherings, circum-Caribbean mobility, and economic opportunities for *libres de color*, along with social and political pressures, also helped enforce a more rigid color line.[24] Unpacking the scholarly discussions and unearthing substantial historical evidence for the Escalera era have enabled me to address unexplored spaces within Spanish imperial policy and race relations in nineteenth-century Cuba. In addition to the vibrant scholarly debate on the Conspiracy of La Escalera, Cuba's rich historiography on nineteenth-century race relations has paved the way for this study. Historians have increasingly analyzed slavery, free people of color, and rebellion in a broader, circum-Atlantic context.[25] Publications on late nineteenth- and early twentieth-century Cuba have illuminated the politics of abolition, independence, and post-emancipation society.[26] In light of the repercussions wrought by the Escalera repression, however, the dearth of scholarship exploring the mid-nineteenth century sparked my intellectual curiosity. Using the repression as a lens for understanding the tense intersections of race, freedom, and resistance in colonial Cuba, I set out to investigate the impact of the repression on *libres de color* and their responses to it. In doing so, I shed light on the clash of imperial politics and the transnational dynamics of race and freedom in a slave regime. I link the Escalera era's legacy of tyrannical, racist policies with creole calls for annexation and separation, political upheaval and reforms in Spain, and economic crisis in Cuba in the 1850s and1860s. These critical developments in resistance, slavery, labor, and colonialism forged the conditions and alliances that would spark the Ten Years' War and its dual struggle for the abolition of slavery and national independence.

As indicated above, in my quest to expose broader and deeper meanings of race, freedom, and politics in Cuba, I do not speculate on whether or not a conspiracy existed. Rather, I focus on the indisputably real repression and its impact on the free population of African descent and colonial Cuban race relations. For example, records from Matanzas, the epicenter of the revolts, indicated that of the 1,836 individuals sentenced, free people of color constituted 1,232; slaves comprised 590. Moreover, *libres de color* constituted almost all of the 435 condemned to banishment, and almost half of the 78 individuals executed.[27] Although those convicted represented just 0.12 percent of the total population, authorities implemented laws that prohibited free people of color from entering local ports, expelled foreign-born free blacks, and dismantled the long-standing militia units of color.[28] In the wake of these oppressive measures, however, free black men and women continued to assert their rights. They petitioned for the release of imprisoned family members, the return of confiscated property, and the reversal of expulsion orders. The early actions of *libres de color* in the face of imperial violence and subjugation indicate that any assumption of their silencing in 1844 has been premature and is in need of revision.

In fact, *libres de color* were anything but silent. Undoubtedly, the Escalera repression shattered the lives of thousands. I argue, however, that the extensive violence, deportations, restrictive legislation, and dismantled institutions did not spell their social, political, economic, or demographic demise. Rather, free men and women of color manipulated the inconsistent, contradictory, and fragmented colonial perceptions, legislation, and unjust treatment. From 1844 to 1868, in acts ranging from lawful to extralegal, they voiced their opposition to colonial policy, negotiated for recognition of their skills and contributions to society, and fostered political and social alliances both inside and outside of Cuba. Drawing on materials from Cuba, Spain, Mexico, and United States, I demonstrate the adaptability and resiliency of *libres de color* as they struggled to counter the repression by rebuilding their economic base and reasserting their identities as free individuals in a slave society. Their collective experience, skill, and knowledge of the colony made them agents of their own survival as the politics of empire in Cuba reverberated across space and time.

The African diaspora is at the heart of this study. Focusing on freedom and resistance within slave systems, this investigation joins the rapidly growing scholarship on the history of the African diaspora in the Americas, particularly on the Caribbean and Latin America. Works focusing on the lives of free blacks in slave societies, especially throughout the Caribbean region, as well as societies with slaves, such as Ecuador and Costa Rica, have created significant avenues for transnational comparisons of freedom within slave systems.[29] Furthermore, scholarship on law and slavery has broadened our understanding of the ways in which people of African descent exercised their juridical knowledge of the slave system, both as slaves and as free individuals.[30] Collections examining social constructions and economic realities of free women of color continue to enhance our knowledge and interpretations of gender relations in the colonial era.[31] Similarly, an increasing number of works detail military service as one of the most visible and well-documented spaces of identity for free black men.[32] Meanwhile, studies of the recurring negative perceptions of free people of color, referred to as "the plague of the colonies" by some colonial officials, highlights discriminatory practices designed to restrict free blacks' economic, social, and civil rights, regardless of their demographic proportion in society.[33] Racism and harsh legislation, however, did not deter resistance and adaptation. Instead, the former mandated the latter.

Whether free by birth for generations or recently freed by manumission or self-purchase, free people of African descent represented a powerful contradiction in slave societies.[34] Studies on nineteenth-century Cuba reflect how that incongruity fostered alliances between free blacks and slaves in revolts, such as the Aponte and Escalera rebellions, but also maintained a wedge between these populations.[35] By concentrating on free people of color in Cuba, their multiple roles, and their understanding of colonial society before and after the repression, this investigation emphasizes the complexities of freedom within slave systems.

Furthermore, as numerous scholars have demonstrated, the rise of slavery in the Americas placed Africans and their descendents at the center of the Atlantic World.[36] Situating free people of color in this framework remains an important but understudied aspect of African diasporic agency, especially as the tide of revolution and antislavery movements swept through the late eighteenth and early nineteenth centuries. Recent works on rebellion and freedom in the Caribbean have demonstrated the level of free blacks' and slaves' involvement in the political processes disrupting colonialism and slavery in the Atlantic World.[37] For free Cubans of color, niche roles as artisans, midwives, teachers, militiamen, artists, domestics, and laborers, and organizational affiliations in *cabildos de nación* fostered the necessary knowledge and skills to negotiate autonomy for themselves and their families. During the Escalera repression and throughout the Escalera era they used their legal understanding to pursue individual and familial justice. Similarly, hundreds who were coerced into emigrating to Mexico, the United States, and parts of the Caribbean claimed Cuba as their homeland and invoked their rights as subjects of the Spanish empire. The mobility of *libres de color* gave them access to people, places, and ideas that intricately linked them to the age of revolution and abolition in the nineteenth century. This previously unstudied exodus illuminates the transpolitical nature of their dispersal from colonial to national and imperial territories. It offers insight into how free blacks reacted to and managed overseas imprisonment and exile. Collectively, these exchanges exemplified the intertwined relationships and dynamics between race and freedom in the Atlantic World.

Viewing free people of color and the Escalera era through an Atlantic World lens reveals the multifaceted impact of the repression at local, regional, and international levels. The Cuban government's brutal response to the conspiracy thrust the episode into the center of the Atlantic World stage. Polemic reactions from the international press revealed the politically charged nature of race, rebellion, and slavery in the nineteenth century. Although most U.S. papers praised the colonial Cuban government for their iron-fist approach, others in the United States, Jamaica, and Britain warned that wanton violence would provoke a Haitian-inspired uprising in the future.[38] Captain General O'Donnell's reports to Spain insisted that suppressing the revolts and unleashing comprehensive prohibitions on *libres de color* guaranteed that those who fled would never want to return. Individual requests, group petitions, and clandestine travel, however, proved otherwise.[39] Furthermore, consuls and informal contacts in Mexico and the United States verified reports that *negros españoles* (black Spaniards) had established networks with other exiles and free African Americans across the Gulf in Veracruz and New Orleans, and up the Atlantic coast in Baltimore, Philadelphia, and New York City.[40] These unexpected activities evoked panic throughout the Caribbean Atlantic World.

Overall, this study documents the multiple forms of resistance and adaptation, especially those informed by the construction and pragmatics of politics and race, in the shifting political and social framework of nineteenth-century Cuba. Whether rooted on the island or cast into the Atlantic World, free men and women of African descent challenged colonial expectations of their codes of conduct. In the face of occupational banning and territorial displacement, they continued to resist governmental attempts to control them. *The Year of the Lash* presents a new perspective on colonialism, freedom, and slavery in Cuba, the Spanish Caribbean empire, and the Americas. It fundamentally transforms conventional scholarship on free people of color in the Escalera era. Rather than leaving *libres de color* on the margins, it places them at the center. In doing so, this investigation contributes to the Latin American, African diaspora, and Atlantic World historiographies on race, slavery, and freedom.

Sources and Chapter Overview

The study draws on fragmentary sources housed in archives in Cuba, Mexico, Spain, and the United States. Petitions, government and personal correspondence, newspapers, manuscript census returns, travelers' accounts, and institutional records compose the range of data used to inform this narrative and analysis. Petitions from free people of color proved to be of particular value. Albeit tempered by notaries, commentaries and assertions in the face of multiple crises resonated throughout these documents. In Cuba, I compiled data from over 500 petitions by black men and their parents who protested forced service in the militia of color reestablished in the 1850s. Similarly, I reviewed correspondence filed by skilled artisans and apprentices to challenge occupational restrictions and bans. Toggling among archives in Havana, Madrid, and Seville, I unearthed dozens of individual and group letters from exiles in Mexico and prisoners in Spain. In addition, careful readings of extensive government documents, particularly the triangular correspondence between Cuba, Mexico, and the United States, shed light on the actions, real and alleged, of free blacks. Collectively, this rich documentation situates *libres de color* within the transpolitical structures of colonialism, imperialism, and nationalism and addresses how they protested and negotiated the military draft, economic displacement, and geographic dislocation in the Escalera era.

* * *

The Year of the Lash is organized both chronologically and thematically. Chapter 1 narrates the roles of free people of color between 1800 and 1843. This section advances my assertion that free people of African descent were both indispensable members of colonial society and potential threats to colonial order. On the one hand, legal prohibitions and Spanish taboos regarding manual labor fostered the predominance of free people of color in certain skilled and unskilled occupations. Regular newspaper solicitations for and by free black and mulatto midwives, teachers, and market vendors indicated their significant functions in colonial society. Government and organizational documents highlight the wealth, networks, and influence of upper-status free blacks. In addition, the demographic strength of the African-descended population in the Caribbean made arming *libres de color* essential to the defense of the Spanish empire. In turn, membership in the militia and an understanding of the legal system among the broader community enabled free men and women of color to voice their concerns on political and social matters that threatened to erode their social and economic standing.

On the other hand, the competition between urban free artisans of color and white workers heightened tensions over employment in the first half of the nineteenth century. Colonial debates over how to restore status and honor to occupations deemed dishonorable, due to associations with workers of color, raged throughout the 1820s and 1830s. Similarly, the growing social and political presence of black and mulatto militiamen coincided with concerns over arming free men of color in a slave society. As multiple slave revolts rumbled across the circum-Caribbean in the first half of the nineteenth century, the specter of race war and imperial devastation rose to new heights. These contradictions, often characteristic of the tenuous nature of freedom within slavery throughout the Americas, took an explosive turn for Cuba in 1844. The rebellions and the repression shook the colony to its core and triggered trans-Atlantic aftershocks that reverberated for the next two decades.

Chapter 2 examines the repression of the Conspiracy of La Escalera from the perspective of colonial authorities, free people of color, and the international media. In response to the Escalera revolts, Spanish authorities in Cuba ignited a sweeping backlash targeting the African-descended population in general and the free community of color in particular. Captain General O'Donnell and the Military Commission used a three-pronged approach to systematically persecute *libres de color* and suppress the alleged scheme to abolish slavery and overthrow colonial rule. First, the colonial regime arrested, tortured, executed, harassed, and banished thousands of people of African descent, dismantled the militia of color, and restricted social organizations. Next, to remove a future threat from free blacks and their allies, authorities coerced hundreds of *libres de color* into "voluntary" exile in Mexico, the United States, and parts of the Caribbean. Finally, officials implemented new legislation that prohibited or restricted free blacks' occupational endeavors, social activities, and insubordinate behavior toward whites. These spectacles of power not only tightened colonial control in Cuba but also revalidated Spanish imperial authority in the Caribbean.

Notably, both free people of color and the press responded to the repression in a range of ways. Still reeling from the wave of violence, many *libres de color* initiated protests. Letters and petitions documented the ways in which they disputed the imprisonment of loved ones and sought to reclaim confiscated property. Furthermore, the brutal uprooting of the plot drew international attention. Whether critical or complimentary, the commentaries of individual travelers, foreign officials, immigrants, the international press, and imperial officials transported this episode to multiple Atlantic shores.

Chapter 3 investigates colonial efforts to rid the island of free people of color, citing their potential for rebellion, and the multiple responses of *libres de color* to these measures. Schemes to remove this sector of the population, which had been gaining strength throughout the first half of the nineteenth century, solidified in the Escalera era. Between 1844 and

1845, the Cuban administration shipped hundreds of free black men and some women off the island. Some were banished from Cuba and Puerto Rico, and others were imprisoned overseas in Spain or Spanish North Africa. Furthermore, faced with continual harassment and surveillance, hundreds of families escaped into exile throughout the Americas.

The expulsions thrust Cuban debates over empire, race, and freedom into the circum-Caribbean and the broader Atlantic World. Despite departing with valid passports, *libres de color* arrived abroad to find that Cuban officials had cast them as tacit co-conspirators and barred any return. In response to travel prohibitions, exiles circumvented restrictions and reentered the island through illegal channels. Furthermore, intelligence gathered from colonial officials, municipal police, and local informants in Spain, Cuba, Mexico, and the United States revealed that *libres de color* had established extensive social and economic networks in the Americas. Moreover, additional reports claimed exiles headquartered in the United States stood poised to ignite a war for independence and abolition. Despite assertions that Cuba had returned to a state of tranquillity, the resulting free black Cuban diaspora forced colonial authorities to grapple with the unexpected international repercussions of black mobility.

Chapter 4 explores officials' efforts to harden racial boundaries and reinvigorate the slave system, in large part, by resubordinating free *pardos* and *morenos*. In particular, the alleged participation of numerous free black artisans and urban workers in the conspiracy compelled authorities to scrutinize this labor sector. Tighter employment restrictions curtailed economic opportunities for people of color, while prominent creoles denigrated *libres de color* as vagrants. Furthermore, officials disrupted established forms of free black individual and group identities and drove social networks underground. Free blacks, especially skilled workers and apprentices, defied these measures by operating without the requisite licenses, presenting written objections, and staging physical protests.

Furthermore, the success of revolutions in the United States (1776–1783), France (1789–1799), Haiti (1791–1804), and Latin America (1810–1825), and of abolition of slavery in Haiti (1794 and 1804), the British Caribbean (1834), and throughout most of the Latin American republics by the 1850s, loomed heavily over Cuba's future prosperity. Both on and off the island, planters called for annexation to the United States, and separatists demanded independence from Spain. To stabilize the colony's vulnerable racial and economic position, the Spanish colonial administration in Cuba used European immigrants and creole workers to escalate the displacement of skilled blacks. By crystallizing the boundaries of race and urban labor, authorities reinforced white supremacy, ethnic hierarchy, and colonial authority in Cuba and abroad.

Chapter 5 addresses the dismantling of the militia of color in 1844 and its subsequent reestablishment a decade later. By disbanding these units, the O'Donnell administration hoped to neutralize the threat of further revolt. Furthermore, this act unraveled a social institution and displaced thousands of former servicemen. Preoccupied with more immediate horrors of the repression, the former militiamen did not directly challenge the initial decree. Rather, their responses emerged during the revival of the institution in the mid 1850s.

Captain General Juan de la Pezuela reinstituted the militia of color in 1854 with contentious results. Years of battling occupational and familial upheaval left *libres de color* suspicious of colonial initiatives. When eligible freemen hesitated to serve voluntarily, de la Pezuela compelled them to do so through forced enlistment. In response, hundreds protested by requesting exemptions on the basis of criteria ranging from poor health to family obligations. Difficulties filling service rosters finally prodded authorities to restore voluntary military participation, with the goal of eventually phasing out militias of color in Cuba and Puerto Rico. Examining the rise and fall of militia service reveals the contested articulation of racial, social, and political boundaries of the Spanish Caribbean.

Chapter 6 scrutinizes how authorities and elites sought to redress Cuba's racial composition and reduce the demographic presence of *libres de color* by promoting immigration. With each slave rebellion in the Caribbean region, particularly those in Haiti and Jamaica, planters and council members pressured Spain to increase Cuba's white population. Cuban officials believed maintaining a white majority was crucial to controlling the island's massive slave workforce. The shrinking slave trade, rising prices for contraband slaves, and heightened competition on the international sugar market spotlighted the dire financial consequences of Cuba's agricultural labor shortage.

Shortly after the Escalera repression began, in conjunction with renewed European immigration schemes, authorities initiated a contract labor trade that introduced over 100,000 Chinese and several thousand Yucatán Indian captives to fulfill cultivation and production demands. Neither group, however, proved to be as docile as some merchants had characterized them. Furthermore, their presence in Cuba exacerbated tensions over race and immigration. For the purposes of fostering Cuba's aspirations for a white majority, officials recorded Asians and Indians as "free" workers and rhetorically "white." They were, however, subjected to the same occupational and living conditions as slaves. Planters even entertained proposals to import free African immigrants as contractual agricultural workers, but such an increase in the free black population revived past fears that Cuba would suffer the same fate as colonial Haiti. Ultimately, the influx of European immigrants diminished the influence of *libres de color*. Cuba's long-desired racial rebalancing finally took hold in the early 1860s when it reached a white population majority (56.8 %, including the Chinese).[41] Although immigration policies had a negative impact on the proportion of *libres de color*, their community had almost doubled in size since 1846. Despite restrictive measures initiated in 1844, political liberalization in the late 1850s gave rise to economic and social stabilization for *libres de color* in the 1860s. By the mid 1860s, the community's commitment to economic and educational programs contributed to a stronger, larger, more literate free population of color. The methods utilized to survive the violence and repression of the Escalera era underscore the knowledge, persistence, and versatility of *libres de color* in negotiating two decades of repression in nineteenth-century Cuba and on foreign shores.

The closing section emphasizes the legacy of the Escalera era as a new generation of free blacks and slaves initiated its struggle for equality. The physical, social, and economic scars from the Escalera repression left an indelible reminder of the tenuous nature of freedom within slavery in Cuba, the Americas, and the Atlantic World. Moreover, it foreshadowed future battles the African-descended population would endure to secure its rights. From the onset of the three-decade struggle for independence in 1868 to the close of Spanish imperialism in 1898, Cubans of color would continue to play significant roles in movements that would overturn the colonial hierarchies of race, politics, and citizenship throughout the Americas.

1 / "Very Prejudicial": Free People of Color in a Slave Society

The free sector of color expands immensely throughout the population without constraint, and without any hope that they or their children will be alleviated from the low condition in which they find themselves.

—FRANCISCO ARANGO Y PARREÑO

"You will be surprised to observe the number of free blacks and mulattoes," wrote Abiel Abott, a Massachusetts minister who visited Cuba from February to May 1828 in a quest to improve his lung condition.[1] Numerous travelers, primarily North Americans and Europeans, who regularly selected Cuba as a destination point for enhancing their health, promoting business, comparing slave systems, and sightseeing in the 1820s and 1830s, reiterated Abbot's observations. In the thriving port city of Havana, visitors noted the black stevedores, sailors, and day workers clustered near the wharf attending disembarking and departing ships and passengers.[2] They passed artisans and washerwomen of color traversing streets lined with shops, stately mansions, and dilapidated huts.[3] Carts loaded with sugar, coffee, and molasses rattled alongside carriages, and *moreno* street vendors walked about selling fruits and other products.[4] On Sundays, black soldiers, dressed in distinctive uniforms, practiced drills in the colony's central plazas.[5] Amid this flurry of activity, some men stood smoking at the outer gates to homes, waiting "to *eye* and answer strangers" approaching the entryway.[6] Music echoed from the heart of Havana as popular *pardo* band musicians entertained those who rode or strolled along the Paseo's broad thoroughfare.[7] Imperial data backed up travelers' observations that a large proportion of these laboring individuals were of African heritage and legally free. According to Cuba's 1827 census, free people of color constituted 15 percent of the island's inhabitants and 27 percent of the African-descended population (see figure 1).[8] Abbot viewed the substantial proportion of *libres de color* as proof of Cuba's progress in race relations under slavery. He predicted that former slaves, "in obtaining their liberty will form those habits which will render them good subjects, and capable of taking care of themselves."[9]

Although Abbot's observations primarily addressed only one category of Cuba's free black population, his commentary and that of other foreign visitors reveals the vital presence of *libres de color*. Cuba's free black community, whether former slaves or free-born, had grown steadily throughout the eighteenth century via manumission, free birth, and immigration. Due to the Spanish empire's traditional practice of prohibiting individuals of color from professional occupations, *libres de color* established niche roles ranging from skilled artisans to midwives. They also defended the Spanish empire as militiamen, maintained community and cultural ties through membership in *cabildos de nación* (sociocultural mutual aid associations based on African-derived ethnicity), and owned businesses, homes, and slaves. Situated between slaves and creoles, and with personal links to both, free blacks established themselves as crucial to colonial society, but also as a potential danger to social and political hierarchies. Would they completely displace white artisans? Would they remain loyal to the Spanish crown during the age of independence? Would they join with slaves and international abolitionists in support of emancipation? The complex and, often, contradictory roles of free people of color, especially as Cuban sugar production escalated and the importation of enslaved Africans increased, produced sharp tensions between colonial officials and elites over how to control the ubiquitous presence and influence of *libres de color*.

From Buenos Aires to Boston, free sectors of color represented an inherent contradiction to the slave system. Nevertheless, by the early nineteenth century, they persisted in varying proportions throughout the hemisphere, enhanced via manumission, natural reproduction, and political immigration streams. The circumscribed conditions of freedom, however problematic, enabled free blacks to carve out a space to bend and maneuver through colonial restrictions. In Cuba, the friction created from being perceived as simultaneously vital and menacing to both slave society and the Spanish empire often aided free men and women of color in negotiating, and, at times, reconstructing established meanings of labor, service, social relations, and politics for their own benefit.

Using the voices and actions of officials, elites, foreign travelers, and free people of color, this chapter examines the anxieties surrounding

FIGURE 1. Mercado de Cristina (Cristina's Market). Samuel Hazard, *Cuba with Pen and Pencil* (Hartford and Chicago: Pitkin and Parker,1871), 87.

race, slavery, and freedom from the late eighteenth century to just prior to the Escalera rebellions in 1843. It emphasizes the transitional nature of Cuba's burgeoning slave society, the Spanish empire's evolving and often contradictory social policies, and the international influences on circum-Caribbean politics. In particular, it highlights existing discourses of race, which simultaneously lauded and vilified *libres de color*. Although colonial authorities, foreign officials, creoles, and visitors produced the bulk of these competing representations, free people of color also contributed their own interpretations, adapting swiftly or resisting vehemently, depending on the situation at hand. As a weakened Spanish empire struggled to maintain political and racial authority over its remaining American territories in the early nineteenth century, the sociolegal status of the free population of African descent and their ability to ally with slaves and foreigners became a menace to colonial authorities and Cuba's social hierarchy. The ensuing conflicts generated waves of violent revolt and retaliation and set the stage for the 1843 Escalera rebellions and the 1844 repression. The ensuing Escalera era, which spanned over two decades, would transform race relations within Cuban society and political relations among Cuba, Spain, and the Americas.

The Dynamics of Freedom in a Slave Society

Libres de color, like visitors, officials, and elites, articulated their own ideas about the meaning of freedom within Cuban slave society. For many, their experiences as slaves fostered intense desires to escape bondage. For example, writer Juan Francisco Manzano, born a slave, "got the idea" of his freedom early on. After one owner's hinted promises of liberation fell through, he remarked "from the moment I lost the illusion of my hoped-for freedom, I was no longer a faithful slave." Rather, "I tried to teach myself many skills," including writing, cooking, painting, and sewing. He would achieve his goal in 1836 from a group of literary benefactors led by Domingo Del Monte, a wealthy creole intellectual.[10] In another case, the African-born *mandinga* and *negra libre* Carlota Molina remained the property of Doña Josefa Molina in Santiago de Cuba until she "freed herself" in 1818. Molina used her skills as a domestic to support herself, and would fiercely defend her legal status in the 1840s.[11] Manazano and Molina represented thousands of former slaves who struggled to acquire and maintain their new legal status.

Those born free also struggled to garner respect for their sociolegal status from broader Cuban society. Monico de Flores, for instance, sought to be treated with the "dignity" he thought he deserved. As a captain in Havana's militia of color, he asserted his contributions to the defense of the Spanish empire and Cuba, in particular, as evidence of his fidelity and honor.[12] María del Pilar Poveda, a free *parda*, took pride in her years of experience and expertise as a midwife in Matanzas. After judges found her guilty of holding conspiratorial meetings in her home and banned her from midwifery, she protested the ruling based on her "distinguished" service to local elites.[13] Although militiamen performed a vital service to imperial defense and midwives played a pivotal role in colonial mortality, these men and women were not above suspicion from the colonial government.

The views of Manzano, Molina, Flores, and Poveda offer telling insights into the complexities of race and freedom. Freedmen and women relished their liberty and recognized the thin line separating them from forced servitude. They would not give up their new status easily, despite being subjected to continued racist practices. Rather, as some elites feared, the manumitted sought to exercise their legal rights and to cultivate the free community of color's expansion. The free-born, especially those within families of multigenerational *libres de color*, worked to gain upward social mobility through participation in the segregated militia, in a variety of skilled manual occupations, and in property ownership, the arts, and membership in *cabildos de nación*.

Although composed largely of former slaves and the offspring of Cuban-born free mothers, *libres de color* also incorporated free black immigrants from throughout Spanish America. Individuals and families from these territories not only contributed to the community's diversity in Cuba, they also heightened officials' anxieties of race and rebellion. The varied quests of *libres de color* to secure and maintain freedom, however, agitated established social hierarchies. By the 1830s, free blacks and mulattos' involvement in these arenas exacerbated imperial and creole apprehensions over how to contain the spread of freedom to slaves and the stifle the demands for fuller equality from the free population of African descent. When the spirit of rebellion spiked in 1843, slaves and *libres de color* all found themselves caught up in the pandemonium of the Escalera era.

Community Contours: Manumission, Natural Reproduction, and Immigration

Cuba's free population of color evolved in ways similar to those in other colonial societies throughout the Americas. Sexual unions between European men and enslaved African and African-descended women, combined with Spanish legal codes, facilitated manumission and *coartación* (self-purchase).[14] Immigration added to this sector as families and individuals resettled from former Spanish territories during Atlantic geopolitical struggles between 1763 and 1825. In Cuba, these distinct origins made for a diverse free black population that included former slaves, locally born free *pardos* and *morenos*, and free blacks born in other Spanish territories and elsewhere in the Americas. Finally, this group's sexual balance proved a crucial feature of its development. Unlike European and African groups, which remained disproportionately male throughout much of the colonial era, *libres de color* in Cuba maintained a gender equilibrium that officials would find increasingly problematic. The virtually unrestricted access by both free men and women of African descent to the city streets and markets enabled them to establish urban and rural networks with the potential to undermine established social hierarchies.

The rise and fall of manumission and self-purchase rates generated varying avenues for freedom. Cuba's traditionally large proportion of young free *pardas* and *morenas* suggests that their manumission was based on a variety of factors. In particular, master-slave relationships tended to produce higher manumission rates for both African and Cuban-born slave women. Scholars have made similar observations about the prevalence of female slaves acquiring their freedom in locales such as Brazil due to "bonds of affection" between slave women and their owners.[15] Trends from seventeenth-century Cuba, which indicated that women represented 65 percent of all slaves who had been freed, continued in the nineteenth century.[16] Cuban officials and elites noted this tendency for women of African descent in the 1830s, remarking how they contributed to the ever-expanding number of *libres de color* because they "easily freed themselves."[17] Despite these figures, particularly for women, the so-called ease of obtaining freedom varied widely in Cuba and throughout the Americas.

One method of self-manumission included the Spanish legal practice of *coartación*, in which the enslaved individual and their master established a fixed purchase price. Once a slave made the down payment for self-purchase, the law stipulated that he or she could not be transferred or sold. As *coartados*, a legal category between slave and freedman, bondsmen and women would continue to make payments over time toward self-manumission.[18] Urban slaves, male and female, often earned these crucial funds either by receiving a portion of the fee their owners earned for renting out a slave artisan, domestic worker, market vender, or tavern operator or by selling the surplus from their garden plots on the plantations.[19] Records for the nineteenth century demonstrate that women constituted 68 percent of slaves on the path to freedom via *coartación*.[20] Havana manumission records of 1810 and 1811 listed 954 slaves who gained their freedom through self-purchase.[21] The efforts of these men and women to achieve their freedom, whether through outright or incremental self-purchase or manumission, demonstrated a conscious and tenacious decision to break from the slave system and improve their lives and that of their families.

Overall, the situation created one of the few colonial sectors with balanced sex ratios, a factor that enabled *libres de color* to become a self-sustaining social group. Cuban censuses from 1792 to 1841 reported the average proportion of male and female *libres de color* at 49.8 percent and 50.2 percent, respectively.[22] Data from 1827 registered one birth for every six free women of color between the ages of twelve and forty. In comparison, white women averaged only one birth for every seven in this age range.[23] Furthermore, the census revealed births by free women of color, *pardas* in particular, had increased by 69 percent between 1817 and 1827.[24] Because the mother's legal status determined that of her offspring, the children of free *pardas* and *morenas* helped reproduce a locally born free community of color in Cuba. Moreover, the large sector of free women of color would make them critical to the development of social and economic networks linking *libres de color*, slaves, and creoles.

Immigration also contributed to the growth and diversity of *libres de color* in Cuba. The tide of imperial war and revolution sparked the movement of refugees and émigrés throughout the Atlantic world. Cuba became a destination point for Spanish colonial subjects throughout the Americas. In North America, the shifting political control of Florida promoted the flow of refugees in the late eighteenth and early nineteenth centuries. In 1763, at the end of the Seven Years' War among Spain, Britain, and France, the Spanish crown relinquished its Florida territory to Britain. This transfer resulted in a stream of over 3,000 evacuees into Cuba. The majority of these new arrivals were connected to Spanish forces and absorbed into Cuban regiments. The remaining 600 individuals included German Catholics, Canary Islanders, Florida Indians, and thirteen free black families. Field Marshall Alejandro O'Reilly, charged with overseeing military and defense reforms in Cuba, sought to transfer these men, women, and children, whom he deemed better suited as farmers than as soldiers, to appropriate agricultural sites. Under this scheme, authorities attempted to resettle seventy-three refugee families to donated lands in Matanzas, including the free *pardos* and *morenos* relocated to the region's new Ceiba Mocha settlement.[25] Similarly, in 1821, as the fledgling U.S. nation secured control over the remaining sections of East and West Florida, former British and Spanish territories, approximately 145 free individuals of color headed to Cuba, including forty black soldiers.[26] The transfer caused families from St. Augustine, Florida, like Tomás Álvarez, his wife Augustina Albaniz, and their young son Tomás, to set sail and reestablish themselves in Havana. Others, like Prince Whitten, a lieutenant in the militia of color, left behind family and property. Spain would subsidize most of these exiles until they became self-sufficient. The militiamen continued serving, and as younger men became eligible they joined Havana's *moreno* battalion.[27] Although numerically few, these *libres de color* acted to preserve themselves and their loved ones against foreign political encroachment by claiming protection as loyal Spanish subjects.

Other emigrants arrived in Cuba from other parts of the Caribbean. In the wake of the Haitian Revolution, thousands fled Hispaniola. From Saint-Domingue, the French side of the island, *gens de couleur*, slaves, and white refugees abandoned the colony in droves. They headed to multiple locales in the Caribbean, the Gulf South, the U.S. Atlantic coast, and France in varying waves between 1791 and 1810. Scholars have estimated that 25,000 to 30,000 refugees, with free blacks representing approximately one-third, arrived in Cuba from 1803 to 1808 to escape insurgent violence and the consolidation of power on the island.[28] In addition, when a shaky coalition between Spain and Haitian rebels dissolved in 1795, after France abolished slavery in its Caribbean territories and temporarily regained authority over Saint-Domingue, a substantial number of Spanish evacuees from Santo Domingo and black rebel auxiliaries sought refuge in Cuba.[29] Among these evacuees was Juan Saldana, who recalled leaving Santo Domingo with his master, Juan Leonard, a Cuban regiment officer, "when he was six or seven years old." Upon Leonard's death, Saldana gained his freedom and went on to marry and have children in his adopted homeland.[30] Teresa Cuello and José Grajales restarted their lives in eastern Cuba in 1808 with the birth of their daughter, Mariana Grajales Cuello.[31] Their relocation would ultimately pave the way for one genealogical line of the Cuban independence leader Antonio Maceo and one of Cuba's most celebrated revolutionary families. As the tide of refugees arrived, they spread not only fears of another Haitian-style rebellion among planters and officials throughout the region but also the hope of revolutionary language among the slave and free black populations.

As noted by Rebecca Scott and J. M. Hébrard, at times the liberty of Haitians in Cuba could be precarious. Due to the needs of Cuban sugar production, some free people of color found themselves captured and sold as slaves. Other newly free individuals, such as Rosalie Vincent, the former slave of Saint-Domingue coffee planter Michel Vincent and the mother of their four children, actively secured documentation to substantiate their free status in Cuba and to safeguard their family.[32] Although the Napoleonic invasion of Spain forced Cuban officials to expel Haitian refugees in 1809 and redirect the migratory stream from Cuba to New Orleans and other U.S. port cities, nevertheless, a substantial proportion of free people of color remained.[33] As they reconstructed their lives on Cuban soil, these *libres de color* helped swell the ranks of the Spanish colony's free black population, particularly in eastern Cuba.

Similarly, the Spanish American wars of independence, between 1810 and 1825, hastened the arrival of *libres de color* from Venezuela, Mexico, and other parts of Spanish America into Cuba.[34] Most had been soldiers in the royalist army and retained an allegiance to the Spanish crown, preferring the familiarity of the colonial system to the chaos and violence of the newly established republics. For instance, Marcos Maceo served in the Spanish Army against insurgents in his native Venezuela until the patriot victory forced him to evacuate with his mother and two siblings, first to Santo Domingo, and then to Cuba. In eastern Cuba, Maceo met and married Mariana Grajales Cuello, and together the couple had nine children, including the legendary Antonio Maceo.[35] Meanwhile, others arrived from the circum-Caribbean. *Moreno libre* Juan Argüí left Vera Cruz, Mexico, bound for Cuba to continue living "under the Spanish flag." Marcos Velásquez fled Venezuela out of "necessity, like many other faithful and loyal emigrants."[36] The convergence of revolution and evacuation forged new communities, expanded existing networks, and sparked revolutionary families. Moreover, the mingling of black immigrants in Cuba spread radical ideas about race, freedom, and equality as thousands struggled to remake themselves in Cuba and beyond.

By the early nineteenth century, Cuba's *libres de color* constituted nearly 17 percent of the colony's inhabitants. In comparative terms, they represented neither the largest nor the smallest proportions of African-descended populations in the Spanish empire: black sectors in Panama, Puerto Rico, Santo Domingo, and Colombia ranged from 60 to 30 percent, and free blacks in Mexico formed 10 percent of the population.[37] Throughout Spanish America, as well as other colonial territories, free people of color came to occupy a particular social space between the slave, creole, and peninsular populations. Colonial laws typically limited the economic opportunitites of those who were legally free but of African ancestry to skilled and unskilled labor, albeit with numerous exceptions. Furthermore, as historian Peter Blanchard has noted, the black population's large presence in Panama and Colombia and their involvement in the Spanish American wars for independence provided the tipping point for regional sovereignty. Meanwhile, established military traditions and a sizeable garrison of Spanish troops effectively maintained Cuba and Puerto Rico as loyal territories.[38] As mainland Spanish America gained its independence, however, Spanish authorities and Cuban elites voiced their concerns over protecting the Spanish Caribbean, the need to expand slavery, and the potential threat free people of color posed as allies of rebellious slaves and dissident creoles.

Tensions of Slavery, Freedom, and Empire in Cuba and the Atlantic World, 1800–1843

Cuba prospered in the early nineteenth century, shifting from a society with slaves to a slave society propelled by sugar production, facilitated by the fall of colonial Saint-Domingue in 1804. Between 1790 and 1820, an estimated 325,000 enslaved Africans arrived in Cuba. Despite an array of international prohibitions, including the 1807 British and 1808 U.S. embargos on the slave trade, the 1817 slave trade abolition treaty between Spain and Britain, and the 1820 establishment of Britain's Mixed Commission for the Suppression of the Slave Trade with sites in Havana, Suriname, Rio de Janeiro, and Sierra Leone to rule on illegal slave trading activities and liberate captives, the flow of slaves into Cuba did not abate. Rather, despite the bans, approximately 100,000 African captives entered the colony between 1817 and 1820. Even with tightened controls between 1821 and 1835, another 169,000 slaves joined Cuba's escalating slave labor force.[39]

In the midst of the expanding slave population, *libres de color* became increasingly vital to Cuba's development through the manual work and services they provided. They not only predominated in urban areas as day laborers and domestics but also constituted substantial proportions of the skilled workforce, as carpenters, masons, and midwives. Free blacks and mulattos also continued to serve in the militia of color in substantial numbers, as they had since the late eighteenth century. Although Iberian customs and colonial laws designed to maintain racial hierarchies thrust free people of color into separate labor sectors and segregated military service, these niche positions garnered many *libres de color* enhanced social status and economic stability.[40] Their access to property, in the form of both real estate and slaves, especially for those who successfully combined skilled employment and military service, troubled colonial elites and officials who simultaneously relied on and mistrusted this sector. Apprehensions heightened as the numerical proportions of free blacks expanded, demanded greater equality and liberty for themselves and their families, and united with slaves to foment rebellion.

Such anxieties did not go unspoken as numerous colonial elites expressed pessimistic interpretations of Cuban race relations. Key social critics included Francisco Arango y Parreño, Félix Varela, and José Antonio Saco. Their writings revealed the tensions surrounding race, slavery, and freedom in Cuba in the 1820s and 1830s. Arango, a landowner, proslavery advocate, and spokesman for Cuba's planter elite, despised people of color. He considered slaves barbaric and ignorant, to be valued only as a cheap labor source.[41] Varela, a professor of philosophy at Havana's Seminary College of San José and San Ambrosio, priest, abolitionist, and representative to the Spanish Córtes from 1821 to 1823, proposed ending the slave trade, and penned numerous memorials on the abolition of slavery in Cuba and how it could be achieved and still support planters' interests.[42] Saco, a student of Varela, aligned himself with the planter class and defended slavery "as a necessary evil."[43] Although their agendas differed, the three men shared concerns over the recent increase in the black population and the impending danger it posed to the colonial government, race and social relations, and whites' economic prosperity.

Arango lamented the dismaying "infinity of people of color," especially free blacks. Among the ideas he conveyed in a multipage commentary to Spain's Fernando VII on how to control slaves, expand slavery, and augment the white population, Arango also included warnings about free people of color. The legal status of *libres de color*, he asserted, often provided only a limited buffer against racist practices in Cuba's social hierarchy.[44] As he cautioned in this chapter's opening quote, "The free sector of color expands immensely throughout the population without constraint, and without any hope that they or their children will be alleviated from the low condition in which they find themselves." The ubiquitous presence of *libres de color* in Cuba, combined with the political realities of Haitian and Spanish American independence, prompted Arango to raise the question, "Wouldn't it be more fitting to gain the will and respect of our people of color with just laws and opportune measures?"[45] His apprehension over how some *libres de color* reacted to their "low condition" spoke to the Spanish empire's long-standing practice of prohibiting individuals of color from professional occupations and relegating them to manual labor. More important, it addressed the recent upturn in revolts from the black population. Worse still, he bemoaned how slaves had acquired "a tendency to liberate themselves," which augmented the free sector of color.[46] The unrestrained spike in the number of *libres de color*, in conjunction with slaves, drove Cuba's black population to new heights, and reached 55.8 percent of inhabitants in 1827.[47] Although Francisco Dionisio Vives, captain general of Cuba (1823–1832), recommended expelling all free blacks, Vives considered the plan impractical because their numbers had grown so rapidly that such a move would surely cause them to rebel.[48] Arango proposed relegating free *pardos* and *morenos* to agricultural work; however, because they constituted a substantial proportion of the population (15 percent), forcefully removing them from urban areas to labor in the countryside was not only logistically "impossible," but had the potential to foment "major disasters" across the colony.[49]

Arango's disdain for free blacks at times seemed in conflict with his commentary; he despised them for their social status, but contemplated how they could be made more submissive under better treatment. Although Arango and Vives disagreed on the best way to handle *libres de color*, either relegating them to field labor or expelling them from the colony, the ideas of both men remained impractical and potentially inflammatory, given the current state of this sector and their roles within Cuba and the Spanish empire.

Although Varela and Saco held different opinions on abolishing slavery, both proposed ending the slave trade. Concerned with the way slave trafficking agitated blacks and increased their numbers, Saco warned "if the slave trade continues, there will be neither peace nor security in Cuba."[50] Similarly, Varela bemoaned how Cuba's involvement in the slave trade made planters believe agricultural laborers "could be supplied without the danger of" shortages and conflicts. How can we do this, he exclaimed, "without danger, with slaves! The fall of Saint-Domingue quickly warned the government of its error, nevertheless, it continued the introduction of blacks" into the colony. Varela proposed liberating slaves with over fifteen years of servitude and establishing funds to purchase the freedom of others.[51] An 1832 Havana newspaper article highlighted similar fears, stating: "Thus far, we have only considered the power which has its origins in the numbers of the population of color that surrounds us. What a picture we might draw if we were to portray this immense body acting under the influence of political and moral causes and presenting a spectacle unknown in history!"[52]

Although a full-scale Haiti-style "spectacle" remained "unknown" in Cuba, anxieties over black rebellion, particularly one that united the colony's slaves and *libres de color*, intensified during the first decades of the nineteenth century. The Aponte Rebellion in 1812, and subsequent revolts in the 1820s and 1830s, would raise the specter of revolutionary insurgency from the united slave and free black populations. From the perspectives of Arango and Saco, as well as colonial officials and newspaper reports, free people of color in Cuba represented a troublesome consequence of slavery. As Captain General Vives observed alarmingly in the early 1830s, the presence of free people of color in close proximity to slaves would prove to be "very prejudicial" in the near future.[53]

Race, Labor, and Honor

Despite exclusion from the professional classes on the basis of race, time and circumstance demonstrated free blacks' aspirations for social advancement. Planter José del Castillo commented that there were numerous *libres de color* with "abundant wealth" who dressed well, imitated white elites, and seemed "fond of reading serious books and even making verse."[54] His observations could have easily been applied to other parts of Spanish American in the early nineteenth century, where large sectors of free black artisans developed in urban areas of Peru, Mexico City, and Puerto Rico due to established hierarchies of race and employment.[55] In Cuba, former slave and author Juan Francisco Manzano and *pardo libre* poet Plácido (Gabriel de la Concepción Valdés) were the most acclaimed writers on the island between the early 1820s and the early 1840s. With the assistance of prominent creoles from Havana's literary community and British abolitionist Richard Madden, Manzano wrote poetry and penned an autobiography, Cuba's only published slave narrative.[56] The Matanzas-born Plácido, son of a free mulatto barber and a Spanish dancer, rose to prominence by promoting his works in Havana's streets and winning poetry contests. Newspapers began publishing his work and he secured a position as literary editor for a Matanzas newspaper two years prior to his death in the Escalera repression.[57]

The literary gains of Manzano and Plácido demonstrated the often flexible nature of Spanish colonial codes of race and employment, albeit within limits. Despite their contemporaneous achievements and historical legacies, both men struggled to support themselves during their lifetimes, primarily as artisans, the main source of employment for most *libres de color*. Manzano held multiple positions as a painter, cook, and tailor, and between poetry contests and performances Plácido worked as a silversmith, printer, combmaker, and carpenter.[58] Rather than do piecemeal work, other free blacks acquired mastery in highly skilled, nonliterary areas. For instance, in the 1820s and 1830s carpenter Ciriaco Acosta, barber Francisco Abrahantes, and mortician Félix Barbosa built profitable businesses. María de la Luz Hernández, María del Carmen Alfonso, and María del Pilar Poveda all established careers as reputable midwives. Doroteo Barba and Juana Pastor dedicated themselves to teaching and created schools for children and adults of African decent, both free and slave.[59] Using their acquired skills, experience, and networks, *libres de color* helped educate and advance their families. As free blacks' goals of equality and social freedom intensified, however, so too did colonial rhetoric regarding the dual nature of their detrimental influence yet vital contributions to society.

ARTISANS

Excluded from professional areas of employment, free people of color gravitated to opportunities as skilled laborers. In the process, many accumulated an array of property that generated additional income for themselves, their families, and their communities. As a carpenter, *moreno libre* Ciriaco Acosta held one of the highest skilled occupations in colonial Cuba. During his forty-four-year marriage to María de Regla Santa Cruz, from 1789 until Acosta's death in 1833, the couple acquired three houses and a workshop, along with four slaves. His slaves were all carpenters who specialized in repairing *volantes*, carriages used primarily by Cuba's social elites.[60] African-born Francisco Abrahantes operated a successful barbershop in Havana, where he owned multiple houses, some of which he rented out, as well as six slaves. He also accumulated earnings by collecting debts from white elites and other *libres de color. Pardo libre* Félix Barbosa's mortuary put him in contact with virtually all levels of society, and like Abrahantes, Barbosa owned numerous buildings and slaves which he used to supplement his income. His lucrative business placed him and his wife, *morena libre* María Juliana de la Merced Reyes, in a privileged economic and social position, which they used to direct philanthropic contributions.[61]

The examples of Acosta, Abrahantes, and Barbosa highlight the success of upper status *libres de color* and the ways hundreds of free black and mulatto men made the most of skilled occupations as an avenue for upward social mobility and economic stability. A group of *morenos* and *pardos* voiced their pride in these achievements, declaring "we perform the skilled arts at the highest level of perfection, admired by the craftsmen of other illustrious nations."[62] Free black men embraced a range of positions disdained by Spaniards and creoles and converted them into avenues for profit, self esteem, and self-respect. As *pardos* and *morenos* garnered important skills, accumulated property, and extended networks, however, their industriousness also generated friction with creoles.

Saco and Varela, less interested in the way free blacks responded to their circumscribed social status, paid more attention to this group's detrimental impact on employment opportunities for whites, particularly the Cuban-born. Creoles, Saco complained, were so worried about improving their social position they had abandoned artisan and other essential labor to *libres de color*. Furthermore, he railed against free *pardos* and *morenos* as the root of white vagrancy. "Among the enormous wrongs this unhappy race has laid at our feet, one of them is having taken away skilled positions from the white population."[63] In his opinion, the government had done little to curtail the situation, which now "had run wild, sinking us into the abyss we find ourselves in today."[64] Varela also decried the situation. "Virtually all free people of color are engaged in the skilled crafts," in effect, "for each white artisan, there are twenty of color." Moreover, artisans typically had some education and knew "how to read, write and count . . . and many of them pursue other classes of knowledge" such that "they don't envy the situation of most whites."[65] The perceived narrowing social gap between creoles and upper-status *libres de color* generated considerable frustration for colonial officials. When Saco questioned Captain General Francisco Dionisio Vives about the status of artisans in the early 1830s, Vives lamented, "people of color occupy this branch of industry" almost exclusively, and added that if whites in Cuba, like those in the United States, did not stop viewing trade work with "contempt," blacks would continue to compose the majority in these areas.[66] These critiques, however, contradicted the colony's established social hierarchy. On the one hand, as noted by Saco and Varela, most creoles had little interest in manual labor, no matter how much skill it required. Moreover, these areas had been specifically slated for blacks and, consequently, considered dishonorable occupations for whites in Cuba. On the other, elites complained how the racial division of labor fostered white joblessness, and in effect, narrowed the social gap between creoles and *libres de color*.

The predominance of *libres de color* as craftsmen and their negative impact on white employment prompted commentary from foreign visitors and officials. During a trip to Havana in 1835, British traveler Charles Murray observed, "There are more idle people in Havana than I ever saw in any place of the same size; there seem to be hundreds of respectably dressed persons who have nothing else to do than to smoke cigars, and play at dominoes or billiards."[67] David Turnbull, the British abolitionist and former British consul in Cuba who would later be expelled from the island and implicated in the Escalera conspiracy, surmised that the very "presence of slavery throws every sort of personal exertion into discredit. Because labour is the lot of slavery, the pride of the freeman is alarmed lest the line of demarcation should not be broad enough between him and the slave, and he therefore abstains from working altogether."[68] From the perspective of Spaniards, residents, and visitors, whites' widespread disengagement from crucial skilled labor fostered idleness and vice, and eroded the island's socio-occupational hierarchy.

Cuban elites and officials offered one overarching solution to the problem of curtailing black artisans: convert manual skilled labor into honorable work by offering whites moral, social, and economic incentives. To put an end to the "deplorable situation," Saco called on creole fathers to encourage one of their sons to pursue work as a craftsman because these skills would "honor his fatherland."[69] In 1836, Ramón de la Sagra, a Spanish economist and head of the Cuban Botanical Garden, declared Cuba's final goal should be to "destroy preoccupations" over the state of Cuba's skilled trades and the white population. To accomplish this, whites would have to discard their misplaced pride and seek occupations typically held by people of African descent.[70] Saco agreed, but complained how, despite incentives to ensure a high status for creoles employed in the skilled crafts, potential *criollo* artisans still considered these occupations to be *degradante* (without honor).[71]

The predominance of black artisans, combined with the escalating presence of *libres de color*, challenged the intertwined notions of honor, race, and labor in colonial Cuban society. Despite appeals to ideas of manhood and fatherland, and warnings of how undue self- righteousness would result in certain poverty, colonial efforts to restore white honor to the skilled crafts did little to balance race and employment in the artisan sector or squelch free blacks' economic and social aspirations.

MIDWIVES

Free women of color, like their male counterparts, also aspired to social advancement. Both racist and sexist practices of the colonial Americas, however, relegated them to work in the domestic realm, ranging from house servants and laundresses to teachers and midwives. Nevertheless, these niche roles enabled many free *pardas* and *morenas* to seek their own version of honor and labor. Some, like Juana Pastor, a free *parda* and native of Havana, became a popular teacher in the 1830s. In 1835, she received permission from the island's Sociedad Económica de Amigos del País (Economic Society of Friends of the Country) to "establish and direct a primary school for persons of her class and sex."[72] Still others, such as María del Carmen Alfonso, María del Pilar Poveda, and María Vicente Carmona, acquired mastery as midwives, a highly skilled women's profession.[73] In effect, they converted occupations involving manual expertise and teaching into new spaces for honor and status. Furthermore, the duties of domestic labor, teaching, and health care afforded free women of color a degree of autonomy not normally extended to Spanish and Creole women. When possible, they combined their work and reputations within the black, creole, and elite communities to further their own social and economic advancement and that of their families.

The activities of free *pardas* and *morenas* challenged white social norms regarding race, labor, and gender. Consequently, they came under constant criticism, particularly for their prominent presence in Cuba's urban streets and public spaces. New Yorker Benjamin Moore Norman noted that the colony's *criollas* were "never seen walking in the streets."[74] Rather, observed British traveler Charles Augustus Murray, "what strikes a foreigner most is the extreme publicity here of domestic life." From behind barred windows, one could observe elite white women, whom he referred to as "inmates," showing off "their occupations, furniture, etc. . . . for the benefit of every passenger" in the streets.[75] In contrast, free women of color regularly traversed the public corridors of Havana and Matanzas. Massachusetts lawyer Richard Henry Dana remarked, "There are no women walking in the streets, except negresses."[76] The notable presence of women of African descent fostered "a paradoxical situation" which granted *libres de color* seemingly greater freedom than white women.[77]

The contrasts also produced a number of frictions over employment. For instance, Varela noted reports of a scarcity of free domestic workers. He hoped to attract more *libres de color* to an occupation normally predominated by slaves, but concluded that they "did not want to mix with slaves." Although poor *criollas* also entered the ranks of household servants, cooks, washerwomen, and maids, Varela complained how whites from Europe, "from the moment they arrive in Havana don't want to be employed in the servant class."[78] Social status and race would play an important role in women's work. Elite Spanish and creole women found manual labor distasteful and dishonorable, while the economic concerns of working-class *criollas* forced them into the ranks of domestic servants. Although relegated to this arena of labor on the basis of racist practices, free *pardas* and *morenas* also attempted to distance themselves from the work of slaves.

The occupation of midwife generated the broadest social critique of free women of African descent. Despite long-standing practices of midwifery in both Europe and Africa, where women predominated in the field, passed down knowledge through oral tradition, incorporated religious rituals, and used medicinal plants, shifts in Western European concepts of medical professionalization in the late eighteenth and early nineteenth centuries sought to displace unlicensed female midwives with formally trained men.[79] Cuba's traditional dependence on women of color in this occupation, however, made it difficult for colonial officials to dislodge its black practitioners. In 1824, Dr. Domingo Rosain, a leader in Cuba's medical community, emphasized the need to bring white women into the profession.[80] Four years later, Havana's *El Diario de la Havana* published an article which claimed that midwifery had been "degraded and abandoned to all the women of color who were the most miserable and destitute."[81] Like their male artisan counterparts, free *pardas* and *morenas* were cast as dishonorable by participating in the field, despite being relegated to this employment sector by colonial Cuban norms of race, gender, and labor. Furthermore, the article posited that midwifery in the hands of black women hindered Cuba's progress among modern societies. In response, Cuban elites attempted to prove their civilized status by embracing the discriminatory shifts in midwife education and recruitment. Nevertheless, given Cuba's diverse population and racial and gender hierarchies, European approaches to midwife standarization proved challenging to copy and implement.

Considered essential to the expansion of all populations, black *parteras* garnered similar condemnation for their efforts throughout the Americas. Slaveholders in the French Antilles saw midwives' work as crucial to the slave population's natural reproduction, but were suspicious of their potential involvement in the high infant mortality that plagued the slave era. Although doctors in Mexico spurned women's "unprincipled" and informal acquisition of knowledge, they conceded that most of these women could not pay the fees for training programs. In the United States, male doctors started competing with female midwives, especially to provide services for elite women. The medical society in Chile foreshadowed the Cuban situation, lamenting that literate white women, who could afford the costs associated with midwife education, eschewed the practice, largely because they would be forced to share the field with "rustic" women of color.[82] In reality, few cities in early nineteenth-century Latin America could boast of having a sizeable cadre of white midwives.[83]

Confronted with similar difficulties in recruitment, Cuba's medical establishment made a concerted attempt to expand the number of trained, white midwives on the island. Doing so would restore the profession's due honor, repair the colony's besmirched reputation, and garner Cuba its proper respect as a modern colony.[84] To pursue these remedies, officials instituted policies designed to dislodge *libres de color* from this employment sector, ranging from establishing a new midwife training program to fining unlicensed practitioners.[85]

The efforts, however, would have little success until the Escalera era took hold.

Recognizing the impact such programs and attitudes would have on their own livelihoods, free women of color use the established race and gender-based policies to counter prohibitive measures. Those licensed by the Real Protomedicato, Spain's medical regulatory authority, advertised their services regularly in the Havana newspaper. María del Carmen Alfonso emphasized her credentials as a "teacher of the art of midwifery." María Vicente Carmona offered similar services "regardless of the hour."[86] Among the six midwives who completed formal training in 1828 in Havana, five were black.[87] Similarly, women of color accounted for four out of the five *parteras* listed as reputable in the1834 visitor's guide. As free women of color attended multiple sectors of society, their responsibilities enabled many to redefine their occupational position as honorable within their families and communities. Their vital roles in the expansion of the population, their advertised services, and their inclusion in selective visitor guides garnered them a level of respect throughout the broader society, bestowing them with influence and leadership among *libres de color*.

The hierarchies of Spanish colonial race relations in Cuba dictated the majority of economic opportunities for all social groups. In turn, *libres de color* used their niche positions for social and economic advancement. By developing essential skills they garnered respect both within their communities and often in the broader society. Despite criticism from officials and elites over the predominance of free blacks in skilled occupations, particularly when they seemed to threaten honorable employment for creoles, *libres de color* continued to make the most of their occupational arenas. Individuals such as carpenter Ciriaco Acosta, midwife María de la Luz Hernández, teacher Juana Pastor, and others like them demonstrated how they appropriated the concepts of honor and labor for their own benefit. Rather than succumb to encroachments on their livelihoods, the realities of race and occupation in a society that prohibited free blacks from professional positions hastened their ability to reformulate the meaning of race, labor, and honor.

The Militia of Color: A Contentious Military Tradition

Juan Francisco Manzano recalled "attending military drills with my godfather, Javier Calvo, a first sergeant in his battalion," in his *Autobiography of a Slave*, penned in 1839.[88] Similarly, Francisco de Paula Aremey recalled the career of his father, Marcelino Aremey Antillero, a decorated militiaman who "enjoyed the benefits" accompanying his position in Havana's *moreno* militia company for over two decades. Given the militia of color's longevity within the Spanish colonial system prior to 1844, particularly in Cuba, the younger Aremey fully expected to continue in the family tradition and serve with honor.[89] Historically, white creole militias and the militia of color, both founded in the early sixteenth century for internal and external defense in the Americas, represented a colonial corporate body with appropriate rights and benefits.[90] For the men of African descent who served, the institution symbolized privilege and prestige, which could be parleyed into opportunities for building personal wealth within the black community and throughout the Spanish empire.[91]

Origin of birth and race delineated Spain's colonial military system. Spanish soldiers constituted regular professional troops. Officers typically received a life appointment, and soldiers served for a fixed period of time. These units, which rotated back and forth between Spain and the Americas, consisted of two divisions, the armies of *refuerzo* and *dotación*. *Refuerzo* units provided relief, particularly during times of political crisis, to the more permanent army of *dotación*. In addition, the criteria of *limpieza de sangre* (blood purity) played a significant role. Men who participation in Spanish regular troops were required to be recognized as legally and racially white.[92] In the Spanish colonies, with their highly diverse populations of non-Spaniards and the racially mixed, imperial requirements of race and birth, already problematic within Spain, encountered new challenges as authorities formed defensive units with American-born men.

Colonial military defense consisted of fixed battalions and militias. Fixed battalions were the creole version of Spain's professional troops and were recruited and maintained in the Americas. Militia units, divided into urban and provincial ("disciplined") battalions, consisted of creoles and were segregated into *blancos, pardos,* and *morenos*. All typically drawn from the artisan classes, they performed weekly military drills. Urban units, often sponsored by guilds, engaged in battle infrequently. Provincial forces were designed to be called upon during emergencies.[93] As the age of revolution and rebellion advanced, militias found themselves serving more regularly and for extended periods.

Although distinguished by color and imperial origin, all those who served received military benefits. Uniforms distinguished soldiers from common workers, promoted discipline, and fostered group identity.

Generally those who enlisted earned regular pay, and officers received meal allowances. Upon retirement, military personnel received pensions, which their widows inherited.[94] In addition, these men gained a range of privileges through *fueros* and *preeminencias*. The Spanish crown extended *fuero* benefits to corporate groups in the form of certain kinds of civic exemptions inaccessible by the common public. These included the use by troops and their families of military courts and detention in local barracks instead of prisons. *Preeminencias* provided additional incentives such as exemptions from local taxes. In 1771, Spain granted these privileges to regular troops and colonial militias, regardless of rank and race.[95] Theoretically, this entitled officers of African descent to use the honorific title "Don" before their names, a practice usually reserved for whites or those who were legally white.[96] Militiamen of color, like their white counterparts, readily accepted *fueros* and *preeminencias*, not only in exchange for service to the empire but also to benefit themselves and their families.

Following the British occupation of Havana (1762–1763), Spanish colonial authorities instituted a series of reforms broadening the role of free *pardos* and *morenos* in the military.[97] By 1770, military troops in Cuba boasted over 3,000 soldiers of African descent among combined peninsular and creole forces totaling 11,667.[98] By the late eighteenth century, some accomplished black officers accumulated substantial money and property. Cristóval Carques, a thirty-eight year veteran of Havana's *pardo* militia, followed in the footsteps of his father, Francisco Javier Carques, a militia captain. Carques's father and his mother, Gabriela Pérez, a free woman of color, made sure young Cristóval became literate and joined the militia at an early age. By the end of his distinguished career and three wives later, Carques owned four houses, one slave, gold jewelry, clothing, and had saved over 6,000 pesos.[99] Such examples continued in the early nineteenth century. *Pardo* officer Nícolas Lanes acquired four houses, a carpentry workshop, and four slaves before his death in 1824. As a sign of their advancing social status, the children of military families frequently intermarried. In 1815, Félix Barbosa, a mulatto officer, married María Juliana de la Merced, the daughter of Franciso Reyes, a sergeant in Havana's *moreno* battalion.[100] Through military service in Cuba, and throughout colonial Spanish America, *libres de color* forged a network of relationships through marriage and community patronage that formed the cornerstone of group identity, solidarity, and upward social mobility.

Despite the benefits of military service for free men of color and the bravery they displayed in countless battles, some Spanish colonial officials remained apprehensive about arming black men. The recruitment of militiamen of color raised concerns over black fidelity and peril. For some authorities, the duties of black and mulatto militiamen, which ranged from protecting Caribbean coastal fortifications to catching slaves, reinforced their image as devoted, self-sacrificing, and honorable.[101] Black and mulatto officers also touted their "loyalty, fidelity, patriotism, and adherence to the governing system," as vital to the empire.[102] But cis-Atlantic struggles for domination reminded officials of the dangers inherent in arming men of African descent. Viceroy Revillagigedo (Juan Vicente Güemes Pacheco y Padilla, Conde de Revillagigedo), the Viceroy of New Spain (1789–1794), blamed the loss of Havana on the widespread incompetence of colonial militias, white and black. With the onset of the Haitian Revolution, Revillagigedo disbanded the bulk of militia of color companies in New Spain.[103] Francisco Antonio Crespo took things a step further. In his 1784 plan to reorganize New Spain's army, he denounced *castas* (persons of mixed racial ancestry) for their detrimental influence on Mexican culture.[104]

Similarly, Francisco Arango y Parreño, a major force in Cuba's expanding slave trade, cautioned against using militias of color. Although he praised free black men for their service to the crown, Arango emphasized their unpredictability. He insisted that veteran militiamen living in the countryside might not aid authorities in suppressing slave uprisings, and even spearhead revolt. To prevent a Haitian-style rebellion, Arango advocated dissolving these companies in the 1790s.[105] In addition, local officials and some abolitionists warned that Cuba's *pardo* and *moreno* militiamen should be viewed as "a potential enemy," claiming that "the best soldier is the most barbaric when he has someone to lead him."[106] Overall, although Cuba remained a stronghold of Spanish loyalism during the revolutionary wars in Spanish America, events during this tumultuous era only heightened local concerns over *pardo* and *moreno* militias. Mounting conflicts between militiamen and the colonial state would come to a dramatic climax in the aftermath of the Escalera rebellions.

The Road to La Escalera

In hindsight, Captain General Francisco Dionisio Vives's ominous remark regarding how the presence of free people of color in close proximity to slaves would be "very prejudicial some day," predicted the future.[107]

Indeed, subaltern struggles to acquire freedom, overcome racism, and dismantle slavery became progressively more volatile. The rapid and turbulent changes of the first decades of the nineteenth century, particularly the success of the Haitian Revolution in abolishing slavery and overthrowing French colonial rule, and the surge of loyalist emigration in the wake of Spanish American independence, had enduring repercussions in the Americas and the Atlantic World. As black rebellion surged in Cuba, Spanish colonial authorities responded with brute force, stiffer legislation, and biting commentary that targeted free people of color. For as much as officials feared slaves, they shuddered at the violent retribution *libres de color* were sure to seek for the freedoms they had been denied by whites.

Often inspired by slave revolts from neighboring Haiti and Jamaica, free blacks and slaves in Cuba forged alliances and fomented rebellions from the 1810s to the early 1840s. Some of the most well known included the Aponte rebellion and the Lucumí conspiracy. The Aponte rebellion shook the island in 1812, as José Antonio Aponte, a free *moreno*, retired military officer, and carpenter, united urban and rural *libres de color* and slaves to end Spanish rule and slavery.[108] In 1835, free blacks Hermengildo Jáurequi and Juan Nepomuceno Prieto, the latter a leader of a *lucumí cabildo* and a retired militia officer, led the Lucumí conspiracy in Havana.[109] Like Aponte, they wanted to abolish slavery and overthrow the colonial government.[110]

Lesser known episodes also represented black resistance. In 1825, over three hundred slaves revolted, setting fire to twenty-four coffee plantations in the Matanzas province.[111] Following an uprising by forty *emancipados* near Havana in July 1833, authorities arrested five *libres de color*, including a free woman of color known in her community as "La Reyna" (the queen), for concealing weapons in her home.[112] As the cycle of insurgency intensified in Cuba during the early 1840s, the uprisings revealed multiple levels of African disasporic agency with the quest for full freedom at their core.

Many authorities in Cuba and throughout the Caribbean blamed the successive uprisings on external agitation. Consequently, the influx of foreign-born free people of color into Cuba amplified apprehensions over rebellion and independence. Although the colony had been considered a bastion of colonial loyalty during the Latin American challenges for political liberty, authorities grew increasingly suspicious of the arrival of free black immigrants. Despite their claims of seeking loyal and honorable lives under the Spanish empire, these men and women came under increasing scrutiny for their mobility and potential to spread rebellious ideas. In the 1830s, Cuban captain generals Mariano Ricafort and Miguel Tacón renewed legislation from 1817 prohibiting foreign-born free people of color and clandestine slaves from entering Cuban ports precisely because they were seen as being "contagious with false doctrines invented by revolutionaries."[113] Some American newspapers cast Cuba, now situated between islands where slavery had been abolished, as the "only barrier that protects the institutions [of slavery] in the Southern States from the insidious attacks of the English abolition forces" in the Caribbean.[114]

These pervasive concerns and crises paved the road for the Escalera rebellions in Cuba. Each challenge to political authority, regardless of the vital positions free blacks held in sustaining and defending societies throughout Spanish America and beyond, reinforced European preoccupations over race, slavery, and freedom. The uprisings that punctuated Cuba in 1843 would unleash the colonial state's deep-seated resentment, racism, and brutality. *Libres de color*, as well as slaves, although forced to endure an era of unparalleled cruelty and constraint, responded with unexpected resiliency and agency.

* * *

The pragmatics of sustaining the Caribbean colony dictated that colonial authorities utilize the labor and services of *libres de color*. Spanish laws and traditions that prohibited women and men of African descent from professional and scholarly endeavors enabled free people of color to secure niches in the artisan, domestic, unskilled labor, and defense sectors. Although their status as free blacks and mulattoes cast them as threatening to Cuban slave society, the vital roles of *libres de color* afforded them the space to revise the intertwined issues of honor, gender, occupation, and ancestry to their own benefit whenever possible.

Free people of color challenged traditional constructions of gender through their public presence and work activities. Visitors noted the proliferation of free women of color in the streets, selling fruits, shopping for daily meals, or doing laundry. As free black and mulatto men traversed the streets during their daily work routine, observers commented on the obvious clustering of free men of color in skilled artisan positions. Although white men regarded these positions as lowly, officials and elites accused free *pardos* and *morenos* of supplanting them in these fields and causing white vagrancy.[115] From Spanish and creole perspectives, the public activities of *libres de color* undermined elite notions of proper female behavior and destabilized white males' participation in the skilled trades.

Militia service also located free men of color in the paradigm of essential, yet threatening. Colonial officials called on them time and again despite fears of arming men of African descent. In return, the legal privileges, status, and personal investment in defending Cuban shores that accompanied military duty bestowed honor and status on male *libres de color* and their families. *Pardo* and *moreno* militiamen, aware of their importance to the Spanish empire, particularly in terms of their personal sacrifices, voiced opinions about their discriminatory treatment in the face of loyal service. Participation in the militia enabled them to test societal boundaries and improve their status, while maintaining a level of protection.[116]

Despite the contradictory opinions they held regarding the occupational and defense activities of *libres de color*, authorities and intellectuals united in their alarm over the numerical expansion of the free sector of color. This "very prejudicial" population in Cuba raised tensions over the potential for *libres de color* to foment rebellion with slaves and creole dissidents.[117] As fears of insurgency became reality, authorities responded with racist legislation circumscribing the activities and disembarkation of free people of color in Cuba. Long-standing debates over how to quell the threat from an alliance between *libres de color* and slaves came to a head in 1843.

The ensuing repression of the Conspiracy of La Escalera struck a devastating blow at the free sector of color. The ways in which free black men and women responded, however, emphasized their perceived importance to and expectations of Cuba's colonial society. Their actions also heightened existing apprehensions over race relations, slavery, and freedom. Moving from 1844 to 1868, the following chapters trace the multiple efforts of *libres de color* to maneuver through the intense violence and dislocation of the infamous Year of the Lash and how they negotiated the Escalera era.

2 / Spectacles of Power: Repressing the Conspiracy of La Escalera

Being of immense goodness, Mighty God!
To thou I turn in my vehement pain . . .
Extend your omnipotent arm,
Scratch off of calumny the odious curtain;
And pull out this inominous stamp
With which the world wants to stain my forehead!
. . . Obstruct them, Lord, for the precious
Blood shed, which guilt shields
Of the sin of Adam, or for that
Candid Mother, sweet and lovely,
When wrapped up in sorrow, sad and crying
Followed your death like a heliacal star
If it suits your Suma Omnipotence
that I perish in such impious wickedness,
And that men insult my cold body

—PLÁCIDO

As guards led Plácido (Gabriel de la Concepción Valdés), celebrated Cuban poet, to his death before a firing squad, he reportedly recited verses from his final work, "A Plea to God."[1] The above excerpt from the poem highlights his grief over the repression of the Escalera revolts and the suffering it caused himself and others. Official allegations and witness testimonies, which accused Plácido of leading a conspiracy, left an "inominous stamp" for all to see. Using words that could be interpreted as either a statement of innocence in the plot or as confirming his actions to abolish slavery and end colonial rule, Plácido proclaimed, "I cannot lie to you, God of clemence/ . . . see through my body and soul." Although Plácido seemed prepared to "perish in such impious wickedness," he also called upon God to "obstruct" the true culprits—the O'Donnell administration, planters, proslavery advocates, and Spanish loyalists—those truly at fault. The blood they shed during the Year of the Lash shields their guilt, asserted the condemned poet. His verses reportedly "thrilled upon the hearts of the attentive masses" that lined the streets. As Plácido moved to sit on the execution bench, he stood briefly to bid the crowd farewell with a solemn "goodbye world." When five bullets failed to kill him, he reportedly turned to the firing squad and pointed to his heart, where two additional shots finally sealed his fate.[2]

Later that day, *Aurora*, a Matanzas-based newspaper, declared Plácido's death by firing squad, and nine others shot with him, an "Execution of Justice." The article justified the public reckoning, in the form of open and deadly punishments, to suppress the slave rebellions and their disruption to social order. Moreover, the executions represented the apex of a broader spectacle of power authorities unleashed to assure metropole officials and international observers that all "evil will be stifled."[3] Spanish colonial officials in Cuba justified virtually all forms of violence and coercion as a means to root out the leaders of the Escalera revolts, suppress potential uprisings, and reassert political, social, and economic control over the colony.

Cuban authorities were no strangers to rebellion or harsh retribution. Revolts throughout the Americas loomed ominously over Cuban slavery. The Haitian Revolution, Gabriel Prosser's Virginia conspiracy, and uprisings organized among slaves of specific African ethnic and religious traditions in Cuba and Brazil were among the more than twenty insurrections that challenged slavery in colonial and republican realms during the late eighteenth and early nineteenth centuries.[4] Decades of revolt in Cuba, particularly from 1812 to 1838, threatened to undermine the colony's burgeoning plantation society. Authorities repeatedly used armed force to quell internal revolts by slaves, *libres de color*, and creoles. They also relied on prohibitive legislation to help prevent any recurrence of unrest. Nevertheless, uprisings persisted. The cycle of rebellion and suppression crisscrossing the Americas in the first four decades of the nineteenth century foreshadowed the brutality initiated by Cuban authorities in the final weeks of 1843. January of 1844 ushered in a repression that engulfed thousands, including slaves, free blacks, creoles, and foreigners.

During the first three months of the Year of the Lash, authorities made mass arrests and tortured suspects on *la escalera*, the ladder, which became synonymous with the rebellions. Military Commission trials followed in April and condemned thousands to imprisonment, banishment, and death. The following month, Cuba's Captain General Leopoldo O'Donnell implemented legislation to expel foreign-born free people of color, coerce black and mulatto natives into exile, and impose new labor restrictions on the general population of African descent. A summer of bloody executions ensued. The socially and politically toxic environment also took its toll on those not directly implicated in the conspiracy. In spite of continued government retribution, reactions ranging from claims advancing annexation to the United States to vindication for individual and material suffering challenged colonial authority.

Some foreign officials and international media praised O'Donnell's methods, while others condemned them. Months before sentencing concluded in early 1845, Spanish colonial authorities in Cuba congratulated themselves for extinguishing dissent, ridding Cuba of rebellious *libres de color*, and restoring tranquillity. But had they? International commentary warned of the possibility, or even probability, that their actions would foment widespread revolt. Examining both the O'Donnell administration's rationale for the extended use of violence and the initial responses of *libres de color* and creoles sheds light on the evolving nature of repression and resistance.

Cycles of Revolt and Suppression

Cuba's political and economic ascendancy took place amid international struggles over colonialism, independence, slavery, and abolition. The "unthinkable" success of the Haitian Revolution fueled Cuban sugar production as the colony filled the void left by the demise of colonial Saint-Domingue. It also strained the delicate racial balance authorities pursued to curtail dissent from slaves and free people of color as Cuba's enslaved population more than doubled between 1817 and 1841, expanding from 199,145 to 436,495.[5] Moreover, by 1821 a substantial proportion of imported African captives were prisoners of war from Yorubaland, a region fragmented after the collapse of West Africa's Oyo empire in the early nineteenth century.[6] This influx evoked fears of organized slave rebellion attributed to the presence of recently arrived *lucumí*, as the Yoruba became known in Cuba. The *lucumí* expanded the influence of *cabildos de nación*, sociocultural mutual aid associations based on African ethnicity.[7] These factors combined to produce a combustible context for Cuban planters, officials, slaves, and free people of color.

Imperial politics also transformed the colony's political position. Independence in Latin America made Cuba the "ever-faithful isle," a bastion for Spanish loyalists and colonial refugees. But the shift came at a high price: loss of the mainland Spanish empire to anticolonial revolutions. Cautiously, and with little choice, Spain attempted to assuage tensions with Caribbean creoles by using military strength. Despite an

American observer's claim that "fear of punishment" governed the island's society, dissidence in Cuba proved constant.[8] As slave revolts and independence plots in the Spanish Caribbean swelled in the late 1820s and 1830s, colonial authorities responded with more violent methods.

The cycle of repression produced two main forms of public spectacle: whippings and executions. Most frequently, planters and officials used whippings to punish slave insubordination. Calculated to inflict anguish, one plantation technique consisted of tying slaves face down and striking them with a braided whip made of raw bullhide or manatee skin. Variations ranged from having the slave enumerate the blows out loud (returning to zero if the pain caused him or her to lose count) to being struck simultaneously by two whips.[9] Wounds from whipping, though agonizing, inevitably healed. Remaining deep scars, however, left permanent physical evidence of the power of the plantation owner to preserve slavery through violence. Moreover, for witnesses of all hues and legal statuses, the lash reinforced the colonial state's broader socio-racial hierarchy.

Prior to the Escalera repression, Cuban authorities increasingly relied on execution, by hanging and firing squad, as a major form of public punishment. In the wake of the 1812 Aponte rebellion, which united a wide range of urban and rural slaves and free people of color in uprisings designed to end Spanish rule and slavery, authorities hanged the accused ringleaders, including free *moreno* José Antonio Aponte, who was a carpenter, retired military officer, and leader of a *cabildo de nación*.[10] James Alexander, a British military officer visiting Havana in the early 1830s, observed how individuals condemned to death by the noose in Cuba "arrived at the fatal tree, where a multitude waited in anxious expectation of the site." Spectators watched the victim climb the ladder and the executioner adjust the rope, and then gawked as the body swung, limp and lifeless.[11] In an effort to heighten the state of terror and submission among slaves and free people of color, authorities shifted from death by hanging to execution by firing squad. As with the public hangings, a large crowd assembled on execution day. The accused emerged from a dimly lit chapel draped in black, where they had been held for twenty-four hours, listening to priests chanting prayers for the dead and viewing their own coffins. At the appointed hour, those scheduled for execution stood or sat with their back to the military guard, awaiting the final shot.[12]

Death by firing squad became more common in the mid 1830s. In Havana in 1835, Hermengildo Jáurequi and Juan Nepomuceno Prieto, the latter a leader of a *lucumí cabildo* and a retired militia officer, organized the Lucumí conspiracy to abolish slavery and colonialism.[13] A firing squad shot these leaders in the back.[14] After another uprising later that same year, officials shot six slaves and promised that "still many more" would be executed.[15] In 1839, the same year as the famed uprising aboard the *Amistad* off the coast of Cuba, militia officers of color, Captain León Monzón, Sergeant José Dabares, Sub-Lieutenant José del Monte del Pino, and Pilar Borrego, a survivor from the Aponte conspiracy, directed a rebellion in eastern Cuba's Guantánamo province.[16] They, too, were executed by firing squad. When slaves revolted on the *Empresa* coffee plantation in 1840, authorities again resorted to armed execution for the main agitators.[17] In addition, whether killed on the scaffold or by bullets, authorities often had the victim's bodies decapitated and mounted their heads on poles for display at the site of the insurgency.[18] The uprisings, often comprising slaves and free blacks, fueled officials' and planters' growing fears over the impact of rebellion and republicanism on Cuban stability, profits, and slavery. This, in turn, provoked more brutal responses. As visions of the colony's transformation into another Haiti multiplied, the cycle of black revolt and colonial oppression worsened.

In addition to creating the violent spectacle of whippings and executions, Cuban administrators punished alleged conspirators by imprisonment overseas. This effectively disposed of rebels, both black and white. In 1809, Cuban-born attorneys Joaquín Infante and Román de la Luz launched a separatist plot that united creoles and *libres de color*. Their new republic, however, would not necessarily abolish slavery or guarantee equality but would overthrow Spanish rule.[19] In response, Cuban authorities deported the accused leaders to Spanish prisons in North Africa.[20] Officials applied deportation again as a punishment three years later. After hanging Aponte and his accomplices in 1812, the government condemned dozens of others to prison in Saint Augustine, Florida.[21] The forced removal of dissidents to jails outside of Cuba eliminated an immediate threat to the island's political stability. By shipping rebel leaders to imperial prisons, where living conditions could turn the ruling into a death sentence, Spanish colonial authorities sought not only to rid the colony of dissidents but also to rip them from their families and potential collaborators.

The methods of suppressing slave revolt and punishing participants were hardly unique to Cuba. After an array of uprisings throughout the Americas, especially in Virginia (1800 and 1831), Louisiana (1811), South Carolina (1821), Guyana (1823), Jamaica (1831–1832), Brazil (1835), and

Puerto Rico (1841), authorities used excessive public violence against insurgents to reassert white racial and political supremacy.[22] Both forms of execution, as well as the parade of rebel leaders' detached heads, generated a bloody theater of capital punishment that simultaneously vilified black insubordination and glorified colonial dominance. In Cuba, as elsewhere, staging state power through death, dismemberment, and deportation enabled authorities to exact retribution, reestablish justice, and reactivate colonial and imperial authority in the aftermath of each uprising. All three forms of punishment, and many other kinds of reprisal, escalated during the Escalera repression.

The multiple rebellions that swept across Cuba in the spring and summer of 1843 intensified colonial preoccupations with revolt from the African-descended population. Experiences in Cuba, as well as examples throughout the Americas, gave the island's colonial administration ample reasons to quell the rebellious spirit of slaves and free blacks. Census data from 1841 fueled fears of black domination by spotlighting Cuba's white minority (41.6%).[23] Faced with an expanding and restless black population, Cuban officials met each challenge with violent assault and coercive policies to erode the position, influence, and activities of people of color. The cycle of rebellion and repression came to a head in 1843. The successive revolts that became known as the Conspiracy of La Escalera unhinged politicians and planters, who released a repression infamous for its brutality and scope.

The Escalera Rebellions and the Year of the Lash

In March, May, and November of 1843, three major slave uprisings reverberated across Cuba. Heightened British enforcement of the abolition of the slave trade and establishment of the joint British-Spanish Mixed Commission in Havana gave rise to conspiratorial links between slaves and English officials in Cuba. On March 25, one day prior to the first insurrection, Joseph Tucker Crawford, the British consul in Havana, recalled receiving an unexpected visit from Juan Rodríguez, a "Coloured man of some respectability."[24] Rodríguez claimed that David Turnbull, Britain's former diplomatic officer, offered to provide weapons in case a rebellion broke out. Crawford dismissed this as "madness," asserting "that emancipation is to be brought about without violence or an open and disastrous war of castes."[25] The next day, an estimated one thousand enslaved workers set fire to crops and structures on five sugar plantations near Matanzas in the Bemba (Jovellanos) and Cimarrones districts.

They also ripped up part of the railroad between Matanzas and Júcaro. By the time military troops arrived, area whites had subdued the rebellion, leaving forty to one hundred slaves dead. The military immediately hanged those apprehended, with no pretense of a trial. Meanwhile, some slaves escaped into the hillsides. In mid-April, one captured rebel, who allegedly had arrived in Cuba with David Turnbull eight months prior to the uprising, reportedly apologized for his crimes before execution on the scaffold.[26] The U.S. media along the mid-Atlantic and Gulf coasts attributed the rebellion to abolitionists, particularly the "incendiary instigations of English emissaries."[27] Although colonial troops and colonists quelled the uprisings, this would not be the end; more disruptions soon followed.

Another large insurrection broke out in May, this time in the eastern part of the island, near Santiago de Cuba. The area's proximity to Haiti, a free black republic less than ninety miles away, and Jamaica, a British colony less than 150 miles away, where slavery had been abolished for a decade, aggravated existing anxieties. Rebels attacked property, planters, overseers, and their families, leaving numerous dead or wounded. Because the uprisings seemed even more organized, and "more desperate and bloody" than those in March, General Francisco Javier de Ulloa, head of the navy, sent a war steamship and four additional vessels to the port.[28] "Such are the bitter fruits of slavery," remarked an article in the *Emancipator and Free American*, a New York City abolitionist newspaper. Of the May rebellions, it concluded, "the constantly recurring insurrections of slaves, proves that the masters' throats are indeed in danger so long as they are occupied in swallowing the fruits of unrequited and whip-exhorted toil."[29] These warnings rang true as minor revolts sprang up across the Matanzas province in the summer and early fall of 1843. Slave uprisings damaged the Flor de Cuba, Concepción, and Ácana sugar mills and plantations in June, and the Arratía *ingenio* in July, and small revolts occurred on numerous plantations in September and October.[30]

These uprisings grew more volatile as the year came to a close, when a final set of rebellions scorched Matanzas again. The renewed revolt in western Cuba was not surprising in a region where thousands of slaves toiled on sugar and coffee plantations. On November 6, nearly five hundred slaves spread rebellion to six estates in Sabanilla.[31] Starting with the Triumvirato sugar plantation, men and women proceeded to the neighboring Ácana estate, where slaves had revolted in June. Insurgent slaves burned property, killed or wounded whites in their path, and dragged hesitant bondsmen with them. By the time rebels arrived at the nearby

Concepción plantation early the next morning, the local magistrate had ordered mounted troops to subdue the uprising. Instead, arriving slaves drove off the forces and, joined by thirty Concepción slaves, set fire to the grounds.[32] Two more sites, San Lorenzo and San Miguel, suffered damage as slaves continued their rebellion for another day. An armed confrontation with a cavalry regimen and civilians finally stopped the revolt. At the end of the struggle, fifty slaves lay dead and seventy-seven were taken prisoner. Officers ordered their men to locate and decapitate rebels who had escaped into the neighboring hills (see map 1).[33]

The matter, however, did not end after slaves had been captured and punished. Rumors of a failed plot circulated. Planters claimed that several thousand slaves and free people of color had organized a massive insurrection, but their plans had been discovered before all parts of it could be implemented. Again, foreign media sources speculated that a foreign abolition agent had encouraged the rebellion, leaving the "poor unfortunate blacks" at the mercy of colonial forces.[34] To "prove" these allegations, local sugar planter Esteban Santa Cruz de Oviedo uncovered information from Polina, Santa Cruz de Oviedo's slave and concubine, who testified she had overheard discussions of the planned revolt in the slave quarters. In response, Antonio García Oña, governor of the Matanzas province, gained approval from Cuba's captain general, Leopoldo O'Donnell, to send troops into the region to quell further revolt and determine the origins of the plot.[35] O'Donnell, planters, and general proslavery supporters could not accept that slaves alone devised the coordinated rebellions.[36] Who were the ringleaders? British and local abolitionists? Slaves? *Libres de color*? An alliance among these groups? O'Donnell set out to determine the conspiracy's origins by any means necessary.

January 1844 marked the start of Cuba's infamous Year of the Lash. By mid-month, authorities extracted slave testimonies implicating free people of color in the uprisings.[37] At the close of January, O'Donnell reported to the Spanish crown that he had apprehended "two whites and several free blacks" involved in the plot.[38] To gain additional evidence, the O'Donnell administration launched an islandwide investigation to uncover the conspiracy's extended roots. He directed Fulgencio Salas, president of the Military Commission, to regain control over the island by almost any means. Furthermore, O'Donnell emphasized the "necessity" of using violence to prosecute "free persons of color under indictment" who refused to name their accomplices.[39] As more coerced evidence emerged, O'Donnell confirmed to the Ultramar, the Spanish

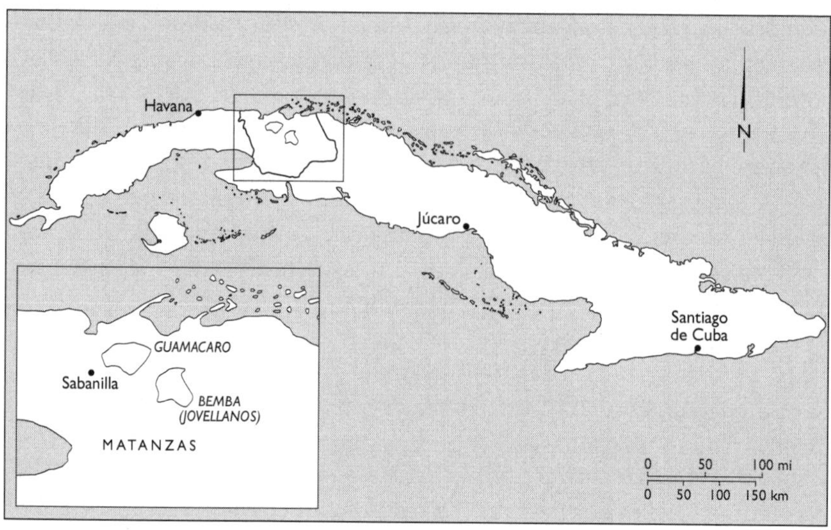

MAP 1. Cuba with markers of major insurrections for 1843.

Overseas Ministry, that "the vast conspiracy that tried to raise a black rebellion . . . was led by . . . a considerable number of free black and mulatto men of color . . . [whose] bad customs and vices are harmful elements in this territory." Once the ringleaders had been identified, O'Donnell planned to execute, imprison, and deport co-conspirators.[40] In March he and Salas accused Gabriel de la Concepción "Plácido" Valdés, a *mulato libre* and acclaimed poet, of being the leader of the conspiratorial plot.

A man of letters, Plácido shared few traits with well-known rebel leaders such as Nathanial Turner, Denmark Vesey, and José Antonio Aponte, who used their ties to the slave community via religion or *cabildo* membership, or their prominence as skilled artisans or militia officers, to rally enslaved men and women. With the exception of his status as a free man of color, like Aponte, Plácido had virtually nothing in common with major insurgent organizers of the era. Although Plácido worked intermittently as a combmaker, silversmith, printer, and carpenter, he did little to distinguish himself in any of these areas.[41] Numerous individuals identified as co-ringleaders proved more in line with the stereotype. Two men executed with Plácido, African-born Franciso Abrahantes, a barber and officer in the *moreno* militia, and Tómas Vargas, a popular phlebotomist and sergeant in the *pardo* militia, possessed more typical affiliations and occupations.[42] Plácido's fame and widespread recognition as a poet, however, may have exacerbated his downfall. When thirty-two witnesses accused Plácido of being "the junta President, a rebel recruiter, instigator, and the primary conspiratorial agent," authorities recast his celebrity as notoriety.[43]

However, rather than concede that the conspiracy had been the complete creation of free blacks and slaves, Military Commission officials accused David Turnbull, the former British Consul in Cuba, of being, at the very least, the plot's "primary motor and source." Cuban authorities vilified Turnbull as an interloper who took "advantage of the aspirations of the population of color," "instilling in them the idea of liberty," and seducing them with promises of "a prosperous future" filled with enhanced employment opportunities, features especially appealing to "pardos." Turnbull then "disseminated his emissaries" throughout the colony. These men, a *junta* (council) composed of Plácido (President), Santiago Pimiento (Treasurer), Tomás Vargas (General), and Andrés Dodge (Ambassador), along with José Miguel Román, Antono Bernoqui, and Pedro de la Torre, germinated the "seed of insurrection." The black population, reassured by the "idea of emancipation and that they would be protected by the English government," sprang into action.[44]

Although debates over whether or not a conspiracy existed or had been manufactured by the government would continue until today, at the time of the repression Cuban authorities pursued only one plausible explanation for the organized rebellions: foreign instigation. External political pressures consisting of British enforcement of the abolition of the slave trade and slave emancipation in the British Caribbean, Haiti, and several Latin American republics bordering the Caribbean region, combined to amplify Cuba's internal anxieties over slavery and rebellion. Only the British, who had promised free blacks fuller freedom and slaves immediate liberation, it was argued, could have enticed the free community of color to lead the slave population in a volatile plot against Cuba. In this paradigm, "President" Plácido, the *junta*, and Cuba's entire African-descended population functioned as scapegoats in the suppression of the revolts.

The repression reached new levels as authorities intensified their quest to identify and punish co-conspirators. Cuban residents and foreigners, free and slave, endured invasive searches, arrests, interrogations, trials, and abuses from January through early April 1844. Authorities traveled throughout their jurisdictions extorting confessions from the African-descended population, and seized furniture, cattle, horses, and other property from *libres de color*. Accounts by foreigners in Cuba often revealed what the O'Donnell administration attempted to downplay in colonial sources. For instance, in Matanzas, island visitors reported that officials gratified their sexual desires with the wives, daughters, and sisters of male victims, while others tortured and hanged victims from a tree, and then took pleasure cutting the ropes and watching the men's bodies fall to the ground writhing in agony.[45] Another described how the countryside echoed with screams of anguish and that in some places the streets were "running with negro blood."[46] Foreign officials, such as Thomas Rodney, the U.S. Consul in Matanzas, preferred to focus on the pragmatics of quelling the revolt. He anticipated harsh punishments for bondsmen and the expulsion or execution of whites and free blacks involved in the conspiracy.[47]

Creoles and foreign officials also found themselves targeted by the Cuban government. Authorities accused Domingo del Monte and José de la Luz y Caballero, two of Cuba's distinguished creole intellectuals, along with David Turnbull, the former British consul, with playing major roles in organizing the conspiracy.[48] Turnbull, who had been expelled from Cuba in 1842 and now held a position in Jamaica on the Court of Mixed Commission, eluded prosecution. Although de la Luz initially avoided arrest, upon his return home from Europe Spanish colonial officials in Cuba placed him under house arrest. Fearing a similar fate, Domingo del Monte eluded apprehension by remaining in Paris in exile.[49] Nevertheless, the Spanish crown labeled all three men enemies of Spain.[50] Lesser known creoles, indicted as accomplices in fomenting rebellion on sugar plantations, received an array of punishments. For instance, the Military Commission sentenced Juan Rivero to six years in public works, fined Juan Novell 200 pesos with an additional stipulation that he be kept under surveillance for one year in Cuba, and offered Rafael Rodríguez the limited choice of exile or confinement on the sugar plantation where he was accused of having fomented rebellion.[51] Although the accusations against Turnbull appeared more symbolic than actionable, the range of penalties imposed on creoles left little doubt that the Military Commission judges sought to make an example of creoles who posed a threat to colonial stability.

Officials also censored and seized an array of contraband literature and ousted creole writers from Cuba. Author Cirilo Villaverde, who would publish *Cecilia Valdés or the Hill of the Angel* during his eventual exile in the United States, corresponded with Domingo del Monte in Paris. His letter characterized the Cuban milieu of 1844 as poisonous for writers and readers. "You are the only one," Villaverde proclaimed, "who can reveal to the civilized world the truth about what happened here" in Cuba.[52] Authorities banned Gertrudis Gómez de Avellaneda's antislavery novel *Sab* and the feminist work *Dos Mujeres* (Two Women), which critiqued marriage and the social oppression of women.[53] When local authorities discovered a creole woman with a copy of poet Pedro Santacilia's "Mi Prisión" ("My Prison"), which compared Cuba's colonial status to that of imprisonment, they charged her with suspicion of supporting a foreign takeover of the colony, or filibusterism. For his part as the author, Santacilia, who was currently living in temporary exile in Spain, found himself permanently banished.[54] Creole writers such as Gertrudis Gómez de Avellaneda, Domingo del Monte, and José Antonio Saco, who already resided in Europe prior to 1843, also witnessed any opportunity for their return to Cuba vanish.[55]

The persecution of creoles during the Escalera repression caused many to also seek refuge in the United States. Some of the most prominent included authors Gaspar Betancourt Cisneros, Juan Clemente Zenea, Miguel T. Tolón, and Cirilo Villaverde, as well as Pedro Santacilia, who traversed the Atlantic from Spain to the United States. These men took up residence among compatriot writers in New York and New Orleans, where they started newspapers and published essays for the growing Cuban exile community. Their writings promoted an array of political agendas ranging from annexation to independence to the abolition of slavery.[56] The New York-based exile periodical *La Verdad*, under the directorship at various times by Betancourt Cisneros, Tolón, Santacilia, and Villaverde, stressed how some creoles sought an alternative political association with the United States under which they could garner a higher level of autonomy, promote U.S. business interests, and deal with the question of slavery without social turmoil. As noted by American observer William Cullen Bryant, the annexation of Cuba to the United States would "rid them of a tyrannical government, and allow them to manage their own affairs in their own way."[57] After breaking with *La Verdad*, Villaverde partnered with Manuel Antonio Mariño to edit the New Orleans newspaper *El Independiente*. Drawing on a broad-based readership that included exiles and immigrants from South America, the articles promoted full Cuban sovereignty through armed revolution, but only for the benefit of white Cubans.[58] In contrast, *El Mulato*, edited by Matanzas-born Carlos de Colins in New York, attacked slavery, urged readers to acknowledge the African influences in Cuba, and argued that natural rights applied to all men, including slaves.[59] Moreover, each group pitched Cuba as central to various international agendas. Annexationists posited Cuba as central to trade routes linking the Atlantic and Pacific. Anti-colonialists feared British and French advances to abolish slavery because this would weaken Cuba's financial stability. Abolitionists took a transnational approach, criticizing not only Cuban but also U.S. slaveholders in the struggle for universal emancipation in the nineteenth century.[60] The disparate perspectives within the exile community echoed sentiments in Cuba and within the Atlantic community. The repression not only aggravated tensions over slavery, freedom, and imperialism, but also raised the stakes over the colony's political and economic future.

The fear of foreign-led machinations against the colony meant that international residents of diverse nationalities also suffered under the repression. Authorities reportedly chained a British man to a log and left him outside for over one hundred days, then threw him in jail, where he died.[61] Monsieur Mollier, French consul in Cuba, complained vehemently that Cuban officials unjustly detained six of his countrymen, at least four of them wealthy planters residing in Matanzas, because of the continued hatred and suspicion surrounding Haitian refugees in Cuba, especially those who remained in the colony after 1808, when Napoleonic forces usurped the Spanish crown.[62] Christopher Boone, an American working as a machinist and engineer in the Matanzas region, was arrested and confined for fifty-one days after a slave testified that Boone controlled a large cache of weapons. Thomas Rodney, of the U.S. consulate, refuted the charges and characterized Boone as "the innocent victim of official tyranny, outrage and abuse."[63] Letters from Havana to Boston warned, "No foreigner in Cuba is safe for an hour, under this state of things."[64]

Although the O'Donnell administration amplified its approach toward punishing slaves and free people of color in 1844, the massive arrests and sentencing of creoles and white foreigners signaled a departure from previous repressive measures. For instance, in 1809, when Cuban-born attorneys Joaquín Infante and Román de la Luz launched a separatist plot uniting creoles and *libres de color*, Cuban authorities sentenced them to deportation to Spanish prisons in North Africa, rather than execution.[65] Officials hesitated to inflict widespread violence on the white population for fear of how that might influence slaves and free blacks. The early months of 1844, however, overrode white exemption from oppression. The wanton cruelty left few untouched. Torture, execution, deportation, and imprisonment defined the Year of the Lash.

Overall, the pervasive violence of the Escalera repression reached far beyond established norms for quelling revolt. In Matanzas, officials arrested over four thousand people. Prisons, jails, and forts overflowed and authorities forced many private residences to house captives.[66] Hundreds died during interrogation. Most of those arrested were denied bail and were unable to ascertain the actual accusation until a court appearance. In striving to simultaneously suppress rebellions, restore social order, and preserve property—slaves, crops, and buildings—the O'Donnell administration aimed to "punish in a severe and exemplary manner the chiefs [of the slaves] and the white and free people of color who have introduced this germ of unrest and insubordination."[67] The cruel process would have lasting, unforeseen repercussions, both in Cuba and abroad.

Strategies of Repression

The O'Donnell administration's goals—to suppress, restore, and punish—targeted conspiracy leaders, accomplices, and potential rebels. Although creoles and foreign whites were implicated and punished, the African-descended population bore the brunt of colonial retribution. Travelers' depictions of torture on the ladder fueled the grisly imagery associated with the repression. Richard Kimball, a lawyer from New York visiting Havana, described an interrogation session as follows:

> [the judge/executioner] ordered his victims to be taken to a room which had been white-washed, and whose sides were besmeared with blood and small pieces of flesh, from the wretches who had preceded them. . . . There stood a bloody ladder, where the accused were tied, with their heads downward, and whether free or slave, if they would not avow what the fiscal officer insinuated, were whipped to death. . . . They were scourged with leather straps, having at the end a small destructive button, made of fine wire. . . . Their deaths were made to appear, by certificates from physicians, as having been caused by diarrhea.[68]

Theodore Phinney, a British landholder in Cuba, who criticized officials for killing and injuring many of his own slaves, gave an equally vile characterization of men "stripped naked and lashed to a ladder on the ground" with their arms and legs stretched in opposite directions until their "joints fairly cracked" and their muscles trembled in anticipation of the lash's agonizing blow or he declared his guilt.[69] Kimball's account of torture on the ladder left little to the imagination. Rather, it emphasized the extreme levels of cruelty, ranging from the mental intimidation of being in a "whitewashed room . . . besmeared with" their predecessor's flesh and blood to the physical terror of the whip outfitted with "a small destructive button" designed to inflict excruciating pain. Phinney's version highlighted the powerlessness of the accused over their situation marked by physical vulnerability, pain, and involuntary confession.

In the cycle of rebellion and suppression, instruments of torture, such as the ladder and the "enhanced" whip, were not uncommon, but rather staples of domination in the plantation zones (see figure 2). Gruesome depictions, however, reveal how proven methods of control intensified during the Escalera repression. To root out the source of the alleged conspiracy, authorities went to new extremes to extract confessions. Government sanctioned torture, and medical fraud paved the way for cruel behavioral excess. These ubiquitous scenes of human flesh secured on a ladder by knotted ropes, helpless to the multiple strikes of the punisher's whip, seared an indelible image into the conspiracy's legacy.

Although some planters and witnesses from England and the United States decried the brutal methods of the Escalera repression, most considered the violence necessary. As one observer declared, "what else can they do? The Government leaves the negro conspirators at their mercy. . . . Can they suffer the slaves to witness the impunity of their crime?"[70] Meanwhile, U.S. consuls in Cuba and American newspapers acknowledged that such "exquisite torture" simply drove slaves and free people of color "to confess, or rather consent to the confession of conspiracies, which exist only in the minds of despotic rulers" in order to relieve their agony.[71] Some victims, however, resigned themselves to pain and death. Andrés Dodge, a free *pardo* and a prominent Havana dentist, endured torture on the ladder on three separate occasions before being executed for refusing to confess to any accusations.[72] By defying investigators at great personal torment, Dodge invoked his last shred of agency. Perhaps as proof of his commitment to personal and political freedom, he accepted death rather than betray the *junta*. Nevertheless, hundreds more were forced to profess or fabricate the truth. By using the ladder and whip to inflict pain and procure anguished declarations, Cuban officials not only stretched previous norms in the cycle of revolt and repression but also revealed their sense of desperation in the colony's battle over antislavery and pro-independence movements.

EXECUTIONS

Execution ushered in the suppression of the 1843 uprisings. Unofficial reports underscore that troops killed dozens of slaves on the spot during the initial confrontations in Matanzas.[73] When formal trials began in April, the Military Commission sentenced accused leaders

FIGURE 2. Whipping Slaves on the ladder. *Harper's Weekly*, November 28, 1868, vol. 12, p. 753. Courtesy of "The Atlantic Slave Trade and Slave Life in the Americas: A Visual Record" website, http://hitchcock.itc.virginia.edu/Slavery, Virginia Foundation for the Humanities and the University of Virginia Libraries.

and co-conspirators to death. On the basis of testimony from twelve to thirty-two witnesses per suspect, judges condemned principal provocateurs to execution by firing squad. In addition to Plácido, they indicted free *pardos* Luis Guigot, listed as a foreign emissary; Santiago Pimienta for leading uprisings in Bermeja, near Matanzas; Pedro de la Torre for organizing revolts in Cienfuegos; and Jorge Lopez, Antonio Bernoqui, José Miguel Román, Andrés Dodge, and *moreno libre* Manuel Quiñones for fomenting rebellion in Matanzas.[74] Slaves Dionisios *carabalí*, Tómas *lucumí*, and Félix *gangá* faced violent executions by quartering and decapitation for killing their white masters and for their "confessions" of leadership in the conspiracy.[75] For inciting revolt on four plantations in Santa Clara, authorities voted unanimously to execute *pardo libre* Manuel Mier by firing squad. Officials then posted his head along the road as a warning to potential insurgents.[76] Official figures from Matanzas listed 38 male slaves and 38 free men of color put to death for complicity in the plot.[77]

The same fate awaited Antonio Marrero and Antonia, the only white man and slave woman to be executed in connection with the conspiracy. Judges indicted them for their independent actions on the Buena Esperanza coffee estate in Matanzas owned by retired lieutenant Pedro Domench. Twelve witnesses accused Marrero, a Canary Islander, of taking part in the conspiracy by fomenting revolt among the slaves. In the case of Antonia, a young slave boy named Matias discovered the plan she devised with three bondsmen—Blas, Patricio, and Melchor—to poison their owner. Another slave, Tomás Robaino, was put to death for supplying the toxin.[78] The roles of Antonio and Antonia struck at the heart of social relations in the colony. As a white immigrant from the Spanish empire, Antonio was expected to conform to colonial hierarchies that privileged both his birth in the Old World and his whiteness. The actions of Antonia, a trusted domestic who had virtually unlimited access to the family's food, challenged master-slave relations at an intimate level. Both Antonio and Antonia violated colonial behavioral codes involving race, ethnicity, and gender. In the minds of officials, the punishment of death matched the crimes.

BANISHMENT AND OVERSEAS IMPRISONMENT

In addition to executing conspirators, officials banished hundreds from the island. For instance, judges sentenced creole José Díaz, indicted for planning the revolt, to expulsion from the Spanish Caribbean or suffer life imprisonment. Five of his own slaves testified against him.[79] Given the cruelty of methods used to extract confessions, it was not uncommon for slaves to implicate whites. Similarly, Rafael Rodríguez and his father Vicente Rodríguez were charged as accomplices in fomenting rebellion on the Santa Ana de Jaspe sugar estate and sentenced to expulsion or confinement at the plantation.[80] Few *criollos*, however, received outright banishment. Just as only one out of seventy-eight was condemned to death, only two white men were recorded in the compilation of Matanzas sentences as being sentenced to banishment.[81] Instead, authorities targeted *libres de color* for expulsion.

Given the key roles of free blacks in the rebellions, the Military Commission actively sought to reduce the number of free people of color, particularly convicted leaders. Judges ruled explicitly that *morenos libres* José Subirá, Alonso *lucumí*, Mateo *carabalí*, and Juan José Perez Barnuevo be deported immediately and barred from setting foot in Spanish Caribbean colonies under penalty of death.[82] The Military

Commission often focused on the black elite—military officers, skilled artisans, and musicians. This included ordinary men, such as bricklayers Agustín Lopez and Félix Justis, carpenters Serafin Lopez and José María O-Farrill, retired sergeant José María Zayas, and those who were more famous, like celebrated *moreno libre* Claudio Brindis de Salas, a militia officer, popular musician, and orchestra leader.[83] At times, trials resulted in the mass expulsion of fifteen to twenty-eight free men of color per session.[84] By the end of the commission sentencing, *libres de color* constituted 99.5 percent (433 out of 435) of those banished from Cuba.[85] This extraordinary proportion demonstrated the government's identification of free people of color as a major source of racial dissent in general and as leaders in the alleged conspiracy in particular. Banishment accomplished two specific goals. First, it removed rebel leaders immediately and permanently. Banning them from returning to Cuba or Puerto Rico severed family ties. These men, forced to relinquish their property and pay court costs, faced the hard reality of starting their lives over, penniless and in exile. Second, deportation achieved the long-standing but unrealized aim of eliminating the negative and disruptive influence *libres de color* had on slaves who aspired to their own freedom.

Authorities utilized overseas imprisonment as yet another method for removing free people of color from Cuba. The Military Commission sent a handful of free blacks, such as José Fertrudis Ramos and Felipe Valdés García, to prisons in Seville and Valladolid, Spain.[86] Judges, however, shipped the majority of convicted prisoners to Spain's presidios in Ceuta, Spanish Morocco. For taking part in revolts on plantations and surrounding farms in the districts of Guamacaro and Lagunillas, *pardos libres* Faustino Benitez, Pascual Elijio, and Guillermo Duarte received verdicts of four to six years of imprisonment in North Africa.[87] Following convictions for instigating uprisings on the Luisa estate and neighboring ranches, *mulato libre* Águstin Jímenez and *negros libres* José María Lopez, Pedro Morales, and Tomás Alvarez were sentenced to the maximum penalty—ten years in Ceuta.[88] Some creoles experienced the same fate, such as Manuel Julio. Condemned for selling poison to Pedro Domench's slaves, Julio was sentenced to four years in a North African prison.[89] Furthermore, these rulings frequently carried stipulations that, in addition to imprisonment in Ceuta, they were also prohibited "from returning to this island and Puerto Rico."[90] If these were violated, some offenders, like Benitez, Elijio, and Duarte, would face life imprisonment.[91] Other transgressors, such as *moreno libre* Juan José Perez Barnuevo, alleged co-conspirator of the Escalera rebellions, and *pardo libre* José Benitez, accused of leading the uprising on the Encanto estate in the Macurijes district, would be executed if "found on Cuban soil."[92]

Despite precedents set in 1809, when officials sentenced creole lawyers Joaquín Infante and Román de la Luz to imprisonment in North Africa for leading an insurgent movement, the council rarely resorted to sending *criollos* out of the country for confinement during the Escalera repression. [93] According to extant records, authorities formally incarcerated only six whites. As with executions and banishments, *libres de color* predominated in overseas imprisonment. Of the over 1,800 individuals sentenced to prison, free people of color made up 70 percent.[94] By exporting the convicted, banning residency in the Spanish Caribbean, and ensuring exile with threats of perpetual incarceration and capital punishment, authorities used the Escalera repression to remove hundreds of alleged co-conspirators—especially *libres de color*—for good.

LOCAL IMPRISONMENT AND PUNISHMENT

Military Commission judges, of course, also relied on local confinement. In general, they stipulated up to ten years in a Cuban jail or on a plantation. For their "complicity in the conspiratorial projects," the council ordered slaves Pedro Quevedo, Gabriel Lopez, and José de Jesus *gangá*, along with six others, to serve ten years in Havana's jail.[95] The accumulated imprisonment sentences included at least 700 free people of color and 500 slaves, ultimately exceeding over 1,200 men and women.[96] The accused all sustained indignities designed to shatter the rebels' spirit. In many instances, property rights compelled officials to remand a large proportion of slaves destined for jail to the plantations. Back in the hands of their owners, bondsmen and women suffered harsh punishments, such at those dictated for Juana, Clara, Joaquin, and Justo. For participating in the revolts, Juana and Clara, two of the eighteen slave women listed in the Matanzas records, were condemned to six months in shackles at Don Juan Bautista Coffigny's farm.[97] Joaquin and Justo, both *lucumís*, suffered stiffer penalties. With eleven accusations for plotting to kill their owners and six more for being rebel leaders, Joaquin spent the next ten years in irons. Justo received four years in the same condition, plus fifty lashes.[98] Plantation owners justified these violent and demoralizing punishments as necessary for reasserting social and political order, especially in the sugar regions.

Because the colonial state incarcerated creoles and returned a large proportion of slaves to their owners, this meant free *pardos* and *morenos* bore the brunt of local jail time and spent a significant proportion of it awaiting trial. As noted previously, the Commission sentenced several hundred more free people of color than slaves into Cuban jails. In addition, *libres de color* often spent up to a year incarcerated before going to trial. For many of these individuals, such as *pardos* José Agustín Puerta and Blas Ordóñez and *morenos* Lúcas Mendiola and Felipe González, the court frequently concluded the matter as time served, but the psychological and physical damage could not be reversed.[99] The experience in Cuban jails was traumatic for all and deadly for some. A particularly egregious example is found in the case of well-known writer Juan Francisco Manzano. Like Plácido, Manzano's status as a poet, the similarity of his name to accused conspirator Manuel Manzano, and his affiliation with Domingo Del Monte, an abolitionist-leaning liberal creole charged with leading the conspiracy, probably influenced judges to extend Manzano's imprisonment several times before his final release. In a letter written while incarcerated during the fall of 1844, he described prison life and its debilitating effects. "Today I have close to seven months [in jail] . . . I have exhausted my methods with which to feed myself in this prison, where each day my health weakens." He asked friends for donations so his wife could feed him and his daughters.[100] For Francisco Uribe, a respected tailor and sergeant in the militia of color, pretrial imprisonment in Havana had a deadly outcome. After being arrested and tortured, Uribe committed suicide.[101] Whether found innocent or guilty, intense pain, indefinite captivity, and flashbacks of the "bloody ladder," vividly described by eye witness and New York lawyer Richard Kimball, surely haunted detainees.[102]

The remaining penalties imposed on individuals of African descent being held in custody, whether slave or free, ranged from hard labor to surveillance. Authorities regularly punished the elderly, minors, and women judged guilty of petty complicity by sending them to work in the colonial hospital, where they were compelled to care for and clean up after the sick and destitute, or to the workhouse, where they would perform a variety of hard labor. The council sentenced *pardo libre* José Domingo Moreno to four years of hospital service due to his "old age." They condemned free mulatto Francisco Cobo to four years of labor with the Department of Industry because of his youth. Judges forced *negra libre* Margarita Morejon to serve a year in a Havana hospital.[103] Clearly, factors such as age or gender only somewhat protected the accused. The hospital's environment of sickness and disease could easily lead to illness in the convicted, and labor for the Department of Industry was tantamount to slavery for free blacks. Moreover, although the Commission absolved over one thousand claimants, a substantial proportion of those deemed innocent had conditions attached to their release. Some rulings subjected free people of color and slaves, such as *pardo libre* Antonio Olivera and bondsman Antonio *mina*, although found innocent, to forced labor on a chain gang before being released.[104] Two years of close surveillance accompanied the acquittals for *negros libres* Tomas Lasonséc and Pablo Oquendo.[105] Despite being placed under close watch at hospitals, workhouses, and at home, overall, these judgments for minor offenses and even innocence did little to abate colonial suspicion of *libres de color.*

By January 1845, the Military Commission had carried out seventy-one rounds of sentencing. Of the colony's population of 1,007,624 inhabitants, authorities sentenced 1,836 people. Among that number, free people of color composed 1,232 (67%), slaves were listed as 590 (32%), and whites numbered 14 (almost 1%). With the exception of those executed, free blacks and mulattoes formed the majority of individuals indicted for rebellion and alleged conspiracy.[106] The punishments—execution, banishment, overseas and local imprisonment, hard labor, and surveillance—severely reduced the financial resources of the population of African descent, separated families, and ensured that free people of color, in particular, would struggle for decades to rebuild social networks and an economic base. Authorities hoped the repression would avert any future threat from slaves and *libres de color.*

Indeed, *libres de color* not formally convicted of conspiracy or fomenting rebellion were left gasping for breath as the O'Donnell administration choked the colony with fear. Nevertheless, numerous free black men and women initiated quests to locate jailed loved ones and petitioned for the return of confiscated items and property. For instance, after authorities arrested María del Francito Flores's brother Miguel, she "demanded [to know] the state of his health."[107] When he secured his release from jail, Serverino Flores requested officials return the money they had taken during his apprehension.[108] Given the horrific conditions for those arrested, María del Francito Flores had ample reason to be concerned about her brother's physical condition. Nevertheless, the inquiry also put her at risk for interrogation. Even after gaining his freedom, Severino Flores, instead of steering clear of officials, sought personal justice by demanding the return of what was rightfully his.

María de los Ángeles Pedroso petitioned for the return of the house and land confiscated from her husband, Lázaro after his arrest. She claimed them as her "exclusive property" and produced documentation verifying that she had acquired the real estate before her marriage.[109] Pedroso's assertion of her right to holdings seized illegally indicated her clear understanding of personal property rights. Moreover, she claimed these rights despite, or perhaps because of, the fact that her husband's unknown fate was in the hands of authorities. Whether or not she lost her husband, she would still need to provide housing and sustenance for herself and the rest of her family. Fortunately, Cuban officials ultimately granted her request. The types of claims presented by Flores and Pedroso demonstrate that, despite intimidating conditions, *libres de color* continued to use proven juridical methods to reclaim confiscated property and money, no matter how nominal these possessions might have seemed to authorities. Early efforts to reconnect with family members and recover material wealth, in the midst of the repression, set the stage for understanding the multiple forms of agency free people of color would engage to negotiate the Escalera era.

International Reaction

As early as February 1844, O'Donnell claimed victory over the conspiracy and declared "tranquillity" had returned to the island: the Military Commission trials were proceeding well, property owners and the general white populace trusted the measures adopted by authorities to handle the situation, and there had been no outbreaks of revolt in the plantations zones, "not even a single fire" since the repression began.[110] By June, O'Donnell boasted to his superiors that he had "punished 1,600 men apprehended in [the conspiracy] with death, imprisonment or deportation."[111] The theater of public power magnified colonial strength and assured the white population and foreign interests of Cuba's stability. Moreover, the display of authority confirmed the government's ability to identify and crush its enemies.[112] The O'Donnell administration's actions sent a powerful warning to people of color and abolitionists throughout the Caribbean region who dared to challenge Spanish colonial rule.

These actions, however, did not go without scrutiny from the international community. As O'Donnell claimed a political, juridical, and moral victory over the Conspiracy of La Escalera, international reaction to the repression reverberated across the Atlantic basin. Proslavery media in the United States proved to be the most supportive of his brutal measures. In New Orleans, a common destination for free people of color banished from Cuba, *The Daily Picayune* praised O'Donnell's efforts, declaring:

> it is fortunate for Cuba that it [the insurrection] reached its crisis when a man of the energy of General O'Donnell was in possession of power. He . . . is determined to eradicate every symptom of disaffection. It is said that he will very materially diminish the number of those engaged in labor on the island, but he will thereby give greater security to life and property.[113]

O'Donnell's heavy-handed approach resonated with many residents in Louisiana. Due to the state's proximity to Cuba, its substantial free black population, and a shared history of slavery and rebellion, elites paid close attention to how the Spanish colonial administration sought to "eradicate every symptom of disaffection" on the island. A journalist from Boston's *Emancipator and Weekly Chronicle* rationalized that despite the gratuitous violence and death, O'Donnell's heavy-handed actions signaled to the world that "Cuba is governed."[114] Furthermore, a contributor for *The New York Herald* concluded the repression would "teach the blacks how desperate is their chance for success against any insurrection against the whites."[115] Across the Atlantic in a London paper, a Spaniard posed the rhetorical question, if the slaves "are not severely chastised, how can the masters maintain subordination?"[116] From the perspective of these staunch slavery advocates, O'Donnell handled the revolts the only suitable way—through violence and intimidation.

Both abolitionist and proslavery outlets, however, readily condemned the captain general's actions. Foreign observers warned that widespread cruelties might set off another Haitian revolution. Statements from a Kentuckian in Havana published in the Boston press cautioned, "should civil war to arise, what would prevent . . . [the] spreading of pillage and devastation through the island? The fate of their neighbor, St. Domingo, is before the eyes of the creoles."[117] Jamaica's *The Spectator* hoped authorities would "see the extreme wickedness and wretched policy of driving the poor slaves to desperation ere it be too late, and scenes of woe, such as were perpetrated in Hayti, become the inevitable result."[118] These admonitions predicted the violent fall of colonial rule to black rebels unless Spain adopted less harsh methods to procure slave compliance and promote political stability.

Much of the international commentary criticized Spain's imperial policies. Noting the long evolution of Cuba's precarious political situation, Boston's *Emancipator and Weekly Chronicle* chided, "The home government in old Spain is imbecile."[119] A letter to the editor of the *New York Herald* argued, only "a prompt and thorough change of measures" in Spanish policy would remedy the rampant conflict and chaos in Cuba."[120] And one Spanish eyewitness account in the *Times* of London proclaimed, "What does it all teach us? That measures of terror are insufficient to all, and that other steps must be adopted for the white man's safety."[121] Critics attributed the unwarranted viciousness of the Cuban administration to Spanish imperial incompetence and despotism. From their perspective, Spain had yet to learn its lesson--that the security of its subjects lay in a more evenhanded approach to political dissent.

The international commentaries on the Escalera rebellions and the way Spanish authorities in Cuba handled them coalesced around issues of race and politics. Spain's "wretched" policies and extreme approach to maintaining slavery provided the catalysts for the surge of uprisings leading up to those in 1843. The multiple references to the Haitian Revolution drew upon elites' fears of a prolonged, destructive race war at the hands of desperate slaves and free blacks. The "scenes of woe" would surely threaten the safety of the white population. Worst of all, a Haitian-style revolt in Cuba would destroy the plantation economy and create yet another black republic in the Caribbean.

Finally, complaints over uncertain economic conditions discouraged confidence in quick resumption of commercial traffic. Arrests of English merchants and French planters, destruction of sugar cane and other agricultural lands, death of cattle due to drought, and reluctance of international shippers to pay advance rates for Cuban goods eroded international confidence in the colony's financial stability.[122] Moreover, foreigners foresaw the collapse of Cuba's economic viability precisely because O'Donnell's repression exacerbated the difficulties of moving commerce from the countryside to the towns and of the exchange of goods in the port cities.

To counter foreign criticism of the repression, Cuban authorities applied censorship and mobilized discourses of moral authority and economic vitality. Colonial officials in Puerto Rico and Spain promulgated laws to prohibit all written material that might "damage the morale and peace" of Cuba.[123] Local media condemned rebel leaders, labeled "lazy Ethiopians," for their barbarism, and glorified Spain's "imperial superiority" at having rooted out the plot.[124] Cuba's Royal Council on the Development of Agriculture and Commerce praised O'Donnell's leadership in suppressing the uprisings as a "brilliant page of service."[125] Cuban newspapers celebrated the return of economic normalcy. "Our ports . . . have never been more crowded . . . shipping, commerce, and mercantile transactions have not been paralyzed," reported the Matanzas newspaper *Aurora*.[126] To many, particularly planters and merchants, the spectacles of violence crushed the Conspiracy of La Escalera and succeeded in reestablishing imperial and economic order.

Simultaneously, Cuban newspapers chastised the international media for questioning Spanish colonial methods. The *Aurora* charged:

> Some foreign newspapers are poorly informed or have sinister intentions; they have taken part in alarming commercial nations regarding the critical state that they imagine our island to be in. . . . The island of Cuba, where its white inhabitants are illustrious and loyal . . . and where a large group of armed forces exists . . . have nothing to fear from those who conspire against our well-being.[127]

Aurora's commentary strove to discredit foreign critiques as misinformed hearsay. Furthermore, editors focused on Cuba's racial and political assets. In their minds, the colony's "illustrious and loyal" white population, combined with the buildup of Spanish and creole troops and the recent dismantling of the militia of color, would prevent any future threat from the slave or free black sectors. Thus, the colony's tranquillity, albeit forged through terror, shielded it from exaggerated claims of turmoil and race war. Cuban officials reasserted their political authority, racial supremacy, and military might on the world stage through the public spectacle of violence, imperial propaganda, and proclamations of moral dominance.

* * *

Cuba's rapid expansion of slavery in the early nineteenth century produced predictable subaltern resistance, especially as abolition gained steam in neighboring Haiti and Jamaica. The mounting succession of revolts by slaves and free people of color dictated harsh imperial retaliation. In many ways, Cuban authorities responded to the 1843 uprisings with the expected trappings of a spectacle of public power—arrests, trials, sentencing, and executions—that effectively restored colonial authority.[128] Captain General Leopoldo O'Donnell's approach, however, went beyond established norms for reasserting power over the island.

The range of insurgents targeted for execution—slave and free, white and black, male and female, Cuban and foreign-born—ushered in a new era of repression. Although the numbers sentenced to capital punishment did not match the 344 executed during Jamaica's rebellion of 1831–1832, the Escalera repression produced a far greater toll in its destruction of lives at the hand of Cuban authorities.[129] The U.S. consul in Matanzas proclaimed "the examination of the blacks and mulattoes whether slaves or free is conducted with a cruelty . . . of the Inquisition."[130] Hundreds died awaiting trial. Thousands of individuals sentenced suffered banishment and imprisonment overseas in North Africa and Spain or incarceration in Cuba. A range of other punishments imposed occupational bans, hard labor, and surveillance. The convergence of repressive measures produced a display of power designed to provide a protective cover for the colony and smother conspirators, especially *libres de color.*

Accounts from witnesses, diplomats, and newspapers attested to the violent milieu and how the repression's impact cast a deep and bloody shadow over much of western Cuba in 1844. Authorities' cruel, controversial, and multilayered measures converted the episode into an expansive tool for asserting and reinstating colonial control both over the island and into the Atlantic node concerning race, slavery, and rebellion. Although international proslavery advocates applauded O'Donnell's heavy-handed actions, much of the U.S. and European media criticized Spanish imperial cruelties and warned of the potential to provoke a Haitian-style uprising that would devastate Cuba's political and economic stability.

When a hurricane pummeled the site of several of the November rebellions and flooded Matanzas, Havana, and Cárdenas on October 5, 1844, it symbolized to some the "divine retribution" promised by Plácido.[131] To others it may have also signaled a cleansing of pain and hope for the future. The subsequent chapters explore the manifestation of these possibilities by examining the ways free people of color responded to the rise in new restrictive measures during the Escalera era in the mid 1840s to the late 1860s. As hundreds abandoned the island, others struggled to remain; groups in Cuba and abroad challenged social and economic displacement. Successful or not, the harsh consequences of the repression did not subdue *libres de color* as completely as elites hoped.

3 / Calculated Expulsions: Free People of Color in Mexico, the United States, Spain, and North Africa

We can certify to the tears we shed over our desolate families, such that we ran with the current of emigration far from Cuba.

—JOSÉ MORENO

On March 19, 1844, José Falgueras, president of the Cuban Military Commission, condemned free blacks Anastasio Ramirez, José Castillo, Mateo *carabalí*, and Alonso *lucumí* to imprisonment in Ceuta, Spain's presidio in North Africa. Moreover, the Commission prohibited them from returning to Cuba or Puerto Rico.[1] These men represented the first of hundreds charged as accomplices in the Conspiracy of La Escalera who would suffer the same fate: overseas incarceration and banishment. Colonial authorities did not stop there. Emboldened by torture and terror, the Leopoldo O'Donnell administration unfurled broader plans to further expunge the island of free blacks. In addition to those formally sentenced to deportation by the Military Commission, O'Donnell devised a strategy for the "prudent and calculated expulsion" of free people of color, targeting three sectors: free blacks who attempted to enter Cuban ports, the foreign-born residing in Cuba, and native *libres de color* living in urban centers in and around Havana.[2] Individuals such as Carlota Molina, who attempted to return to Cuba via Jamaica, Vicente Pacheco, a native of Caracas living in Havana, and José Moreno, an exile in Mexico, would all become caught up in the colonial administration's determined efforts to purge Cuba of racial strife. These measures, however, proved far from uniform and would often produce results contradicting the stated aims of Cuban officials.

O'Donnell's desires to reduce the number of *libres de color* renewed previous debates over the dangers of having so many free and enslaved men and women of African descent in the colony. In the wake of the

1843 rebellions, O'Donnell took up the mantle of former captain general Francisco Dionisio Vives. In the 1830s, Vives had ardently supported the expulsion of all free people of color from Cuban shores, but had hesitated to implement this idea. Doing so, he reasoned, could potentially lead to a labor shortage and greater dissidence among free blacks and slaves.[3] The 1843 uprisings and the subsequent conviction of over 1,800 people, the majority of whom were *libres de color*, however, forcefully revived the issue.[4]

The harassment and removal of hundreds of free blacks underscored the crisis of slave rebellion that engulfed Cuba in the mid 1840s. The revolts in the Matanzas province jeopardized the colony's prosperity. Abolishing slavery, however, was not an option; planters, officials, and merchants had too much at stake. Without a coerced and controllable agricultural labor force, profits would plummet and lead to Cuba's demise. Consequently, free people of color suffered irreversably from the colonial government's attempts to remove them via legislation and coercion in the Escalera era. Although some regional officials questioned the purpose of the mass relocations to Mexico or challenged the legality of aiding Spain in the surveillance of Cuban subjects on American soil, Cuban authorities pushed these issues with threats and covert activities in both locales.[5] Fueled by the fear of conspiratorial black plots from within and without, the O'Donnell administration facilitated the departure of free blacks as a means to weaken their alleged rebellious influences in the colony and pursued evidence of an insidious network poised to conquer Cuba from afar. Accused of leading the rebellions, *libres de color* became easy scapegoats in the continuing repression and a powerful example to erode lingering creole dissidence.

Above all, coerced removal struck at the heart of the free black community. Economic stability unraveled as authorities compelled some families to separate from their loved ones on what would surely be difficult and dangerous journeys into prison and exile. However, as the imposed embarkations thrust free people of color into unfamiliar Atlantic World settings, many responded with established negotiation tactics. *Libres de color* sentenced to banishment and imprisonment in Morocco and Spain petitioned for family reunification. Individuals and ship crews seeking to enter Cuban ports challenged bans prohibiting disembarkation. On Cuban soil, those born elsewhere protested anti-immigrant expulsion orders. During the coerced relocations to coastal Mexico and American port cities such as Philadelphia, New Orleans, and New York, *libres de color* forged transregional linkages within a new black

Cuban diaspora that would subvert colonial Cuban political authority in unexpected ways. An exploration of their strategies of negotiation at home and abroad reveals the multiple methods by which *libres de color* responded to the Escalera era's sharp shifts in social policy.

Banishment

During the initial wave of expulsions, Military Commission judges banished 433 free men of color for their explicit or implicit connection to the conspiracy.[6] Authorities vacillated between imposing direct deportation and dispensing overseas prison terms ranging from two to ten years. For instance, after judges convicted *negro libre* Ciriaco Consuegra, an officer in the militia of color, of being a conspiracy leader and spreading subversive language, they voted unanimously for his immediate deportation.[7] *Pardo libre* Pedro Nolasco Baergas and *moreno libre* Domingo Ceballos suffered the same fate after authorities accused them of being among the first to spread "alarming expressions" about the plot.[8] In these instances, authorities did not explicitly designate where those convicted should be sent, although dozens relocated to New Orleans, Louisiana, and Pensacola, Florida.[9] Rather, officials prohibited *libres de color* sentenced to banishment from residing in Cuba and Puerto Rico, Spain's only remaining territories in the Americas.

In contrast, those sentenced to overseas imprisonment were bound for specific destinations in North Africa and Spain. Session one of the Military Commission trials set the tone early. After convicting thirteen *negros libres* of planning and instigating the slave rebellion on the Encantado plantation and surrounding farms, authorities condemned these men to Ceuta in Spanish Morocco for six to ten years.[10] Meanwhile, *libres de color* like José Fertrudis Ramos, Jose Carbo, Damian de Fleites, and Damaso Ramos would endure imprisonment in the southern Spanish town of Seville.[11] Similarly, *pardo* Felipe Valdés García faced a ten-year sentence in a Valladolid prison in north central Spain.[12] Whether condemned to deportation or confinement across the Atlantic, individuals thus punished were prohibited from living in Cuba or Puerto Rico. The penalty for transgressing these boundaries was death. By adding residential restrictions and capital consequences, officials anticipated a definitive reduction in what they considered the island's more rebellious elements.

Escalera convicts bound for Spain and North Africa were destined for misery. An account from the early nineteenth century characterized Spanish prisons as an "earthly hell." Thousands of vermin scurried across the floors and walls as prisoners breathed "mephitic air" and wasted away on "miserable and insufficient" food.[13] In Seville, "criminals of every degree" passed their days in a gravel yard "wholly unoccupied," and spent their nights locked in cramped compartments where aged filth and stench permeated the senses.[14] Escalera prisoners bound for Ceuta, in North Africa, faced additional hardships. Since the mid-eighteenth century, Spain had regularly condemned criminals to hard labor in presidios in Spanish Morocco. Those sentenced to Ceuta constructed, repaired, and maintained military facilities and fortifications. Meager rations, scarce potable water, unsanitary conditions, and poor health were endemic to both overseas locales.[15] Although similar conditions existed in Havana jails, in Cuba the Escalera inmates at least had access to family and friends. As strangers and convicts in Spain and North Africa, these networks vanished (see map 2).

These descriptions suggest that those who served their terms abroad would have virtually no resources and no hope of return to Cuba. Having completed their two-year prison terms in Seville in 1847, convicted co-conspirators José Gertrudis Ramos and Damian de Fleites pursued authorization to reenter the island, but officials denied their requests.[16] And although policies against political prisoners began to thaw in the 1850s, Cuban officials remained suspicious. In 1854, at the end of *pardo* Felipe Valdés García's ten-year jail sentence in Valladolid, he petitioned to return to Cuba to put his business affairs in order and reunite with his wife and children. Spanish colonial authorities allowed a brief visit with his family, but refused to allow permanent residency in Cuba.[17] Clearly, in the late 1840s and early 1850s, Cuban officials remained cautious of *libres de color* convicted in the Escalera plot. Permitting those imprisoned overseas to return would have contradicted the colonial rationale of removing conspirators and would have exacerbated already heightened concerns over restoring social and economic tranquillity. Although tensions eased in the mid 1850s, unless former overseas prisoners could procure permission for fleeting family reunions or secure resources to relocate with loved ones beyond Spain's Caribbean territories, the politics of empire, race, and rebellion forced these men to remain separated from their families indefinitely.

Bans on Port Entry

In the aftermath of the Escalera rebellions, authorities expanded the banishments and overseas imprisonments for seditious co-conspirators by renewing legislation designed to prevent free people of color abroad

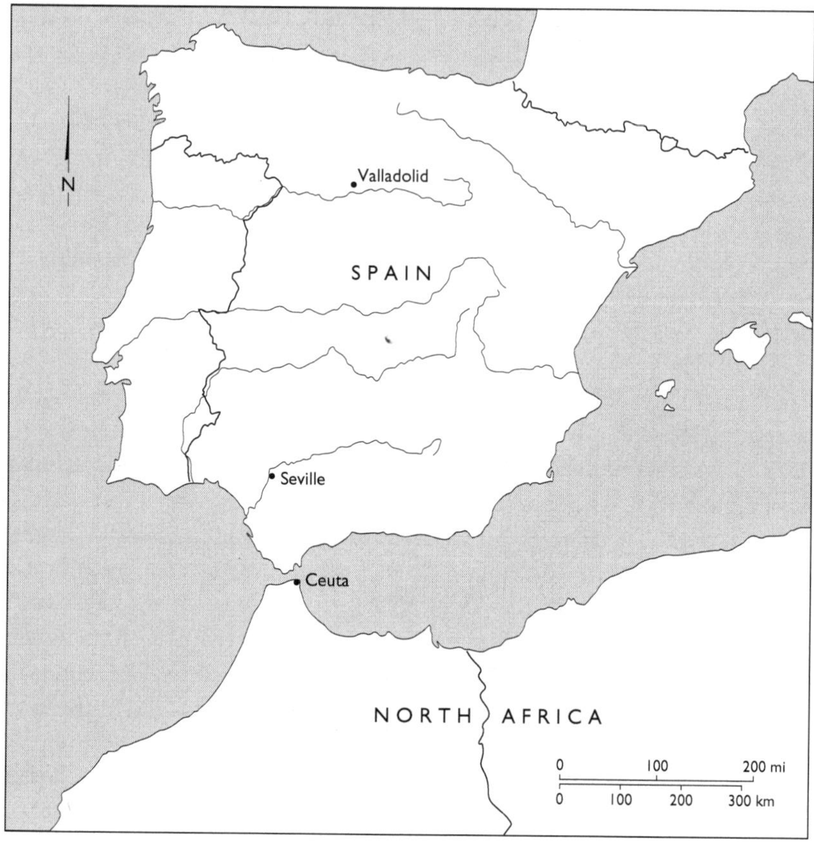

MAP 2. Nineteenth-century Ceuta, North Africa and Spain.

from gaining access to the colony and creating more turmoil among the slave population. Laws promulgated in the 1830s initiated Cuba's, and Puerto Rico's, general ban on free black disembarkation. Jamaican freedmen, whom Cuban officials considered to be "a dangerous class," became an early target.[18] Legislation established in 1832, one year prior to Britain's Abolition of Slavery Act, called for authorities to scrutinize free blacks and mulattoes arriving from Jamaica.[19] With full emancipation in the British Caribbean imminent, Cuba reinforced the prohibitions on free blacks' access to Havana and other port cities in 1837.[20]

Cuba's tactics paralleled many of the bans on the general entry of free people of color throughout the early nineteenth-century Atlantic.

In the decade following the Haitian Revolution, numerous southern legislatures, particularly in Virginia, North Carolina, and Louisiana, as well as in Maryland, outlawed black immigration, fearing that free blacks' mobility would provoke slave insurrection in the United States.[21] These prohibitions persisted following the Spanish American wars for independence. Several states on the eastern seaboard refused to admit free people of color from Mexico, South America, and the Caribbean, again for fear of spreading the turmoil of rebellion.[22] For instance, one British traveler noted how Charleston harbor authorities locked up a black servant arriving from St. Vincent "for no other reason but that he was free, and not white."[23] By the 1830s, travel between American ports proved equally problematic for free individuals of African descent in the United States such as Andrew Durnford, a free black planter from Louisiana, who feared "being detained" as he sought passage from Baltimore to New Orleans.[24] In the revolutionary era of the late eighteenth and early nineteenth centuries, free people of color sought locales for refuge and opportunities to advance their equality. The overlapping Atlantic tensions of race, politics, slavery, and rebellion, however, collided with expanding levels of black mobility. In this context, officials and elites considered free blacks and slaves provocateurs of revolt which, in turn, cast individual and group movements of blacks from port to port as dangerous and suspicious.

Furthermore, additional legislation aimed at curtailing the spread of subversive ideas specifically targeted black sailors in North America and the Caribbean. After the failed revolt led by Denmark Vesey, a free black man, in 1822, South Carolina instituted the Negro Seamen's Act, which permitted Charleston officials to incarcerate black sailors landing in the local port until their vessels were prepared to leave. In 1835, South Carolina and Louisiana reiterated this law. Authorities jailed black crewmen when their incoming ships docked, fined them, and if they did not pay, threatened to sell them into slavery.[25] In 1837, Cuban authorities confiscated an abolitionist pamphlet printed in Spanish by a London publisher that had been circulated by crewmen of color from the Bahamas.[26] In that same year, an African American newspaper, *The Colored American*, warned black sailors arriving in Cuba from the United States that they would be immediately incarcerated and held until their vessel stood ready to depart. It also cautioned readers that those convicted of seditious behavior would be "executed or else sold into slavery."[27] Even when vessels had no intention of landing, sailors came under fire. When a Haitian ship became stranded on the South Carolina coast in the late

1830s, officials seized the crew and imprisoned them until the vessel had undergone sufficient repairs to depart.[28]

Given the sustained upheavals involving empire and slavery throughout the Americas in the opening decades of the nineteenth century, the measures taken by U.S. and Cuban officials were hardly surprising. Previous revolts led by free blacks in the circum-Caribbean and the international circulation of British abolitionist propaganda in multiple languages fueled the dissemination of revolutionary ideology. In turn, imperial and republican governments responded with restrictive laws and threats of imprisonment, death, and chattel servitude to further harass free people of color. Nevertheless, the repeated passing of intimidating laws did little to assuage elites' fears of the powerful notion of freedom among the slave population.

By the early 1840s, Cuba's battle to suppress the spread of revolt, abolition, and liberty took on new urgency. In 1842, one year prior to the Escalera rebellions, Cuban authorities reinforced efforts to confine sailors of color to their ships and restrict their contact with local port workers.[29] In the wake of the 1843 uprisings, colonial authorities intensified existing restrictive travel codes. On May 13, 1844, O'Donnell reinstated the royal order banning free people of color from disembarking, and article four of the revised slave code of the same year incorporated this directive.[30] In this context of rebellion and from the perspective of colonial authorities in Cuba, all free people of color, especially foreigners and *marineros*, were viewed as purveyors of antislavery agitation and rebellion.

The reality that not all *libres de color* sought to foment rebellion, however, left some free blacks in a precarious situation, especially those who traveled through Jamaica en route to Cuba. Carlota Molina, a free *morena* and native of Santiago de Cuba, provided a case in point. In 1835, she had left her home to care for a "sick relative" who resided in Curaçao.[31] After her loved one's death in 1843, she prepared to return home via Jamaica. News of the uprisings and the brutal repression gave greater urgency to Molina's efforts to be reunited with her family in Cuba. When she approached the Spanish consul in Kingston to authorize the final segment of her trip, however, he responded that he could "not consent to her request."[32] Reinforced legislation severely curtailed the disembarkation of free people of color from Jamaica.[33] Molina's situation put her in a perilous position. On the one hand, as a Cuban native who had not resided on the island for eight years, Molina clearly had not been involved in the rebellions. On the other hand, the tumultuous events on the island and the regulations denying free people of color entry cast her under a spotlight of suspicion. The combination of Molina's legal status, racial ancestry, and travel from Jamaica made her a prime target as the Escalera repression took hold.

Molina, determined to be reunited with her children, would not be deterred. She asked that Carlos Duquesnay, a Spanish consulate official, prepare a character reference on her behalf. His letter attested that Molina had "always behaved honorably" and that she had a sincere desire to simply "return to her family in Santiago de Cuba."[34] This written acknowledgement of Molina's respectable behavior and family loyalty by a government official bolstered her claim to return to Cuba. By confirming that Molina maintained key attributes of Spanish colonial codes of honor, Duquesnay validated her public and personal reputation.[35] Timing also proved significant. Officials acknowledged that Molina had been away from the island during the revolts in Matanzas. Furthermore, she received leniency because her request arrived several months before authorities had fully implemented the new legislation and other plans devised to ban free people of color from entering Cuba. Whatever the official motives, Molina's written request and references represented one of numerous strategies thousands of *libres de color* would pursue to circumvent the restrictive laws regarding free black oceanic mobility. Her success at circumventing the disembarkation ban also suggests the flexibility of colonial laws despite the O'Donnell administration's seemingly adamant position on curbing the flow of free people of color, especially native Cubans, into the colony.

Expelling the Foreign-born

In addition to the suspicions surrounding black travelers and sailors, distrust persisted regarding the influence of free black immigrants residing in Cuba. So much so that, in April 1844, O'Donnell called for the expulsion of all foreign-born free people of color. A month later, a royal decree by the Spanish monarch enforced O'Donnell's plan.[36] As noted in chapter 1, the free community of color comprised a fusion of diverse groups. Immigrant waves spanned from those who had emigrated from Florida during the Seven Years' War to more recent arrivals during the Spanish American revolutions. Because foreign and native *libres de color* had forged strong kinship relationships, they reacted strongly to the expulsion order's clear intention to disrupt black social networks, which would rip apart families in the process.

Initially given only fifteen days to leave the country or be expelled, numerous free blacks viewed the order as a threat to their livelihoods, an affront on their loyalty to the Spanish empire, and an insult to their personal honor.[37] In response, between April and August 1844, ninety-three foreign-born *libres de color* in Havana submitted petitions protesting the expulsion directive. These documents illustrated the multiple origins, arrivals, and occupations of Cuba's free African diaspora. Some, like former refugees Pedro Calvo and Juan Saldana, had fled from the upheavals in Haiti to Spanish Santo Domingo and then to Cuba as children in the 1790s.[38] These men had distinct legal statuses; Calvo, *nación carabalí,* arrived as a free man, and Saldana disembarked as a slave. Over time, Calvo establish himself in Havana as a cook. Saldana gained his freedom upon the death of his owner and supported his family selling estate property. Furthermore, both now had families; Saldana's wife was pregnant with their second child and Calvo was already a grandfather.[39] Although they had not been born on Cuban soil, these men hardly considered themselves foreigners. For them, Cuba was home.

When the Transcontinental Treaty of 1819 between the United States and Spain transferred Florida to American control, hundreds resettled in the Spanish Caribbean. In 1821, these circumstances prompted *morenos libres* Diego Domingo and Juan Bernardo Marrero to set sail for Cuba from St. Augustine. In Cuba, they found employment in the port of Havana as a cooper and a dockworker, respectively. Because Domingo and Marrero had arrived in Cuba due to legal shifts in political authority over Florida, they did not consider themselves to be foreigners.[40] Like Calvo and Saldana, they, too, claimed Cuba as home. Although all four men had been born in the Spanish empire, the restrictive policies now required even greater territorial specificity for permanent residency. Domingo, Marrero, Calvo, Saldana, and many more were forced to prove their right to remain in Cuba.

Overall, the predominantly male petitioners advanced a variety of reasons for the government to exempt them from expulsion. Several highlighted military service as the most compelling motive to maintain residency in Cuba. For instance, Venezuelan León de Rojas and Luís Pivas of Costa Firme declared that their service in the "Royal Spanish Army" should remove them from suspicion.[41] Similarly, Veracruz-born Juan Arregui proclaimed his service in Havana's *pardo* militia proved his loyalty to the crown. Arregui added that his Spanish language and customs made him well suited to remain on the island.[42] The exaggerated claims of Rojas and Pivas as participating in the regular troops aside—in reality, their African ancestry would have dictated their actual service in the militia of color, which supplemented professional Spanish forces—claims of military participation resonated with the colonial government. Indeed, the Spanish crown had long acknowledged militiamen of color as vital to the empire, often characterizing these men as devoted and self-sacrificing.[43] Although the segregated units reinforced color and race distinctions, militia service enabled *pardo* and *moreno* servicemen to embrace a recognized corporate colonial identity.[44] Despite the incidents of black officers who led uprisings in 1812, 1835, and 1839, all attributed to Cuban natives, Spanish authorities concluded that incorporating *libres de color* into state service would solidify their loyalty to the crown.[45] Moreover, despite the rhetoric of repression, immigrant militiamen seemed readily able to evade O'Donnell's policies. When foreign-born soldiers of color invoked their fidelity to Cuba, they did so in accordance with the traditions cultivated under Spanish colonialism. Imperial recognition of the rights and privileges of military defense bestowed public honor to black militiamen that could not be withdrawn by Cuban officials.

The long history of native and immigrant free blacks as artisans and proprietors emerged as another prominent claim used by foreigners to secure their residency. Cartagena-born José Ramón Ortega highlighted his career on the island as a shoemaker.[46] Francisco Noven asserted that his expertise as a carpenter and ownership of a coffee plantation, not his birth in Spanish Santo Domingo, should be considered in granting his petition to stay in Cuba.[47] Vicente Pacheco, a native of Caracas, argued that because he had spent the past thirty-seven years working as a bricklayer in Havana, and now managed sixteen apprentices and owned several houses, he was an asset to the island.[48] Cuban native Eusebia Josefa Courbille, one of the few female petitioners, advocated on behalf of her two adult children, both born in Pensacola in the 1820s. Although Courbille had no specified occupation, her children did. Carlos worked as a shoemaker and Patricio was a tailor.[49] As their Cuban-born counterparts had demonstrated in the decades leading up to 1843, foreign-born free black artisans emphasized how their skilled occupations enabled them to support their families and how their status as business and property owners permitted them to make valuable economic contributions to the colony.

Authorities ultimately viewed foreign artisans in a positive light, much like those with militia service. Although local advocates asserted that the predominance of free black craftsmen degraded these fields, the colonial occupational hierarchy expressly prohibited men of color from accessing legal and administrative professions.[50] Since the 1830s, Cuba's governors conceded that black skilled workers, especially those who owned land and slaves, were respectable colonial subjects.[51] Thus, thousands of *libres de color,* natives and immigrants, sought to enhance their social status by acquiring skilled trades. When possible, they parlayed the profits from their small businesses into real estate. Their success as artisans provided them with avenues for both economic stability and upward social mobility as they purchased houses, coffee plantations, and rented out land and accommodations to other free people of color. These factors played an important role in the success of immigrant petitioners. By virtue of their material accomplishments in Cuba, these individuals now claimed a position of trust that resonated with the economic and social sensibilities of colonial officials in 1844. Moreover, as in the case with foreign-born soldiers, the success of petitions by immigrant artisans also directly contravened the colonial government's expulsion orders, suggesting that native Cubans ultimately had more to fear from the repression than did the foreign-born.

Finally, and similarly to the case of Carlota Molina, immigrants residing in Cuba posited honor as an overarching factor in their protest against expulsion. Petitions illuminating the claimants' honor through their behavioral patterns in Cuba, obligation to family, and activities of self-sufficiency made their way to the captain general's office. *Negro libre* José Verde, who hailed from Uruguay, submitted letters of reference attesting to his "good conduct" since arriving in the early 1820s, after he fled from the South American wars for independence.[52] Pedro Calvo, mentioned previously, asserted his childhood arrival and strong ties to the community as proof of his strong character. He was nearly sixty years old in 1844, and witnesses concurred that Calvo had always conducted himself "honorably."[53] New Orleans-born Antonio Merlin, a blacksmith and Cuban resident for twenty years, cited the importance of his role as an honorable husband and father as imperatives for granting his request.[54] In petitioning for her Pensacola-born sons, Carlos and Patricio, Cuban native Eusebia Josefa Courbille upheld her respectability as a mother: after having lived in Florida with her children's father, an Anglo American, she later returned to Cuba with her sons. Local baptismal records and references validated her story.[55] During Brazilian José González's twenty-nine years on the island, he had married a Cuban woman and lived happily with her for fourteen years until her death during a cholera epidemic in the 1830s. Despite his advanced age of sixty-nine, González maintained himself financially by working on the docks.[56] Although colonial elites considered honor a tangible trait reserved exclusively for themselves, the masses recognized, challenged, and asserted their own representations of honor.[57]

For foreign-born free blacks, the expulsion order amounted to an affront to their public reputation, which could only be reinstated by public authority. By emphasizing the high quality of their character in an array of social arenas, free immigrants of color fused their understanding of Spanish colonial culture and the malleability of honor to protest expulsion from Cuba. By asserting honor through the interwoven threads of conduct, kinship, and self-reliance, dozens of free black immigrants successfully repelled the attack on their respectability. Doing so enabled them to retain their lives in Cuba and regain their personal and public status despite O'Donnell's plans for removal.

Just as successful appeals established a pattern of qualities that resonated positively with the colonial administration, authorities rejected others they perceived as negative or suspicious. Free black immigrants with cultural and social connections to the British empire were seen as especially objectionable. In particular, Cuban authorities grew uneasy after Jamaica's Protestant-influenced Baptist War of 1831–1832 hastened Britain's passage of the Abolition of Slavery Act in 1833.[58] In response, Cuban officials marked Jamaican freedmen as "contagious with the false and fictitious doctrines of revolutionaries," and instituted legislation to bar them from entering the colony.[59]

These sentiments and legal prohibitions played a prominent role in requests by those deported to Anglophone locales or who were somehow associated with Britain. For instance, José María de la Peña, a free man of color, languished in Jamaica after being deported in 1844. Meanwhile from Cuba, his wife Soledad Vargas, a *criolla* and native of Holguin, petitioned twice, in 1847 and 1851, requesting permission for her husband's entry into the island. While married to Vargas, de la Peña had acquired the title of "Don," which gave him legal whiteness in the Spanish empire.[60] Like immigrants, he had firmly established his social and economic position in Cuban society by residing with his family in Holguin for twenty years, working as a watchmaker, and owning numerous properties. In this instance, however, the case fell on deaf ears. His deportation to Jamaica slammed the door on negotiations; authorities denied both of his wife's requests for reunification.[61] Unlike Carlota Molina, who successfully petitioned to return to Cuba from Jamaica several months prior to the onset of the Escalera repression, de la Peña would have no such luck.

Similarly, two English-speaking petitioners had little success. Adam Rayt and José Manuel Rivas attempted to stress their solid morals, but character references discredited their behavior. Even though both had served as militiamen in Spanish Florida, relocated to Cuba in 1821, and participated with loyalist revolutionary forces in Venezuela, a Barrio commissioner in Havana negated these factors by accusing them of being able to speak English. In addition, Rayt received charges of frequenting the company of foreigners, and Rivas was condemned for his repeatedly licentious and drunken behavior.[62] Assertions of bad conduct, particularly being bilingual in English, using foul language, being inebriated, and associating with foreigners, instantly destroyed these men's chances to remain in Cuba. In addition, the denials to individuals connected linguistically to the British empire represented political prudence from the perspective of colonial officials. Despite personal and economic ties to Cuba, men like Rayt and Rivas continued to be viewed as a potential menace to society. Moreover, given the dual threats of British antislavery activities and these agents' links to the Escalera rebellions, virtually anyone who had contact with Britain or with British Caribbean territories became persona non grata in Cuba.

Considering the colonial government's anti-immigrant legislation against free individuals of color, foreign-born petitioners experienced a high success rate. The O'Donnell administration granted 72 of their 93 requests (77.4%). Although these numbers denote a small sample of the free population of color, nevertheless, the results seemed to contradict the expulsion order's prime directive: to remove all foreign-born men of African descent. Moreover, it is clear that foreign free blacks' use of petitions, successful or not, represented a traditional legal avenue to challenge colonial authority. Time and again they appealed to the O'Donnell government's sense of loyalty, economic viability, and honor. Petitioners asserted their allegiance to Spain through military service, prior to and during their settlement in Cuba. Claims granted on the basis of economic achievements such as those of skilled craftsmen and property owners suggested that colonial officials favored the ability of *libres de color* to support themselves and contribute to the wealth of the colony as accomplished artisans and plantation owners. Finally, their attachment to Cuba through kinship ties and personal references bolstered claims of honor. In spite of mounting legislation designed to remove and bar foreign-born free people of color, many black immigrants who managed to present themselves as ideal subjects of the Spanish empire accomplished their goal to remain in Cuba.

A "Prudent and Calculated Expulsion": Cuba's Free Black Diaspora

The final phase of O'Donnell's plan to eliminate black dissension called for the mass emigration of Cuban-born free people of color. Still reeling from the initial repressive measures and fearing further persecution, hundreds of free black men and women searched for avenues to escape the harsh restrictions on their employment and social activities. When the O'Donnell administration announced that it would grant passports to all native *libres de color* who requested to leave the island, hundreds jumped at the chance for respite.[63] Scholars have calculated that at least 739 *libres de color* left Cuba under these conditions between March 1844 and June 1845. The bulk of those who secured official documents fled to Mexico, Brazil, the United States, Africa, Europe, and other parts of the Caribbean.[64] Port cities in Mexico and the United States became primary destinations, due largely to Havana's long-standing regional, commercial, and historical connections with Veracruz, New Orleans, and New York. Although these 739 emigrants represented a small percentage of the total 152,838 free people of African descent on the island, authorities interpreted their flight as another means of restoring order and control to the slave society.[65] As the emigrants arrived in foreign ports, the government's dubious plan emerged: Cuban authorities branded the emigrants co-conspirators in the Escalera plot and requested host governments to intern the exiles or keep them under close surveillance.[66]

And so the cleansing of so-called rebellious free blacks began. By the summer of 1844, O'Donnell reported the "voluntary" departure of over three hundred *libres de color* in the previous ten weeks and heartily anticipated more in the coming months.[67] Spanish consuls in Mexico confirmed the arrival of Cuban *expulsados* (expellees or exiles) in the Yucatán, Veracruz, and Campeche. Agents in the United States scrutinized their disembarkations in New Orleans, New York, and Philadelphia, traditional sites of Cuban exile communities since the 1820s, as well as in Baltimore.[68] In correspondence between the Cuban government and Spain's Ministro de Estado (Ministry of State), the cumulative exodus marked Cuba's definitive "opportunity to purify the class of color, which is contaminated in general."[69] In letters to the Ultramar (Ministry of Overseas Affairs), O'Donnell reasoned that the departure of free blacks would stifle influences on slave demands for freedom.[70] In addition, he insisted that the Escalera-era prohibitions and the coerced emigration would ensure that none of the free *pardos* or *morenos* who left would even want to return. Furthermore, he concluded that purging the island of rebellious blacks and mulattoes would also stop creole attempts to liberate the island from Spain through annexation or independence.[71]

By summer 1845, the combined banishments, overseas imprisonments, and coerced emigrations had ousted nearly 1,300 *libres de color.*[72] On the surface, these departures characterized a successful extirpation. In reality, the victory rang hollow. Colonial officials soon realized they had not adequately prepared for policing free blacks abroad. Removing allegedly rebellious *pardos* and *morenos* from the island may have curtailed a localized threat, but regional communications revealed potentially greater machinations such as covert voyages to Havana and secret plots to take over Cuba.

Indeed, Cuban free black emigrants had other ideas about their lives in exile. Hundreds considered emigration only a temporary solution. Many, determined to return home, did so legally and illegally. Reports from Mexico and the United States documented their clandestine travel, access to financial resources, and alleged ties to an international rebel network poised to take over the colony. In other words, the expulsion may have "cleansed" the political wounds of the Escalera rebellions, but the removal of *libres de color* spread the free black "contagion" beyond the island--an issue that had plagued not only Cuba but also much of the Americas in the nineteenth century. It would continue to vex colonial and American authorities for decades to come. In the Escalera case, the free black Cuban diaspora redefined the spatial dynamics of the politics of race. What Spanish colonial officials had previously considered a threat from within became a threat from without.

NEGROS EXPULSADOS IN MEXICO

In the opening weeks of May 1844, a steady flow of *libres de color* boarded ships to traverse the 930 miles between Havana and Veracruz, ultimately totaling at least 416.[73] Accustomed to accepting travelers from Cuba, for several weeks Mexican authorities processed travelers' valid passports normally. However, the May 15 arrival of a British steamship carrying twelve "negros expulsados" connected to the "horrid conspiracy" finally prompted officials in Veracruz to question the continuous disembarkation of free blacks from Cuba. Pedro Pascual de Oliver, Spain's consular officer in Mexico, addressed the situation by asking José María de Bocanegro, Mexico's minister of foreign relations, to intern these *expulsados*, and all subsequent groups, at a "convenient distance from the coast."[74] Bocanegra reminded de Oliver that his government valued an individual's rights and that "the laws of the Republic [of Mexico] did not permit him to reject these men because they had not been convicted of any atrocious crime." In response, de Oliver hastily referred Bocanegro to the "secret article" in an 1836 treaty between their two countries for "cases of this nature," which called for political compliance. He then reminded Bocanegro that it was the Mexican government's "duty" to obstruct any potential plot that might threaten the security of the Mexican state or Spanish dominions.[75] Given the terms of the 1836 treaty, Mexican officials begrudgingly acquiesced to Spain's request. They confined the twelve men and agreed to do the same to subsequent groups of color from Havana. From the persective of Spanish colonial officials, they were all to be treated as criminals, regardless of their official documentation. Doing so would strip them of any assumed legal rights as Spanish subjects and interning them would curtail their potential ability to foment dissent that would harm Cuba.

Mexico, however, soon had far more pressing concerns than Cuba's *negros expulsados*. On June 19, de Oliver communicated to Cuba's naval commander the "critical state" of U.S.-Mexican relations over the annexation of Texas. President Tyler of the United States had established a blockade and deployed seven war ships to the Gulf of Mexico "to block the ports of this Republic or at least impede the arrival" of additional troops to the Texas border.[76] The situation in Mexico deteriorated rapidly. Within a year, the United States acquired Texas; from 1846 to 1848, the two nations would be fully engaged in war. These events would severely hinder Mexico's interest in or ability to enforce previous agreements with Spain, particularly those regarding Cuba's concerns over free people of color.

Furthermore, on June 20, one day after the first rumblings of war between Mexico and the United States, de Oliver noted that another 108 *expulsados* had arrived from Cuba. At this point, even the Spanish consul began to question the rationale behind interning so many free people of color. They all held valid passports issued by O'Donnell, and most carried no other "note of explanation" as evidence of their innocence or culpability in the plot. Surely, de Oliver reasoned to Francisco Martínez de la Rosa, the Spanish Minister of State, not all of them were co-conspirators. Pushing the issue, he asserted, "it seems to me an opportune time" to pose three important questions: why did O'Donnell decide to give them passports; did "said blacks merit being interned"; and "with whom in the Spanish consulate in Veracruz could they request to be registered as Spanish subjects"?[77] The case of *pardo* Bernardo de la

Rosa offered a prime example for de Oliver's line of questioning. De la Rosa had recently approached the Spanish consulate to record his status as a "Spanish citizen." He also presented documentation from O'Donnell attesting to his "good conduct and respectable circumstances" prior to leaving Cuba.[78] To de Oliver, Spain's demands in this case seemed to make little sense. Why should de la Rosa, or any Cuban *libre de color*, be detained without probable cause? Moreover, he concluded that detaining those with valid passports would be "contrary and offensive" to promoting cordial political relations between Mexico, Spain, and Cuba.[79]

O'Donnell vehemently addressed the issues head on. He accused virtually all free people of color of being involved in the conspiracy, and reasoned that the best way to reduce this populations' influence was to facilitate their departure. Furthermore, the colony's overflowing jails and the political and financial ramifications of the trials necessitated the removal of *libres de color* as quickly as possible. To that end, he distributed legitimate passports and then banned most recipients from returning to Cuba. Regardless of what free blacks told Spanish officials in Mexico, their "tendencies and intentions," asserted O'Donnell, were "contrary to the tranquillity and security" of the island, and their presence in Veracruz required constant vigilance.[80] As for Bernardo de la Rosa's case, O'Donnell considered it an exception to the rule. Although it is unclear how he came to be judged as sufficiently honorable with respect to the conspiracy, de la Rosa had been granted permission to remain in Cuba or, alternately, receive a passport to Mexico, without penalty.[81]

As for the questions posed by de Oliver and other Spanish officials in Mexico, in September 1844, Spain's Ministry of State returned a forceful and definitive response, issuing a royal order for internment by Spanish consulates, and closed the matter to further discussion.[82] Furthermore, the indignant tone behind O'Donnell's statements gave weight to his desperate quest to not only remove *libres de color* from Cuba but also to command authority on the matter in neighboring countries. That both the Mexican minister of foreign relations and the Spanish consul in Veracruz questioned the legal, moral, and political validity of his approach forced O'Donnell to rely on Spanish imperial authority to enforce his policies. *Libres de color* would take note of this chain of command in their efforts to circumvent O'Donnell's restrictive travel regulations.

With all-out war looming, Mexican and Spanish diplomacy dictated that both should tread carefully in discussions of mutual cooperation pertaining to territorial security. A temporary ease in tensions between Mexico and the United States in late August 1844, accompanied by the appointment of M. C. Rejón as the new minister of Mexican foreign affairs to replace the retiring José María de Bocanegro, seemed to facilitate cooperation between the two countries.[83] In one of Rejón's first official measures, he ordered his coastal governors in Veracruz, Tampico, Tabasco, Campeche, and the Yucatán to detain all Cuban free blacks entering these ports and intern them at least ten leagues (thirty miles) from the Mexican shores (see map 3).[84] However, he also began to doubt the legality of interning *libres de color.* Rejón posited that Spain had overstepped the intent of the 1836 treaty; in other words, enforcing reciprocal policies should be reserved for true allies, not ones that strong-armed their officials as Cuba had done.[85]

By October, Spanish officials in Mexico had grown increasingly anxious over the situation, and with good reason. The number of Cuban *expulsados* now confined in Veracruz had doubled to over two hundred, and tensions began to flair between officials and exiles. Exasperated that they had traded an oppressive situation in Cuba for a similar one in Mexico, *libres'* mounting frustration brimmed over. On a muggy evening in September, individuals within a crowd of irritated internees reportedly shouted "Death to all Spaniards! Death to the tyrants!" Fearful of the potential physical destruction these words implied, local officials wasted no time in breaking up the gathering. The thick cover of night, however, made it impossible to apprehend and punish the instigators.[86] This episode only intensified officials' scrutiny of Cuban exiles. Shortly after the incident, Spain's Ministry of State reiterated the ban on free blacks attempting to return to Cuba, especially from Mexico.[87] The volatile situation prompted *libres de color* to take matters into their own hands.

Over time, dozens of exiles in Mexico returned to a tried and tested method of procuring justice: the petition. In 1846, José Moreno wrote to the Ministro de Gracia y Justicia (Ministry of Justice) on behalf of himself and twenty other Cuban *libres de color* living in exile in Campeche. They included his African-born wife Merced Santa Cruz and their son Jacinto, along with five other households: the families of Pedro González and Justo Bobadilla, Juan Bautista Arango and his son Domingo, Pedro García and his wife Tomasa Alburqueque, Juliana Castro and her three young sons, as well as several other individuals. After two years of living under difficult circumstances in a "foreign land," deteriorating conditions in Mexico compelled the cadre of artisans, laborers, and their families to take action. They made a formal appeal for authorities to allow them to return to Cuba. Their letter, which wound its way through

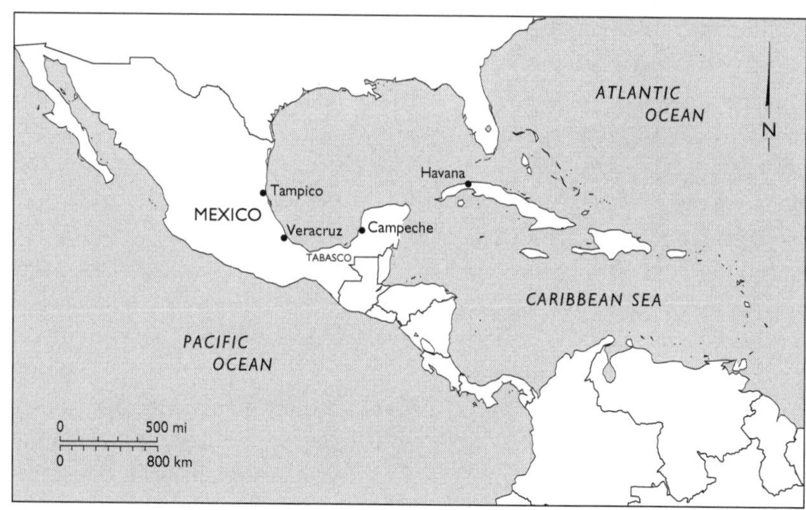

MAP 3. Nineteenth-century coastal Mexico and Cuba.

the hands of the Spanish consul in Mexico, the captain general in Cuba, and the Ministro de Gracia y Justicia and the Ultramar in Spain, detailed the tragic circumstances of their departure and the impact of deterritoralization on their lives.

> We were not among the people of color who planned the secret conspiracy, that was fortunately discovered, but we trembled at the [military] commissions, for they never were about justice . . . and we can certify to the tears we shed over our desolate families, such that we ran with the stream of emigration far from Cuba, a blessed land, sweet like sugar, a land consecrated by the work with which our fathers earned Christian freedom, and which they then gave to us.
>
> . . . Freely, and with legal permission, we came to this foreign land, and have been here for two long years, during which time we have honorably sought to support ourselves with meager resources . . . we reverently request that you lift the prohibition, opposing the orders of the Captain General in Cuba. . . . The investigations determined that we are innocent; we have in no way been involved in the conspiracy.[88]

The group's request highlighted several reasons for the government to end their exile. First, they appealed to the authorities' sense of justice, proclaiming they had nothing to do with the conspiracy and had left Cuba legally as innocent victims of the repression. Next, they emphasized their families' Christian, rather than African-based, religious connections and strong work ethic established by their fathers as additional proof of their loyalty to the Spanish crown. Furthermore, the letter underscored the group's honor. As respectable members of Cuba's free community of color, they had exhibited diligence and humility as they scraped to support themselves in exile. Finally, they addressed imperial hierarchy. Giving deference to Spanish power, the families asked officials in the metropolis to override decisions made by colonial officials in Cuba in the matter, and implored authorities in Spain to facilitate the group's safe passage back to Havana.

José de la Trinidad Oquendo also prepared a collective request. He arrived in Veracruz on November 15, 1844, on board the British steamer *Fourth*. The ship's thirty-six–person manifest listed passengers hailing from Mexico, England, Spain, and Morocco. Those from Cuba included Oquendo, his wife and mother-in-law, *pardo* Pedro Quiñoz, *moreno* Domingo Castro, *moreno* Juan Bautista Arango, *pardo* Manuel del Rey, and *morena* María de las Vagas. The ship's captain also recorded their occupations as skilled artisans, including several tailors, shoemakers, a carpenter, and a seamstress.[89] Given the dire circumstances of their exile, Oquendo's petition not only sought a homecoming for himself and his wife, Agustina Geralda, but also for Agustina's sister, Francisca Franeito Oliva, and their friends' families, including José María Padezo and his son Santiago, and José Valentine Martínez. Oquendo explained that they were all *libres de color*, natives of Havana, and wanted to return to their homes. Like hundreds of others, they had fled Cuba with valid passports, following the "stream of emigration" into Mexico in the aftermath of the conspiracy.[90]

Oquenda's petition, like those of other foreign-born free blacks, rang with the language of honor. They characterized themselves as honorable men who sought to protect their families in the face of adversity. Furthermore, the Spanish consul in Campeche verified that since Oquendo group's arrival in 1844, they had "behaved very well, focused only on . . . working in their respective occupations."[91] Successful or not, claims of occupational industriousness and social responsibility proved common strategies among free people of color in exile or foreign-born. The petitions by Moreno, Oquendo, and others were forwarded to the Ministry of Justice for further consideration. They would wait months for a final decision.

A lengthy debate regarding the petitioners ensued among Spanish authorities. Officials in the Ministry of Overseas Affairs pointed out that two years after the conspiracy, "very few of the men of color who initiated the insurrection had fled the island."[92] This suggested that local free people of color, not *expulsados*, posed a threat. On the other hand, Spanish consuls and operatives in Mexico and the United States had intercepted correspondence and tracked activities of Cuban *libres de color*. The extensive links between dissident residents and exiles confirmed the emigrants' suspicious "tendencies and desires." The conflicting evidence appeared to weigh heavily on the ministers' minds. Even though the council agreed that some free blacks had nothing to do with the conspiracy, they feared the return of these groups might ignite a chain of events that could destroy the colony. Furthermore, they had to consider that granting *expulsados*' requests might encourage petitions from overseas prisoners and the banished. Rather than undermine the prohibitions on free black entry into Cuban ports, the Ministry of Overseas Affairs came to a final decision: under no circumstances would "any men of color" be allowed to return to the island.[93] In effect, despite claims of loyalty, honor, diligence, humility, and deference made by *libres de color* in exile, officials summarily denied all petitioners, individuals and families, the right to return to Cuba.

Meanwhile, despite coordinated efforts to contain exiles in Mexico, Cuban authorities began receiving new reports about subversive exile activities. When Havana officials discovered that *moreno* Claudio Brindis de Salas, a celebrated orchestra leader and militia officer, and *moreno* Lino Lamoneda had returned illegally, the government had them removed.[94] When José de los Angeles Inocencio reentered Cuba clandestinely from the Yucatán, authorities captured, jailed, and deported him to Veracruz.[95] At least one ship, the *Abon*, had aided the exiles. The vessel repeatedly slipped past Mexican port authorities and carried free blacks back to Havana.[96] According to local sources in Cuba, passengers from the *Abon*, all free persons of color, had taken up residence in the capital and established a dissident cell. Informants noted that the illegal returnees included several members of their central unit headquartered in New York City, which officials dubbed the *junta revolucionaria* (revolutionary council). Moreover, they warned that these men planned to organize the "systematic, daily killing of a white person."[97] The Spanish consul in Veracruz verified all allegations.[98] The O'Donnell administration quickly realized that, despite their intentions to remove their problem, the recent expulsions had only exacerbated racial and political tensions with the exiles. The illegal travel of free blacks, combined with confirmation of a *junta revolucionaria* with branches in Veracruz and Havana, its financial backing and connection to a *junta* in New York, and its plans against whites in Cuba, revealed how intensely Cuban officials had underestimated expellees during the repressive Escalera era.

Obviously, Cuban requests that Mexico confine exiles thirty miles from the Gulf coastline had proven insufficient. In an effort to safeguard Cuba, O'Donnell ordered all English vessels, regardless of their destination, be detained at the main jail depot and searched for foreign passengers.[99] Moreover, Spain issued yet another royal order to their consulates to confine all Cuban *negros expulsados* they encountered.[100] Despite these instructions, however, many *libres de color* were not interned for more than a year, particularly in the Yucatán. The Spanish consul there confessed he never received the Spanish crown's internment order.[101] Consequently, Cubans in the Yucatán had the ability to move freely in this region for over a year, giving them access to travel beyond the Caribbean. In January 1846, the Mexican minister of foreign relations finally demanded the Yucatán governor to enforce the confinement order.[102] Yucatán compliance, however, was too little, too late.Although O'Donnell's reports to the Ultramar maintained that all was well on the island, his communications with Secretary of State Francisco Martínez de la Rosa in Spain revealed how serious he considered the potential threat from Cubans of color abroad.[103] The international nature of exile activities prompted Spanish authorities in Mexico and the United States to launch an intense investigation to verify the plans, movements, networks, and resources of *negros expulsados*.[104] The triangular correspondence and the actions taken by colonial authorities in Cuba, the United States, and Mexico between 1845 and 1847 demonstrated that Cuba's status was far from tranquil. Behind the veneer of calm crafted by O'Donnell stood a political powder keg that threatened Cuba's stability, Spain's colonial authority and influence, and foreign relations in the region.

NEGROS EXPULSADOS IN THE UNITED STATES

According to Cuban historian Pedro Deschamps Chapeaux, approximately forty *libres de color* fled voluntarily to the United States. These individuals, all men, arrived primarily in the New York City and New Orleans.[105] Although not as many in number as the four hundred who fled to Mexico, free Cubans of color bound for the United States reportedly entered the country with substantial financial resources and connections to New York abolitionists. They quickly established ties with their countrymen and American free blacks in Philadelphia and Baltimore.[106]

Since the 1820s and 1830s, white Cuban exiles had also established a growing presence in the east coast port cities. Father Félix Varela fled to the United States in 1823 due to his critique of colonialism and proabolition stance. In New York City, he established *El Habanero*, a Spanish-language newspaper, which advocated the overthrow of Spanish colonialism in Cuba through revolution.[107] In 1844, Cuban authorities arrested writers and censored printed materials to suppress creole dissent. Creole authors, whether they advocated annexation, independence, or abolition, fled the island and joined burgeoning Cuban exile communities in the United States. Radicalized, they produced an array of newspapers that advanced competing political positions. By the late 1840s, Cuban annexationists and anticolonialists arrived and organized in Washington, D.C., and New York City. They spread their political agendas through periodicals such as *La Verdad* and *El Independiente*.[108] An annexationist *junta* also formed during this period to promote both revolutionary and diplomatic solutions for advancing Cuba through a political association with the United States.[109] Although evidence of the interaction between creole exiles and *libres de color* is sparse, the parallel migration patterns, as well as the activities U.S. informants uncovered regarding *negros expulsados*, suggests that each group must have been aware of the other.

Francisco Stoughton, the Spanish consul in New York City, worked fervently to verify the existence of the *junta revolucionaria*. Denied diplomatic assistance from the U.S. government to infiltrate the group, Stoughton resorted to collaborating with personal contacts in the local police department. His informant, a trusted New York City police officer, made regular visits to African American neighborhoods in the city and investigated activities and meetings held there. In February 1845, the officer unexpectedly encountered his target group. While attempting to pick up a fugitive from justice, he stumbled upon twenty *negros españoles* (black Spaniards) among a street celebration. Surveying the crowd, he spotted an American woman of color whom he recognized, and pulled her aside for questioning.[110]

The officer claimed he had previously met this woman, dubbed La Mulata by officials in correspondence between Cuba, Spain, and the United States, when, as a slave, she informed authorities about plans for an uprising. In exchange for the information, she obtained her freedom.[111] Given that Pennsylvania implemented the gradual abolition of slavery in 1780, and New York instituted full emancipation by 1827, it is most likely that La Mulata had been a slave in Maryland.[112] The Nat Turner slave rebellion in neighboring Virginia in 1831 struck at the heart of slaveholders across the upper and lower south and provoked dissention among slaves. Simultaneously, free blacks and slaves were encouraged, via promises of personal freedom or payment, to provide information on schemes for conspiracies and revolts.[113] This suggests that La Mulata may have offered such information to secure her own freedom and then fled the state. In response to the officer's inquiries about her acquaintances, La Mulata responded guardedly that she was dating one of the *negros españoles*. She confirmed they had been spending a lot of time together, but he had not mentioned anything about a *junta revolucionaria*. Sensing the officer's eagerness for information, however, and his potential as a useful ally, she agreed to keep him informed about the movements of her lover and his companions.[114]

A few days after their chance encounter, La Mulata met the policeman at his home. She reported that her lover, whom his associates often called El Secretario due to his business acumen, and four other men had spent the prior weekend "writing incessantly." She described the men he worked with all as Spanish: three mulattoes, and the fourth, "tall" and "almost white." The latter, she said, spent a lot of time traveling and attended all of the group's activities in Philadelphia. In fact, in the midst of a trip to Philadelphia with her lover, La Mulata provided more substantial information. El Secretario had left her in the city while he accompanied his four comrades to Washington, D.C. In his absence, La Mulata hastily returned to New York with new data for the officer. She claimed his companions planned to travel to New Orleans for a one-month stay. Furthermore, her lover had begun investigating how to withdraw their money from Cuba.[115] Eager for additional intelligence and to avoid arousing suspicion in El Secretario, the officer arranged for his informant's morning train passage back to Philadelphia.[116] Unbeknownst to La Mulata, this news helped confirm the existence of a *junta revolucionaria* reportedly poised to ignite a race war in Cuba. Moreover, her news shed light on crucial clues to the *expulsados*' financial status, networks in the United States, and transregional connections in Cuba.

As expected, La Mulata carried additional news about the exiles when she returned to New York. The men had scheduled yet another trip to Philadelphia in a few weeks. La Mulata announced that she intended to accompany them and laid out her financial requirements as an informant. Not wanting to lose momentum, police officials agreed to pay for her travel so she could keep abreast of the suspects' activities. In addition, several New York officers were called in to coordinate surveillance with the city's local authorities. In total, La Mulata, the officers, and additional agents observed forty-three *negros españoles*—twenty from New York, twenty from Philadelphia, and three from Baltimore—gather to meet for five consecutive nights on the outskirts of the city. Filled with interest, but unable to attend the sessions, the young woman questioned her boyfriend repeatedly about the meetings. His response, however, abruptly ended her inquiries. His retort that she had a "singular curiosity" resonated with suspicion.[117] Not wanting to expose her duplicity, and sensing the tenuousness of her relationships with both El Secretario and the police officer, the young woman prepared to give her final report.

As the rapport between La Mulata and El Secretario unraveled, she managed to deliver a crucial piece of intelligence about him and his comrades to her contact in New York. El Secretario had begun receiving correspondence from New Orleans and anxiously awaited another letter expected to arrive in a few days. The Spanish consul in New Orleans, who had been tracking Cuban free blacks, confirmed similar activities among these men in Crescent City. By February 1845, with assistance from La Mulata and local American police, the Spanish consulate considered the data gathered sufficient evidence to confirm an extensive network of Cuban *libres de color* in the United States. Authorities concluded that the groups indeed aimed to foment a revolution among free people of color in Cuba.[118] With the worst of their suspicions validated, officers severed their links with La Mulata. From their perspective, her services as an informant had been worth every penny. Although largely unaware of the depth of her role, La Mulata had become the center of intelligence activities surrounding Cuban free blacks in the United States. According to the letters that circulated among the Cuban captain general, the Spanish consul in the United States, and the Ultramar, La Mulata held the key to unearthing an international plot by *expulsados* against colonialism and slavery in Cuba. Moreover, she revealed the level of literacy, political motivation, and coordinated communication *negros españoles* in the United States exercised in what appeared to be a quest to overthrow Spanish colonial rule in Cuba.

DISMISSALS, POTENTIAL ALLIANCES, AND VINDICATIONS

In spite of evidence verifying the network of *negros españoles*, Spanish consul authorities in the United States opted not to take further action. Remarkably, they concluded that, due to the irregularity of the group's movements and meetings, these *libres de color* posed no real threat to Cuba. Instead, the Spanish consulate dismissed the activities as the "typical rumblings against slavery in [Cuba] from a few poorly behaved blacks."[119] Shocked by the turn of events, O'Donnell refused to comply. He considered the coalition of Cuban free blacks in the United States, especially their mobility and established linkages in major American port cities, a very real threat. Frustrated, he urged Spanish officers in Washington, D.C., and New York City to, at the very least, continue scrutinizing the *expulsados*; he would do the same to protect Cuban stability and prosperity.[120]

In fact, O'Donnell took matters into his own hands. He circumvented colonial officials and maintained secret communications with local police in Washington, D.C. Anxious to see the situation for himself, in April 1845 he traveled to the United Stataes to meet with his contact personally, from whom he received alarming news. According to his informant, various secret societies of blacks and mulattoes still existed in the city. Moreover, they and their affiliates in Philadelphia and New Orleans were preparing ways "to emancipate their race and give a repetitive and simultaneous attack on the Antilles." In addition, British abolitionists, who had been spotted attending the meetings, seemed poised to forge an alliance with the *libres de color*.[121] Confidential accounts from Jamaica and Haiti corroborated American reports, and confirmed a surge of conspiratorial plans against Cuba by British abolitionists and slaves in the Caribbean.[122] The reliability of these reports, however dubious, fueled O'Donnell's fears. On the one hand, although a variety of sources tracked the *negros españoles*, hard evidence of their actual plans remained elusive. On the other hand, the reports from Jamaica and Haiti, where slavery had been abolished, may have served to purposely alarm Cuba. True or fabricated, in the context of the Escalera era, they could not be ignored.

Furthermore, disparate pockets of white Cuban dissenters exacerbated the situation. Among these exile cadres, some sought intellectual freedom from Escalera-era censorship. Others promoted Cuban annexation to the United Statea to preserve slavery, while an opposition sector called for the abolition of slavery. Another demanded Cuba's full independence. In the late 1840s and 1850s, when these groups began circulating their views via newspapers in New York City, Philadelphia, and New Orleans, exiled Cuban free men of color like El Secretario and his associates most likely read or heard about the most prominent of these periodicals, such as *La Verdad*, which supported annexation to the United

States; the anticolonial *El Independiente*; and *El Mulato*, which called for abolition and challenged exiles to make race a key issue in the fight for *Cuba libre*.[123] Cuban authorities dreaded the volatile combination of *expulsados*, annexationists, abolitionists, and anticolonialists. If an alliance of these groups succeeded in overriding Spanish political, social, or economic authority, O'Donnell reasoned, Cuba would be ruined.[124]

With this new set of developments among exiles, the Spanish crown and colonial officials in Cuba took action. Spain braced Cuba for black rebellion and creole revolt from abroad by sending warships and troops to permanently protect the island. Meanwhile, the Treasury Department allocated a monetary reserve to fund defense activities.[125] Seemingly vindicated, Captain General O'Donnell promised to continue transmitting news of thwarted schemes to emancipate the island, secure in the knowledge that the crown's "valiant and disciplined army" would swiftly "suppress any disturbances."[126]

Yet, how could Cuban officials know the true intentions of free people of color? In some instances, especially in Mexico, local authorities had warily processed passports and witnessed black emigrants' simmering aggravations bubble over. In other cases, *libres de color* responded directly with letters declaring their innocence, allegiance, and desires to return to Cuba. Contacts in the United States, although considered reliable, proved less substantive, so much so that Spanish consulate officers failed to take the threat of organized rebellion from *negros españoles* seriously. Not until O'Donnell became personally involved in surveillance activities in Washington, D.C. did Spain validate the captain general's suspicions. However, if *expulsados* in the United States plotted an attack on Cuba, it never materialized. Rather, instead of conspiring to destroy Cuba, the majority of exiles, both *libres de color* and creoles, resumed their quest to return home legally.[127] As mothers, fathers, spouses, children, and friends, they forged a community inseparable from Cuba. Nevertheless, most would spend ten arduous years abroad before shifts in colonial policy opened ports for a relatively safe homecoming.

Tentative Homecomings

Significant changes in Spanish imperial and local Cuban politics emerged to shift the dynamics of the Escalera era seemingly in favor of the exile community. In 1848, four years after initiating the Escalera repression, O'Donnell returned to Spain. By 1854, he led a revolution to restore Spain's Progressive Party to power. Ironically, the new government eased the repressive measures O'Donnell had implemented in Cuba in the previous decade. In addition, it placated creole slave owners, who feared abolition and annexation.[128] Meanwhile, increased Spanish immigration to Cuba strengthened the demographic proportion of Spaniards and gave the colonial administration more control over creole elites in the form of military defense. Since the outbreak of the Escalera rebellions in 1843, Spanish regular troop figures had jumped by 36 percent in 1853 (from 14,484 to 19,759) and by 64 percent in 1855 (23,802). The rapid militarization of Cuba in the early 1850s helped stave off separatist attempts.[129]

In Cuba, the new leadership embraced reforms emanating from Spain. Juan de la Pezuela, the captain general in 1853, stimulated the liberalization of politics in Cuba. His controversial policies chipped away at the slave trade, authorized interracial marriage, and reinstated the militia of color. Considered too radical, his tenure lasted under a year. His replacement, José de la Concha, reversed some and augmented others of his predecessor's policies. On the one hand, the de la Concha administration loosened the slave trade prohibitions to appease plantation owners and pro-annexationists.[130] On the other hand, he expanded the size of creole and black militias. Additional measures softened labor and association policies, which included relaxing indentured apprenticeship regulations. Furthermore, the de la Concha government authorized creole artisan associations to provide mutual-aid services and the re-formation of black mutual-aid organizations that had been outlawed during the Escalera repression. Intellectual freedom increased, allowing literary publications and societies to flourish.[131] Moreover, in 1854, Spain initiated a limited amnesty for colonial exiles.[132] Despite the advent of an economic crisis in 1857, the colonial trends in political reform set the stage for a long-awaited full pardon of the *expulsados*.

On December 12, 1857, the Spanish crown declared a general amnesty for all "who had taken part, directly or indirectly in conspiracies, rebellions or foreign invasions with the goal of promoting disturbances or committing any other type of political crime in the overseas provinces."[133] Articles Two and Four of the decree ordered the immediate release of political prisoners jailed in Spain or Spanish territories in North Africa, as well those being held in the Americas.[134] For those who had been banished, however, the residency caveat still applied, unless they could obtain written permission from the captain general.[135] Although wary of the governments' motives, hundreds of black and white exiles set sail for a tentative homecoming in Cuba.

Among the first to take advantage of the new law were Havana natives Francisca Santa Cruz and Pedro de la Guardia. In August 1857, Santa Cruz, a seamstress, and de la Guardia, a tailor, requested to return from Veracruz, Mexico.[136] In November, officials approved their passage to the island.[137] In 1861, authorities released *moreno libre* José Claudio Pieda at the end of his seventeen-year imprisonment and banishment in Asturias, Spain. He had been indicted for taking part in planning a slave rebellion on three sugar plantations, La Merced, La Isabel, and El Fundador, in the Matanzas district. Under the terms of Article One of the amnesty, officials excused his actions as "racial crimes," and not "truly political" in nature. Furthermore, officials appeared willing to grant Pieda's request because he had completed his jail term.[138] Not surprisingly, those who presented themselves as skilled artisans experienced the least difficulty. Exiles like Santa Cruz and de la Guardia, and ex-convicts like Pieda suddenly posed no threat to Cuba. By the 1850s, the expansion of Cuba's white population, through Spanish immigration programs, and the trade in Asian indentured labor combined to help dampen the looming menace of annexationists and separatists, and rebellion fomented by slaves and free people of color.

* * *

The social and political realities of Cuba's slave society dictated boundaries of race designed to maintain white control over a sizeable African-descended population. Although intricately linked to the slave and white sectors, the island's substantial free community of color compromised established hierarchies. The threatening influences of *libres de color*—their legal status in the midst of a large slave sector and their ability to lead and join with slaves and creole dissidents in rebellion against slavery and colonial rule—had sparked decades of debate over how to suppress them. Time and again, island governors considered expulsion as an effective, albeit impractical, method to relieve this potential danger to the colony. Yet, colonial officials acknowledged that free people of color filled vital roles in society. As skilled artisans, laborers, and militiamen, they provided services that Spaniards and creoles were reluctant to perform. Although authorities preferred to remove *libres de color* from the island, doing so would jeopardize the economic stability Cuban leaders and elites fought to maintain.

In the wake of the Conspiracy of La Escalera, island authorities gained a new opportunity to reduce the menace posed by *libres de color*. Using a three-pronged approach, Leopoldo O'Donnell's administration purged the colony. First, the Military Commission sentenced over six hundred free men of color to imprisonment overseas or banishment from the island. Second, the Cuban government enforced anti-immigrant laws to expel foreign-born *libres de color*. Finally, the government extended passports to Cuban-born free men and women of African descent. In search of refuge from the repressive measures, those who hesitantly accepted quickly realized the dubious nature of emigration as officials denied pleas to return from exile.

The expulsions gave rise to new spatial contours between colonial Cuba, *libres de color*, and the Atlantic World. Formerly contained to the island, Cuban authorities found themselves reacting to the claims of overseas free blacks that the island was their homeland. Immigrants asserted a legitimate connection to Cuba as militiamen, property owners, and craftsmen, and emphasized their honorable behavior. Exiles, particularly those located in Mexico, submitted group petitions to return, or had contacts in Cuba request permission on their behalf. Overseas prisoners in North Africa and Spain asked for term reductions and sought to negotiate banishment prohibitions. Eager to dismiss *libres de color* upon physical departure, officials had underestimated free blacks' attachment to Cuba from afar. From displacement in foreign territories and Spanish prisons, free men and women of African descent stretched, and often broke, colonial codes of conduct by continuing to undercut and challenge imperial mechanisms of control from abroad.

Over a decade after the Escalera era began, Spanish imperial political reforms facilitated amnesty for everyone connected to a political crime, rebellion, or conspiracy. Although there is insufficient evidence to know how many *libres de color* returned to Cuba under the 1857 decree, the examples in this chapter make clear that free people of color pursued a variety of methods to reclaim their lives in Cuba long before amnesty took hold. Whether foreign born, imprisoned overseas, or expelled to foreign territories, free people of African descent claimed Cuba as home. In doing so from exile, they maneuvered through the severe spatial, racial, political, and social conditions that defined the Escalera era. Tracing the paths of *libres de color* from Cuba to Spain, Morocco, Mexico, and the United States reveals multiple levels of African diasporic agency in motion. Moreover, their actions within these specific contexts emphasized how the issues of race, rebellion, slavery, abolition, and independence continued to resonate across the Atlantic during the mid-nineteenth century.

4 / Acts of Excess and Insubordination: Resisting the Tranquillity of Terror

Give that to your mother!

—JOSÉ ELIAS MENDIOLA

As the Military Commission sentencing came to a close in January 1845, Captain General O'Donnell had begun sending carefully crafted correspondence to the Ultramar affirming Cuba's peaceful state of affairs. Twenty-two of the twenty-five letters he penned between January and December 1845 asserted the island's "tranquillity"; all was safe in the colony.[1] Cuban elites especially desired a return to a state of affairs that would further subordinate blacks to whites and displace free black workers, particularly in skilled and domestic urban labor sectors. With this characterization of colonial "normalcy" in mind, Escalera era legislation limited geographic mobility between urban and rural areas and curtailed economic opportunities for *libres de color*. In many instances, the tightened restrictions combined to drive their social networks underground and disrupt established forms of free black individual and group identities. Just as the public executions generated spectacles of white supremacy and authority, and the expulsions attempted to remove seditious behavior that could foment violent dissent, local legislation circumscribing the lives of people of color attempted to harden racial boundaries and reinvigorate the slave system. Blanketed in what one foreign observer called the "tranquillity of terror," Cuba's revised black codes of 1844 extended the Escalera repression into the decades to come--not, however, without opposition.[2] Despite trauma from the "Year of the Lash," some *libres de color* contested governmental attempts to direct and restrict their lives, indicating that the calm veneer O'Donnell constructed for the Spanish metropole had already started to crack and splinter. In November 1845, regional authorities complained of insubordination from free men and women of African descent. According to the lieutenant governor of Puerto Príncipe, their persistent "acts of disrespect and excess" undermined white privilege and domination. Recently, free pardos and morenos in this jurisdiction claimed local judges had violated their rights by jailing them for longer than the maximum thirty days without formal charges. As precedent, they called attention to the original regulation, promulgated in 1842, which applied to "all persons without exception," black or white. This legal demand, on the heels of the Escalera uprisings and repression, gave rise to one Puerto Príncipe official's assertion, "never more than now we must try to limit" the black population's actions and restrict their behavior.[3] Just as intense harassment drove hundreds of *libres de color* beyond Cuban shores, the repression also had a severe impact on those who remained behind. This chapter addresses the impact of the Escalera era on those without the means to leave. Their previous understandings of colonial society, and of the contradictory policies being enacted, compelled many free people of color to stand their ground and claim justice in Cuba.

O'Donnell's reports of peace and stability deeply contrasted with the realities of the repression. To be sure, violence was an endemic feature of slavery, especially in restoring order after revolts. However, the consequences of the Escalera repression left many men and women of African descent in desperate social and economic conditions, particularly in the urban areas where most *libres de color* resided. The terror used to generate tranquillity would force *pardos* and *morenos* to become more creative and persistent as they worked to rebuild their lives and safeguard their families.

Just as exiles demonstrated their ability to negotiate the politics of race from abroad, *libres de color* who remained in Cuba sought ways to redress the extremes set in motion by the Military Commission trials, racist legislation, and economic displacement. Individuals such as María del Pilar Poveda challenged the ban on her work as a skilled midwife.[4] José María Pacheco struggled to retain his profession as an undertaker in the face of stricter licensing requirements.[5] Apprentices Merced Valdés and José Elias Mendiola rejected their respective extended assignments as domestic and cigar-maker trainees.[6] Similarly, leaders of *cabildos de nación* undermined restrictions on community-based activities. Individual and group struggles to overcome racist practices underscored how black resistance, albeit fragmented, worked to destabilize the repression's totalizing impact.

Restoring Order to a Slave Society

Colonial officials in Spain and Puerto Rico, and Cuban newspapers, government councils, and planter elites rallied behind the success of the Escalera repression. Above all, they used the episode to reinforce the institution of slavery. As noted by historian Robert Paquette, O'Donnell aspired to "return the slaves to their habitual state of discipline and servitude without grave damage to the proprietors."[7] According to Captain General O'Donnell and proslavery advocates, Cuba needed African labor to produce the colony's "rich fruits": sugar, coffee, and tobacco. Any alternative would spell ruin for the island.[8] These concerns and aims paralleled previous rebellious episodes in Cuba and the Americas during the first half of the nineteenth century. After uprisings in Brazil, Cuba, Jamaica, New Orleans, and Virginia, authorities instituted a range of harsh restrictions and violence to restore state control.[9] In each instance, officials sought a return to elite ideas of normalcy by inflicting harsh restrictions on slaves and free people of color. The measures initiated in 1844, however, generated cruelty and prohibitions far beyond the norm for Cuba. Rather than return to the status quo after they had vented their anger through torture and displayed state power through trials and public executions, Spanish colonial officials in Cuba endeavored to do more than contain the revolt, destroy rebel leaders, and purge the island of potential conspirators. In addition, the government pursued a course of action to crush black social and economic opportunities, and harass those who remained into total submission.

The measures taken to quell the Escalera rebellions, however, did little to alter the importance of slavery and the acquisition of slaves in Cuba. Despite a significant dip in African imports from 10,000 to 5,000 a year in 1845, due primarily to Spain's new agreement with Britain to abolish and suppress the slave trade, imports rebounded quickly. By the close of the decade, the figures had jumped to 9,000. In 1850, a spike in plantation and mill construction renewed calls for coerced labor, and slave importations soared, averaging 12,000 annually between 1851 and 1860. Simultaneously, the cost of slaves also climbed. Although the average price between 1835 and 1850 remained approximately 400 pesos, at times this figure more than tripled. The rising expense of slaves and increased sugar exports going to the United States compelled Cuban planters to acquire an enslaved labor force through both legal and contraband methods.[10] In other words, post-rebellion policies advanced slavery largely at the expense of the existing slave and free black populations. Moreover, despite the impact of the Escalera rebellions, safeguarding the profits produced by slavery outweighed the threat of potential uprisings.

In addition to targeting slaves and *libres de color*, the government's restoration of order included measures to curtail dissenting social and political commentary and reinforce Cuba's dependent colonial status. Creole critiques, especially those developed in the 1820s and 1830s, came under heavy fire during the Escalera era. Cuban writer Cirilio Villaverde noted the difficulties of life during the repression. In a letter written in September 1844 to friends in exile, he characterized Cuba's atmosphere as toxic, especially to men of letters.[11] In effect, the repression intensified divisions within the white population, pitting plantations owners against nonslaveholders, Spaniards against creoles, and annexationists against abolitionists.

Stabilizing Cuba after the revolts implied suppressing dissent among all segments of the population; nevertheless, the resubordination of the black sector remained a primary goal. To help stem the flow of slaves into the free population of color, the O'Donnell administration suspended issuing *cartas de libertad* (freedom papers). Claiming the "undeniable fact" that free men of color had led the conspiracy, he hoped to curb this group's expansion by denying slaves access to freedom and revoking the requisite documentation of those newly freed.[12] To this end, O'Donnell reversed the course of his predecessor, who had authorized more than three hundred freedom papers. In doing so, he aimed to reinforce colonial authority, appease planters, and limit contact between slaves and *libres de color*. These actions, he predicted, would suppress future racial dissent.

To restore order on a broader scale, the colonial administration also revised existing ordinances pertaining to black mobility and revolt. O'Donnell and the Junta de Fomento (Development Council) altered the 1842 Slave Code established by the former governor, Geronimo Valdes. The updated General and Estate Regulations limited both the movements of free people of color and their interaction with the slave population. The first seven articles of the General Regulations targeted free blacks for continued surveillance. In particular, officials applied overarching occupational restrictions and bans to hamper free blacks' economic viability and social influence on slaves. The dual approach of scrutinizing the movements of free *pardos* and *morenos* and reducing their occupational resources shrouded the Escalera era in a tranquillity forged by terrorizing the African-descended population.

UNDER A WATCHFUL EYE

A first step in implementing the colonial elites' aim to reestablish order involved a heightened scrutiny of people of color, especially *libres de color*. "Any crime against whites" was to be harshly punished, as exemplified in the case of *morena libre* Dolores Ruiz and her son, Andres Poveda. Ruiz, a widow, earned a living by renting out rooms in her Havana home. No doubt subjected to racist insults from her clientele on occasion, Ruiz most likely noticed an escalation of such episodes during the Escalera era. In the late summer of 1848, Andres witnessed a white man verbally assault his mother and stepped in to defend her. For his protective actions, judges sentenced Andres to three months on the Isle of Pines located off the coast of Cuba. During the nineteenth century, part of the Isle of Pines served as a penal colony, and it developed a reputation as the "dumping ground" for Cuba's unwanted elements.[13] Measures like this, which compromised a mother's and property owner's respectability and tore apart a family, revealed the persistent and personal affront free people of color endured during the Escalera era.

To monitor and track the black population, officials began requiring this sector to carry special identity papers called a *cédula de seguridad* (security document). In 1854, just as colonial authorities granted limited amnesty to political prisoners, they also sought to "establish and regularize" a slave registry by issuing *cédulas de seguridad* to urban and rural slaves. On April 2, 1855, the José de La Concha administration began enforcing *cédulas* for male *libres de color* over the age of fifteen.[14] Three years later, in March 1858, officials expanded the order, and required all free people of color—men, women, and children—to carry these special identification papers, color coded according to gender.[15] The certificate, which described the holder's physical characteristics, marital status, age, occupation, and address, also recorded the individuals they lived with and their relationship to them.[16] Furthermore, the March decree forced all free people of color, not just men, to renew their paperwork annually and report any changes of address.[17] In theory, data collected from the *cédulas de seguridad* created a census from which officials could track the movements of the entire black population. Moreover, by extending identification papers to include all *libres de color*, the government could systematically account for an ever-evolving and mobile segment of the population.

Furthermore, authorities used the identity papers to boost colonial revenues and exact punishment. The 1858 order raised the *cédula* tax from two *reales* for men to a scale based on age for the broader population. With the exception of those who were blind, deaf, or invalids, taxes ranged from half a *real* for those younger than seven and over sixty to four *reales* for everyone between the ages of fifteen and sixty.[18] Punishments for those found without the proper documentation also augmented government coffers. Transgressors were to be fined five *reales* and could be jailed for an unspecified amount of time. According to the 1855 reports, authorities registered over 50,000 *cédulas de seguridad* for free black men.[19] However, data from 1858 indicated a sharp decline, down to just under 23,000. The drop in registrants suggests the ineffectiveness of the *cédula* system. Most free people of color, as well as slaveholders, undermined the elaborate identification and tax scheme by simply refusing to provide personal or residential information.

In fact, the system began breaking down almost as soon as it started. As reflected in the updated order, numerous "abuses" plagued the project, especially the "falsification" of *cédulas de seguridad*. To eradicate the proliferation of fake documents, particularly among the slave population, colonial officials ordered slaveholders to retain the identity papers for safe keeping. Officials noted that, as the property of others, slaves could not "legitimately" own anything. *Libres de color* also confounded authorities by exploiting their seeming lack of permanent residencies, which further eroded the government's combined plan of surveillance and revenue.[20] If slaves could access and circulate false papers for themselves, most likely aided by free people of color, the next step—creating freedom papers—would not be far behind. The inability of authorities to pinpoint the location of free blacks suggests both their transient tendencies, based on economic and social inequalities, and outright noncompliance with the state's new security system.

Moreover, data from 1858 indicated that thousands of *libres de color* were actually exempted from carrying *cédulas de seguridad*--in particular, militiamen, firemen, and registered sailors. Reports calculated a total of 182,919 men and their families affiliated with these areas of employment.[21] Meanwhile, population estimates put the free sector of color at 205,866.[22] In other words, the identity papers applied to only 11 percent of *libres de color* because, presumably, the exempted 89 percent could be tracked through their specific associations with the colonial state. Furthermore, there is scant evidence that *cédulas de seguridad* ever gained widespread usage in the colony. Deprived of data and revenues from security papers, officials turned their attention to subordinating the urban labor force.

URBAN LABOR UNDER ATTACK: ARTISANS, APPRENTICES, AND MIDWIVES

In the aftermath of the Escalera rebellions, the O'Donnell administration acted quickly to fuse race and labor into plans for the restoration of colonial order. A restructuring of the urban labor force took center stage. First, Spanish colonial authorities banned *libres de color* from a variety of medical and crafts areas and sought to push this sector into agricultural labor. Second, officials struggled to infuse white creoles into a wide range of urban occupations. In fomenting plans, O'Donnell insisted how "indispensable" it would be to have whites "replace blacks as skilled artisans, domestics, cooks, and carriage drivers." More important, he reasoned that supplanting free black workers in the cities would reestablish white dominance in these fields and suppress further political upheaval.[23]

O'Donnell's recommendations clearly carried weight. In July 1844, Spain issued a royal order capping the number of black domestics in the colony and imposing a one-peso tax for each person of color employed as a household servant.[24] In addition, regulations from the revised Slave Code directly impeded free blacks' employment opportunities, with one explicitly barring *libres de color* from practicing as pharmacists.[25] Similarly, the Military Commission trials banned dozens from working as skilled artisans. These actions, combined with the deportation of thousands of prisoners to serve time in North African and Spain, and the flight of several hundred free black artisans and their families to Mexico and elsewhere in the Americas, eliminated substantial numbers from the skilled workforce.

In a sweeping move to monitor and erode employment avenues for free *pardos* and *morenos* after 1844, authorities tightened qualifications for obtaining operating licenses for established and new businesses.[26] Shortly afterward, the Sociedad Económica de Amigos del País (Economic Society) in Matanzas reported a 67 percent rise in the number of white artisans between 1846 and 1849.[27] Prominent creoles in the 1820s and 1830s, particularly José Antonio Saco and Félix Varela, who were now in exile, envisioned *criollos* working as carpenters, masons, and blacksmiths as a means to infuse manual occupations with honor and curtail white vagrancy. Their agenda finally began to take hold during the Escalera era as revised colonial codes circumscribed the number of black proprietors and reinforced white supremacy in skilled craft employment.

Nevertheless, free people of color challenged these threats to their economic survival. For instance, in 1848, José María Pacheco, an undertaker who had been "operating without a license for twelve years," encountered difficulties when he applied for a permit. He explained he started his venture through Joaquin Muños, an established mortician, at the same location. After much debate, and a reference for Pacheco from the town mayor who vouched for his good conduct, officials fined Pacheco fifty pesos and granted his license.[28] Similarly, when José Lamarra asked for a certificate to legitimate his barber shop, authorities charged him fifty pesos before approving his request.[29] The fines levied by officials suggests both their frustration over being unable to deny these licenses and also a way to penalize *libres de color* economically. The fact that these men had established practices, in some cases for over a decade, nevertheless, demonstrated their skill in circumventing legalities and maintaining a certain level of autonomy over their livelihoods before and after the repression.

Others, however, proved less successful than Pacheco and Lamarra. When Ramón Campos requested permission to open a mortuary in 1848, officials assessed his space simply as "unsuitable." Campos rejected this appraisal, claiming that he had previously registered for a license without difficulty. His request went unanswered.[30] José Isidoro Hernández faced a similar situation. He wrote to obtain a license for the carpentry workshop he had been operating for over eight years. When authorities investigated the site, however, they described it as being in a "miserable state." Hernández countered, saying this had little to do with his actual business because he "almost always left the shop closed to work in the homes" of his customers. Similarly to Campos, Hernández's petition remained unsettled.[31] Left in limbo, some *libres de color* had little choice but to continue working in unauthorized businesses.

In addition to harassing established and new business owners, authorities also targeted apprentices, a substantial proportion of whom were free people of color. Established in the early 1830s under the direction of the Economic Society, apprenticeships initially required slaves, free people of color, and creoles to labor without wages at a workshop ranging from two to five years. Moreover, officials designed the system to play a persistent role in tightening the labor conditions for free workers at a time when Cuba experienced significant economic growth. According to creole intellectual Antonio Bachiller y Morales, architect of the revised system in 1835, apprenticeships aimed to diminish vagrant behavior and reinforce colonial control of urban laborers. Two years later, at the urging of Bachiller y Morales, the Economic Society instituted regulations that enabled them to extend apprentice status even after the required training period ended.[32] Doing so reduced competition for master artisans and limited the ability of slaves and free workers to begin collecting the substantial earnings of which they were deprived during their instruction.

During the Escalera era, authorities prolonged the length of apprenticeships and created a new Apprenticeship Council to oversee the program.[33] These actions facilitated even more state control over the skills free *pardos* and *morenos* acquired, and created greater colonial leverage in thwarting the expansion of black businesses. In 1849, new apprenticeship regulations increased the typical two- to five-year training period to a maximum of ten years for women and twelve years for men, more if authorities determined an individual had been excessively ill or defiant. Punishments for disobeying these new rules often included shackling, whipping, or placing the offender in stocks.[34]

In response, *libres de color* confronted the new restrictions with increasing insubordination. Some, like Merced Valdés, ran away from their appointments. Valdés fled from her white instructor, Merced Orduña, five times in four years.[35] Onlookers condemned Pedro Veitia, a carpenter-in-training, for his threatening behavior and the possession of a weapon. Witnesses reported that he carried a small rock and prepared to throw it at Andres Dapena, "without respect for him [Dapena] being a white man." Although Veitia never physically assaulted anyone, he was arrested and charged for shouting insults.[36] Tensions also ran high for José Elias Mendiola, who worked for Narciso Jímenez, an abusive creole cigarmaker. One day Mendiola lost his temper and flaunted his feelings with the vehement outburst, "give that to your mother!" For his insolence Mendiola spent eight days in jail. Upon his release, Jímenez returned Mendiola to the apprenticeship director for reassignment.[37] These examples of disruptive behavior suggest that many *libres de color* had far less choice during the Escalera era about becoming apprentices, choosing an occupational trade, or selecting a master craftsman to work with than they had prior to the 1844 repression. Once placed, they became, at best, indentured servants for a decade or longer. Acts of insubordination signaled their dissatisfaction, frustration, resistance, and agency during the Escalera era.

Moreover, the sharp numerical reduction among free people of color dramatically changed the occupational landscape for free blacks and creoles. In 1846, *libres de color* between the ages of sixteen and sixty had decreased by 8 percent islandwide. As to be expected, given the epicenter of the rebellions, the most striking reductions occurred in western

Cuba, where men and women in this age group declined by 18 percent. Not surprisingly, men bore the brunt, with a 12 percent decrease.[38] For authorities and other interested parties, the shifts marked progress in their goals to usurp economic opportunities from free blacks. Data collected by the Economic Society in Matanzas in 1849, which revealed only 34 percent of free men of color among their 1,266 craftsmen, supported this trend. Content at the near success of their goal to establish a 3-to-1 ratio of white to black artisans, society members exclaimed "we were not looking for the cause" behind these figures.[39] In addition, when trade guilds emerged in the late 1840s, they supported male Spaniards and creoles only. In the 1850s, to placate disgruntled white artisans and elites who promoted annexation to the United States as a means to maintain slavery and obtain political opportunities, Captain General Federico Roncalí allowed only white artisans, professionals, and immigrants to establish associations.[40]

The occupational erosion that left thousands of male *libres de color* hard pressed to find work also made them vulnerable to recategorization as a menacing subclass. Authorities labeled those found idle and unable to provide evidence of regular employment or property ownership as vagrants, and had them jailed or subjected to state labor projects.[41] For instance, officials charged Juan García Feblita for vagrancy and sentenced him to six months in public works, after which he would be transferred to the Royal Jail, most likely for hard labor.[42] In addition, Captain General O'Donnell proposed establishing a private tribunal for these individuals because of their alleged danger to society.[43] In other words, the policies of the Escalera era attacked free blacks in the urban areas from multiple angles. New regulations prohibited access to certain skilled areas of employment, extended unpaid apprenticeships, and recruited white workers to supplant black artisans. Inevitably, these actions made it difficult for male *libres de color* to obtain gainful employment, which then enabled colonial officials to treat them as a danger to the colony.

Legislation restricting the movements and occupations of free black males also severely affected the work of skilled *pardas* and *morenas*. The revised slave codes of 1844, which reduced opportunities connected to the medical field and established special prohibitions on practicing as apothecaries or making prescriptions, along with the Military Commission's rulings, also targeted midwives for surveillance and occupational displacement.[44] Since the early nineteenth century, the colony had struggled to shift midwifery into the hands of white women, but with little success.[45] Just as free men of color had come under fire for dishonoring artisan positions, free women of color suffered the same accusations for their predominance as midwives. When the Military Commission discovered María del Pilar Poveda, a respected Matanzas *partera* (midwife), to be an accomplice to the Escalera rebellions, she became the catalyst for a renewed push to reverse the field's racial composition.

Authorities charged María del Pilar Poveda, a free *parda*, for allowing her son-in-law, Plácido, to hold political meetings in her home. Judges condemned her complicity in the conspiratorial plan and her knowledge of "the crimes and their consequences."[46] Furthermore, because of her familial links to the rebellions and her prominence as a midwife in Matanzas, the council viewed Poveda as a potential threat to both the colonial state and the white women and children she attended. Judges sentenced her to a year of labor in Havana's San Francisco de Paula Hospital, banished her from living in Matanzas with her family, and barred her from working as a *partera* under the threat of life imprisonment.[47] Poveda's string of punishments represented the harshest for free women of color delivered by the Military Commission. By targeting her medical expertise and position in the community, officials sought to eliminate Poveda's social standing and cast a damning example for the free sector of color.

Like many of her fellow skilled artisans and apprentices, Poveda protested the prohibition on her livelihood and family contact. After completing her sentence in Havana in 1845, she wrote to the Captain General to lift the employment and residential restrictions. Poveda explained how her three sons and "aging and ailing husband . . . had been reduced to the greatest misery" without her income as a midwife. As proof of her respectability, Poveda underscored how the "elite ladies" of Matanzas had never criticized her behavior and had always paid "her at the level to which her expertise distinguished her."[48] Unable to counter the commendations made by Poveda's supporters and acknowledging she had served her one-year hospital term without incident, authorities granted her request. Nevertheless, this action, like the favorable decisions for foreign-born *libres de color*, seemed a direct contradiction to Cuban officials' goal of curtailing the roles of free black skilled workers.

Poveda's success in reversing the ban on her occupation as a midwife, however, fueled the medical community's desires to displace midwives of color. Between the mid 1840s and the late 1860s, the medical establishment made gradual gains in shifting midwifery out of the hands of *libres de color*. At the start of 1845, officials appointed a director to supervise a new obstetrics program for women at the Havana hospital.[49] Although the program admitted *criolla blanca*, *parda*, and *morena* students, the series of eligibility requirements revealed dubious motives. Entry was based on documents attesting to an applicant's moral character, piety, and literacy, and subject to the approval of her husband. Widows could not skirt the issue; they had to present their husband's death certificate to complete the admissions process.[50] On the one hand, the medical council recognized it had to, at least initially, include free black and mulatto women, given the latter's traditional involvement in the field and the societal taboos on white female employment. On the other hand, by imposing standards of honor considered unattainable for women of African descent—moral character, literacy, and legal marriage in particular—the medical board ultimately aspired to exclude as many free *morenas* and *pardas* as possible.

Efforts to establish additional midwife schools and regulate candidates' character persisted over the next two decades. In the late 1850s, legislation and public commentary over the need for more white midwives began to show progress, and creole and Spanish women finally began submitting requests to become *parteras*.[51] By 1862, Havana boasted eight white midwives and six free black practitioners. In Matanzas, however, where María del Pilar Poveda had resumed her practice, *parda* midwives continued to outnumber *criollas*. In this case, women of color represented eight of the nine midwives.[52] Clearly, some cities outside of Havana had a more difficult time recasting midwifery as a desirable occupation for white women.

A final round of prohibitive matriculation fees in the late 1860s brought about the full exclusion of registered *parteras* of color.[53] The increased program costs made it excessively difficult for potential *parda* and *morena* candidates to afford attending midwife schools and steadily siphoned them from the applicant pool. By 1869, government records listed no women of color as licensed *parteras*.[54] Nevertheless, given that the free and slave populations continued to increase, numerous unlicensed free women of color must have continued to practice. Midwives of color soon discovered, however, like their fellow male artisans, that authorities' continual use of racist employment practices, however fragmented, eroded the pride, honor, and economic support *libres de color* derived from skilled occupations for both men and women.

Spanish colonial authorities celebrated the pronounced reduction of black artisans and midwives. Although the attack on urban labor took hold unevenly, by the early 1860s, repressive policies and practices had thwarted economic opportunities for a substantial number of skilled black workers in major cities and towns. With their individual and family well-being at stake, artisans, midwives, and apprentices did their best to survive the economic backlash. Many would turn to their communities for assistance even as social organizations fell under attack.

Targeting Cabildos de Nación

In addition to destroying economic opportunities and placing *libres de color* and slaves under intense scrutiny, Spanish colonial authorities further complicated urban workers' struggles by suppressing *cabildos de nación*. These sociocultural mutual aid associations, in existence in Spanish and Portuguese America since the late sixteenth and early seventeenth centuries and sanctioned by colonial authorities, united segments of Cuba's slave, free ethnic African, and native black Cuban populations.[55] Under the direction of elected male and female officers, these dues-collecting organizations often acquired real estate and rented out rooms, made loans to members, purchased the freedom of slaves, cared for the sick, and buried the dead.[56] Although authorized by Spanish colonial authorities to facilitate Africans' religious and cultural assimilation under Spanish colonialism, *cabildos de nación* became fertile spaces of ethnic cohesion to subvert white supremacy and the slave system.

Increasingly, *cabildos de nación* became implicated in Cuban revolts. The most prominent included the *cabildo* Shangó Teddún led by José Antonio Aponte in 1812 and the *cabildo* Lucumí Eyo under the direction of council officer Juan Nepomuceno Prieto in 1835. Authorities summarily executed these men, and subsequent legislation in 1837 restricted *cabildo* gatherings to Sundays and only approved their celebration of Catholic holidays outside of Havana's walled perimeter.[57] Unrest persisted. In 1839, Havana authorities disrupted a meeting at the home of Margarito Blanco, a dockworker and leader in a Carabalí *cabildo*. Those in attendance, who included quarry and wood laborers, domestic slaves, militiamen, and artisans, were members of Abakuá and other secret societies. Fearful of their intentions, officials arrested the men and sent most of them to Spain for permanent banishment. A revolt involving fifty *lucumís* erupted on the Aldama sugar plantation in 1841 and resulted in the participants' arrest and death.[58] Despite repressive measures to stamp out dissent, these associations continued to multiply, amplifying colonial apprehensions over the potential of future plots designed to overthrow slavery and Spanish rule.

As pockets of revolt intensified across Cuba in 1843, authorities quickly implicated *cabildos de nación*. Even foreign newspapers noted how each episode of revolt seemed "more extensive and deeply organized" than the last.[59] Out to prove their suspicions, the Military Commission extracted testimony to corroborate these observations. Slaves such as Dimas from the San Ignacio sugar estate in Matanzas acknowledged that rural *cabildos* had elected kings and queens "with the sole objective of the conspiracy."[60] Witnesses accused Jaime, a slave and a king in the *cabildo* Mandingo, of persuading others to join the plot. In neighboring Cárdenas, officials uncovered a separate scheme to overthrow Cuba under their noses. *Pardos libres* Juan Flores Cañizo and Francisco Espinosa, denounced at the Military Commission trials as ringleaders by fourteen accomplices, ultimately confessed to facilitating "seditious meetings" in the public spaces of Cárdenas. Witness testimony revealed cockfights and African *tangos* (dances) as sites where the men passed messages to *cabilido* affiliates and secret societies, like the Abakuá.[61] The intertwined identities of *cabildo* members as community leaders, artisans, and militiamen, as well as slaves and *libres de color*, made these organizations a prime target of the repression. Using coerced testimonies and confessions, government officials identified *cabildos de nación* as primary forces linking the convergence of uprisings in 1843.

As the Escalera repression began, Cuban authorities moved swiftly to suppress *cabildos de nación* and their members. The Military Commission persecuted an array of individuals associated explicitly with *cabildos* in the urban sectors. These included well-known free people of color, such as prominent dentist Andrés Dodge and Tómas Vargas, a popular phlebotomist and sergeant in the *pardo* militia, as well as lesser known individuals, including Juan Flores Cañizo and Francisco Espinosa. All of them were executed. Commission judges also implicated numerous plantation slaves with ethnic African affiliations in their names which typically connected them with the associated *cabildos*. Authorities sentenced Dionisio *carabalí*, Tomás *lucumí*, and Patricio *gangá* to death by firing squad for leading revolts on the Encanto plantation and neighboring farms. Jaime, the elected officer of the *cabildo* Mandingo mentioned previously, suffered perpetual exile from the Spanish Caribbean.[62] In a quest to reduce African cultural influences on Cuban-born blacks and broader Cuban society, authorities established laws preventing *libres de color* from holding meetings, unless authorized by the government, and passed codes limiting their interactions with slaves.[63] Taken together, the repression of *cabildos de nación* indicated both their significance to *libres de color* and their potential threat from the perspective of Spanish colonial officials in Cuba. These organizations played a crucial role in forging an intricate web connecting free people of color and slaves, African and creole, in the cities and the countryside. The presumed involvement of *cabildo* members in the Escalera uprisings emphasized their quest for freedom. For elites and colonial administrators, however, *cabildos de nación* forged alliances between free blacks and slaves that clearly had the potential to destroy Cuba's slave society if these relationships could not be restrained.

Creole elites also weighed in on the best means to foster separation between free blacks and the slave population. Several pushed to split the groups by place of birth to prevent future political and cultural alliances between *bozales* (newly arrived Africans) and *criollos*. They warned that the union of these sectors in Cuba, and influences from Haiti and Jamaica where slavery had been abolished through black agitation, would strike a "fatal blow" to the colony.[64] In particular, the rise of slave imports in the late 1840s heightened elite fears over the colony's Africanization. From the perspective of Spanish elites, the continuities and fusions in African cultural practices among *bozales* and *criollos* subverted Hispanic Cuban norms. To lessen the impact, Cuban thinker José Antonio Saco repeatedly called for the end of the slave trade, both before and during the Escalera era, although not the abolition of slavery. Rather, Saco advocated this approach as a means to reduce the demographic proportion of blacks and their cultural impact on whites, and to prevent "another Haiti." Anything less, he warned, and Cuba would achieve neither "peace nor security."[65]

Evidence indicates, however, that *cabildo* prohibitions were not strictly enforced, and in some cases, authorities facilitated activities. For instance, in 1845, the *cabildo* Carabalí Ugrí petitioned the government to remove an operating ban. The case lagged, in part due to a law suit brought by Maria de Regla Farjado. She sued the association because it had defaulted on a loan issued in 1820 by then leader José Morejón. Officials ruled against the *cabildo* Carabalí Ugrí in 1847 and ordered it to pay 2,700 pesos immediately or cease functioning. Even this threat proved negotiable. Ultimately, *cabildo* leaders pressed for and received an extension, finally repaying the loan in 1850.[66] Again, official actions contradicted repressive policies.

Furthermore, the organizations' officers invoked their right to hold meetings authorized by local administrators. In 1848, the Havana *cabildo* Nuestra Senora de Monserate (Our Lady of Monserate)–Congo Massinga pursued this action. Their king or queen had died and they needed to gather for elections. Although it is unknown whether officials approved this request, other *cabildos* would make similar appeals and receive approval into the 1860s.[67] This suggests that although some gatherings had to be sanctioned, increasingly most did not. More important, it indicates that *cabildos de nación* remained a vital part of the black population's social and cultural network throughout the Escalera era.

In fact, *cabildos de nación* reemerged in significant numbers starting in the mid 1850s. The return of hundreds of free people of color from exile, coupled with a rising economic crisis throughout the colony, prompted the expansion of *cabildos*, as well as the establishment of *sociedades de socorros mutuos*, mutual aid societies. Unlike *cabildos*, these associations welcomed membership regardless of ethnic affiliation or origin, although they were primarily joined by free people of color, and tended to foster black assimilation into Spanish cultural norms.[68] Names such as the *socorro* Sociedad de Caridad de Nuestra Señora de los Desamparados (Charitable Society of Our Lady of the Helpless) revealed explicit aims.[69] *Socorro* applications also addressed overarching goals. For instance, *morenos libres* José María Armenteros and Vencelad Manresa sought to found the mutual aid society Our Lady of El Cobre for free *pardos* and *morenos* as a "pious" *socorro* for male artisans who had no other resources "but the fruit of their personal labor." Their goals included providing assistance "in cases of illness and death," as well as Christian religious instruction to its members.[70] Despite the proscribed aims of *socorros*, ethnic-based *cabildos* continued to be established, such as the *cabildo* Nuestra Señora de Regla (Our Lady of Regla) initiated in 1859 by Antonio Bonilla and other members of the Congo Mombanba nation.[71] A decade after the prohibitions were initiated, a report to the Ultramar listed forty-seven Havana *cabildos* and *socorros*.[72] The escalation of *socorros* revealed free blacks' concerted responses to the dire economic and social realities of race and unemployment during the Escalera era. Moreover, the upsurge in both associations offers evidence that ethnicity and familial ties between slaves and liberated Africans continued to play an important role in sociocultural adaptation and resistance.

By the early 1860s, although Escalera policies helped shrink the black population's proportions in Cuba, nevertheless this sector also underwent an increase of just over 28,000. Although the combined slave and free black sectors represented just 36 percent of island inhabitants in 1861, the growth trends, especially among free blacks, troubled authorities and elites. Census data reported a 36 percent surge among *libres de color* and a 13 percent rise in the number of slaves. Dissatisfied with these figures, Spanish colonial officials enacted a new wave of prohibitions on *cabildos de nación* and *sociedades de socorros mutuos*.[73] Aware that the African-descended populations would seek out these organizations for social, cultural, and financial support, in 1864 Cuban officials authorized the formation of *cabildos* islandwide, but with a major caveat. African natives could establish *cabildos de nación*, but Cuban-born free people of color were barred from forming or joining these societies.[74] In particular, Antonio Zambrana, a member of Cuba's Administrative Council, moved to restrict cultural exchange between the two groups by banning black Cubans from attending African cultural celebrations. Zambrana claimed native-born blacks "had enough distractions" in their own dances, the *cunas*, which were "almost equal to those of whites." The last thing he wanted to encourage was free people of color parodying "African's entertainment" practices.[75] Complaints by elites, such as Dr. Jorge Marsden, buttressed government opinion. He opposed the establishment of the new *cabildo de nación* Gangá on his street, proposed by *moreno libre* Antonio Veita y Zayas, because he "would not stand for the bothersome" activities, especially the music they made on "Sundays . . . and festival days."[76] By hardening the distinctions between organizations for the African-born versus the Cuban-born, officials fostered the spread of fragmented black associations, which colonial authorities hoped would further divide the free and enslaved populations.

The arrival of Francisco Lersundi as captain general renewed the Cuban government's oppressive stance toward *cabildos*. In August 1866, he "began a brutal persecution of the Abakuás," a black secret society. Members of this association represented a substantial percentage of the hundreds he had arrested as vagrants and deported. He reiterated his campaign against "outlaws, vagrants, and undesirables" during his second term (1867–1868) by forcefully prosecuting those who fell into this category.[77] Just after the U.S. Civil War culminated in the abolition of slavery, Spain enforced a ban on the Cuban slave trade in 1867. Surrounded by slaveless societies in the 1860s, Cuba's reactionary laws, attitudes, and actions worked to denigrate African and native-black Cubans' cultural and social ties, and reassert white supremacy within its shores.

* * *

After the Military Commission trials and coerced migration siphoned thousands of *libres de color* from the colony, authorities turned their attention to those who remained. The social and economic restrictions of the Escalera era eroded opportunities for free people of color on multiple levels, ranging from economic bans and racial exclusion from trade organizations to forced ethnic divisions between *cabildos de nacion* and *sociedades de color*. Furthermore, *libres de color* were compelled to live their lives under intense scrutiny. They had limited ability to gather informally, travel to visit slave relatives, or secure gainful employment. Meanwhile, officials, elites, and intellectuals used the Escalera repression as a powerful catalyst for reshaping traditional understandings of race and labor. Displacing black artisans enabled officials to spearhead programs attracting upper- and middle-status white women and men to skilled occupations that they had typically cast as inferior. Whether carried out loosely or to the letter, the new laws sanctioned black resubordination to white authority.

Nevertheless, free people of color made their opposition known. Some formally protested the new licensing procedures or secured documentation to challenge occupational bans. Others, dissatisfied with apprenticeship assignments, vented their frustrations verbally. The desperate escaped intolerable situations by running away. Through acts of insubordination and claims to legal equality, *libres de color* struggled to defy the Escalera era's injustices.

In response, the Military Commission rulings made an example out of some free people of color, stripping them of income, family, honor, and social status. Restrictive legislation curtailed free black men's access to skilled and semi-skilled occupations. Segregated trade guilds displaced a range of workers. The overall impact left the free community of color frustrated, destitute, and vulnerable to new vagrancy laws. The breakdown of long-standing associations and economic practices disrupted established forms of black individual and group identities, reduced manumission possibilities, and for a time, drove social networks underground. The 1850s ushered in a combination of leniency and restriction, especially in the segregated reformation of mutual aid societies. By the late 1860s, prohibitions targeting employment and social ties had crystallized ethnic, racial, and social divisions among the black population. By all official accounts, Cuban authorities had indeed restored order by terrorizing the black population, especially artisans, apprentices, militiamen, landlords, midwives, and *cabildo* members.

Throughout the Escalera era, elites and subalterns struggled to refashion race relations. Existing tensions surrounding race, slavery, freedom, urban labor, and colonial authority were exacerbated by the prolonged repression's goals of preserving slavery and resubordinating free people of color. *Libres de color* responded by circumventing legislation and fomenting rebellion. In the subsequent outbreak of another "black conspiracy" in 1853, involving *libres de color,* slaves, and Cuban whites, authorities condemned the leaders to death by garroting, and banished and imprisoned co-conspirators.[78] The return of armed revolt a decade after the Escalera uprisings signaled the continued and volatile collision of white supremacy and black resistance. As the cycle of revolt and suppression surged forward, it also revealed that black agency would never be fully subdued.

5 / The Rise and Fall of the Militia of Color: From the Constitution of 1812 to the Escalera Era

Antonio Vazquez had the luck of being drafted as a pardo militiaman . . . but according to the published regulations . . . I request that he be exempted from service . . . because he is my only son and my only source of support.

—URSULA VIVIANA

In March 1844, the same month the O'Donnell administration initiated the targeted expulsion of *libres de color* from Cuba, officials also disarmed *moreno* and *pardo* battalions. Over the next few months, the Military Commission trials convicted or detained an array of militiamen as co-conspirators in the Escalera rebellions. Judges accused Ciriaco Consuegra, first corporal in Havana's *moreno* battalion, of using subversive language to help foment the conspiracy and had him expelled.[1] They also sentenced African-born Francisco Abrahantes, a lieutenant in the *moreno* militia, to banishment, but he died in prison before he could be sent into exile. Because of Félix Barbosa's position as a sublieutenant in the *pardo* battalion, his status as a wealthy and well-known mortician, and his regular contributions to charities, authorities arrested and detained him for almost a year before finally acquitting him.[2] Convinced of the black and mulatto militiamen's complicity in the Escalera revolts, Cuban authorities dismantled the institution in June. In September 1844, Spain finalized the process by issuing a royal order authorizing the extinction of the militia of color in Cuba.[3] These actions ended the participation of *libres de color* in a centuries-old military practice until its reinstatement a decade later.

A colonial corporate body, the military had come to symbolize privilege and prestige for Spaniards, creoles, and free people of color who served. Within the free community of African descent in particular, colonial militia service offered imperial benefits, social status, and the public acknowledgment of free blacks and mulattoes as valuable defenders of the Spanish empire, despite their racial background. In turn, these attributes helped shape the social and cultural identities of *libres de color* by infusing military service with colonial honor and imperial loyalty, which they used to pursue upward social mobility and advance racial pride.[4] As the language of freedom and equality circulated throughout the Atlantic, however, free *pardos* and *morenos* began demanding rights beyond those tied to military service. By the early nineteenth century, black soldiers would take a leadership role in challenging colonial hierarchies of race and social status.

Meanwhile, arming *libres de color* remained a point of contention in the Spanish empire. Prominent creoles, including Viceroy Revillagigedo of New Spain and Cuban planter Francisco Arango y Parreño, characterized militias of color on a sliding scale from the most reliable to the most dangerous soldiers.[5] Spain's 1812 constitution, informed by debates over nationality, slavery, citizenship, and imperial unity, chipped away at free blacks' previous colonial recognition for proven fidelity to the empire. In addition, the build-up of regular Spanish troops in Cuba after the loss of mainland American colonies in the early 1820s, meant to prevent the spread of revolution and abolition in the Spanish Caribbean, also contributed to the erosion of colonial militias.[6] Fears gave way to reality as *pardo* and *moreno* officers, such as Juan Nepomuceno Prieto, José Dabares, José del Monte del Pino, and León Monzón, led a series of revolts in the 1830s.[7] The indictment of numerous soldiers of color in the Escalera rebellions escalated these concerns to a breaking point; colonial authorities banned military opportunities for men of African descent and, simultaneously, expanded the existing number of permanent Spanish troops in Cuba "to conserve order and tranquillity."[8]

The demise of the militia of color during the Escalera repression would have a damaging impact on its representation a decade later, when Captain General Juan de la Pezuela reestablished *pardo* and *moreno* units in 1854. De la Pezuela's decision not only rekindled previous arguments about the risks of arming men of African descent but it also fueled unexpected defiance from the free community of color. Although authorities insisted free blacks and mulattoes were "obligated to armed service," difficulties in filling the rosters prompted the government to institute a draft for all young, male *libres de color*.[9] In response, in the 1850s hundreds of draftees and their parents objected to compulsory enlistment. Using established exemption rules, mothers like Ursula Viviana, quoted in the opening of this chapter, demanded the release of their only son from military service.[10] Her petition, like that of many other parents and draftees, both incorporated and rejected the colonial rhetoric of fidelity; Viviana referred to her son Antonio's "luck" at being drafted, but declined such an opportunity because it disrupted her family's economic stability. Others staked their claims to health and age exceptions. Successful or not, collectively the protests revealed how, despite the restrictive realities of race and gender, free black men and women challenged what they considered an assault on their rights as legally free subjects of Spain. Furthermore, the petitions demonstrated *pardos'* and *morenos'* ability to maintain a social identity beyond one predicated on the militia. Just as *libres de color* disputed foreign-born expulsion orders, coerced emigration, and prohibitive urban employment codes, they also negotiated the boundaries of the military system during the Escalera era. These efforts reflected yet another important aspect of their resistance to colonial policies informed by the politics of race, freedom, and empire.

Colonial Conflicts, the 1812 Spanish Constitution, and the Erosion of the Militia of Color

By the late eighteenth century, free men of color, as well as their creole and Spanish counterparts, had clearly incorporated military service as a core part of their personal and group identity. In particular, the intense militarization of Cuba that took place after the British occupation of Havana in 1762 enabled *libres de color* to expand their access to the militia and its privileges.[11] Nevertheless, politics and the hierarchies of race remained important issues throughout the Spanish empire. Over time, fears of rebellion and revolution would prove significant factors in the erosion of the militia of color.

By the 1790s, political tensions in Europe and social conflict in the colonies began to have a detrimental impact on military service, especially in Cuba. Although Spain's new monarch, Charles IV, inherited a flourishing and peaceful empire after his father's death in 1788, internal competition among disgruntled royal officials and Charles IV's incompetence helped unravel his predecessor's reforms. Meanwhile, regional conflicts rearranged European alliances. The French Revolution transformed France into Spain's enemy and Britain into a wary ally. The spread of revolutionary ideology across the Atlantic and into the minds and hearts of creoles, slaves, and free people of color produced even greater disarray with the onset of the Haitian Revolution.[12] Charles IV's appointment of Manuel de Godoy, a relatively inexperienced military officer, as head of the newly formed Consejo de Estado (Council of State), did little to alleviate political difficulties.[13] As soldiers retired, deserted, or died, few enlisted to replace them, which lead to a sharp decline among Spanish troops. These changes would also have serious repercussions in Cuba.[14]

Indeed, social and political conditions in Cuba had begun to unravel. A forced-labor draft instituted by Captain General Luís de Las Casas in 1790 was met with widespread resistance from creoles and free people of color. Due to the entrenchment of military culture, large proportions of free society had access to *fuero* benefits that protected them from being compelled into forced labor for the colonial state. An attack on *fuero* privileges ensued, enforced by Las Casas and supported by several elites, including Francisco de Arango y Parreño, Havana's deputy governor José de Ilicheta, and Spanish merchants. Together, the Spanish colonial government in Cuba set about to alienate creole military personnel and its families. In particular, Illicheta complained the *fuero militar*'s broad application to nonranking militiamen and retired servicemen deprived him of essential city revenue.[15] Arango echoed these sentiments, but pointed to the civil threat of former black and mulatto soldiers. "The veterans who retired in the countryside" retained military privileges, but because they were no longer attached to active units, authorities had far less control over these men's activities and actions.[16] While officials in Spain debated these issues, colonial authorities in Cuba broadly applied repressive reforms in 1792 to individuals or families who had served the Spanish crown for multiple generations. These included the general violation of traditional *fuero* rights, the denial of pensions to widows and orphans, and the destruction of military careers.[17] In response to these tensions, Charles IV organized a special commission to address the issue of military privilege. Its recommendations to curtail military benefits in both New Granada and Cuba, however, were ultimately rejected, and the *fuero* traditions were reaffirmed in 1804.[18]

Meanwhile, a simultaneous drop in peninsular troops and the cessation of rotating Spanish soldiers to the Americas, keeping them in Europe to fight losing battles with Republican France and British forces, eliminated the participation of experienced Spanish personnel within Cuba, in both regular and militia forces. By 1799, regular troops garrisoned at Havana had dwindled from 1,879 to 801. Militia forces took up the slack, but their involvement in continuous warfare in the Caribbean region (in Hispaniola during the Haitian Revolution, in Louisiana, and with British forces) would take a heavy toll. For Cuban militiamen, such activities generated extended time away from home. Furthermore, the economic drain of war on the Spanish military budget resulted in dwindling financial support for servicemen's families. Despite the honor and privilege military service carried, these would provide small consolation for those who endured prolonged deployment and economic hardship. Increasingly, those serving refused to report for drills, and men eligible for enlistment skirted recruitment. By 1802, the Spanish crown resorted to a draft to fill the militia ranks, a move that would reappear during the Escalera era targeting *libres de color*.[19]

Arango noted these circumstances, but moved beyond *fuero militar* privileges in his attack on blacks in the military. He heralded those in Cuba's militia as "indisputably some of the best soldiers in the world" but, nevertheless, asserted there was little need for *moreno* and *pardo* battalions. Although he acknowledged militiamen of color had been a "necessary resource" for foreign military defense in the past, he claimed that Cuba now furnished a "sufficient number of whites" to protect the colony's domestic interests, and it would be prudent to "substitute the black militia" with white servicemen. Furthermore, in the colonial Atlantic World in which black and mulatto militiamen had taken part, Arango warned of the volatile influence Spanish imperial "political and military aims" might have on them, and, in turn, the demands for military favor these men might seek.[20] In 1799, Havana authorities reitered Arango's concerns about controlling black veterans in the countryside. Furthermore, these city officials appealed to Spain to "diminish or extinguish the militia of color, or at least the black regiments."[21] In addition, Cuban planters noted how the expansion of slavery both eroded the prestige free *pardos* and *morenos* derived from the militia of color and promoted racial solidarity over corporate identity.[22] Although Spain's Council of State concurred with many of these sentiments and advised caution regarding the use of black soldiers, the realities of war between Spain and France and the protection of colonial territories in the Americas took precedence. Ultimately, authorities in the late eighteenth century concluded that the benefits of retaining black and mulatto battalions far outweighed their potential danger.[23]

Given the activities that militiamen of color participated in by the late 1700s, however, imperial concerns proved well founded. During the American Revolution, black battalion captains José Antonio Aponte and Gabriel Doroteo Barba, among other militiamen of color, battled the British in campaigns in Florida and the Bahamas. These experiences, as well as cosairing voyages within the Caribbean, brought Havana's *pardo* and *moreno* soldiers, and their civilian associates, into direct contact with the evolving language of liberty and equality sweeping through Europe and the Americas.[24] Revolutionary ideology evolved into action in 1795, when *mulato libre* Nicolás Morales, a rural property owner, collaborated with creoles in a plot to secure greater equality for free people of color. Ironically, Pedro Calunga, a member of the Battalion of Mulattoes in Bayamo, denounced the plan in 1796, and his actions significantly improved his social and financial status. He was granted the *gracias al sacar*, the right to purchase legal whiteness, offered by Spain to free individuals of partial African ancestry. This right gave those who obtained the document such privileges as access to a university education, admittance into the clergy, and marriage to a white spouse.[25] For his "loyalty," Cuban authorities also awarded him six *caballerías* of land (approximately 200 acres) and 300 pesos to purchase a slave to help cultivate it.[26] For *libres de color*, the intersections among military service, upward social mobility, and racial politics produced a variety of contradictions that highlighted the complexities of race and identity. As exemplified by Morales's plot and Calunga's willingness to expose it to authorities, free people of color struggled over the realities of racial discrimination and rewards of imperial fidelity. To be sure, free black men like Calunga used military service to advance their personal, racial, social, and economic interests. However, as Morales's behavior suggests, the intricacies of colonial race relations could not be swept away by military identity. Without the benefits of military privilege, Morales experienced even higher levels of circumscribed freedom than his soldier compatriots. His actions indicated an allegiance to a new ideology that transformed individuals of African descent into whites' social equals. Increasingly, those with strong links to imperial defense and the free community of color used their leadership positions to push the established boundaries of race and freedom. By the early nineteenth century, the pursuit of greater equality would resonate at a rapid pace among both Cuba's civilian and military populations of African descent. Simultaneously, Spanish officials and colonial representatives sought to strengthen established social hierarchies by curtailing privileges for militiamen of color.

THE 1812 CONSTITUTION OF CÁDIZ: DEBATING SLAVERY, RACE, AND CITIZENSHIP

In both Spain and its colonies, 1812 became a momentous year for the politics of race, slavery, and freedom. In 1810, peninsular and creole representatives at the Córtes in Cádiz had initiated debates over the political status of its American subjects. The recent restoration of the Spanish throne after Napoleon's usurpation of power in 1808 left Spanish authorities keen on maintaining political harmony with its American and Pacific territories, and also on retaining dominance over regions whose approximately sixteen million inhabitants outnumbered the roughly ten and a half million in the peninsula. Furthermore, Spanish America's large populations of Indians, Africans, and the racially mixed made for a multifaceted racial and caste hierarchy. The combined numerical and ethnic imbalance in the colonies prompted Spanish officials to devise a constitution that sustained slavery and excluded as many free inhabitants as possible from full colonial citizenship. Creole delegates voiced their concerns for and against these issues, depending on the context. For instance, participants concurred that the slaves' legal status made them ineligible for political participation. They then turned their attention to the free populations. As Spanish representative Ramón Utges observed in early January 1811, "some American delegates admit that certain castas should be included as equal and others excluded."[27] Since long-standing laws had granted Indians nominal equality and freedom, heated debates regarding the free population of African descent ensued.[28] The discussions revealed not only blatant discrimination against *libres de color* on both sides of the Atlantic but also how the denial of citizenship to free people of color contributed to the erosion of the black militia. With few exceptions, the Córtes would offer little legal or political satisfaction for populations of African descent in the Americas.

Concerns over slavery revolved around issues of human rights versus political order. In early April 1811, inspired by the British, chief of the Spanish delegation Agustín de Argüelles proposed ending the slave trade. A month later, José Miguel Guridi y Alcocer of New Spain agreed and also called for a plan to institute the gradual abolition of slavery. José Mexía Lequerica from New Granada, an ardent defender of both slaves and free people of color, declared "slaves too are men, and some day policy, justice and the Christian Religion will show us how they also should be considered." Their pleas, however, would be drowned out by slavery proponents. Representatives from major slaveholding areas in Venezuela and the Caribbean, as well as New Granada and Peru, advocated the continuation of slavery and the slave trade to maintain planters' and merchants' economic interests and to prevent political upheaval. For example, Esteban Palacios of Caracas, Simón Bolívar's uncle, a self-professed "lover of humanity," feared the potential turmoil abolition could produce.[29] Juan Nicasio Gallego, a delegate from Cartegena, rejected abolition on the grounds that slaves, although human, were property, and it would be "unjust to deprive an owner of his possessions." Such commentary from the Córtes exposed the inherent contradiction of slaves as human property, especially in the context of delegates' claims of liberty and equality within the empire.[30]

Furthermore, representatives from Cuba vehemently opposed abolition. On April 2, 1811, Andrés Jauregui, the spokesman for Cuban planters, reminded the Córtes that similar discussions over slave emancipation that had taken place in the French National Assembly resulted in the disastrous Haitian Revolution. The same fate, he warned, would surely take hold in the Spanish Americas if they did not put an end to the debate. In response, the Córtes removed the issue from open deliberation and relegated it to secret sessions.[31] In July, delegates in the closed Córtes reviewed a letter from Salvador de Muro, Marqués de Someruelos, the captain general of Cuba. He claimed that the disputes in the Cádiz over the abolition of the slave trade and slavery, and their potential to foment a Haitian-style rebellion, had been reported in the *Diario de la Havana* and circulated by word of mouth across the colony. The resulting rumors of emancipation agitated the slaves and produced a chaotic atmosphere on the island. Moreover, the abolition of slavery in the Spanish empire proved to be a transatlantic issue. The intertwined concerns connected masters interested in protecting their property rights, Spanish officials who sought to retain colonial control, European and U.S. authorities who hoped to gain a geopolitical advantage at Spain's expense, and, of course, the slave population that aspired to freedom.[32] Ultimately, slave emancipation did not take concrete form in the Constitution of 1812. Instead, the debates reaffirmed the maintenance of slavery and racial hierarchy. Slavery and abolition, however, would remain important issues as tensions between the American colonies and Spain erupted in volatile and prolonged battles for independence everywhere but in Puerto Rico and Cuba.

Apprehensions over race and politics did not end with struggles over slavery. Discussions of citizenship for free colonial subjects, particularly *libres de color*, also fostered substantial debates. For the purpose of electing future representatives, a core group of American delegates, led by José Mexía Lequerica from New Granada, supported free black suffrage.[33] He passionately declared, "Grant equality to the free colored castes. . . . Why should their blood be deemed impure? . . . The blood of colored men is red, and so is that of warriors, of healthy men: of pure and noble blood." The majority of attendees, however, opposed the extension of electoral rights to *libres de color*. Influential Peruvian delegate Vicente

Morales Duárez contended that granting such equality would produce "grave disadvantages" to the established social hierarchy.[34] Agustín de Argüelles, chief of the Spanish delegation, offered the concession that African-descended men who possessed the qualities of "virtue, merit, and diligence" could potentially enjoy the "rights of citizenship," but appeals for more a definitive statement ground to a halt. Ultimately, Spain's 1812 constitution split the categories of subject and citizen. Article 5 defined "Spaniards" as "all free men born and domiciled" in Spanish territories, their offspring, naturalized foreigners, and "freedmen, from the moment they acquired liberty in Spanish territory." This included individuals of African descent born in overseas possessions as colonial subjects; however, it did not qualify them as citizens.[35]

Rather, Article 22 subjected *libres de color* to stricter requirements. The constitution granted conditional imperial citizenship to free *pardo* and *moreno* men who had "rendered eminent services to the fatherland or to those who distinguish themselves by their talent, application and conduct." In other words, men who performed extraordinary service to the empire. In addition, *libres de color* had to be children of free, married parents, have a free spouse, and have gainful employment to support their families.[36] Had the requirements not been tied to such strict combinations, several individual conditions would have paved the way for thousands of black and mulatto men to be recognized as Spanish citizens. For instance, the Spanish crown repeatedly recognized militiamen of color for their meritorious and virtuous contributions to the defense of the empire. Furthermore, in many American locales, free blacks comprised substantial proportions of the artisan class, owned property, and supported their families, which qualified them as talented and honorable craftsmen. The final stipulation, however, would have proved difficult to fulfill because the vast majority of *libres de color* were the offspring of slave women or unmarried parents. Ultimately, the language of merit and virtue worked to exclude free people of color based on areas over which they had little control—the condition of their birth.

Several creole delegates voiced their objection to the denial of citizenship for militiamen of color. José Simeón de Uría of Guadalajara rejected the rationale for categorizing black men as Spaniards but not as citizens, especially since they provided a "robust column" of Mexican military defense in the past and the present. Similarly, Francisco Salazar of Peru noted how black and mulatto soldiers helped suppress the Túpac Amarú rebellion in the 1780s and they now comprised the bulk of the militia garrisoned in Callao. Furthermore, these men currently served as protective troops for the cities of Quito and Guayaquil and combated dissident forces in Buenos Aires. Another Peruvian, Ramón Feliú, warned that denying men of color citizenship would lead to civil unrest, and Spain's exclusion would only alienate them further. Despite these arguments, the delegates passed Article 22's conditional citizenship with overwhelming support.[37] The completed constitution, adopted by the Córtes on March 18, 1812, united the Spanish colonial world in unprecedented ways. For example, it ended Indians' tribute payments and forced labor, and abolished the feudal system.[38] Nevertheless, the outcome of the Córtes debates over slavery and citizenship rang hollow for those of African descent. Evidence of free blacks' and slaves' discontent over the denial of freedom, equality, and citizenship had already begun to manifest in Cuba, and militiamen of color led the way.

THE EROSION OF THE MILITIA OF COLOR: FROM THE APONTE REBELLION TO THE ESCALERA REPRESSION

The debates and decisions in the Córtes resonated violently across Cuba. From January to March 1812, a series of actual and thwarted uprisings, which became known as the Aponte Rebellion, signaled not only an urgency among sectors of the African-descended population to dismantle slavery and inequality but also revealed the extensive involvement of militiamen of color in the plots. In mid January, slaves and free people of color revolted for two days in Puerto Príncipe, in eastern-central Cuba, where they damaged five plantations and killed eight whites. Those who escaped execution or imprisonment in Saint Augustine, Florida, fled to the mountains, where plans for another uprising, this time slated for neighboring Bayamo, took shape. Before it could begin, in early February, a slave named José Antonio informed his owner Lorenzo Vásquez Tamayo of a plot that included attacking "military headquarters to seize gunpowder, bullets, and rifles." Bondsmen and *libres de color* united in another revolt in mid-March, this time near Havana. The rebels attacked four plantations, where they killed overseers and their families. Interrogations of those captured led officials to the home of free *moreno* José Antonio Aponte. There they found evidence of his background as a captain in the militia of color, a leader in a *cabildo de nacion*, and as an artisan (sculptor). Of particular interest was the discovery of a hidden book of drawings that contained maps of Cuban military garrisons and images of black militiamen defeating white soldiers. Officials also noted portraits of Haitian revolutionary leaders throughout Aponte's house. Authorities executed Aponte, along with four other militiamen and over a dozen slaves, and exhibited his decapitated head as a warning to other potential rebels.[39] The damage to the social and political landscape, however, had been done. The island's disorderly atmosphere as a result of the public debates over the abolition of slavery, described in Cuban Captain General Someruelos's correspondence to the Córtes in the previous summer, had come to fruition. Moreover, so had delegates' concerns that denying citizenship to *pardo* and *moreno* militiamen, despite their proven protective and combative strength, would provoke social strife. In the aftermath of the Aponte Rebellion, black soldiers would experience even greater scrutiny.

The tradition of service, which enabled soldiers of color to fuse military participation, colonial identity, and artisan employment to improve their social status and create substantial wealth, fostered an elite sector of *libres de color*, often unmatched throughout much of the Spanish empire. For instance, Nicolás Lanes, a *pardo* lieutenant in Havana, also operated a lucrative carpentry business. By the time of his death in 1824, he owned property and slaves with an estimated value of over 10,000 pesos.[40] Captain Gabriel Doroteo Barba of Havana's *moreno* battalion was a decorated soldier and veteran of Spanish campaigns in Florida, with over twenty years of service in 1844. He also operated a school for free women of color and slave women to acquire domestic skills. In terms of property, he and his wife, *morena libre* María Isabel Aróstegui, owned two houses and one female slave. Like many other officers, Barba and Aróstegui encouraged their children to maintain links to the military. Their son, José Silverio Guadelupe, became a sublieutenant in the black militia, as well as a carpenter, and their daughter, María Tranquilina, extended the military family network by marrying Manuel Salazar, a captain in the *moreno* battalion.[41] These examples highlight some of the ways soldiers of color, especially the Barba family, used military privileges and marriage to build a strong social network. Moreover, it fostered greater knowledge of their rights as imperial subjects. The formal marriages between free families of color laid the groundwork for their offspring to be recognized as citizens. Nevertheless, although military service afforded *libres de color* in Cuba an advanced level of social recognition and influence, it did not shield them from the inherent prejudices of their nineteenth-century colonial context.

Given the way military affiliation intertwined with identity, it is no surprise that free blacks fervently defended themselves from charges of untrustworthiness and dishonor. When attacked by the South American newspaper *La Fraternidad* in 1823 for alleged disloyalty to Spain during the Spanish American wars of independence, a cadre of *pardo* and *moreno* officers responded with a powerful manifesto disputing the erroneous claims. Led by Captain Monico de Flores and signed by twenty-four militia officers ranging from captain to second lieutenant, the document asserted their bravery and sacrifice despite being "both denied and governed by the same laws" that benefited Spaniards and creoles. In addition, the officers laid claim to the interdependent relationship between militiamen of color and Spain, asserting that "we place our forces and bravery against any invasion that might rashly set foot on our [Cuban] ground with depraved visions of domination."[42] Despite charges of treachery, black soldiers continued to seek the benefits of armed service. In 1830 Marcos Rodríguez requested a promotion to the rank of sergeant and its corresponding salary in Havana's *moreno* battalion, which he received after a local official attested to Rodriguez's honorable conduct.[43] In general, however, political turmoil of the early nineteenth century would wreak havoc on the public honor and imperial trust *libres de color* had worked so hard to gain over three centuries of experience defending the empire. Colonial distress over arming men of African descent, despite their record of loyalty, would accelerate steadily until the demise of the militia of color in 1844.

Atlantic warfare and the expansion of slavery in Cuba chipped away at the benefits for *pardo* and *moreno* servicemen. In 1789, four officers from Havana's *moreno* battalion accused their white commander and his assistant of constant abuse. The charges included verbal assault, unjustly confining soldiers, and the murder of a fellow militiaman. From the soldiers' perspective, the commander had treated the men as if they were slaves. As recompense, the petitioners urged Spanish authorities to create another *moreno* battalion with a colonel and lieutenant colonel who would outrank the existing white officers. Although ministers in Spain appeared to take the matter seriously, Cuban Captain General Luís de Las Casas dismissed the complaint as an arrogant "mixture of ignorance and malice" and discharged the petitioners. In 1812, black officers in Havana renewed their request for a second battalion of color and the greater respect and equality it would command, again to no avail. Rather, the petition only raised officials' ire. Francisco Montalvo, sub-inspector general of the Cuban army, abhorred the potential repercussions that granting greater rights to officers of African descent might bring, but also feared the potential threat of the *pardo* and *moreno* militias, especially given their connection to the Aponte Rebellion of the same year. Again, colonial authorities shelved the request and then relocated three of Havana's *moreno* companies to Florida to protect imperial interests.[44] Accusations and demands by soldiers of color and the dismissal of their concerns by officials revealed the changing meanings of black military service. Although *libres de color* eagerly pursued the institution's corporate benefits, royal honors, the right to use weapons, and the status these components conveyed, nevertheless, *pardo* and *moreno* militiamen grew increasingly irritated with the derogatory attitudes and actions directed at them in spite of their loyalty.[45]

With the success of the Haitian Revolution at the beginning of the nineteenth century, slaveholders and colonial authorities in Cuba reiterated anxieties concerning black male participation in militias.[46] Cuban authorities violated *fuero militar* privileges by prosecuting black and mulatto militiamen without regard to military regulations.[47] For example, in 1807, Felipe Aristiga, a soldier in Havana's *moreno* battalion, was arrested for an unspecified crime. Typically, soldiers served their sentences in a military prison, but because Cuba had no such structures, judges condemned Aristiga to several months in public works, most likely repairing roads. Instead of serving time with fellow soldiers, this punishment required the offender to work with slaves. Other affronts to black soldiers' corporate and social status included authorities' demands to see documentation verifying the freedom and service records of *pardo* and *moreno* militiamen.[48] These kinds of actions eroded the legal and social distance between free men of color and slaves, and reinforced the racial supremacy of whites. Moreover, they chipped away at the colonial identity fostered by military participation.

Problems escalated in the 1820s, as Cuba's Military Commission indicted an array of *libres de color* for using subversive language and gathering in secret meetings. In 1826, the commission charged former sergeant of the *pardo* militia Pedro Córtes with using rebellious speech. A year later, officials accused *moreno* sergeant Domingo Suntas of organizing clandestine meetings.[49] In response, Félix Varela, although a priest and abolitionist, characterized Cuba's militiamen of color as "a potential enemy," noting that "the best soldier is the most barbaric when he has someone to lead him."[50] Although the privileges of militia service promoted imperial solidarity, the simultaneous decline of these benefits and the rise in discriminatory practices targeting soldiers of color continued. So, too, did the existing rifts among colonial politics, race, and the probability of organized rebellion from black and mulatto militiamen.

Revolts led by militiamen of color following the Aponte Rebellion cemented colonial elites' worst fears. In 1835, *libres de color* Juan

Nepomuceno Prieto, a retired militia officer and a leader of a Lucumí *cabildo*, and Hermengildo Jáurequi plotted another revolt in the jurisdiction of Aguacate, in the countryside east of Havana.[51] The uprising became known as the Lucumí Rebellion because many of those captured and interrogated were identified with the *lucumí* ethnic and *cabildo de nación* designations, such as the recently freed Simon *lucumí*, African-born slave Luís *lucumí*, and creole bondsman Florencio *lucumí*. Reportedly, thirty to forty men, armed with machetes, attacked area plantations.[52] As in the Aponte Rebellion, the Lucumí Rebellion aspired to abolish slavery and end Spanish rule.[53] Officials responded as they had in 1812 by repressing the revolt, then executing the leaders and displaying their decapitated heads as a warning to the slave and free black populations.[54] In 1839, Captain León Monzón, Sergeant José Dabares, Sub-lieutenant José del Monte del Pino, and Pilar Borrego, a survivor from the Aponte Rebellion, orchestrated uprisings in eastern Cuba composed of soldiers, slaves, dock workers, and artisans.[55] Authorities accused Monzón of holding secret meetings at his home with members of the militia of color and the *cabildos de nación*. Like preceding insurgencies, Monzón's sought to abolish slavery and colonialism. Borrego, although not affiliated with the military, proved particularly menacing to officials. After being sentenced to four years of imprisonment in Puerto Rico for his involvement in the Aponte Rebellion, Borrego returned to Cuba to help rekindle Aponte's vision of freedom and sovereignty.[56]

The repeated collaboration of *pardo* and *moreno* soldiers, slaves, craftsmen, and laborers produced a new wave of condemnations and precautions regarding the militia of color. Following the revolt led by Monzón, Spanish officials sent an urgent and confidential communiqué to Cuba's Captain General Joaquín de Ezpeleta y Enrile (1838–1840), directing him to engage in "active vigilance over" the colony's militia of color, and "to make the necessary adjustments to these units as he saw fit." If any of the soldiers displayed symptoms of sedition, Spanish officials in Cuba had royal authorization "to extinguish those who attempted to veer from the path of loyalty."[57] Since the early 1830s, bolstered by royalist troops retreating from the Latin American wars for independence, Spain garrisoned Cuba with a professional, peninsular army of between 15,000 to 20,000 men, which they maintained until the late 1860s. Although the militia of color had also expanded since the 1760s from sixteen to twenty-six companies and three battalions, the influx of regular troops dramatically reduced the proportion of black soldiers, and in turn, their potential danger to Cuba.[58] By acquiring imperial permission "to extinguish" *pardo* and *moreno* soldiers for acts deemed treasonous, Cuban officials revealed their heightened apprehensions over the complexities of race and military defense. Fears of black militiamen mounting an attack against the colony escalated as concerns over arming men of African descent collided with black militia officers' demands for equality through both military channels and rebellion. The combined decline of military privileges, the denial of full, imperial citizenship, and militiamen's challenges to slavery and the colonial order set the stage for the institution's outright destruction in 1844.

Dismantling and Reestablishing the Cuban Militia of Color

Following the 1843 revolts, the O'Donnell administration swiftly disarmed free men of color to neutralize impending dissent. Initial efforts included deporting foreign-born militiamen like Simo Jerodes, a native of Santo Domingo, who served in Havana's *moreno* battalion, and expelling Claudio Brindis de Salas, a Cuban-born militia officer and well-known musician.[59] In June 1844, sweeping measures replaced piecemeal actions as O'Donnell dismantled the militia of color. Three months later, Ultramar legislation legalized the institution's official "extinction" in Cuba.[60] In the past, black soldiers' pivotal roles generally prohibited such a drastic approach, with exceptions for locales like New Spain, where colonial authorities dismantled militias of color in 1792 because the companies had not met imperial expectations to supply adequate security for the interior regions or supplement regular army forces during times of crisis.[61] Cuban battalions, however, stood in stark contrast. In the 1820s, soldiers praised themselves for their "loyalty, fidelity, patriotism, and adherence to the governing system."[62] Similarly, historians have characterized reforms to the institution, especially reorganization and expansion of the black and white militias, in Cuba as a "success," particularly until the early nineteenth century.[63] The Year of the Lash would dramatically alter this dynamic. Debates over arming men of color came to an abrupt halt as rebellion engulfed the western sugar-growing region in 1843. Moreover, the discovery that numerous militiamen participated in yet another insurgency made the decision all the more urgent. Spanish officials congratulated the O'Donnell administration for its quick and decisive action against black troops. Moreover, they proclaimed the colony's white creole militias would "not lack soldiers nor officers with good service records" to replace those of African descent.[64]

The dissolution of black and mulatto battalions, combined with the crippling repression, stunned the island's free community of color. With the exception of petitions by foreign-born militiamen fighting expulsion orders, there is little evidence to suggest that African-descended servicemen challenged the decree, despite previous examples of protest. Past appeals, such as those in 1789 and 1812 for increased benefits, higher rank, and fairer treatment, followed military channels, albeit with limited success. Demands via revolt, however, garnered only governmental resentment and anger. To counter dissent from militiamen, white and black, in 1850 Cuban Captain General Federico Roncalí eliminated creole militias. A year later imperial officials established an armed royalist police force in Cuba, akin to Spain's civil guard, which had both civilian and military functions, composed of eight hundred cavalry and infantry troops.[65] The Escalera repression and its social and economic aftershocks, combined with the expansion of peninsular forces in Cuba, forced militiamen of color and the free black community at large to recast militia service as a low priority. Plagued with torture, imprisonment, expulsion, occupational bans, and coerced emigration, *libres de color* would have had scant energy to contemplate collapsed military careers. Moreover, they had little choice. With the successive involvement of *pardo* and *moreno* soldiers in revolts against slavery and colonialism, and crippling militia legislation instituted by O'Donnell and the Spanish crown, claims of loyalty and sacrifice would have fallen on deaf ears. Instead, free people of color now focused on managing economic destabilization, physical displacement, family dispersal, and overwhelming personal loss.

Ten years later, colonial authorities reversed their decision. Along with the limited amnesty granted to *expulsados* and other political prisoners in May 1854, Captain General Juan de la Pezuela (1853–1854) reauthorized the militia of color.[66] A variety of reasons factored into his decision, in particular, how the pressures of warfare in Europe constrained attempts to expand peninsular forces. Consequently, predictions of "no lack of soldiers" rang hollow, and officials remained concerned about island defense.[67] In addition, during the previous year, British visitor James Phillippo estimated the number of *libres de color* "capable of bearing arms" in Cuba totaled as many as 40,000. Phillippo considered combining existing peninsular troops with various forms of local defense a necessity, "not less as a security against the insurrection of the slaves than against American aggression" in the form of annexation.[68] Echoing these sentiments, de la Pezuela also used the militia of color's restoration to intimidate creole elites and suppress threats of annexation to the United States. To those ends, the captain general revived the black militia by establishing two voluntary companies of color, one *pardo* and one *moreno*, totaling two thousand men initially active for two years. To entice new recruits and assuage previous apprehensions regarding race and military service, his administration again extended free men of color "the same advantages and obligations" as their peninsular counterparts, which included *fuero* and *preeminencias* benefits.[69]

A year later, in 1855, José Gutiérrez de la Concha replaced de la Pezuela. Under his rule, the number of black militia companies expanded to sixteen, consisting of eight each for *morenos* and *pardos*, with six based in Havana.[70] British traveler Amelia Matilda Murray noted the revived presence of "negro soldiers in straw hats," during her visit to Havana in early March 1855. Despite the garrison of Spanish troops, a few weeks later she lamented, "Military uniforms are visible in every direction, and the fortresses bristle all around this city, yet there is no such thing as public confidence, or a sense of general security."[71] Though she was new to the city, Murray's comments touched on key issues surrounding imperial defense and the black militia's restoration. Although officials promoted the presence of Spanish troops to improve the social milieu for residents and visitors, this seemed to do little in the way of reassuring the public of their safety in the midst of *libres de color* returning from exile and elite calls for annexation to the United States to safeguard slavery.

Furthermore, the reestablishment of Cuba's militia of color resurrected prior debates and concerns. Some leaders and intellectuals interpreted the move as more than the reorganization of a defunct institution to supplement scarce troops and fatigued soldiers. Proslavery advocates read it as a nod toward the abolition of slavery. Meanwhile, annexationists considered it an attempt to strengthen the Africanization of the island and Spanish imperial rule.[72] To placate detractors on both sides, *pardo* and *moreno* units and their officers would report to white superiors, just as they had done previously, to ensure the careful control of the new units.[73] Despite official rationale for restoring the militia of color as a means to augment regular troops and enhance colonial defense, it remained an organization based on the politics of race. In response, free people of color also expressed their misgivings about the new militia. For some of them, memories of the repression and the institution's unilateral disbanding made them cautious about the new battalions. Unsurprisingly, many *libres de color* viewed the new militia with extreme skepticism. Despite official claims and the restoration of military privileges, they recognized that the prestige and status attributed previously to armed service would be difficult to restore. As these competing interests converged, they produced both anticipated and unexpected results for colonial authorities.

Problems surfaced immediately during early recruitment efforts. In spite of promises to renew *fuero* benefits indiscriminately, government attempts to attract soldiers proved insufficient to fill the ranks. In response, military leaders hesitantly prepared to make enlistment mandatory for *libres de color* if the numbers remained low.[74] By 1859, exasperated officials began investigating roster deficiencies. Reports made in early July revealed the dismal state of the units. Only 332 (196 *pardos* and 136 *morenos*) served in Havana's six militia companies.[75] Baffled as to why free people of color respond so unfavorably to voluntary recruitment, the de la Concha administration resorted to compulsory participation. In August 1859, the government began drafting young *libres de color*, particularly unemployed men between the ages of eighteen and thirty, to fill the new battalions of color.[76]

As expected, the move instantly increased militia rosters. In Havana, the number of militiamen tripled to 1,000. The forced enlistment seemed particularly slanted toward increasing the number of *moreno* soldiers. Within one month after officials initiated compulsory service, Havana's *moreno* draftees quintupled, rising from 136 to 703. Meanwhile, *pardo* enlistment doubled, increasing from 100 to 200.[77] The mandatory participation of free people of color mirrored previous recruitment efforts in Spanish America. For instance, in Peru in 1779, officials ordered free men of color to enroll immediately or be enslaved.[78] Desperate for men during the prolonged revolutionary wars in Spanish America, royalist and patriot leaders forcibly recruited free men of all hues between the ages of fifteen and forty-five and conscripted slaves into service as military servants, construction workers, and armed soldiers.[79] Those called to the militia, however, often had their own motivations for participating, particularly when enhanced by offers of citizenship or freedom. In the case of Cuba in the mid-nineteenth century, officials considered the *fuero* and the tradition of black service as sufficient incentives. When these proved inadequate, authorities declared "men of color on this island are obligated to armed service."[80]

Forced enlistment in Cuba would have major consequences. As their mainland counterparts discovered, the draft heavily negated the institution's honor and status.[81] Despite centuries of loyal defense, *libres de color* found they could just as easily decline military participation if hardships outweighed the benefits. In Cuba, hundreds of free *pardos* and *morenos* now viewed service in the militia as a burden, not a privilege.

When officials published exemption rules in Havana's *La Gaceta* and other local newspapers in August 1859, hundreds of free people of color manipulated the regulations to oppose the draft.[82]

PROTEST

In response to the draft, young free men of color and their families flooded colonial authorities with formal exemption requests. Between August 1859 and November 1860, nearly five hundred exemption claims in the forms of letters and reports arrived in Havana, Matanzas, Cienfuegos, and Santa Clara. Despite the substantial number of official protests, the military shortages forced authorities to scrutinize petitioners' requests carefully. They subjected *libres de color* to physical exams, questioned draftees and their families, and often demanded written proof, such as medical documentation or birth certificates, to verify a variety of claims. The petitions brought to light complainants' deep dissatisfaction with forced military service, their understanding of the colonial legal structure, and their ability to forcefully and creatively assert their rights. In doing so, free people of color effectively turned the widespread exemption regulations, detailed in the new *Reglamento para las milicias disciplinadas de color*, to their own advantage.[83] Ultimately, their resistance to service worked to destabilize colonial officials' plans for the reestablished militia.

As soon as Captain General de la Concha publicized August 15, 1859, as the initial date for exemption hearings, *libres de color* began submitting their petitions.[84] Before the close of August, for example, *pardo* Marcelino Lamadrón from Matanzas, *morena libre* Margarita Chacón from Havana, *moreno liberto* Francisco Perez de Alejos of Santa Clara, and *moreno libre* Manuel Silvestre Congo from Cienfuegos all sought release from service for themselves or their sons.[85] These individual requests represented the *Reglamento*'s three main exemption categories: poor health, family hardship, and age ineligibility. *Libres de color* rarely used the forth area, substitution, which permitted a potential draftee to provide a willing volunteer in his place.[86] Rather, given the potential impact of the draft on their individual freedom and personal obligations, free men and women of African descent especially targeted declining health and family adversity as the primary means to evade military service. Poor health emerged as the most varied and well-documented of the exemption requests, at 213 (48%). Free blacks declared a range of health deficiencies—from chronic physical pain to mental instability—to circumvent the draft. Marcelino Lamadrón requested a release based on his chronic seizures. After Matanzas doctors examined him and officials interviewed his black and white skilled artisan references, Lamadrón won an exemption.[87] Despite having a heart defect, Santiago Ramos was conscripted twice for Havana's new *pardo* militia company. Doctors diagnosed him with an enlarged heart in 1859 and again in 1860, before officials finally removed him from the draft rolls as unfit for service.[88] *Moreno* Florencio Quesada, age twenty-four, asked to be exempted because he was prone to "bouts of insanity."[89] Meanwhile, Matanzas military reports listed *pardos* Baltazar Benítez, José Hernández, and Federico Mato y Palacio simply as "useless." Although officials did not provide detailed records in every case, the lack of information typically meant draftees' had obvious physical limitations, such as missing or deformed limbs, or clear behavioral problems.[90] Prior to the Escalera repression, men like Lamadrón, Ramos, and Quesada might have hidden their health issues in order to join the militia. However, in the context of the draft, declaring physical or mental afflictions that withstood close scrutiny became crucial to avoiding service.

Family hardship offered yet another major arena for exemption, although they represented only 8.81 percent (42 requests) of requests. Bids for a family release may have received relatively little attention, in large part, because hardship cases often required an array of evidence. Nevertheless, it became a vital argument as dozens of men and their parents drew attention to the difficulties military service would have on dependent relatives. For instance, in Havana, *pardo* Emilio Navarro claimed he was the only adult left to care for his two sisters, Antonia, age six and Dolores, age ten, after the death of their mother in 1856. Authorities granted his request only after Navarro produced his mother's death certificate.[91] Ana Consnegra, a fifty-two-year-old *parda*, petitioned on behalf of her son, nineteen-year-old Antonio Demetrio Ignacio Díaz, because he supported her and his five young siblings. Authorities released Díaz from service after Consnegra presented her son's birth and baptismal records, and a certificate attesting to her own "good character."[92] *Morena libre* Lorenza Reyes bent the truth to garner an exemption for her son, Francisco Ramos. Reyes claimed her status as a widow and her inability to work as a seamstress due to advanced age as rationales for exempting her son from the draft. According to Reyes, Ramos's income as a tobacco worker now supported her. Further investigation, however, revealed that Reyes had lied about being a widow. Investigators quickly discovered her husband, Ambrosio Ramos, but concluded that he, too, could no longer work. Ultimately, authorities approved Reyes' petition.[93]

Similar scenarios emerged throughout western Cuba. *Moreno* Juan Velches of Cienfuegos and *pardo* Joaquin Pirson of Matanzas took care of their aged mothers, and *moreno* Gabriel Benítez of Santa Clara supported his seventy-year-old father.[94] Juan Fardio petitioned to continue supporting his sixty-year-old mother and five younger siblings in Cienfuegos.[95] The occupational bans and the stricter racial constraints on employment instituted in 1844 made securing a job and supporting a family difficult. Concerns over family stability indicated that *libres de color* had not fully recovered from the harsh economic effects of the repression. Moreover, militia service offered virtually no monetary assistance. As in the past, enlisted men would have to provide their own personal effects, including shirts, shoes, and blankets; only officers received a modest regular salary.[96] For those dependent on their sons for financial and emotional support, military participation represented a economic serious loss for families. As enlistments dropped in the late eighteenth and early nineteenth centuries, Spanish officials noted how militiamen's extended tours of duty resulted in an array of family "hardships" for "the want of the husbands and sons who support them by means of their labors, whose fruits are denied them when they are mobilized."[97] Roughly fifty years later, similar issues couched in radically different circumstances eroded militia rosters. Whereas in the past, active duty and long deployments curtailed soldiers' abilities to support their families, by the late 1850s, the repercussions of the Escalera repression, particularly the dismantling of the militia of color and employment restrictions, set the stage for renewed resistance. Despite official attempts to stimulate participation, hundreds of *libres de color* now proved unmotivated to endure personal sacrifice for the sake of colonial defense in the Escalera era.

In addition to poor health and family hardship, *libres de color* submitted thirty-six petitions (7.42%) based on age ineligibility. Although used less than the previous categories, age exemptions for men over the age of thirty and under eighteen proved effective when substantiated with appropriate documents. The bulk of these (twenty-two petitions) came from Havana. For example, forty-three-year-old *pardo* José de los Angeles Acosta included his baptismal record from the Havana church, Our Lady of Guadalupe, as proof of his ineligibility. Similarly, *moreno* Ciriaco García submitted his birth record as evidence that his thirty-three years made him ineligible to serve. *Pardo* José Enrique from Matanzas, age thirty-six, and thirty-nine-year-old Francisco Pérez de Alejos, a *moreno* from Santa Clara, did likewise.[98] Given the current age of Ciriaco García in 1859, he would have just turned eighteen when colonial authorities dismantled the militia in 1844, and most likely never served in the militia. Although records do not indicate whether José de los Angeles Acosta, José Enrique, and Francisco Pérez de Alejos had prior experience in the military, they would have been in their late twenties in 1844, suggesting that they might have been soldiers in the late 1830s. If so, the militia of color's disbandment would have come just as their careers had begun, cutting short their access to military privileges and opportunities for upward social mobility.

Numerous men also petitioned for being too young for service. Rafael Vicasio Morales, *nación gangá*, and José de la Caridad Perez contested their draft notices because they were only seventeen.[99] *Moreno* Regino Ordar attempted to do the same, even though he had just turned eighteen. Because he straddled the draft age threshold, Ordar bolstered his claim with family obligations. Odar's father had recently died and, as the only son, he insisted he could not abandon his mother. The petition included not only his baptismal records but also the newly established *cédula de seguridad*, identification papers the government now required free people of color to carry.[100] The petition and supporting documents showed that Ordar had complied with new regulations for free people of color, but also how he combined age regulations and family hardship to manipulate the militia exemptions to his advantage. Whether they were too young, like Regino Ordar, or too old, like José de los Angeles Acosta, draftees used age ineligibility, often in combination with other regulations, to strengthen their cases, and when possible, to bend exemption rules to suit their needs.

In addition to petitions based on health, family, and age, some *libres de color* took advantage of other exemption guidelines. These included employment exclusions, substitutions, and even mistaken identity. For instance, numerous free people of color received occupational exemptions from military service because they worked as local firemen. Registered firefighters, like Máximo Valdés and Domingo Lima, had no difficulty avoiding military service.[101] Nor did *pardo* José Antonio Peña, who petitioned for an exemption based on his livelihood as a musician at the Havana Cathedral, where he had worked for the previous eight years. As proof, Peña produced a copy of the royal decree that had created four positions for imperial musicians who, like firemen, were excluded from military service.[102] Article 15 of the exemption rules stipulated that draftees could substitute or change draft numbers with another person.[103] Examples of successful substitution requests surfaced from Secundino de la Hoz and José de la Rosa Valdes, both from Havana's fourth district. De la Hoz recommended Rafael Parra take his place in the *pardo* militia, but when officials declined his request, de la Hoz contested due to illness. De la Hoz explained that, although his condition had somewhat improved, he needed to support his family, which included five young children.[104] When authorities called José de la Rosa Valdes' *sorteo* (draft) number, his work in the countryside prohibited him from leaving, so he contacted Rafael Gomez. Gomez, recently called for service, agreed to extend his military assignment in Valdes's place. Naturally, Valdes gave him a glowing reference, saying he had known Gomez for eight years and attested to his friend's physical fitness to continue serving.[105] Although exemption by substitution was an uncommon option for free men of color, in some respects it may have been easier than claims based solely on health. Substitutions did not require documentation, only the corroboration of a willing proxy. Still, given the climate of forced enlistment, locating an eager replacement could prove more difficult than producing written evidence of ailments or family obligations. Fortunately, de la Hoz and Valdes found agreeable alternates. Although successful substitutions offer another way some *libres de color* rejected service, it also sheds light on how others welcomed the opportunity to participate in the militia.

Finally, on rare occasions, draftees proclaimed mistaken identity to escape military service. Typically, these errors surfaced due to common names and inaccurate recording of an individual's color or race. For example, *moreno libre* Magdeleno García claimed he had been drafted by mistake. The roster called for someone with his name, but who was a *pardo*. He stopped short of requesting a full exemption, possibly in fear of state retribution, and instead, asserted his willingness to serve when his *sorteo* number for the *moreno* militia came up.[106] José Marcos Mora, a twenty-eight-year old tobacco washer, faced a similar situation. Mora explained that although he and the actual draftee had the same name, the accompanying documentation proved he was white—not *pardo*, making him ineligible for service in the militia of color.[107] García and Mora's petitions highlight the intricacies of race and color for militia draftees in the Escalera era. In the context of opposition to militia duty, petitions involving mistaken identity offer another layer of protest based on naming practices, color, and race. Magdeleno García and José Marcos Mora's experiences with duplicate names indicated the penetration of Hispanic traditions among *libres de color*. In terms of color and race, the often blurred boundaries between *moreno*, *pardo*, and *blanco* sharpened under the draft and further emphasized faltering interest in militia duty.

Not all those who petitioned would be granted an exemption. Some of these individuals took desperate measures, especially if they lacked the proper documentation of health deficiencies, family hardships, or occupational exclusions. Juan Rodríguez claimed an accident had left him unfit for duty, but physicians declared he met all the physical requirements for militia service.[108] Authorities also denied Pedro Pablo de Rojas's request to exempt his twenty-one-year old son, Ramón, who apprenticed with him to become a teacher.[109] Francisco Javier Pita asserted he had not yet completed his apprenticeship as a shoemaker, but after investigating his case, officials discovered Pita was not registered as an apprentice in any district.[110] If unable to secure a formal release, hundreds of men simply fled after being drafted. In September 1859, Doctor José Ramón Cabello reported that 27 percent of the healthy draftees he examined had deserted their post.[111] For those men unable to secure an official exemption and unwilling to participate in the militia, abandoning service proved their only recourse.

Ultimately, a large proportion of *libres de color* who petitioned the draft won their claims. Cuban officials granted 91 percent of the nearly five hundred exemption requests. This high approval rating may be attributed to the ways free *pardos* and *morenos* interpreted their military options and then supported their claims. Free men and women paid close attention to the exemption rules. Using their knowledge of the legal system and the particulars of the *Reglamento para las milicias disciplinadas de color*, hundreds of free blacks opted to protest military service. They substantiated petitions with a range of evidence, including baptismal, marriage, and death records. Parents often reinforced these claims by asserting how economic hardship would destabilize the family without theirs sons' contributions to the household. By November 1860, authorities had spent several months scrutinizing petitions and interviewing family and neighborhood witnesses to verify a range of declarations. Nevertheless, the combined exemptions and desertions countered the draft's goal to fill the militia rosters. The difficulties in securing *pardo* and *moreno* soldiers would force officials to reconsider their approach to recruiting *libres de color*.

The Fall of the Militia of Color

By the 1860s, Spain's efforts to maintain military defense and social order in Cuba renewed concerns over arming soldiers of African descent. During his stint in Cuba in 1859, Boston lawyer Henry Richard Dana noted planters' growing impatience over what he characterized as the "favoring of free blacks." "Slaveholders," he asserted, perceived the reestablished militia as a means of securing "the sympathy and cooperation of free blacks, in case of a revolutionary movement."[112] To counter these sentiments, Spanish authorities again expanded royalist troop levels. Records for 1862 enumerated 19,561 veteran Spanish soldiers or officers serving in Cuba. In comparison, the combined number of militiamen, black and white, totaled only 4,170. Within this group, soldiers of color accounted for approximately 1,003.[113] Given these proportions, the Cuban militia, particularly *pardo* and *moreno* soldiers, played an increasingly diminished role in colonial defense over the decade.[114] Meanwhile, perplexed by the resistance to the draft, but bolstered by the size of royalist forces, elites and imperial authorities contemplated the final fate of the militia of color.

Warfare pushed some officials to rethink the formation of militia units obtained by a draft and consider the possibility of raising a full voluntary battalion of *pardos* and *morenos*, particularly in Havana. Heavy losses midway through Spain's war with Morocco in 1859–1860 over Ceuta's borders prompted a plan by Martín de Arredondo y Oléa, a member of the Havana elite. In February 1860, Arredondo proposed supplementing the peninsular army with voluntary units of color. As previous advocates of black soldiers had done, Arredondo emphasized race and military tradition. Blacks' and mulattoes' racial heritage, he argued, made them "familiar with the rigor of the summer climate" and "burning dessert winds" of North Africa. Stereotypically, he predicted these attributes would make them far more successful than European troops. Furthermore, Arredondo heralded *pardos* and *morenos* as "good soldiers, uncomplaining and valiant in the face of the enemy." The units, he also pointed out, had been especially useful in previous military campaigns in Mexico and Florida, where they had proven their importance and loyalty time and again. Arredondo's plan for the voluntary battalion of color, however, would ultimately fall on deaf ears. The military aide who brought the idea to the attention of Leopoldo O'Donnell, now head of the Spanish Army, expressed several reservations. Major obstacles included the recent recruitment deficits in Cuba and the expense of transporting troops from Havana to Morocco. Consequently, military officials abandoned Arredondo's proposal, which left Cuba's military contribution to the conflict in Africa primarily in the form of financial donations made by various units and individuals.[115] Ignoring Arredondo's plan, however, would leave the issue of what to do about the militia of color unresolved until the mid-1860s.

The colonial government's abrupt destruction and problematic reconstitution of the militia of color had a serious impact on the institution's future. Prior to the 1840s, Arredondo's plan would have been given far more consideration. In fact, authorities had steadily expanded voluntary militia units from the 1760s to the late 1820s, although not without debate. The outbreak of revolts involving militiamen of color in the 1830s, however, dampened claims of *pardo* and *moreno* loyalty to the Spanish crown. The militia's dissolution in 1844 brought an abrupt end to black military careers, access to benefits, family traditions, and an important layer of social status to several generations of free *pardos* and *morenos.* For many *libres de color,* the reestablishment of the militia of color in 1854 proved too little, too late. A decade of social coercion and discrimination, both within and outside the colony, combined with economic restrictions, gave free blacks and mulattoes little incentive to pledge their loyalty to the Spanish empire through forced participation in the restructured militia units. The stream of exemption petitions by men of color and their parents, and outright desertions by draftees, attested to the reluctance and resistance toward serving in the military. Furthermore, their responses forced officials to question both the draft's effectiveness and, ultimately, the viability of the militia of color.

In September 1865, Havana's Consejo de Administración (Administrative Council) commenced discussions "with the object of proposing several alterations" to the current status of the militia of color. They acknowledged that the enlistment of *libres de color* in the reestablished units, first through voluntary participation and then through the draft, had been largely unsuccessful, in part because the majority of *pardos* and *morenos* continued to constitute a substantial proportion of the skilled artisan and agricultural sectors. The forced enlistment interfered with their "need of daily employment to sustain themselves and their families," especially given the ongoing occupational restrictions of the Escalera era.[116] Consequently, for some on the Council renewing the institution's former honor became a top priority. Several members suggested, as Arredondo had a few years prior, making the troops voluntary, as they had been in the past. Doing so, reasoned the Consejo, ensured that those who participated in the militia did so of their own volition. Ultimately, it would be to the military's "advantage" to enlist men who "willingly" embraced the "fatigues" associated with service. These attributes would, in turn, foster the enlistment of men with high "morality." Council members also reviewed the relationship between residence and service. They recommended only enlisting individuals who lived in or near their home city's battalion so militiamen could remain near their families and attend to personal affairs. These combined components aimed at raising the militia's status and restoring it as an "honorable force."[117] These reconsiderations of the draft, employment concerns, and family obligations suggested the willingness of some members of the Consejo to concede to the priorities of *libres de color*. A return to voluntary enlistment, albeit dubious given the institution's destruction and restoration in the span of ten years, had the potential to attract desirable servicemen. Making it easier for soldiers to retain familial ties might also entice *pardos* and *morenos*, especially given the complaints by petitioners. Indeed, the combined impact of these approaches might well have restored the institution's honor, if not for the detractors on the Council.

Not everyone on the Consejo agreed with the proposed concessions to *libres de color*. Several councilmen adamantly countered the pros of using militiamen of color asserted by Arredondo and other reform-minded members. Fears of arming thousands of men of color remained a core concern. They acknowledged the question over whether or not to retain black soldiers was crucial, not only because of their past "importance" to the defense of the empire but also for the "consequences" they had wrought over the years and for what impact these troops might have in the future. Nevertheless, the twists of past loyalty and recent protests to service reminded conservative leaders just how easily *moreno* and *pardo* soldiers could shift their allegiance to the empire. They complained that although Spain had "flattered" *libres de color* by extending all the "exceptions, benefits and privileges," including the "*fuero* and other distinctions," the crown had to offer, it had proven pointless. "The militias of color are more dangerous than useful," asserted council leader Virgil de Quiñones. Furthermore, given the build up of royalist troops and police, many claimed there was simply no "great necessity" for the militia of color. To that end, the Consejo recommended the "pan-Latin extinction" of the militia of color, as well as their white counterparts in Cuba and Puerto Rico. Despite the numerical strength of peninsular forces, authorities feared black militiamen because their knowledge and experience in weaponry and deployment might "one day serve as the nucleus of a great army" of opposition, as they had during the revolutionary wars. Moreover, they had become a financial drain. Dismantling the units would enable the Spanish crown to redirect these funds toward other state uses. By the end of September 1865, the committee voted unanimously to minimize and, ultimately, dissolve the *pardo* and *moreno* militias.[118]

The militia of color's second disbandment, just ten years after being reestablished, reflected the deep fissures within Spanish imperial control across the Atlantic. Free blacks' resistance to military recruitment, voluntarily or through the draft, renewed fears of scattered revolt from the 1830s and the more coordinated rebellions of 1843. Despite the build-up of Spanish forces across the colony, elites and visitors remained apprehensive about the potential of the free population of African descent, as well as creoles, to pursue armed revolt, or worse, revolution. The exemption petitions submitted by hundreds of *libres de color* expose the irreparable damage the Escalera era had on the status and honor of military service for free families of color. In turn, their resistance rekindled disputes over the roles of black and mulatto militiamen and their significance to the defense of or detriment to Spanish imperial interests. By the mid 1860s, colonial authorities had concluded that the problems of maintaining the militia of color outweighed the benefits.

* * *

Centuries of participation in colonial militias of color in Cuba and throughout Spanish America had garnered free men of African descent honor, prestige, and respect within their own communities and among colonial authorities. Opening military service to free *pardos* and *morenos* required Spanish authorities to modify existing prejudices. In the process, numerous officials recognized and praised these men for their loyal service under arduous conditions. The segregated nature of the units and soldier's strong ties to their communities also worked to reinforce group unity. Service, albeit circumscribed by race and color, offered *libres de color* opportunities to access privileges which enhanced their social status and gave them opportunities for upward mobility. Nevertheless, apprehension over arming black men resonated throughout the late eighteenth and nineteenth centuries. Militiamen's demands for fairer treatment, the impact of revolutions in Haiti and Spanish America, and the exclusion of *libres de color* from Spanish citizenship heightened officials' fears of social and political upheaval at the hands of soldiers of color.

The Escalera rebellions, which linked some *pardo* and *moreno* soldiers to the broader plot, unleashed a massive effort to extinguish the power and influence of *libres de color* across the island. Disbanding the black militia became one of the most comprehensive methods authorities used to rid Cuba of the threat from agitated dissent from the population of African descent in 1844. Although evidence of how militiamen reacted to this crushing blow to their identity and honor remains sparse, their responses to the reestablished militia of color a decade later sheds light on their concerted efforts to circumvent military service. After enduring a decade of hardships under the Escalera era, hundreds of *pardos*, *morenos*, and their parents resisted participation in the reestablished militia of color, both as volunteers and as draftees. They petitioned for exemption based on a variety of issues, particularly family obligations and economic hardship.

Like the expulsion of free people of color discussed in chapter 3, dismantling the militia also produced unexpected consequences for the colonial government. The wide dissemination of military exemption rules, combined with the legal sophistication of the free community of color, enabled hundreds to circumvent service. By filing exemption petitions, *libres de color* rejected colonial assumptions about their desire to serve based on past experiences and traditions. Their actions demonstrated a definitive shift in the meaning of militia duty. In this redefined understanding, forced service negated the incentives offered. Individual and group identity and agency now worked to undermine previous participation in imperial defense. The actions of free black men and women compelled authorities to, first, reconsider the merits of a voluntary corps. Intriguingly, some council members expressed the need to return the militia of color to an honorable status, even as they attempted to strip black and mulatto artisans of respectability and replace them with white skilled workers. Ultimately, regional conflicts between Spain and North Africa and the potential role of black soldiers forced Spanish officials to rethink the institution's overall viability. They concluded that phasing out militias of color throughout the Spanish Caribbean was the safest way to avoid future dissent. In the meantime, Spanish colonial officials, elites, planters, and merchants directed their attention to agricultural profitability by developing immigration and migrant worker plans they hoped would reduce the proportion of Cuba's African-descended population and nullify the threat of rebellion.

6 / Balancing Acts: The Shifting Dynamics of Race and Immigration

> *It is indispensable that the white population be expanded successively. . . . This expansion must always be bound to the political idea of sustaining an equilibrium of the castes in order to prevent the notion that the reduction of the black race might encourage those who wish to fuel and promote ideas of independence and complete separation from the Metropole.*
>
> —LEOPOLDO O'DONNELL

In April 1844, Captain General O'Donnell urgently reminded officials in Spain of the political importance of "sustaining an equilibrium of the castes" in Cuba. In particular, he sought to undermine the positions of "black skilled craftsmen, maids, cooks, and coachmen" and replace them with white workers. He held the same attitude about the agricultural sector, although he conceded that "only Africans" could tolerate Cuba's harsh, tropical climate. These sentiments, however, would change within a few years. Overall, O'Donnell asserted that augmenting the white population offered two solutions to the problems exacerbated by the Escalera rebellions. First, expanding Cuba's white sector would help prevent "ideas of independence and complete separation from the Metropole" and bolster loyalty to the crown in Spain's fractured nineteenth-century empire.[1] Second, and more important, the presence of white workers would reduce the proportion of free people of color and slaves in Cuba and the island's dependency on blacks for agricultural and urban labor. In other words, "equilibrium" meant reducing the proportion of blacks and increasing that of whites.

Despite O'Donnell's ambitions, several factors aggravated existing internal and external strains. Although the displacement of free black workers by whites in the cities had garnered some success, the recent reductions in this population created a void in the skilled crafts. Raising the number of *libres de color* in the countryside had also proven difficult. Furthermore, agricultural labor shortages threatened to disrupt planters' economic stability and profits. To alleviate anxieties, officials and plantation owners in the 1840s returned to the theme of white immigration fostered by prominent creoles such as Franciso de Arango y Parreño and Félix Varela in the 1830s. Noting the labor crisis ushered in by emancipation in the British Caribbean in 1834, planters in Cuba aimed to avoid the virtual collapse of sugar production experienced by their Anglo counterparts. Moreover, the renewed colonization schemes not only fostered European immigration but also tapped into the new stream of rhetorically "white" Asian indentured workers flowing into the Americas, as well as Mexican prisoners displaced by the Caste War in the Yucatán. Supplanting the African-descended population with Spaniards, Canary Islanders, Chinese, and Amerindians represented colonial Cuba's attempt to suppress racial upheaval and political dissidence during the Escalera era. Spanish officials and creole businessmen in Cuba hoped the introduction of this array of colonists and contract workers, often to toil alongside slaves, would invigorate the plantation workforce, divide racial alliances among the slave and semi-free, supplant *libres de color*, and rebalance the colony so that whites tipped the scales as the majority.

Officials had pursued several aspects of these goals with zeal. As discussed previously, between 1844 and 1845 colonial authorities blocked hundreds of free *pardos* and *morenos* from entering Cuba, expelled many of those born abroad, and used extralegal means to purge the native-born from the colony.[2] The execution and overseas imprisonment of bondsmen also served to reduce the proportion of slaves in the workforce.[3] The official, albeit contested, census figures of 1841 and 1846 revealed that the number of slaves had plunged by 112,736 (25%) and *libres de color* by a more modest but nonetheless significant 3,612 (2.3%).[4] Using the Escalera era's hallmarks—terror and retaliation—Spanish colonial authorities in Cuba sought to dramatically alter the former demographic and economic trajectory of free blacks, and by extension slaves.

By the late 1860s, race-based immigration and contract labor programs complemented Escalera-era restrictions. These would significantly impact the economic, social, and political destiny of Cuba's African-descended population, particularly free people of color. Preferential treatment for white colonists, conflicts between Chinese contract workers and slaves, tensions between "free" Chinese and *libres de color*, and overarching racist policies directed at free blacks revealed the multiple factors informing the transformation of race relations. In response to these dramatic shifts, free people of color used their shrinking influence and opportunities as rallying points for the community of African descent. Individuals such as Antonio Medina y Céspedes created schools for students of color. Others like Antonio Mora established mutual aid societies. Furthermore, despite the expanding white population, the number of free blacks rose dramatically during the Escalera era, doubling between 1846 and 1861. As *libres de color* created more educational and social opportunities and gained strength in numbers, imperial political forces converged and enabled free blacks and slaves to forge new cause for revolt.

White Immigration and the Fear of Another Haiti

Cuban elites had advocated plans to whiten the colony since the early nineteenth century. In 1821, Father Félix Varela bemoaned the fact that Cuba's massive agricultural base, and much of its domestic service, remained in the care of enslaved Africans, which effectively eliminated the participation of free, white workers in these arenas. He noted how household work was "relegated to free blacks because . . . this class does not want to mix with the slaves, and only when they are unable to secure other work [in the skilled crafts] do they turn to domestic service." Moreover, he stressed how the black population "exceeded the white population by three to one."[5] As others would do time and time again, Varela raised the specter of Haiti as the epitome of black resistance in which slaves vastly outnumbered whites. He also observed that rebellious slaves could ruin Cuba through work stoppages and renewed resistance. "Let us not deceive ourselves," he wrote in a *Memoria* to the Spanish Cortes. "Constitution, liberty, equality are synonymous; and their very names repudiate slavery and inequality of rights. In vain do we seek to reconcile these contradictions." The resolution to this problem, he reasoned, lay in augmenting Cuba's European population.[6]

Influential creoles echoed his call in the 1830s, although their proposals varied. Planter spokesman Francisco de Arango y Parreño recommended simultaneously raising Spanish immigration and enslaved African importation as the solution to curtailing the expanding free sector of color. Arango's plan proposed accelerated miscegenation as a driving factor. He envisioned settlements composed of male European workers and women of color who would produce racially mixed offspring. They, in turn, would form unions with other European immigrants and beget whiter children. According to Arango, racial mixing would hasten Cuba's whitening process, rapidly reduce the existing proportion of free blacks, and gradually eradicate discrimination based on color.[7] José

Antonio Saco, a leading creole proslavery supporter, advocated whitening the colony through accelerated Spanish immigration and reducing slave imports. To ensure Cuba's security and prosperity, Saco urged Cuban officials to "close its ports to blacks forever and open them freely to all whites."[8] Saco advocated whitening on the basis of cultural and racial issues. He asserted that, regardless of miscegenation levels, Africans and their descendents retained ineradicable cultural traditions and dark complexions. These elements, warned Saco, maintained an impassible racial divide. From Europe, where Captain General Miguel Tacón exiled him because of his procreole stance in 1834, Saco proposed that the colony experiment with staffing sugar plantations with salaried European workers and free blacks.[9] Aspects of both proposals appeared too broad to be viable. Arango's plan seemed simplistic and unrealistic, especially given the intricacies of Spanish colonial configurations of race, particularly in Cuba, and considering his expressed animosity toward the African-descended population (slave and free). Meanwhile, the sociocultural separation of Saco's scheme failed to take into account the colony's nearly four-hundred-year history of slavery, Spanish colonialism, multicultural exchange, and racial hierarchies. His ideas about experimenting with paid agricultural labor, however, took hold and a flurry of programs promoting white immigration and free labor ensued.

Encouraged by British investors in Cuba, who had contracted Irish and Germans as railroad workers since the early 1830s, local planters pushed for white immigrant labor in the agricultural sector.[10] In 1835, Tomás de Juana y Soler prepared a report calling for the importation of free white agricultural contract workers to supplement slaves.[11] European colonists, called *colonos*, primarily from Spanish territories, were directed toward Cuba through a variety of incentives, including free trans-Atlantic travel and "guarantees against contract abuses."[12] Plantation owner José María Dau saw the benefits of Juana y Soler's report. Building on the precedent set by the Junta de Fomento de Agricultura (Agricultural Planning Council), which permitted the importation of over 500 *isleños* (Canary Islanders) to work on the Havana-Güines railroad in 1836, Dau recommended Canary Islanders as a potential source for large-scale immigration. The *isleños*'s Spanish language, Catholic religion, and roots in a traditionally agricultural economy, currently in economic crisis, made them an ideal immigrant group for the Cuba. These factors, asserted Dau, would promote cultural continuity and facilitate the interests of the empire and plantation owners by whitening the island, stimulating economic growth, and creating a more desirable and controllable agricultural work force.[13]

Foreign travelers also took note of Cuba's racial agenda. "The great object of the Creole patriots of Cuba," noted David Turnbull, a British abolitionist who visited Cuba in the late 1830s, "is at once to increase the white population, and render the further importation of Africans unnecessary." The influx of over 8,000 white immigrants to Cuba during this period ran the gamut from poor *isleños* to convicts, with the bulk arriving from Spain (46%), the Canary Islands (33%), and the United States (12%), with most destined for plantations, as well as the railroads and copper mines. Nevertheless, Turnbull cautioned, the numbers proved deceiving, in large part because many of the recent arrivals were returnees.[14] Despite Turnbull's concerns, by the late 1830s, approximately 35,000 assorted white immigrants had landed in Cuba.[15] Given the volume of white arrivals, whether returnees or new *colonos*, Cuba appeared well on its way toward achieving its ambitions.

By the early 1840s, workers from northern Spain joined the list of preferred immigrants. Authorities from the Ultramar wrote to military leaders and the Council for Agricultural and Commercial Development in Cuba stressing the necessity of adopting measures to "replace the . . . workers of color with white laborers."[16] Although many officials agreed that bringing in such workers was vital to maintaining Cuba's security and wealth, they wondered whether "four or five hundred thousand Europeans" could be enticed to substitute for slaves in agricultural and domestic activities.[17] Northern Spanish officials from Lugo and Pontevedra in Galicia suggested targeting existing agricultural workers from the region, who had already established a migratory pattern to South America, particularly to Montevideo, Uruguay.[18] They deemed this particular stream of immigrant families preferable to the existing flow of single young male artisans and shopkeepers currently arriving in Cuba.[19] By March 1841, the Ultramar approved plans to expand the importation of individuals and families from both the Canary Islands and northern Spain to Cuba and the rest of republican Latin America.[20] With preferences established and expanded plans underway prior to 1843, the racial balance desired by authorities finally seemed within Cuba's grasp.

Actual efforts to introduce white laborers and servants, however, had proved problematic before the Escalera era. For instance, immigrants transported from the Canary Islands to work on Cuban railroads complained of numerous abuses, especially poor provisions and inadequate housing.[21] One plan to import workers from northern Spain in the early 1840s failed, as Catalan laborers came close to rioting because of Cuba's harsh tropical climate and the strenuous working conditions. The bulk of these immigrants deserted the plantation for domestic or trade opportunities in the cities.[22] These impediments led Cuban authorities to dissolve the White Population Council, which had been administering immigration activities, and establish the White Population Commission as a branch of the Junta de Fomento (Development Council) in 1842. To bolster the White Population Commission's charge to increase the number of white sugar workers, the Development Council established a bank designed to award funds to plantation owners who brought in twenty-five families or more or acquired contracts to transport Cuban sugar to India. Furthermore, officials secured additional financial resources for white colonization by requiring slaveholders to pay taxes on each person of color they employed in domestic services.[23] These funds supplemented the arrival of *isleños* to Gaspar Betancourt Cisneros' plantation, where he claimed the fifty to sixty Canary *colonos* laboring on his extensive land holdings worked side by side "with my blacks, without distinction," and were "perfectly content."[24] His idyllic depiction of free and slave labor, however, clashed with harsh realities. For instance, although Canary Islanders acquired the reputation of being "a hardy race, better able than Europeans to support the heat of a tropical climate," they were unaccustomed to the labor conditions in Cuba and fell prone to the ravages of cholera's "malignant fever." A similar fate met Irish workers from the United States.[25] Misrepresentations, tropical working conditions, and disease took a heavy toll on the whitening project in the 1830s and early 1840s, despite the arrival of thousands of immigrant workers.

Statistically, the 1841 census cast an ominous shadow over the success of white migration. The data revealed that the population of African descent had risen to 58.5 percent of the colony's total inhabitants (15.2% *libres de color* and 43.3% slaves).[26] In other words, the influx of Europeans combined with the natural reproduction of creoles failed to yield the anticipated racial balance. Part of the problem rested in the concurrent flow of forced African immigration. Between 1831 and 1840, more than 180,000 Africans arrived as slave labor for the expanding sugar industry.[27] These numbers were more than five times the level of white immigration. Furthermore, the free population of color also increased from 106,494 to 152,838.[28] Thus pre-1843 plans to whiten skilled urban employment sectors garnered fragmented success. Efforts to redistribute the racial dynamics of Cuba's general population and its agricultural labor force would not succeed until after the Escalera repression took hold.

WHITENING CUBA IN THE ESCALERA ERA

The Escalera rebellions reignited long-standing concerns over how to increase the white sector and reduce the black population. Given the material value of slaves, *libres de color* bore the brunt of the deaths, deportations, coerced migrations, and port entry prohibitions initiated in the 1844 repression. As the Escalera era restrictions targeting the black population gained strength and the sugar and coffee industries expanded, officials and planters amplified plans to promote white immigration. Colonial authorities and businessmen pursued this objective using a rationale centered on race and labor. The anticipated influx of cheap European immigrant workers would achieve key goals: to offset the existing black population and fill labor shortages in the agricultural economy.[29]

To that end, officials in Spain completed a report in 1845 entitled *The Development of the White Population in Cuba and Progressive Slave Emancipation*. It noted how Cuba needed to shift its focus from attracting single white male workers to recruiting families. This move would create a solid base on which to establish a stable and natural increase in the white population. Furthermore, immigrant families, the bulk of whom would be directed toward plantation work, would ultimately replace slaves and, potentially, free people of color. In essence, the colonial state envisioned the immigration of "hardworking and honorable families" as a means to diminish Cuba's dependence on slaves for agricultural production, and on the artisanal and semi-skilled labor of free people of color. This would, in turn, curtail the possibilities of widespread revolt from the black population.[30]

The arrival of a new wave of Canary Islanders in 1845 initiated this revised approach to whitening. José María Gutiérrez and Bernardo Forstall, businessmen from the region, agreed to transport three hundred families to the Spanish Caribbean, sending two hundred to Cuba and the remainder to Puerto Rico, where they would receive a horse and a plot of land to cultivate.[31] The following year, Domingo Goicuria, a Havana merchant, joined the renewed push for free, white labor. From his perspective, European workers would instantly solve existing shortages in sugar production because they were considered intellectually superior to and more mechanically inclined than Africans. With the aid of white agricultural workers, Cuban planters aimed to expand the quantity and quality of the sugarcane they produced for the world market.[32] Not surprisingly, this latest plan for white immigration coincided with the forced exile of hundreds of *libres de color* and overseas imprisonment and banishment of thousands of free blacks and slaves sentenced during the Escalera Military Commission trials in 1844. As ports closed their doors to free blacks who attempted to gain entry into Cuba, they openly welcomed European men and their families.

Conditions in Europe, and in the Canary Islands, continued to propel immigration to Cuba and elsewhere in the Americas, which in turn helped erode the proportion of free people of color. Over sixteen thousand *isleños*, predominantly poor and illiterate, sought refuge across the Atlantic Ocean, desperate to escape the hunger and misery brought on by a famine in 1847 and a cholera epidemic in 1851.[33] The combination of poverty in the Canary Islands and Cuba's ideological agenda and material incentives propelled an average of 1,000 *isleños* per year into Cuba.[34] By 1846, Canary Islanders made up 32 percent of the Europeans in Cuba, second only to Spaniards.[35] The 1846 census also revealed dramatic reductions in the free sector of color. In the western provinces at the epicenter of the rebellions, the number of *libres de color* dropped by 3,612 (21.7%). Havana bore the brunt, with the proportion of free blacks and mulattos plummeting by almost one-quarter; the number of free black men declined by almost one-third.[36] Massive European immigration, combined with the colonial state's explicitly racist and repressive policies, steadily chipped away at the influence and demographic growth free people of color experienced prior to the Escalera era.

These promising figures, from the perspective of officials, planters, and merchants, catapulted plans in the 1850s. In 1856, Havana property owner José Lorenzo Odoardo established a sugar processing plant on his property with the hope of recruiting one hundred "hardworking, robust" *isleños* to operate it. In exchange for working ten hours a day, he agreed to front the passage expenses for men and their "able-bodied" wives and sons. He planned to be reimbursed out of the men's monthly twelve-peso salary. Odoardo also guaranteed these families healthy meals and free medical care. José de la Cruz Castellanos, a creole plantation owner, gained approval to implement a similar plan. Rather than Canary Islanders, he targeted *colonos* from Spain and other European countries. His incentives included a twenty-year tax exemption, free transportation to Cuba, and the necessary tools for agricultural production.[37] Whether Odoardo and Castellanos lived up to their promises is difficult to say for certain; however, immigration figures between 1845 and 1859 indicate that nearly 5,000 Canary Islanders, along with groups from Catalan, Galicia, and the Basque region, albeit in comparatively small numbers, sought better opportunities for themselves and their families in Cuba and elsewhere in the Americas.[38]

In addition to material enticements, strained political relations between Spain and the new Latin American republics also influenced immigration to Cuba. Between 1838 and 1853, Spain sought to prohibit emigration to anywhere other than Cuba, Puerto Rico, and the Philippines.[39] Some *colonos* disembarked in Venezuela, but the majority, at least 97 percent, headed to Cuba. These factors enabled Spanish emigration to peak in the late 1850s, with just over 10,000 men and women directed toward the Spanish Caribbean.[40]

Nevertheless, despite the steady immigrant flow and hefty colonial promises, the actual working and living conditions European immigrants encountered in Cuba ignited a stream of grievances from both *colonos* and plantation owners. Workers complained of malnutrition and inadequate shoes, clothing, and housing. Landowners grumbled that these laborers left the fields for the city once they accumulated enough savings.[41] In other words, the immigration problems of the 1830s and early 1840s, such as severe working conditions, disease, and general discontent, persisted into the Escalera era. Two decades of whitening now intertwined with the urgency to quell black revolt and stem agricultural and urban labor shortages. After 1844, efforts to remake Cuba's population dynamics shifted from single to family programs for European settlers, albeit with varying results.

Additional factors fueled the difficulties in whitening and racial imbalance. First, the push for European immigration in the 1850s coincided with Spain's general amnesty for political prisoners initiated in 1853.[42] Returnees to Cuba included hundreds of *libres de color*, as well as creoles, who had fled into exile or were imprisoned overseas following the Escalera uprisings. For example, in 1852, Cuban-born Leandro Valdes, who had resided in Mexico for several years, requested a passport "to return to the country of my birth to reunite with part of my family."[43] Those who arrived in Cuba found themselves displaced from a variety of employment and service sectors. Second, Cuba's local free black population experienced its own demographic surge. Between 1846 and 1851, the number of *libres de color* increased by over 15,000--a figure that surpassed the arrival of European immigrants during the same time period.[44] It would take another decade before the Cuban government could boast of reaching a white majority. Finally, regardless of claims heralding European immigrants' hearty work ethic and intelligence, officials had not resolved Cuba's perpetual shortage of agricultural labor. In another bid to augment the plantation work force and reduce the overall proportion of blacks, elites turned to a new trend in the free labor arena: Asian contract workers. These new laborers, officially categorized as white, but treated as slaves, rhetorically expanded Cuba's white population.

SHADES OF WHITE: CHINESE AND YUCATÁN CONTRACT WORKERS

Difficulties in retaining sufficient numbers of European immigrants for the agricultural sector and the high cost of acquiring enslaved Africans compelled Cuban planters to seek alternative sources for augmenting the sugar industry's workforce. In 1847, just two years after the Escalera Military Commission trials ended, planters turned to Asian contract workers to supplement slave, free black, and white laborers.[45] Spanish colonial officials, Cuban planters, and former slave traders facilitated the arrival of these predominantly male indentured workers. A year later, Yucatán Indian prisoners of war entered Cuba as pawns in Mexico's political efforts to secure the republic and the peninsula. By 1874, approximately 125,000 Chinese and over 2,000 Yucatán Indians had arrived in Cuba.[46] Characterized as rhetorically white for the sake of tipping Cuba's racial scales and considered temperamentally more docile than workers of African descent, thousands of laborers from both the Atlantic and the Pacific converged in Cuba. Their presence challenged the slave society's existing boundaries between white and black, and slave and free.

China's military defeat at the hands of the British during the Opium Wars (1839–1842 and 1856–1860) led to lopsided trade treaties, political encroachment, and war indemnities favoring Western powers. The ensuing economic crisis and social unrest in China resulted in the explosive Taiping Rebellion (1851–1864) that destroyed hundreds of cities and resulted in the death of over twenty-five million people in southern China before being suppressed by European powers.[47] The subsequent external and internal strife set the stage for the mass dispersal of Chinese migrant workers, known as coolies.

The nineteenth-century coolie trade cast approximately one million Chinese, primarily men from southeast China, around the world. Hundreds of thousands landed in Dutch, French, and British Southeast Asia, western Samoa, Hawaii, Tahiti, New Zealand, Australia, and Mauritius. On the other side of the Atlantic, the British abolition of slavery pulled Chinese laborers into the Caribbean, as well as Latin America and North America, primarily into the British, French, and Dutch Caribbean, Cuba, Peru, Mexico, Brazil, the United States, and Canada.[48] In particular, in the West Indies emancipated freedmen would not work on the plantations without the constraints of slavery. Black peasants in Trinidad, Jamaica, and British Guiana refused the poor wages of plantation labor and bought land for subsistence farming.[49] These actions by freedmen provoked a labor crisis for British Caribbean planters and, in 1842, Lord Stanley, British Secretary of State for Colonies, in agreement with Caribbean plantation owners who formed the West India Company, stressed the importance of the Chinese as "a fresh labouring population" that would foster "competition for employment."[50] Despite such assertions, British legislation combined with the loss of slave labor continued to diminish profits. The 1846 British Sugar Duties Act, which removed protective tariffs and forced British Caribbean planters to compete on the world sugar market against locales where slavery still existed, such as Cuba, Brazil, and Louisiana, resulted in what officials throughout the region characterized as the "failure of emancipation."[51]

The dismal result of abolition in the British Caribbean from the perspective of plantation owners, combined with the Escalera revolts in Cuba and the colony's numerical black majority, prompted planters there to use the British model of indentured Asian labor to augment the slave workforce and diminish the proportion of slaves and free people of African descent. A network of prominent families, businesses, shipping companies, and their representatives, many of whom had trafficked in slaves, carried Chinese contract workers to Cuba. In particular, cousins Pedro Zulueta, the son of a London-based slave trader, banker, and planter, and Julián Zulueta, a plantation owner, worked in conjunction with Spain's Real Junta de Fomento (Royal Planning Council) to initiate the importation of Chinese contract workers into the colony. Both men had deep connections to the slave trade. The powerful Zulueta family had built its wealth in the agricultural and transportation industries, particularly sugar production, railroads, and shipping. Their established offices in Havana, London, Liverpool, Spain, and Amoy (Xiamen) formed the key networks to import Asian workers to the Caribbean.[52] Although plans faltered in 1847, they resumed with intensity in 1853 until 1874, when the Chinese Commission halted the flow of its workers after collecting extensive testimonies regarding the abuses these men suffered under the slavelike indenture system.[53] The two-decade presence of Chinese workers, primarily indentured, but increasingly "free" from contracts, worked to further complicate Cuban race relations by augmenting the white population, at least in census reports, and also expanding the "controllable" workforce.

The arrival of Yucatán Indians added yet another small layer to Cuba's racial and ethnic mixture. Conflicts between the independent and relatively autonomous Yucatán Peninsula and the Mexican Republic sparked this immigration. In July 1847, in the mist of the Mexican-American War (1846–1848), Maya *caciques* (leaders) launched an enormous rural uprising that became know as the Yucatán Caste War (1848–1853). Shortages of food and arms, combined with internal strife, governmental shifts, and foreign incursions by U.S. troops left indigenous residents vulnerable.[54] In response, Yucatán governor Miguel Barbachano y Tarrazo initiated the sale of 140 rebel Indians as contract workers to Cuban authorities in 1849.[55] As the Caste War came to a close in the early 1850s, Mexican authorities in the Yucatán ordered a ten-year expulsion of virtually all Indians who had been prisoners of war in the recent conflict. This legalized removal numerically reduced Mayan rebels and eliminated their political leadership. Meanwhile, the arrival of Yucatán planters fleeing the war prompted Cuban colonization officials to consider allowing creole Mexican families and their Maya servants to establish farms in Cuba with the hope that their proximity to coastal Mexico would facilitate family colonization.[56] Authorities in Havana and Mérida, Mexico, however, struck a different deal. Given Mexico's political situation, Spanish consular representatives in the Yucatán suggested the use of Mayan prisoners of war as contract workers. Between 1848 and 1871, over 2,000 *yucatecos*, primarily male, became contract laborers in Cuba.[57] Although indentured Mexicans represented only 1.5 percent of the number of Chinese migrant workers, they would also contribute to Cuba's intersecting discourses on race, population dynamics, and labor.

In the Escalera era, planters increasingly expressed a desire for an agricultural work force more compliant than African-descended slaves. Some Cuban merchants, plantation owners, authorities and foreign visitors rationalized the subjugation of Asian and Indian workers. Government reports cast the Chinese as hardworking and more passive than slaves.[58] The Administrative Council described the arrival of the first six hundred coolies who disembarked in Cuba as "robust, agile, and experts in agricultural labor."[59] After decades away from Cuba, Spanish economist Ramón de la Sagra returned to the island in 1860. He assessed Chinese workers as having "the highest level of happiness and pleasure in the countryside."[60] Colombian merchant Francisco de Paula de Castro offered perhaps the most telling attitude of the era. In a letter designed to convince Matanzas planter Francisco de Ximeno to participate in the coolie trade, de Castro reasoned, "there are no dangers whatsoever and nothing that will disgust your fearful conscience. It is [simply] about bringing Asians to Cuba."[61] The Chinese diaspora of the nineteenth century expanded as merchants, planters, and officials from Mauritius to Peru bolstered these sentiments. In Cuba, representations of the Chinese as an ideal mixture of robust, diligent, and docile workers offered clear contrasts to Cuba's rebellious slave and free black populations. Moreover, these notions fueled the idea that the coolie trade offered a business alternative that was less personally offensive but just as profitable as dealing in slaves.

As for the Maya, Governor Barbachano rationalized their sale to Cuba and other parts of Mexico by arguing that as rebels, they would be condemned to execution if caught in the Yucatán. Colonel Pedro Acereto's burgeoning trade in Indian captives for indentured labor for Cuba's sugar industry demonstrated how profits accrued to the individual.[62] Cuba took advantage of these war prisoners; although planters considered the Maya physically weak for plantation labor, they nevertheless had other positive attributes. Spanish consulate officers commented that Indians, under Spanish colonialism, had acquired a gentle demeanor and sound moral values. Moreover, with the proper direction, they could enhance agricultural profits.[63] These sentiments conflicted with certain aspects of the rationale for enslaving Africans, whom planters such as Arango perceived as ignorant and uncivilized, only fit for menial labor. Ultimately, however, they resulted in some form of bondage.[64] In other words, the Maya had been sold almost expressly for agricultural labor. The shared conceptualization of Asians and Indians as ideal, submissive workers justified their enslavement.

Although Cubans considered indentured workers a part of the "free labor" system, Asians and Indians worked under coerced conditions facilitated by slave trading networks, regulations, and infrastructure. Most observers and officials agreed that the system was tantamount to slavery. British visitor Henry Murray considered Asian men "admirably suited to all the mechanical labour, but far inferior to the negroes in the fields."[65] His compatriot, Amelia Matilda Murray characterized coolies as a "miserable race," and questioned their ability to survive servitude. She also observed that "they do less work, but are the slaves of slaves."[66] Visiting Italian writer Antonio Carlo Napoleone Gallenga echoed these sentiments: "The Chinaman, thus left to the planter's discretion, has become to all intents and purposes a slave."[67] Mexico's Barbachano, who trafficked in Maya prisoners, seemed fully aware that in reality servitude under contract still amounted to slavery.[68] The simultaneous representation of Asian and Indian workers as a supplemental and alternative indentured agricultural labor supply and as free white men contributed to "a discourse of legal slippage" in which race categorization and colonial violence reinforced Cuba's fragmented application of political authority.[69]

The rhetoric of coolie and slave system comparison also permeated social constructions of race, particularly whiteness, throughout the Americas. Complex patterns emerged in the late nineteenth century. In Peru, where slavery was abolished in 1854, Chinese laborers replaced former slaves, often working on plantations as the sole labor force or in the highlands with free men of color and Indians. Their use informed Peruvian discussions surrounding free labor and nationalism, which frequently posited Chinese culture as a positive counterweight to the nation's African and indigenous heritage.[70] Instead of competing with understandings of whiteness, the Chinese acquired legal protection codified in a series of laws, albeit with limited reinforcement, in the 1840s and 1850s, governing their importation, treatment, and rights.[71] In the United States and Cuba, where the introduction of Asian workers had the potential to impact white supremacy, the rhetoric on race intersected with that of the coolie trade. In the late 1850s, U.S. commissioner to China William Reed defined the Chinese as "people of color" due to the coolie trade's similarity to slavery.[72] In the United States following the Civil War, the possibility of Chinese immigration produced regional and political concern. In the southern United States, the ending of the slave system and the rise of universal male suffrage exacerbated the perceived threat to white social, legal, political, and economic domination. Writers from periodicals such as the *Galveston Times*, the *New Orleans Times*, and the *West Baton Rouge Sugar Planter* rejected to the "importation and admixture of the inferior breeds of men" and insisted on "men of the Caucasian race and, no others, as a reinforcement to our population."[73] Despite Peruvian discourses of inclusion and American rhetoric of exclusion, the separation of Chinese immigrants into a distinct category maintained historical and emerging racial hierarchies.

In Cuba, officials also emphasized that "the Chinese race is thought to be purer than the African race" and although "considered as whites, public opinion and custom places them in a position inferior to whites."[74] Nevertheless, the Cuban context produced a feature not found in the United States or Peru. Whereas U.S. anti-coolie advocates warned that Chinese workers eroded employment opportunities for whites, Cuban elites' racial classification of the Chinese as white worked to expand the size of the white population.[75] In 1854, the Spanish crown issued the

"Reglamento para la introducción y regimen de los colonos españoles, chinos, o yucatecos en la isla de Cuba" (Regulations for the Introduction and Control of Spanish, Chinese, or Yucatán Indians in the Island of Cuba) to address European, as well as Asian and Indian, immigrant workers.[76] In 1864, questions concerning how to categorize Chinese immigrants baptismal and marriage records prompted Spain's Administrative Council to address the matter of race directly. Their conclusion, that both Indians and "the Chinese were to be considered as whites," provided the basis for the rhetorical construction of whiteness for the Chinese and the Yucatán Indians in Cuba.[77]

The discrimination and racism suffered by these workers exposed the fictive nature of the "whiteness" posited by the Spanish colonial government. Despite assertions that Asians represented an intermediate space between free and slave labor, they were not treated as whites in terms of either social privilege or legal status.[78] Given the nature of the coolie trade, in which contracts were sold without regard for the laborer and no provisions made for him to return home, "the coolly," reiterated Commissioner William Reed in reference to the Caribbean, is clearly "a man of color, to be disposed of and held in Cuba."[79] American visitor Richard Dana, who witnessed the landing of Chinese workers in Cuba in 1859, reflected on what he called a "strange and striking exhibition of power." In particular, he noted the racial contrasts of "two or three white men, bringing hundreds of Chinese thousands of miles, to a new climate and people . . . to work at unknown trades, for inscrutable purposes!"[80]

Chinese workers' testimony recorded in the 1874 *Cuba Commission Report* also attested to racial inconsistencies and abuse. After taking statements from over 165 laborers, Chinese officials concluded, "the owners . . . administrator . . . and overseer . . . only think of profit and are indifferent to our lives."[81] One worker, Chuang A-i, described how discrimination continued after completing his contract. In the general store he owned, "a white soldier entered my shop and endeavored to remove a number of articles without payment, and on my resisting beat me with a stick."[82] The commentary provided by U.S. officials, visitors, and the Chinese highlighted the actual, rather than discursive, treatment of Asian laborers in stark relief. Chinese testimony and the visible treatment of Asians as inferior to Spaniards and creoles contradicted official rhetoric and legislation that gave them status equal to whites. Nevertheless, such a classification of indentured Asians and Indians helped authorities accomplish their goal of increasing the proportion of whites in the colony.

The conditions of the indentured, which often matched those of the enslaved, also produced social unrest and served as a constant reminder of the empty promises of rhetorical whiteness. Stereotypes of Asians and Indians' alleged passivity gave way to outright resistance. Italian writer Antonio Carlo Napoleone Gallenga acknowledged the Chinese laborers' "superior intelligence and high temper," but claimed this is what made them "unmanageable" on the plantations.[83] Spanish economist Ramón de la Sagra commented that the Chinese seemed to have no religion and their consequent departure from the plantation on Sundays exposed them to the potentially "harmful" influence of outsiders they encountered in nearby towns.[84] In 1858, just three years into the renewed trade, Havana's *Diaro de la Marina* published an article lamenting the recent rise in Chinese criminal behavior, which included suicide, homicide, theft, and attempted robbery. Moreover, the author concluded, "individuals of this race have . . . little regard for life." The tensions over Asian "passivity" and "volatility" would persist over the next two decades, until Chinese officials banned the trade to Cuba in 1877.[85]

Cuba's turn to Chinese and Mexican laborers, nevertheless, had both economic and demographic advantages. From the perspective of planters faced with a curtailed slave trade and the rising costs of acquiring enslaved Africans, the supplemental workforce of indentured Asians and Indians was relatively much less expensive and easier to obtain. The average cost of a Chinese contract between 1847 and 1875 was 297 pesos, versus 512 pesos for a slave, and Yucatán contracts started out at 25 pesos per person.[86] The contradictory depictions of Asian and Indian indentured laborers shed light on the problematic dynamics of race and immigration in nineteenth-century Cuba. Planters and overseers found ways to subdue, humiliate, and control these contract workers. More important, in terms of balancing population dynamics, by introducing these two groups Cuban elites sought more than a temporary fix for labor shortages, and in the process, aspired to remake the colony's socioracial underclass. Moreover, the arrival of Chinese immigrants in combination with European colonists and Cuba's urgent goal to expand the white racial sector chipped away at the colony's proportionately dominant black population.

From Slave Labor to "Free" African Workers

Ironically, plans to resolve Cuba's agricultural labor demands did not stop with Europeans, Asians, and Maya Indians. Using the same principles of indentured labor, Cuban planters and businessmen proposed to contract free Africans, so-called apprentices, to work on sugar and coffee plantations. What proponents of free African labor in the 1840s and 1850s conveniently seemed to forget was that elites in Cuba had used a form of free black labor in the 1820s and 1830s known as *emancipados*, Africans who had been liberated from ships seized for illegally transporting slaves. The schemes undertaken in the Escalera era resulted from the networks of merchants, planters, and Spanish colonial officials involved in European colonization, coolie importation, and the slave trade. African immigration, however, would prove far more difficult to develop as a viable source of free labor, given the multiple categories within the black population and the co-existing systems of coerced labor.

As with coolie labor schemes, plans to import free Africans derived from Anglo-Spanish relations and labor experiments in the Caribbean. Treaties initiated by Britain in 1817 with Spain, Portugal, Brazil, and the Netherlands established the Mixed Commission for the Suppression of the Slave Trade, a set of bilateral courts designed to assess the legal status of the cargo of ships caught engaged in the now illegal slave trade. Unfortunately, the judges had no power to punish slavers, only to seize vessels and free the African captives.[87] Between 1820 and the mid-1830s, Havana's Mixed Commission liberated and processed over 20,000 Africans. Although a large proportion of *emancipados* were redistributed to the British Caribbean, particularly Trinidad and the Bahamas, several thousand remained in Cuba. The majority of these men and women remained under the control of Spanish colonial authorities, many of whom represented some of the major slaveholders in the colony. In other words, instead of acquiring freedom, they were subjected to an ambiguous but highly exploitable status between free and slave. For example, Spanish judge José Buenaventura Esteva, whom his British counterpart James Kennedy characterized as "perhaps the largest proprietor of slaves" in Cuba, acquired hundreds of liberated Africans for his personal use. *Emancipados*, who cost the government nothing to obtain, were also often sold into servitude for a fraction of the slave market price. Frequently, these men and women were delivered to other individuals as political favors or rented out as short-term or seasonal labor.[88]

In the aftermath of the Escalera rebellions, colonial authorities targeted liberated Africans in the revised slave codes of 1844 by requiring that "all *emancipados* on the island who have finished their civil and religious education and instruction shall be taken by the government as soon as they have been placed in liberty in order to furnish them with the provisions and means with which to leave the country."[89] Hundreds in Cuba sought to return to West Africa, such as the "78 free blacks who desired to return to their country" who awaited authorization for the ship *San Antonio* to sail for Africa in January 1845.[90] Scholars, however, have indicated that those who did so relied on their own resources or the assistance from the British, not the Spanish government.[91] Overall, *emancipados*, who were technically neither free nor slave, emerged simultaneously as a vulnerable and accessible labor source and as another threat to Cuba's social hierarchy.[92]

In the 1850s, as another wave of *emancipados* sought repatriation to Africa, thousands of Chinese and Indian indentured workers and European immigrants arrived, and hundreds of free blacks returned from exile or imprisonment with the political amnesty, Cuban officials and planters refocused their attention on how to expand and control the agricultural labor force.[93] Several businessmen proposed importing free African immigrants to fill Cuba's labor needs. For example, in 1853, merchant Ignacio María Zangroniz requested permission to introduce five thousand free African "apprentices."[94] Spanish officials reacted to his proposal negatively, unlike their reaction to proposals for other migrant workers. They claimed introducing free Africans in the midst of slavery would undermine the tranquillity of the island, not to mention offset efforts to expand the white population. Given the racial nature of slavery, choosing free Africans to toil side by side with slaves would create a precarious situation. Moreover, they argued, as long as Cuba maintained its slave system, "Britain would not believe . . . that introducing free people of color would diminish the nature of slavery on the island."[95] The government's rebuff of Zangroniz's proposal made sense. For decades *libres de color* had symbolized the possibility of liberty for the colony's slaves. Hosting yet another "free" black population that would gain its freedom after completing a short contract would only create more havoc for slavery and race relations.

Nevertheless, seeing a lucrative business opportunity, others pressed the issue. In 1857, Ramón Mandillo, a navigator and businessman from Santa Cruz de Tenerife in the Canary Islands, requested permission to bring 10,000 free African immigrants from the Canary Islands to augment Cuba's supply of workers. He claimed, "these men, of the black race, are naturally fit for cultivation and the climate of Cuba; the idea of slavery, condemned by the forces of morality, humanity, civilization, and justice, must be substituted by the colonization of the same black race."

Despite the contradictions in replacing African and African-descended slave laborers with free African immigrant workers in a coerced labor system, Mandillo assured his detractors that he had the best interests of both the government and immigrants in mind.[96]

Officials in the Canary Islands submitted letters in support of Mandillo. Reminiscent of Francisco de Paulo de Castro's comment that there would be "no dangers whatsoever" associated with the coolie trade, administrator Félix Fanlo observed that the project could result in "incalculable advantages" for Cuba, without any "inconvenience."[97] Officials supporting Mandillo's plan called the African immigrants "the most appropriate [choice] for enduring the rigors of Cuba's climate and the hard labor of cultivation."[98] Although officials, businessmen, and merchants disagreed on the question of slave abolition, they conceded that servile men of African descent would secure elites' wealth and Cuba's prosperity. Expectations ran high on the prospects of fulfilling these proposals. In 1859, Ruiz Lacasa wrote to the Ultramar requesting support for his company to be the primary carrier for African immigration to Cuba. His project, which he characterized as "highly humanitarian," proposed to introduce 20,000 free African workers over the course of two to four years. According to Lacasa, free Africans would be much more beneficial than the Chinese immigrants currently working on the plantations. Citing Spain's use of African migrant workers in Fernando Pó (present-day Bioko, Equatorial Guinea) and Corsico Bay (Gabon), islands off the coast of West Africa, he reasoned Spain could and should contract Africans for Cuba.[99] To lend credibility to his plan, Lacasa outlined over thirty-five regulations to insure the endeavor's success, and drew up a sample worker's contract.[100] Others, such as merchant José Suárez Argudin, echoed Lacasa's plans, noting disease as another factor that should compel Cuban authorities to contract African labor. The cholera epidemic of 1853 had caused the death of more than thirty thousand slaves. Outbreaks of yellow fever a few years later compounded health problems.[101]

As Mandillo, Lacasa, Suárez, and others waited for an official response to their proposals, colonial media weighed in on the issue. A fierce debate in the *Diario de la Marina* and *La Prensa* newspapers during the end of January and early February of 1855 highlighted Suarez's point regarding the urgent need for supplemental workers. The articles called for a remedy to the shortage of agricultural labor, with a "main preference, above all others" for workers from Africa.[102] Suarez, of course, agreed, commenting that the pragmatics of the situation forced planters "to look for indirect methods, since the direct methods are insufficient." From his perspective, the best "indirect method" was to introduce enough African immigrants to at least reduce the labor problem. Furthermore, Suárez pointed out that there were no laws prohibiting this type of migration. He argued, "if Cuba permits European, Yucatán, and Chinese immigrants, African immigrants should be allowed." It would, he surmised, breathe new life into Cuba's agricultural industry.[103] By the 1860s, Suárez had joined forces with Cuban plantation owners Manuel Basilio de Cunha Reis from Portugal and Luciano Fernández Perdone from Asturias, Spain, in a final attempt to bring African migrant workers into Cuba.[104]

Spanish officials finally took up the matter with England, with disastrous results. As predicted, Britain vehemently opposed the idea. Cabinet members asserted that because slavery still existed in the Spanish Caribbean, it would be easy for Cuba to convert these free workers into slaves. The Spanish consul, distressed at the news, lamented that the "wealth of Cuba will disappear with the slaves."[105] The negative British reply provoked some Spanish authorities and Cuban planters to become more vocal on the issue of contract labor.

A renewed debate over the issue of nonwhite labor took hold. The Junta Informativa (Information Council) of the Ultramar posed a series of questions to colonial politicians and plantation owners in Cuba and Puerto Rico. The responses informed a massive report. The 350-page document included sections dedicated to *negros libres* responding to the question, "On what basis can the work of free blacks be established as obligatory?" In other words, how could they force the island's existing free population of color to engage in plantation labor and offset the shortages?[106] The answers caused a split among officials and planters. Not all Spanish Caribbean officials agreed it was possible to force free individuals of African descent to work. For instance, commissioners from Puerto Rico José J. de Acosta, Ruiz Bélvis, and Francisco Mariano Quiñones all agreed that it would be impossible to sustain the forced labor of *libres de color*. They concurred that "the population of color in Puerto Rico, primarily the workers . . . is . . . not only one of the most important elements in production, but also merits the most respect for their constant desire to improve their social position." In other words, coerced labor hindered individual development and economic production. Furthermore, Puerto Rican commissioners claimed that any move to establish new legislations forcing *libres de color* into a slavelike labor system would be "dangerous and profoundly disturbing" to the "tranquillity and progress" of the island.[107]

Cuban planters, however, strongly disagreed. Suárez, known for his adamant position on using contract laborers of color, stressed the need for free blacks to be "useful" employees; otherwise they would become burdensome vagrants. Those who did not meet these standards should be "forced to work" in areas stipulated by the government, such as public works.[108] Manuel José de Posadillo, a member of Havana's administrative council, agreed with Suárez. Posadillo followed a typical line of argument regarding African immigrants, stating "their robustness and resistance [to disease] are the most appropriate and useful for cultivating sugarcane."[109] He added that the island needed two kinds of immigrants—*colonos* and *braceros*, migrant workers. *Colonos* would come as families, work the land, and establish residency on the island, like many Europeans. The importation of *braceros* amounted to a business transaction for seasonal labor. Other governments, he concluded, had no right to speculate or interfere in Cuba's internal affairs. As for local unemployment or vagrancy within the free population of color, Posadillo conceded Cuba should adapt several of Puerto Rico's guidelines, such as the *libreta*, a booklet where employers recorded workers' wages, and use local authorities to closely monitor and control free laborers, black and white, to curtail vagrancy.[110]

Due to these controversial and compelling debates, plans to introduce African contract workers never materialized. Rather, slavery persisted alongside the existing immigration streams. Meanwhile, anxious rhetoric on race and immigration continued to fuel Spanish colonial desires of whitening Cuba's population. Cuba's white sector finally achieved this goal in the early 1860s. The 1861 census confirmed the White Population Commission's success. It reported whites as the majority, at 56.8 percent of the colony's total inhabitants.[111] Nearly twenty years after the Escalera repression, Spanish colonial officials in Cuba could finally boast of creating a racial equilibrium in which whites outnumbered the nonwhite and nearly white sectors.

The Impact of Escalera-Era Immigration on Free People of Color

By the 1850s and 1860s, Cuba's foreign visitors observed numerous changes from the milieu of the 1820s and 1830s. "The character of the general population is extremely varied, both as to physical features and costume," observed English native James M. Phillippo on a visit to Cuba in 1853. "Circumstances which add greatly to the picturesque effect of the whole scene, -- Spanish, French, American, Italian, Dutch, African, Creole, Indian, Chinese, presenting every shade of colour and variety of countenance that can be imagined."[112] *Libres de color* figured prominently among the population, at 16.6 percent. According to American Samuel Hazard, who traveled to Cuba in the mid 1860s, "a great proportion of the market is filled with negroes, most of them free."[113] Almost twenty years of white colonization and labor migration, however, had produced an international "white" sector which represented a competitive 11.5 percent of the total population, and included 116,114 Spanish immigrants, 34,046 Chinese, and 743 Yucatán Indians.[114] When combined with creoles, these groups helped create the desired white majority. Closer examination, however, reveals that free people of color had a growth spurt of their own during the Escalera era. Fueled by balanced gender ratios, rising birth rates, and the return of several hundred *libres de color* from exile and imprisonment, the size of this sector almost doubled, from 149,226 to 232,493.[115] Although supplanted by white workers in the cities and indentured agricultural laborers in the countryside, free people of color renewed social networks and took advantage of opportunities to pursue community advancement. The new social and political conditions of the 1860s provided important spaces, however limited, for their struggle for greater equality.

A surge in the number of mutual aid associations accompanied the expanding immigrant sector. To help maintain Spanish authority and cultural dominance, imperial policy favored Cuba's peninsular population. As racial whites from Spain, they were granted by colonial authorities a variety of privileges and liberties far above those of creoles, and inaccessible to the population of African descent or to the legally white Asians and Indians. The Spanish immigrants benefited from the exclusive right to form associations. For instance, Catalan immigrants in Cuba directed commerce and frequently became the proprietors of large tobacco factories and extensive sugar plantations. They created a highly influential mutual aid association called the Charitable Society of the Natives of Catalonia. The only such organization in Cuba until 1848, the society's mission was to provide financial assistance to needy Spanish immigrants and creoles. A second organization influenced cultural affairs. The Havana Artistic and Literary Lyceum, founded in 1844 and open to Spaniards and creoles only, facilitated gatherings for the island's elites. Not until the late 1850s would creoles, as well as Asians and *libres de color*, have the opportunity to form associations, although multiracial membership remained prohibited.[116]

According to Cuban-born Afro-Chinese author Antonio Chuffat Latour, former indentured Chinese laborers, primarily from southern

China, established two major associations in the late 1860s. Hen Yi Tong (Brothers), created in 1867, established a social space for indentured and noncontract Chinese men in Havana. In 1868, the Kit Yi Tong (Union) was instituted by Cantonese workers who arrived in the 1850s and completed their contracts in 1867. They sought alliances among the Chinese community in Havana. A third organization, also organized in 1868, the Yi Seng Tong (Second Alliance), united the Hakka Chinese, an Asian minority who arrived in 1847. Their ethnic and regional distinction created conflict within the Chinese community.[117] As historian Juan Pérez de la Riva has noted, the Chinese during this time period seemed to "divide themselves, subdivide, regroup and divide again," which hindered social cohesion.[118]

Libres de color also expanded the number of *sociedades de socorros mutuos*. In 1858, free *pardo* Antonio Mora established the Sociedad de Socorros Mutuos Gran Poder de Díos (the Great Power of God Mutual Aid Society), located in Havana.[119] Two years later, *morenos libres* José María Armenteros and Vencelad Manresa created the society Nuestra Señora del Cobre (Our Lady of Copper) to support members in another Havana parish. They described themselves as humble artisans who sought to unite under a "pious institution" to "support each other in times of sickness, [and] death."[120] These organizations, and others of the era, held members to high standards. They required affiliates to adhere to colonial codes of social respectability, which included stable employment, whether as a skilled craftsman or semi-skilled laborer, the resources to provide for their family, and the practice of Catholicism.[121] As noted in chapter 4, the *sociedades de socorros mutuos* provided another source for support at a time when colonial authorities prohibited free blacks from joining African ethnic-based *cabildos de nación*. Although interracial membership remained illegal, as in previous instances, these kinds of alliances took place secretly. Free black associations often modeled themselves along the lines of their Spanish and Asian counterparts in their mission to uphold personal honor and provide a social space for their members. Race relations, however, would remain tense as whites resented any change to the slave system, and as *libres de color*, the Chinese, and slaves pushed for greater equality and abolition.

Free blacks' pursuit of literacy and education emerged as a powerful indicator of their desire for self-improvement. As Atlantic debates over the abolition of slavery in Cuba and Puerto Rico gained strength during the 1860s, Rafael María de Labra y Cadrana, a leading Spanish abolitionist, compared the literacy rates of free blacks in Cuba to those in Puerto

Rico, and to whites in Spain, as evidence of the colony's potential for development as a society based on free labor rather than slave labor and of the strong possibilities for Cuba's smooth transition from slavery to emancipation. In support of *libres de color,* Cadrana noted the group's high literacy rates—11.5 percent in 1861, as compared to 25 percent in Spain in 1860, and 9.4 percent of *libres de color* in Puerto Rico in the late 1860s. For Spanish abolitionists, Puerto Rico's large free black population (42%), small slave sector (5%), and absence of Chinese workers, stood as a model for the future of Cuba.[122] Cuba's dependence on slavery could be diminished by free labor that did not inherently require any coercive framework. Expanding the free sector of color, not suppressing it, could be considered one way to achieve the goal of reducing Cuba's dependence on slavery.

During the Escalera era, free blacks promoted opportunities for their community's educational advancement, as they had done in the 1820s and 1830s. Individuals such as *pardo* Matías Velazco, first sergeant of a batallion of color in Havana, reopened his primary school in 1856.[123] In 1861, writer Antonio Medina y Céspedes instituted a school for children of color that educated hundreds, including well-known figures such as Juan Gualberto Gómez, who became an outspoken abolitionist, journalist, and revolutionary, and Afro-Chinese author Antonio Chaffat Latour.[124] In the previous decades, Medina had also started two newspapers for people of African descent, the first in 1842 entitled *El Faro* and the second in 1856 entitled *El Rocío.*[125] Manuscript census data taken in 1861 of the barrio Arsenal in Havana's Jesús María district provides a sample of the literacy rates of a multiracial community, which included white and black artisans, slaves, *emancipados*, and Mexicans. Of the 177 individuals listed, 41 free people of color (23.1%) were recorded as literate. For instance, in Dominga Laquer y Barbosa's Havana household, seven of the nine adults—eight of whom were women working as seamstresses—were listed as literate. The closest comparable white household, that of lawyer Antonio Valdes Heredia, enumerated eight whites who could read and write, which included his wife and daughter, mother, mother-in law, and several other extended family members. None of his fifteen domestic and skilled slaves had these abilities.[126] For households like that of Dominga Laquer y Barbosa, education offered greater personal and economic autonomy. The efforts of men like Velazco and Medina, albeit limited in scope, nevertheless represented a decades-long patient commitment to preparing the black population for new freedoms of the future.

Government reforms of the 1860s expanded educational opportunities for free blacks.[127] The 1863 *Plan de Estudios*, initiated by Captain General José Gutiérrez de la Concha in the 1857 Law of Public Instruction, formally recognized the necessity of providing primary education for children age six to nine. Article 182 facilitated the establishment of schools of color based on the needs of the population.[128] By 1861, 12 percent of free people of African descent had received instruction, as compared to 30 percent of the white sector. The total number of registered students for that year almost tripled, increasing from 486 to 1,256.[129] Nevertheless, thousands of *libres de color* remained without access to primary education, particularly due to the lack of schools in the countryside.[130] For decades to come, free blacks continued to face an uphill battle for greater opportunities.

Despite free blacks' individual accomplishments, reformist initiatives from the Spanish government, and positive commentary from foreign visitors to Cuba, conservative Spanish officials, planters, and creole thinkers remained staunchly opposed to changes that would expand the rights of the African-descended population. From exile in Paris in an 1868, José Antonio Saco warned creoles in Cuba to remember the disasters of Haiti. Even though more than sixty years had passed since the revolution and founding of the first black republic, the refrain continued to resonate among Cuban whites. Saco asserted that Spain's proposal to emancipate thousands of slaves in Cuba would put the colony's security and its social and political hierarchy at extreme risk. With anything other than gradual abolition "slaves would abandon the plantations to enjoy liberty in their own brutal manner." Moreover, because "neither Spain nor Cuba had the resources to indemnify masters," Saco also cautioned colonial officials that slaveholders would retaliate with force to maintain their rightful human property.[131] In that same year, insurgent factions in eastern Cuba made political sovereignty and the abolition of slavery key issues, and sparked the Ten Years' War (1868–1878), the colony's first war for independence. The insurgency would mobilize thousands of slaves and free people of color in the name of Cuban liberty and emancipation. At the close of over two decades of the Escalera era's repressive measures, alongside European immigration and Chinese labor programs that culminated in a white majority, colonial authorities and elites in Cuba had yet to resolve concerns over black revolt or political alliances formed among dissident creoles, slaves and *libres de color*.

* * *

Anxieties over the expanding size of the black population and mounting slave rebellion prompted schemes promoting whitening in Cuba from the 1820s to the early 1840s. To neutralize the potential for another Haitian-style revolution, planters and colonial officials sought to augment the white population through European immigration. Doing so, they reasoned, would infuse the colony with loyal subjects who would help suppress creole dissidence. The addition of Spanish immigrants would also augment the existing population so that whites would quickly become the colony's majority. In short, whitening through immigration offered the solution to Cuba's political and economic stability, at least in theory. In reality, this goal fell short. Despite a healthy stream of workers, particularly from Spain and the Canary Islands, harsh labor and poor health conditions caused massive plantation desertions. Furthermore, the rise in slave importation and the expansion of the free sector of color skewed white immigration totals. By the early 1840s, Cuba's African-descended population reached an all-time high. This forced Spanish colonial officials to change tactics. Before new projects could gain footing, however, the Escalera rebellions shook the colony.

The uprisings in 1843 inflamed previous apprehensions over race. Whitening projects gained new urgency, particularly those designed to fill shortages in agricultural labor and aimed to supplant slaves and *libres de color*. Factors of attraction included the direct recruitment of families and incentives such as tools and transportation, while famine and unemployment in Spain and the Canary Islands helped propel these workers to Cuba and other parts of the Americas. The decades-long repression enabled elites to fuse whitening aims with coercive practices targeting free blacks and slaves. These tactics removed thousands of *libres de color* from the colony, barred free blacks from attempting to disembark, and subjected those who stayed on the island to an array of economic and social prohibitions. Meanwhile, Cuban ports welcomed the arrival of Europeans and indentured workers from China and the Yucatán. Although colonial rhetoric categorized Asians and Indians as white and preferable to workers of African descent—whether slave or free—the realities of plantation labor contradicted this legal distinction. Some claimed old stereotypes of African resiliency in the tropics, and pitched schemes for African contract labor. Concerned about the introduction of yet another free black population into Cuba and sensitive to British objections of trafficking Africans, however, Spanish colonial officials balked at these plans. Nevertheless, authorities continued to exploit coolies, *yucatecos*, *emancipados*, slaves, and *libres de color* precisely because they were not white.

By the 1860s, the elites' whitening goals had come to fruition. On the surface, the white population, excluding Asians and Indians, held a comfortable majority. Race relations, however, had grown more complex. Although the slave sector diminished substantially during the Escalera era, the free population of color had expanded. *Libres de color* used *socorros mutuos* to carve out community spaces and fostered educational opportunities. Simultaneously, Chinese immigrants, particularly those who had completed their contracts, also established mutual aid associations to help cultivate social cohesion. Despite these outlets for self-improvement, free blacks, slaves, as well as the Chinese, remained dissatisfied with their low status and inequality within Cuba's social hierarchy. When creoles rebelled in eastern Cuba and called for independence and abolition, free blacks, slaves, and Asians joined the cause. In response, Spanish officials and creole thinkers invoked the old refrain "remember Haiti."

The Ten Years' War, however, did not stop the flow of immigrants and indentured workers, particularly in the western sugar regions. Merchants brought in additional Yucatán and Chinese contract laborers and Spanish immigrants throughout the 1870s. By 1877, Asians numbered 47,439 and Spaniards 151,000.[132] Reformist policies like the 1870 Moret Law, which declared free all children born to slaves after September 1868 and all slaves over the age of sixty, slashed the proportion of bondsmen and women to 13.6 percent and swelled the ranks of free blacks to 19.2 percent. By the close of the Ten Years' War, Cuba's white majority soared to 63.2 percent.[133] These results highlight the shifting dynamics of race and immigration during the Escalera era. Decades of programs designed specifically to expand Cuba's white sector and reduce the population of African descent produced the desired aim, but at a high cost to the political and social cohesion of Spanish colonial officials, merchants, planters, and creoles. Legally white Asian and Indian indentured workers supplemented plantation slaves in a system that replicated slavery. Caught in the middle, *libres de color* defied perceptions of their passivity posited by contemporaneous observers and historians. When possible, free blacks reclaimed and rebuilt their lives amid oppressive policies. Their perseverance during the Escalera era forged a strong foundation for a new period of struggle for freedom and equality.

Conclusion

"Every visitor to Havana notices the variety in appearance, as well as the numbers of the negro population," noted American writer Samuel Hazard, who traveled to Cuba in late 1860s. Englishman Henry Latham not only reiterated these sentiments but offered a positive appraisal of black residents. After touring American East and Gulf Coast port cities in 1867, he observed, "The condition of the negro population in this city [of Havana] strikes one at the first glance as being better, as far as material comfort goes, than in any part of the United States. . . . The splendid apparel of some of the nurses, housekeepers, and I suppose, freed women, is quite startling. . . . These ladies of coulour are well-to-do and shining in the sun."[1] The commentary by these visitors echoed those made by travelers in the 1820s and 1830s. Free black street vendors continued to sell sweets and hawked their wares, laundresses delivered finished orders, and dock workers attended disembarking ships.[2] These images, although limited in scope, nevertheless offer evidence suggesting not only that free people of color had recovered from the devastating impact of the Escalera era but also that they had made significant strides in securing avenues for economic stability, despite competition from creoles, Spanish immigrants, and Chinese who had completed their contracts. Above all, at the end of the Escalera era, *libres de color* persisted in making their presence felt in Cuban society by continuing to carve out spaces for autonomy, community, and freedom.

As an approach to understanding this process, the *Year of the Lash* has detailed and analyzed the decades between 1844 and 1868 and the impact of the repression on *libres de color*. By exploring free blacks' varying levels of agency in response to the Escalera era's shifting political dynamics, this work has exposed the evolving nature of race relations, slavery, and freedom within nineteenth-century Cuba, the Americas, and the Spanish empire. An examination of the sociopolitical context in which free blacks lived during the years preceding the 1843 uprisings revealed the dual colonial conceptualization of free men and women of African descent as both essential and threatening to nineteenth-century Cuban society. In the wake of the rebellions, colonial administrators implemented prohibitive legislation and dismantled institutions and social organizations as a means to further marginalize the population of color, but officials also contradicted these measures. As dozens of foreign-born free men of color discovered, such as shoemaker José Ramón Ortega of Cartegena, bricklayer Vicente Pacheco of Caracas, and militiaman Juan Arregui of Veracruz, they could successfully protest expulsion orders on the basis of evidence of their ability as skilled artisans, property owners, or soldiers.[3] Others, like midwife Pilar Poveda, managed to have occupational bans lifted.[4] When authorities reinstated the militia of color in the 1850s, hundreds of potential militiamen, such as Marcelino Lamadrón and Gabriel Benítez, proved the most successful at using exemption regulations to their advantage on the basis of poor health and family hardship.[5] Scrutinizing the array of free blacks whose requests for exemption from these same policies were approved sheds light on the complex, multidirectional negotiation process between free blacks and the state. These inconsistencies emphasized the range of ways in which free people of color circumvented, accommodated, or directly resisted coercive and racist practices. Situating *libres de color* at the center of the Escalera era has not only unearthed an important, yet previously untold, perspective on the aftermath of the alleged conspiracy but also provides a vital understanding of the lengths the Spanish colonial state went to as they reasserted control over key political and social elements in Cuba, particularly those pertaining to race, slavery, and rebellion.

This study offers numerous insights into the history of nineteenth-century Cuba, the African diaspora, and the Atlantic World, and their intersections. Moving beyond the existing historical literature on the Conspiracy of La Escalera, which has focused exclusively on verifying the subaltern authenticity or government fabrication of the conspiracy, this project reexamined key sources, such as the Military Commission records, not for proof of a plot, but rather for evidence of African diasporic agency in confronting state authoritarianism in Cuba and abroad.

Piecing together shards of information from archival sources in Cuba, Spain, Mexico, and the United States produced results that radically depart from prior assumptions about both the immediate and long-term impact of the repression on *libres de color.* As the comments of visitors attested, free people of color appeared as ubiquitous in the streets of Cuba in the 1860s as they did in the 1820s. Undoubtedly, the Escalera era had a traumatic impact on Cuba's free black population, but it did not paralyze them. Whether they were free women of color petitioning for returned property, skilled artisans objecting to tighter operating restrictions, or black soldiers protesting military service, collectively these actions revealed how free men and women of African descent clearly comprehended the fissures between colonial policy and practice, an understanding they continued to use to assert their rights during the Escalera era. Despite the deliberate and violent ways colonial officials and elites reinforced political authority and white supremacy, free *pardos* and *morenos* continued to seek out avenues for self-preservation, community survival, and economic stability. This work thus serves as a critical bridge between the existing scholarship on Cuban race relations that focuses on the opening and closing decades of the nineteenth century.

Engaging the African diaspora in the context of the Escalera era also emphasizes the multiple levels of black agency at work among *libres de color.* Although not uniform in their approaches—some struggled to stay in or return to Cuba while others fled the colony—the individual and group actions help us grasp the complexities of freedom in a slave society. Free, but by no means equal to creoles or Spaniards, with varying degrees of legal liberty, and of diverse territorial origins, *libres de color* in early nineteenth-century Cuba learned to negotiate the constraints and contradictions of race and empire by eluding, undermining, or collaborating with the colonial system. Witnesses confessed to crimes they did not commit to save themselves from further torture on the ladder, while others attempted to challenge rulings of banishment and overseas imprisonment. Some appealed to authorities for information on the status of loved ones arrested in connection to the conspiracy, and numerous free black parents sought to exempt their sons from military service. In a world circumscribed by Cuban society and its preoccupations over slavery and empire, free people of color confronted the repression armed with proven legal and extralegal strategies acquired before 1844 and deployed them the best ways they knew how in the name of equality, justice, and freedom.

Reconstructing dominant meanings of race, gender, labor, and colonial service became key in the formation of black identity during the Escalera era. Spanish cultural traditions transported to the Caribbean equated honor with whiteness, a formula that secured white prosperity and dominance in Cuba. Meanwhile, free people of color frequently deployed a counter-representation that infused their work in skilled occupations with personal respectability. Although the areas in which they predominated were deemed dishonorable employment avenues for whites, such as midwifery and masonry, free people of color used these niche roles to foster personal and public integrity. The process transformed their expertise into new social spaces that derived honor from the free black and slave communities. Only as a result of the Escalera era's concentrated policies did creoles and Spaniards finally supplant black artisans and midwives from their traditional occupations in Cuba. Military participation also took on a distinct meaning in the Escalera era. For centuries the militia of color had been recognized as both honorable and critical to colonial defense. The dismantling of these battalions left a permanent scar on free men of color and their families. By the time officials reestablished units of color, a new generation applied its own measure of respectability and recast service as less than honorable, even as colonial officials sought ways to attract black soldiers. These multiple applications of honor highlight it as a malleable but crucial component in colonial social relations.

In the agricultural sector, officials, elites, and merchants pooled their efforts to counter the threat of black rebellion by whitening the plantation workforce and the colony's broader population. The process produced new shades of legal whiteness for indentured Asians and Indians, which grated against Cuba's existing socioracial hierarchy. This racial construct, however, succeeded only rhetorically; the contract labor system mimicked slavery in virtually every way. Coolies suffered much of the same trading networks, working conditions, punishments, and abuse as slaves. This new layer of legally white but economically and socially enslaved workers did little to assuage the plight of free blacks. There was little honor within the plantation complex. Rather, *libres de color* shared their exploitable labor position with Chinese, Indians, and slaves.

Moving beyond Cuban shores, a circum-Atlantic framework added structure and depth to understanding the impact of oceanic crossings in the form of black emigration, overseas imprisonment, banishment, and exile. Foreign-born free people of color avoided deportation by fusing understandings of honor derived from skilled labor and military service to successfully stake their claim to Cuba. From prison and exile, *libres de color* in several countries and on both sides of the Atlantic appealed to the highest Spanish colonial courts to reduce prison sentences, lift banishment rulings, and simply return home to Cuba. Albeit unsuccessful, José Moreno and his compatriots exiled in Mexico, and José Gertrudis Ramos and many others like him imprisoned in Spain and North Africa, petitioned to reside in Cuba.[6] Others took a more covert approach. Men like "El Secretario" took part in a network among free black Cubans in New York, Philadelphia, Baltimore, and New Orleans, while some of those exiled in Veracruz slipped into Havana aboard ships traveling clandestinely.[7] From Mexico and the United States, the free black Cuban diaspora forged new social and political linkages that facilitated transnational communication and surreptitious passage to the island. From these Escalera-generated diasporic spaces, free blacks' varied, but determined, responses demonstrated how they manipulated and maneuvered through fragmented imperial and international policies and adapted to diverse social contexts. Their time in exile or prison, however, would not relieve colonial Cuban officials' apprehensions over race and rebellion.

As the Escalera era came to a close in the late 1860s, free blacks faced a Cuba altered by the brutal policies of empire, race, and slavery that had direct connections to the events of 1844. Two decades of "white" immigration combined with economic, social, and political restrictions helped facilitate the transformation of race relations from its more fluid and flexible nature prior to the Escalera rebellions to a less porous form in the second half of the nineteenth century. Although *libres de color* made a striking recovery from the era of repression, the twenty-four years had taken a heavy toll on their former social influence and economic stability. The loss of loved ones by torture, banishment, imprisonment, or exile, and the siphoning off of employment opportunities eroded the hard-fought status and modest wealth *libres de color* had acquired prior to 1844. Nevertheless, free black men and women continued to rebuild their communities, through mutual aid societies and the pursuit of literacy and education, in preparation for a world that, despite the rhetoric of slave rebellion echoing the fear of Haiti, moved closer to abolition.

The year 1868 marked the close of the Escalera era in Cuba and the start of a new phase in politics, race relations, and slavery in the late Spanish empire. The triple revolutions of that year united Spain under a new civilian-military alliance and liberal constitution that touted widespread civil rights and universal male suffrage, and advocated the abolition of slavery. These changes modified the structures and trajectory of Spanish imperial hegemony.[8] In Puerto Rico, colonial Spanish authorities uncovered and quickly suppressed the Boricua independence plot.[9] Marginalized eastern Cuba planters, whose interests took a back seat to western sugar planters' concerns, also severed relations with Spain. The resulting insurgency, known at the Ten Years' War, gained the support of *libres de color*, slaves, Chinese, and creoles, primarily in eastern Cuba. The multiracial rebel army, led by white and black officers, compelled the movement's leadership to abolish slavery and the coercive apprenticeship system imposed during the Escalera era.[10] The subsequent Little War (1879–1880) rejected the negotiated peace of the Ten Years' War and continued the separatist insurrection led by free blacks Antonio Maceo, Juan Gualberto Gómez—whose free families of color survived the Escalera era—creole José Martí, and Dominican Calixto García until their arrest, imprisonment, and exile in the United States and the Caribbean.[11] For many in Cuba, the legacy of the Escalera era informed how the African-descended population would take part in the colony's determined entrance into the age of revolution and abolition. The insurgencies brought free people of color and slaves, as well as Chinese and creoles, into the armed struggle for independence, abolition, and equality on an unprecedented scale.

Thousands of Cuba's marginalized population, particularly *libres de color* and slaves, joined the revolt. Although royalist forces halted rebel advancement toward the western provinces, the fact that people of African descent had joined the uprising and leaders instituted the abolition of slavery raised western planters' worst fears.[12] In an effort to combat the racially mixed army, colonial officials once again resurrected visions of a Haitian-style revolt that would lead to racial warfare. Ever aware of the potential danger of emancipating slaves who later might not join the army on their own, rebel leaders mobilized slave workers and called for an end to slavery, albeit gradual and indemnified.[13]

Libres de color and slaves were not strangers to the insurgent language, principles, and pronouncements unleashed in the Ten Year's War, which set the stage for the ideals of freedom, citizenship, and nationhood espoused in the final War for Independence (1895–1898). Rather, black perseverance throughout the Escalera era buoyed their involvement in these armed conflicts to come. The legacy of the repression served as an ominous reminder to free women and men of African descent of their tenuous position in Cuba's slave society, and that the struggle to secure their rights would be an uphill battle. The memory of the twenty-four-year repression left an indelible mark on free blacks' individual, racial, and political identities. Despite staggering personal and professional losses, *libres de color* carried their healing scars into new struggles as they continued to maneuver through an evolving system that created, sustained, and bound them.

Notes

Introduction

1. *Aurora*, 29 June 1844, Archivo Nacional de Cuba, Havana, Asuntos Políticos (hereafter ANC-AP), Leg. 42, Exp. 5, p. 5.

2. I use the following terms to refer to the greater free African-descended population in nineteenth-century Cuba: "of color," "of African descent," and *libres de color*. The terms "free" and *libres* are used interchangeably to indicate individuals or groups who are not legally slaves. During the nineteenth century, individuals were denoted in the records I examined for this study as *pardo*, *parda*, *mulata*, and *mulato*, referring to persons who physically appeared to have partial African ancestry, typically a mixture of African and European heritage. Similarly, the terms *moreno*, *morena*, and "black" refer to persons recorded as appearing to be of full African ancestry or dark in complexion. I also use the term "free blacks" to reference the broader population of African descent, on the island or in the diaspora, or to reference issues involving colonial race relations. I use the terms "white," "Spanish," and "creole" (or *criollo*) when referring to individuals and groups recorded or recognized as European or having European parentage in Cuba.

3. Leopoldo O'Donnell to Secretario de Estado y del Despacho de la Gobernación de Ultramar, Havana, 30 March 1844, Archivo Histórico Nacional, Madrid, Ultramar, Gobierno, Cuba (hereafter AHN-UGC), Leg. 4620, Exp. 33, folio 1.

4. José Moreno to Ministro de Gracia y Justicia, Campeche, Mexico, 26 June 1846, Archivo Nacional de Cuba, Havana, Cuba, Real Órdenes y Cédulas (hereafter ANC-ROC), Leg. 159, Exp. 106.

5. Cuba, *Colección de los fallos pronunciados por una sección de la Comisión militar establecida en la ciudad de Matanzas para conocer de la causa de conspiración de la gente de color* (Comisión Militar Ejecutiva y Permanente, 1844). The Military Commission in Matanzas listed sentences for 1,836 individuals (67% *libres de color*) as following: 78 executed (48.7% *libres de color*), 1,165 imprisoned (52.9% *libres de color*), 435 banished (99.5% *libres de color*), 31 sentenced to workhouses and lighter

punishments (58% *libres de color*); Kenneth F. Kiple, *Blacks in Colonial Cuba, 1774–1899* (Gainesville: University of Florida Press, 1976), 88–90; Spain, Superintendencia General Delegada de Real Hacienda, 1841, *Informe fiscal sobre fomento de la población blanca en la isla de cuba y emancipación progresiva de la esclava con una breve reseña de las reformas y modificaciones que para conseguirlo convendría establecer en la legislación y constitución coloniales . . .* (Madrid, 1845), 6. The 1841 census breaks down the 1,007,624 inhabitants as follows: 152,838 (15.1%) free people of color, 436,495 (43.4%) slaves, and 418,291 (41.5%) whites.

6. Celia María Parcero Torre, *La pérdida de la Habana y las reformas borbónicas en Cuba, 1760–1773* (Spain: Junta de Castilla y León, 1998); Nicholas Tracy, *Manila Ransomed: The British Assault on Manila in the Seven Years War* (Exeter: University of Exeter Press, 1995).

7. Jorge I. Dominguez, *Insurrection or Loyalty: The Breakdown of the Spanish American Empire* (Cambridge: Harvard University Press, 1980), 76, 79. Percentages calculated from Tables 6.1 and 6.2—approximately 20,758 black militiamen; total militia for Mexico, Cuba, and Venezuela listed as 51,897; total regular army comprised 15,129; total for all forces approximately 67,026.

8. Dominguez, *Insurrection or Loyalty*, 77.

9. Mónico de Flores, Francisco Abrante, Marcelino Gamarra, et al., *Justo sentimiento de pardos y morenos españoles libres de la Habana* (Havana: Oficina Filantrópica de Don J. M. de Oro, 1823), p. 5, Archivo Nacional de Cuba, Comisión Militar, Leg. 60, No. 2.

10. Robert L. Paquette, *Sugar Is Made with Blood: The Conspiracy of La Escalera and the Conflict between Empires over Slavery in Cuba* (Middleton: Wesleyan University Press, 1988), 177–179, 201–210, 214–215; Jonathan Curry Machado, "Catalysts in the Crucible: Kidnapped Caribbeans, Free Black British Subjects and Migrant British Machinists in the Failed Cuba Revolution of 1843," in Nancy Priscilla Naro, ed., *Blacks, Coloureds and National Identity in Nineteenth-Century Latin America* (London: Institute of Latin American Studies, University of London, 2004), 122–124.

11. Leopoldo O'Donnell, Cuba Captain General, to Secretario del Estado y del Despacho de la Gobernación de Ultramar, Havana, 1 December 1843, Archivo General de Indias, Digital Collection, Archivo Histórico Nacional, Ultramar (hereafter AGI-AHNU), Leg. 8, Exp. 14, No. 2, folios 1–2; Paquette, *Sugar Is Made with Blood*, 209, 210, 214–215.

12. Paquette, *Sugar Is Made with Blood*, 217.

13. Susan Gilman, "The Epistemology of Slave Conspiracy," *Modern Fiction Studies*. 49.1 (Spring 2004), 104; Christopher Schmidt-Nowara, *Empire and Antislavery: Spain, Cuba, and Puerto Rico, 1833–1874* (Pittsburgh: University of Pittsburgh Press, 1999), 29; Ferrer, *Insurgent Cuba*, 2; Paquette, *Sugar Is Made with Blood*, 4.

14. Paquette, *Sugar Is Made with Blood*Franklin W. Knight, *Slave Society in Cuba during the Nineteenth Century* (Madison: University of Wisconsin Press, 1970); Ada Ferrer, *Insurgent Cuba: Race, Nation, and Revolution, 1868–1898* (Chapel Hill: University of North Carolina Press, 1999); Aline Helg, *Our Rightful Share: The Afro-Cuban Struggle for Equality, 1886–1912* (Chapel Hill: University of North Carolina Press, 1995); Aisha K. Finch, "Insurgency at the Crossroads: Cuban Slaves and the Conspiracy of La Escalera, 1841–1844" (Ph.D. diss., New York University, 2007).

15. Francisco González del Valle, *La conspiración de la Escalera: I. José de la Luz*

y Caballero (HavanaEl Siglo XX1925), 29–34;Vidal Morales y Morales, *Iniciadores y primeros mártires de la revolución cubana* (Havana: Avisador Comercial, 1901); José Luciano Franco, "Introducción al proceso de la Escalera," *Boletín del Archivo Nacional* 67 (January-December 1974): 54–63; José Luciano Franco, "Las rebeldías negras," in *Tres ensayos: Alejandro Serguéievich Pushkin. Los pintores impresionistas franceses. Las rebeldías negras* (Havana: Ayon, 1951), 88; Pedro Deschamps Chapeaux, *El negro en la economía habanera* (Havana: UNEAC, 1971), 24–25.

16. Herbert Klein, *Slavery in the Americas: A Comparative Study of Virginia and Cuba* (Chicago: University of Chicago Press, 1967), 193–222; Klein somewhat revises his view in his *African Slavery in Latin America and the Caribbean* (New York: Oxford University Press, 1986), 212. See also Franklin W. Knight, *Slave Society in Cuba*, 81, 96.17. José Manuel de Ximeno, "Un pobre histrión (Plácido)," in *Primer Congreso Nacional de Historia*, 2 vols. (Havana: Sección de artes gráficas, C.S.T. del Institúto cívico militar 1943), 371–377; Daisy Cué Fernández, "Plácido y la conspiración de la Escalera," *Santiago* 42 (June 1981): 145–206—see reprint in Salvador Bueno, ed., *Acerca de Plácido* (Havana: Letras Cubans,1985), 427–483; Rodolfo Sarracino, "Inglaterra y las rebeliones esclavas cubanas: 1841–1851," *Revista de la Biblioteca Nacional José Martí* 28 (May-August 1986): 81; Jorge Castellanos, *Plácido, poeta social y político* (Miami: Ediciones Universal, 1984); Enildo García, *Plácido: Poeta mulato de la emancipación, 1809*–1844New York: Senda Nueva de Ediciones, 1986; Walterio Carbonell, "Plácido, ?Conspirador?" *Revolución y cultura* 2 (February 1987): 57.

18. Hugh Thomas, *Cuba: The Pursuit of Freedom* (New York: Harper & Row, 1971), xxi; 81, 96, 200–206; Arthur Corwin, *Spain and the Abolition of Slavery in Cuba, 1817–1886* (Austin: University of Texas Press, 1967), 81; Gwendolyn Midlo Hall, *Social Control in Slave Plantation Societies: A Comparison of St. Domingue and Cuba* (Baltimore: Johns Hopkins University Press, 1971), 57–62; David R. Murray, *Odious Commerce: Britain, Spain and the Abolition of the Cuban Trade* (London: Cambridge University Press, 1980), 172, 178.

19. Philip S. Foner, *A History of Cuba and Its Relations with the United States* (New York: International Publishers, 1962), 1: 214–228.

20. Paquette, *Sugar Is Made with Blood*, 248–249.

21. Finch, "Insurgency at the Crossroads," 8.22. Deschamps Chapeaux, *El negro en la economía habanera*, 24–25; Pedro Deschamps Chapeaux and Juan Pérez de la Riva, eds., *Contribución a la historia de la gente sin historia* (Havana: Editorial de Ciencias Sociales, 1974), 5–27, 55–110.

23. Helg, *Our Rightful Share*, 3–4; Aline Helg, "Race and Black Mobilization in Colonial and Early Independent Cuba: A Comparative Perspective," *Ethnohistory* 44.1 (Winter 1997): 55.

24. Many of the restrictions on economic opportunities are detailed in Appendix II of Paquette, *Sugar Is Made with Blood*, 273–274. The following archival sources address prohibitions on international mobility and social institutions: order banning black disembarkation in Cuba: Leopoldo O'Donnell, Havana, 13 May 1844, ANC-ROC, Leg. 133, Exp. 220; order dismantling Cuban militias of color: Leopoldo O'Donnell to Ministro de Estado, Havana, 15 June 1844, ANC-AP, Leg. 42, Exp. 3, folios 1–2.

25. See, in chronological order of publication: Fernando Ortiz Fernández, "Los cabildos afro-cubanos," *Revista Bimestre Cubana* 16 (January-February 1921): 9–15;

Knight, *Slave Society in Cuba during the Nineteenth Century* (1970); Pedro Deschamps Chapeaux, "Historia de la gente sin historia: testamentaria de pardos y morenos libres en la Habana del siglo XIX," *Revista de la Biblioteca José Martí* 63 (May-August 1971): 45–54; Deschamps Chapeaux, *El negro en la economía habanera* (1971); Franklin W. Knight, "Cuba," in *Neither Slave nor Free: The Freedman of African Descent in the Slave Societies of the New World*, edited by David W. Cohen and Jack P. Greene (Baltimore: Johns Hopkins University Press, 1972), 279–308; Deschamps Chapeaux, *Contribución a la historia de la gente sin historia* (Havana: Editorial de Ciencias Sociales, 1974); Herbert S. Klein, *African Slavery in Latin America and the Caribbean* (New York: Oxford University Press, 1986); Paquette, *Sugar Is Made with Blood* (1988); Consuelo Naranjo Orovio and Armando García González, *Racismo e inmigración en Cuba en el siglo XIX* (Madrid: Ediciones Doce Calles, S.I., 1996);Philip A. Howard, *Changing History: Afro-Cuban Cabildos and Societies of Color in the Nineteenth Century* (Baton Rouge: Louisiana State University Press, 1998); Christopher Schmidt-Nowara, *Empire and Antislavery: Spain, Cuba, and Puerto Rico, 1833–1874* (Pittsburgh: University of Pittsburgh Press, 1999); María Elena Díaz, *The Virgin, the King, and the Royal Slaves of El Cobre: Negotiating Freedom in Colonial Cuba, 1670–1780* (Stanford: Stanford University Press, 2000); Daniel E. Walker, *No More, No More: Slavery and Cultural Resistance in Havana and New Orleans* (Minneapolis: University of Minnesota Press, 2004); Manuel Barcia Paz, "Fighting with the Enemy's Weapons: The Usage of the Colonial Legal Framework by Nineteenth-Century Cuban Slaves," *Atlantic Studies*3.2 (October 2006): 159–188; Matt D. Childs, *The 1812 Aponte Rebellion in Cuba and the Struggle against Atlantic Slavery* (Chapel Hill: University of North Carolina Press, 2006);Alejandro de la Fuente, "Slaves and the Creation of Legal Rights in Cuba: *Coartación* and *Papel*." *Hispanic American Historical Review* 87.4 (2007): 659–692;Alejandro de la Fuente, *Havana and the Atlantic in the Sixteenth Century* (Chapel Hill: University of North Carolina Press, 2008).

26. For the abolition of slavery, post-emancipation society, and race relations in twentieth-century Cuba, see: Rebecca J. Scott, *Slave Emancipation in Cuba: The Transition to Free Labor, 1860–1899* (Princeton: Princeton University Press, 1985); Rebecca J. Scott, *Degrees of Freedom: Louisiana and Cuba after Slavery* (Cambridge: Belknap Press of Harvard University Press, 2005); Tomás Fernández Robaina, *El Negro en Cuba, 1902–1958: Apuntes para historia de la lucha contra la discriminación racial* (Havana: Editorial de Ciencias Sociales, 1990); Helg, *Our Rightful Share*; Alejandro de la Fuente, *A Nation for All: Race, Inequality, and Politics in Twentieth-Century Cuba* (Chapel Hill: University of North Carolina Press, 2001). For the independence struggle, see Ada Ferrer, *Insurgent Cuba: Race, Nation, and Revolution, 1868–1898* (Chapel Hill: University of North Carolina Press, 1999); Rodrigo Lazo, *Writing to Cuba: Filibustering and Cuban Exiles in the United States* (Chapel Hill: University of North Carolina Press, 2005); Teresa Prados-Torreira, *Mambisas: Rebel Women in Nineteenth-Century Cuba* (Gainesville: University Press of Florida, 2005).27. Cuba, *Colección de los fallos*; Paquette, *Sugar Is Made with Blood*, 229.

28. Kiple, *Blacks in Colonial Cuba*, 88–90; Spain, Superintendencia General Delegada de Real Hacienda, *Informe fiscal sobre fomento de la población blanca en la isla de cuba y emancipación progresiva*, 6. The 1841 census lists the total Cuban population at 1,007,624; the 1,230 free people of color sentenced represented 0.12 percent of the total population.

29. Works on free people of color in slave societies in the circum-Caribbean and Latin America include Barry Gaspar and Darlene Clark Hine, eds., *Beyond Bondage: Free Women of Color in the Americas* (Urbana: University of Illinois Press, 2004). In the United States: Kimberly S. Hanger, *Bounded Lives, Bounded Places: Free Black Society in Colonial New Orleans, 1769–1803* (Durham: Duke University Press, 1997), and Ira Berlin, *Slaves without Masters: The Free Negro in the Antebellum South* (New York: New Press, 1974). In the Spanish Caribbean: Deschamps Chapeaux, *El negro en la economía habanera*; Deschamps Chapeaux, *Contribución a la historia de la gente sin historia*; and Jay Kinsbruner, *Not of Pure Blood: The Free People of Color and Racial Prejudice in Nineteenth-Century Puerto Rico* (Durham: Duke University Press, 1996). In the British Caribbean: Edward C. Cox, *Free Coloreds in the Slave Societies of St. Kitts and Grenada, 1743–1833* (Knoxville: University of Tennessee Press, 1984); Jerome S. Handler, *The Unappropriated People: Freedmen in the Slave Society of Barbados* (Baltimore: Johns Hopkins University Press, 1974); and Mavis C. Campbell, *The Dynamics of Change in a Slave Society A Sociopolitical History of the Free Coloreds of Jamaica, 1800–1865* (London: Associated University Presses, 1976). In the French Caribbean: Stewart R. King; *Blue Coat or Powdered Wig: Free People of Color in Pre-Revolutionary Saint Domingue* (Athens: University of Georgia Press, 2001); and John D. Garrigus, *Before Haiti: Race and Citizenship in French Saint-Domingue* (New York: Palgrave Macmillan, 2006). In South America: A.J.R. Russell-Wood, "Colonial Brazil," in *Neither Slave nor Free: The Freedman of African Descent in the Slave Societies of the New World*, edited by David W. Cohen and Jack P. Greene (Baltimore: Johns Hopkins University Press, 1972), 130; Christine Hunefeldt, *Paying the Price of Freedom: Family and Labor among Lima's Slaves, 1800–1854* (Berkeley: University of California Press, 1995); Zephyr Frank, *Dutra's World: Wealth and Family in Nineteenth-Century Rio de Janeiro* (Albuquerque: University of New Mexico Press, 2004); and Mariana L. R. Dantas, *Black Townsmen: Urban Slavery and Freedom in the Eighteenth-Century Americas* (New York: Palgrave Macmillan, 2008), Recent debates have emerged over recategorizing urban Spanish American areas of the sixteenth and seventeenth century, such as Mexico and Ecuador, as slave societies, rather than societies with slaves. See Rina Cáceres Gómez, *Negros, mulatos, esclavos y libertos en la Costa Rica del siglo XVII* (Mexico City: Instituto Panamericano de Geografía e Historia, 2000); Ben Vinson III, *Bearing Arms for His Majesty: The Free-Colored Militia in Colonial Mexico* (Stanford: Stanford University Press, 2001); and see Herman L. Bennett, *Africans in Colonial Mexico: Absolutism, Christianity, and Afro-Creole Consciousness, 1570–1640* (Bloomington: Indiana University Press, 2003); and Sherwin K. Bryant, "Slavery and the Context of Ethnogenesis: Africans, Afro-Creoles, and the Realities of Bondage in the Kingdom of Quito, 1600–1800" (Ph.D. diss., Ohio State University, 2005).

30. De la Fuente, "Slaves and the Creation of Legal Rights in Cuba," 659–692; Barcia, "Fighting with the Enemy's Weapons,"159–188; Laurent Dubois, *A Colony of Citizens: Revolution and Slave Emancipation in the French Caribbean, 1787–1804* (Chapel Hill: University of North Carolina Press, 2004), 74; Díaz, *The Virgin, the King, and the Royal Slaves of El Cobre*.

31. Gaspar and Hine, eds., *Beyond Bondage*; David Barry Gaspar and Darlene Clark Hine, *More than Chattel: Black Women and Slavery in the Americas* (Bloomington: Indiana University Press, 1996); Bernard Moitt, *Women and Slavery in the French Antilles, 1635–1848* (Bloomington: Indiana University Press, 2001); Luis Martínez

Fernández, "The 'Male City' of Havana: The Coexisting Logics of Colonialism, Slavery, and Patriarchy in Nineteenth-Century Cuba," in *Women and the Colonial Gaze*, edited by Tamara L. Hunt and Micheline R. Lessard (New York: New York University Press, 2002), 104–116; Teresa Prados-Torriera, *Mambisas: Rebel Women in Nineteenth-Century Cuba* (Gainesville: University Press of Florida, 2005); Félix V. Matos Rodríguez, *Women and Urban Change in San Juan, Puerto Rico, 1820–1868* (Gainesville: University Press of Florida, 1999); Eileen J. Suárez Findlay, *Imposing Decency: The Politics of Sexuality and Race in Puerto Rico, 1870–1920* (Durham: Duke University Press, 1999).

32. Ben Vinson III and Stewart King, eds., "Introducing the 'New' African Diasporic Military History in Latin America," Special Issue, *Journal of Colonialism and Colonial History* 5.2 (Fall 2004); Vinson, *Bearing Arms for His Majesty*; Peter M. Voelz, *Slave and Soldier: The Military Impact of Blacks in the Colonial Americas* (New York: Garland, 1993); Hendrik Kraay, *Race, State, and Armed Forces in Independence-era Brazil: Bahia, 1790's–1840's* (Stanford: Stanford University Press, 2001). See also Zachary Morgan, "Legislating the Lash: Race and the Conflicting Modernities of Enlistment and Corporal Punishment in the Brazilian Military during the Empire," *Journal of Colonialism and Colonial History* 5.2 (Fall 2004)1–47.33. Neville A. T. Hall, *Slave Society in the Danish West Indies: St. Thomas, St. John, and St. Croix* (Baltimore: Johns Hopkins University Press, 1992), 159; Dubois, *A Colony of Citizens*, 74; Patrick J. Carroll, *Blacks in Colonial Veracruz: Race, Ethnicity, and Regional Development* (Austin: University of Texas Press, 2001), 86; Kinsbruner, *Not of Pure Blood*, 19.

34. Douglas R. Cope, *The Limits of Racial Domination: Plebian Society in Colonial Mexico, 1660–1720* (Madison: University of Wisconsin Press, 1994), 15.

35. Childs, *The 1812 Aponte Rebellion*, 48, 63;Paquette, *Sugar Is Made with Blood*,125, 127;David Sartorius, "My Vassals: Free-Colored Militias in Cuba and the Ends of Spanish Empire," *Journal of Colonialism and Colonial History* 5.2 (2004): 2.36. For a detailed discussion, see John Thornton, *Africa and the Africans in the Making of the Atlantic World, 1400–1800* (Cambridge: Cambridge University Press, 1998); David Eltis, *The Rise of Africans in the Americas* (Cambridge: Cambridge University Press, 2000); David Brion Davis, *Inhuman Bondage: The Rise and Fall of Slavery in the New World* (New York: Oxford University Press, 2006); Phillip D. Curtain, *The Rise and Fall of the Plantation Complex: Essays in Atlantic History* (Cambridge: Cambridge University Press, 1993).

37. Laurent Dubois, *Avengers of the New World: The Story of the Haitian Revolution* (Cambridge: Belknap Press of Harvard University Press, 2004); Dubois, *A Colony of Citizens*; Childs, *The 1812 Aponte Rebellion*; David P. Geggus, ed., *The Impact of the Haitian Revolution in the Atlantic World* (Columbia: University of South Carolina Press, 2001); Aline Helg, *Liberty and Equality in Caribbean Colombia, 1770–1835* (Chapel Hill: University of North Carolina Press, 2004); Gelien Matthews, *Caribbean Slave Revolts and the British Abolitionist Movement* (Baton Rouge: Louisiana State University Press, 2006).

38. *Emancipator and Weekly Chronicle*, 1 May 1844, and *The Liberator*, 9 February 1844, Nineteenth Century U.S. Newspapers Database, Woodruff Library, Emory University, Atlanta, Georgia (hereafter NCUS-Emory); *The Daily Picayune*, 20 April 1844, Latin American Newspaper Collection, National Archives and Records

Administration, Washington, D.C. (hereafter NA-LANC); *The Spectator*, 25 April 1844, Archivo General de Indias, Seville, Digital Collection, Archivo Histórico Nacional Ultramar, Seville, Spain (hereafter AGI-AHNU).

39. O'Donnell to Ministro de Estado, Havana, 15 June 1844, ANC-AP, Leg. 42, Exp. 3.

40. José Moreno to Ministro de Gracia y Justicia, Campeche, Mexico, 26 June 1846, Archivo Nacional de Cuba, Real Órdenes y Cédulas (hereafter ANC-ROC), Leg. 159, Exp. 106; "Los individuos José Gertrudis Ramos, Jose Carbo, Damian de Fleites y Damaso Ramos, soliciten indulto," 1847, Archivo Histórico Nacional, Madrid, Ultramar, Gobierno, Cuba (hereafter AHN-UGC), Leg. 4627, Exp. 9, Nos. 1–3; Angel Calderon de la Barca, Spanish Consul in U.S. to O'Donnell, Washington, D.C., 31 December 1844, ANC-AP, Leg. 140 Exp. 39.

41. Kiple, *Blacks in Colonial Cuba*, 95–96. The total 1,396,530 inhabitants enumerated in the 1860 census are broken down as follows: 793,484 (56.8%) whites, 232,493 (16.7 %) free people of color, and 370,553 (26.5 %) slaves.

1 / "Very Prejudicial"

1. Abiel Abbot, *Letters Written in the Interior of Cuba, between the Mountains of Arcana, to the East, and of Cuscu, to the West, in the Months of February, March, April, and May 1828* (Boston: Bowles and Dearborn, 1829), 99.

2. James Edward Alexander, *Transatlantic Sketches: Comprising Visits to the Most Interesting Scenes in North and South America, and the West Indies. With Notes on Negro Slavery and Canadian Emigration* (London: Richard Bentley, 1833), 1: 320.

3. Antonio Gallenga, *The Pearl of the Antilles* [1873] (New York: Negro Universities Press, 1970), 26, 28; Robert F. Jameson, *Letters from the Havana*, in Louis A. Pérez, Jr., ed., *Slaves, Sugar, and Colonial Society: Travel Accounts of Cuba 1801–1899* (Wilmington, Del.: Scholarly Resources, 1992), 5; John G. F. Wurdemann, *Notes on Cuba* (Boston: James Munroe, 1844), reprinted in Robert M. Goldwin, ed., *Physician Travelers* (New York: Arno Press, 1971), 40.

4. Gallenga, *Pearl of the Antilles*, 26, 28; Jameson, *Letters from the Havana*, 5; Wurdemann, *Notes on Cuba*, 40; Luis Martínez-Fernández, *Fighting Slavery in the Caribbean: The Life and Times of a British Family in Nineteenth-Century Havana* (Armonk, N.Y.: M. E. Sharpe, 1998), 68.

5. Pedro Deschamps Chapeaux, *Los batallones pardos y morenos libres* (Havana: Instituto Cubano del Libro, 1976), 42; Childs, *The 1812 Aponte Rebellion*, 86.

6. Jameson, *Letters from the Havana*, in Pérez, *Slaves, Sugar, and Colonial Society*, 6. Italics in the original.

7. Abbot, *Letters Written in the Interior of Cuba*, 244.

8. Kiple, *Blacks in Colonial Cuba, 1774–1899*, 88. The 1827 census lists at total population of 704,487, with 106,494 free people of color, 286,942 slaves, and 311,051 whites.

9. Abbot, *Letters Written in the Interior of Cuba*, 99; B. Huber, Aperçu statistique de l'ile de Cuba, précédé de quelques lettres sur la Havane (Paris, 1826).

10. Juan Francisco Manzano, *Autobiography of a Runaway Slave* [1840] (Detroit: Wayne State University Press, 1996), 13, 15, 119, 125; ANC-AP, Leg. 140, Exp. 36.

12. De Flores, *Justo sentimiento de pardos y morenos*, 1.

13. Pilar Poveda to Cuba Captain General, Havana, 27 August 1845, ANC-IP, Leg. 40, Exp. 2114.

14. See David W. Cohen and Jack P. Greene, eds., *Neither Slave nor Free: The Freedman of African Descent in the Slave Societies of the New World* (Baltimore: Johns Hopkins University Press, 1972); Arthur Stinchcombe, *Sugar Island Slavery in the Age of Enlightenment: The Political Economy of the Caribbean World* (Princeton: Princeton University Press, 1995), 159.

15. See Mary C. Karasch, *Slave Life in Rio de Janeiro, 1808–1850* (Princeton: Princeton University Press, 1987); James Sweet, "Manumission in Rio de Janeiro, 1749–54: An African Perspective," *Slavery and Abolition* 24.1 (April 2003): 60.

16. De la Fuente, *Havana and the Atlantic*, 174. See also Klein, *African Slavery in Latin America and the Caribbean*, 227.17. Francisco Arango to King of Spain, Havana, 30 August 1830, Codigo Negro, No. 2, Archivo General de Indias, Seville, Spain, Indiferente, Leg. 2828, folio 5 (hereafter AGI-Indiferente 2828).

18. Stinchcombe, *Sugar Island Slavery*, 159; Alejandro de la Fuente, "Slaves and the Creation of Legal Rights in Cuba: Coartación and Papel," *Hispanic American Historical Review* 87 (2007), 4Childs, *The 1812 Aponte Rebellion*, 65.19. Alejandro de la Fuente, *Havana and the Atlantic in the Sixteenth Century* (Chapel Hill: University of North Carolina Press, 2008), 171, 174, 255 n. 68; Childs, *The 1812 Aponte Rebellion*, 64,116; Philip A. Howard, *Changing History: Afro-Cuban Cabildos and Societies of Color in the Nineteenth Century* (Baton Rouge: Louisiana State University Press, 1998), 4920. Laird W. Bergad, Fe Iglesias García, and María del Carmen Barcia, *The Cuban Slave Market, 1790–1880* (New York: Cambridge University Press, 1995), 122–142.

21. Klein, *African Slavery in Latin America*, 194–195.

22. Kiple, *Blacks in Colonial Cuba*, 84. Census data is reported as follows. 1774: total free people of color 30, 847, with 16,152 men (52.3%) and 14,695 women (47.6%); 1792, total free people of color 54,152, with 25,211 men (46.6%) and 28,941 women (53.4%); 1817, total free people of color 114,058, with 58,885 men (51.6%) and 55,173 women (48.4%); 1827, total free people of color 106,494, with 51,962 men (48.8%) and 54,532 women (51.2%); 1841, total free people of color 152,838, with 75,703 men (49.5%) and 77,135 women (50.5%).

23. Ramón de la Sagra, *Historia económico-política y estadística de la isla de Cuba o sea de sus progresos en la población, la agricultura, el comercio y rentas* (Havana: Imprenta de las Viudas de Arazoza y Solér, 1831), 21.

24. Cuba's 1827 census lists 54,532 free women of color out of the total 300,582 women on the island (142,398 white females and 103,652 slave females). The 1827 census states that the birth ratio for free women of color between the ages of twelve and forty was 1:6. In comparison, the white birth ratio was 1:7. Furthermore, free black women, *pardas* in particular, experienced a 79.2% increase in births between 1817 and 1827. The breakdown is as follows: *pardas* 57.7%, *morenas* 11.5%, slave women 44.3%, white women 48.7%. Sagra, *Historia económico-política y estadística*, 21, 23; Paquette, *Sugar Is Made with Blood*, 121, Kiple, *Blacks in Colonial Cuba*, 91, 93–94.

25. Sherry Johnson, *Social Transformation of Eighteenth-Century Cuba* (Gainesville: University of Florida Press, 2001), 47–48, 50; Jane Landers, *Black Society in Spanish Florida* (Urbana: University of Illinois Press, 1999,) 59, 62, 64.

26. Jane Landers, *Atlantic Creoles in the Age of Revolution* (Cambridge: Harvard University Press, 2010), 167.

27. Tomás Álvarez to Cuba Captain General, Havana, 30 April 1844, ANC-AP, Leg. 140, Exp. 31; Landers, *Atlantic Creoles in the Age of Revolution*, 116, 118, 168.

28. Nathalie Dessens, *From Saint-Domingue to New Orleans: Migration and Influences* (Gainesville: University of Florida Press, 2007), 15, 19, 18, 20; Susan Branson and Leslie Patrick, "'Étrangers dans un pays étrange': Saint-Domingan Refugees of Color in Philadelphia," in *Impact of the Haitian Revolution in the Atlantic World*, edited by David Geggus (Columbia, S.C.: University of South Carolina Press, 2001); Duvon Corbitt, "Immigration in Cuba," *Hispanic American Historical Review* 22 (May 1942): 287; Rafael Duharte Jímenez, *El negro en la sociedad colonial* (Santiago de Cuba: Editoral Oriente, 1988), 91.

29. David P. Geggus, *Haitian Revolutionary Studies* (Bloomington: Indiana University Press, 2002), 179–181.

30. Juan Saldana to Cuba Captain General, Havana, 6 May 1844, ANC-AP, Leg. 140, Exp. 35.

31. James D. Henderson, "Mariana Grajales: Black Progenitress of Cuban Independence," *Journal of Negro History* 63.2 (April 1978): 136.

32. Rebecca J. Scott and J. M. Hébrard, "Les papiers de la liberté: Une mère africaine et ses enfants à l'époque de la révolution haïtienne, " *Genèses* 66 (2007): 4–29.

33. Gabriel Debien, "The Saint-Domingue Refugees in Cuba, 1793–1815," 89–90 in *The Road to Louisiana: The Saint-Domingue Refugees 1792–1809*, edited by Carl A. Brasseaux and Glenn R. Conrad (Lafayette: University of Southwestern Louisiana, 1992); David Brading, *The First America: The Spanish Monarchy, Creole Patriots, and the Liberal State 1492–1867* (Cambridge: Cambridge University Press, 1991), 540. Between April and August of 1809, a total of 6,060 individuals left on 40 ships listed as follows: whites, total 1,887 (989 men, 455 women, 443 children under age 15); free people of color, total 2,060 (282 men, 926 women, 852 children under age 15); slaves, total 2,113 (603 men, 905 women, 605 children under age 15). Another 605 people departed on three ships in early August 1809, but no breakdown was provided; Dessens, *From Saint-Domingue to New Orleans*, 27. The final total of Haitian refugees leaving Cuba included 2,731 whites, 3,102 free people of color, and 3,226 slaves.

34. "Solicitudes de negros extranjeros para que no se les deporte," ANC-AP, Leg. 141, No. 6, 1844.

35. Philip S. Foner, *Antonio Maceo: The "Bronze Titan" of Cuba's Struggle for Independence* (New York: Monthly Review Press, 1977), 7–8.

36. Juan Arregui to Cuba Captain General, Havana, 4 May 1844, ANC-AP, Leg. 140, Exp. 17; "Solicitudes de negros extranjeros para que no se les deporte," 1844, ANC-AP, Leg. 141, Exp. 6.

37. *Libres de color* in Cuba represented the following proportions: 1817, 20.6% or 114,058 out of a total population of 553,0331827, 15.1% or 106,494 out of a total population of 704,487; 1841, 15.2% or 152,838 out of 704,487 island inhabitants; Kiple, *Blacks in Colonial Cuba*, 84–86, 88–90. Percentages for Puerto Rico are as follows: 1802, 43.8%, 1812, 43.6%, 1835, 43%; David W. Cohen and Jack P. Greene, eds., "Introduction" to *Neither Slave nor Free: The Freedman of African Descent in the Slave Societies of the New World* (Baltimore: Johns Hopkins University Press, 1972), 4; Kinsbruner, *Not of Pure Blood*, 31; George Reid Andrews, *Afro-Latin America, 1800–2000* (New York: Oxford University Press, 2004), 41.

38. Peter Blanchard, *Under the Flags of Freedom: Slave Soldiers and the Wars of*

Independence in Spanish South America (Pittsburgh: University of Pittsburgh Press, 2008), 35.

39. Bergad, Iglesias García, and Barcia, *The Cuban Slave Market*, 26; Landers, *Atlantic Creoles in the Age of Revolution*, 206; Martínez-Fernández, *Fighting Slavery in the Caribbean*, 42; David Eltis, "The Nineteenth-Century TransAtlantic Slave Trade: An Annual Time Series of Imports into the Americas Broken down by Region," *Hispanic American Historical Review* 67.1 (1987): 122–123.

40. Paquette, *Sugar Is Made with Blood*, 119; Knight, *Slave Society in Cuba*, 94; Teresa Ortiz, "From Hegemony to Subordination: Midwives in Early Modern Spain," in *The Art of Midwifery: Early Modern Midwives in Europe*, edited by Hilary Marland (London: Routledge, 1993), 100, 102; Sarah C. Chambers, *From Subjects to Citizens: Honor, Gender, and Politics in Arequipa, Peru, 1780–1854* (University Park: Penn State University Press, 1999), 167–168; Ann Twinam, *Public Lives, Private Secrets: Gender, Honor, Sexuality, and Illegitimacy in Colonial Spanish America* (Stanford: Stanford University Press, 1999), 32.

41. Paquette, *Sugar Is Made with Blood*, 83, 85; Dale Tomich, "The Wealth of Empire: Francisco Arango y Parreño, Political Economy, and the Second Slavery in Cuba," *Comparative Studies in Society and History* 45.1 (January 2003): 1, 19; Christopher Schmidt-Nowara, *Empire and Antislavery: Spain, Cuba, and Puerto Rico, 1833–1874* (Pittsburgh: University of Pittsburgh Press, 1999), 18.

42. Joseph J. McCadden, "The New York-to-Cuba Axis of Father Varela," *The Americas* 20.4 (April 1964): 376, 378; Landers, *Atlantic Creoles in the Age of Revolution*, 166.

43. Schmidt-Nowara, *Empire and Antislavery*, 18; McCadden, "The New York-to-Cuba Axis of Father Varela," 378.

44. Kiple, *Blacks in Colonial Cuba*, 88; Francisco Arango y Parreño to King of Spain, 30 August 1830, AGI-Indiferente 2828, folio 4.

45. AGI-Indiferente 2828, folios 4, 6.

46. Ibid.; AP, Leg. 140, Exp. 36.

47. Kiple, *Blacks in Colonial Cuba*, 88; AGI-Indiferente 2828.

48. José Antonio Saco, *Historia de la esclavitud de la raza africana en el Nuevo mundo y el especial en los países américo-hispanos* (Havana: Cultural S.A., 1938), 4: 350–352.

49.Kiple, *Blacks in Colonial Cuba*, 88; AGI-Indiferente 2828.

50. José Antonio Saco, *La supresión del tráfico de esclavos en Cuba* (Paris: Imprenta de Panckoucke, 1845), 50.

51. Eduardo Torres-Cuevas, Jorge Ibarra Cuesta, and Mercedes García Rodríguez, eds., *Félix Varela: El que nos enseñó primero en pensar* (Havana: Imagen Contemporánea, 1997), 2: 115, 120–121.

52. Richard Burleigh Kimball, *Cuba, and the Cubans; Comprising a History of the Island of Cuba, Its Present Social, Political and Domestic Condition; Also, Its Relation to England and the United States. By the author of "Letters from Cuba." With an appendix, containing important statistics, and a reply to Senor Saco on Annexation, etc.* (New York: Samuel Hueston, 1850), 57.

53. Saco, *Historia de la esclavitud*, 4: 350–352.

54. Sibylle Fischer, *Modernity Disavowed: Haiti and the Cultures of Slavery in the Age of Revolution* (Durham: Duke University Press, 2004), 80.

55. Lyman Johnson, "Artisans," in *Cities and Society in Colonial Latin America*, edited by Louisa Schell Hoberman and Susan Midgen Socolo (Albuquerque: University of New Mexico Press, 1986), 239, 241;Kinsbruner, *Not of Pure Blood*, 79.

56. Juan Francisco Manzano, *Poems by a Slave in the Island of Cuba, Recently Liberated*. Translated by R. R. Madden (London: T. Ward, 1840); Manzano, *Autobiography of a Runaway Slave*, 6.

57. Gabriel de la Concepción Valdés, *Poesias completas de Placido* (Paris: C. Denné Schmitz, 1856); Fischer, *Modernity Disavowed*, 77, 79.

58. Manzano, *Autobiography of a Runaway Slave*, 15; Fischer, *Modernity Disavowed*, 9; Paquette, *Sugar Is Made with Blood*, 110.

59. Deschamps Chapeaux, *El negro en la economía habanera*, 65, 67, 74, 122, 128, 173; Instrucción Pùblica, ANC, Leg. 40, No. 2115.

60. Deschamps Chapeaux, *El negro en la economía habanera*, 67–68; Martínez-Fernández, *Fighting Slavery in the Caribbean*, 73.

61. Deschamps Chapeaux, *El negro en la economía habanera*, 65, 67, 74–79.

62. Mónico, et al, *Justo sentimiento*, 208, Archivo Nacional de Cuba, Comisión Militar (hereafter ANC-CM), Leg. 60, Exp. 2, folio 208.

63. José Antonio Saco, *Colección de papeles científicos, históricos, políticos, y de otros ramos sobre la isla de Cuba* (Havana: Ministerio de Educación, 1960), 1: 216.

64. Saco, *Colección de papeles científicos*, 216–217.

65. Torres-Cuevas, Ibarra Cuesta, and García Rodríguez, eds., *Félix Varela* 2: 116.

66. Saco, *Historia de la esclavitud*, 4: 350–352, 354.

67. Charles Augustus Murray, *Travels in North American during the Years 1834, 1835, & 1836: Including a summer residence with the Pawnee tribe of Indians in the remote prairies of the Missouri and a visit to Cuba and the Azore Island* (London: Richard Bentley, 1835), 2: 210.

68. David Turnbull, *Travels in the West. Cuba: With Notices of Porto Rico and the Slave Trade* (London: Longman, Orme, Brown, Green, and Longmans), 266.

69. Saco, *Colección de papeles científicos*, 1: 216–218.

70. Orovio and González, *Racismo e inmigración*, 105.

71. Saco, *Colección de papeles científicos*, 1: 216–218.

72. Deschamps Chapeaux, *El negro en la economía habanera*, 128; Matt D. Childs, "'Sewing' Civilization: Cuban Female Education in the Context of Africanization, 1800–1860," *Americas* 54:1 (July 1997): 83. A royal decree by the Spanish crown at the turn of turn of the nineteenth century established the Sociedad Económica de Amigas del País to administer public education in Cuba. The Sociedad members comprised twenty-seven large landholders.

73. Deschamps Chapeaux, *El negro en la economía habanera*, 173.

74. Benjamin Moore Norman, *Rambles by Land and Water, or, Notes of Travel in Cuba and Mexico; including a canoe voyage up the river Panuco, and researches among the ruins of Tamaulipas* (New York: Paine & Burgess, 1845), 29.

75. Murray, *Travels in North America*, 2: 201–202.

76. Richard Henry Dana, Jr., *To Cuba and Back: A Vacation Voyage* (Boston: Ticknor and Fields, 1859), 35.

77. Martínez-Fernández, *Fighting Slavery in the Caribbean*, 68–69.

78. Torres-Cuevas, Ibarra Cuesta, and García Rodríguez, eds., *Félix Varela*, 2: 115–116; Turnbull, *Travels in the West*, 210.

79. Suzanne Lebsock, *The Free Women of Petersburg: Status and Culture in a Southern Town, 1784–1860* (New York : Norton, 1984),169; Matthew Ramsey, *Professional and Popular Medicine in France, 1770–1830: The Social World of Medical Practice* (Cambridge: Cambridge University Press, 1988), 79; Hilary Marland, *Medicine and Society in Wakefield and Huddersfield, 1780–1870* (Cambridge: Cambridge University Press, 1987), 302, 303; Harriett Deacon, "Midwives and Medical Men in the Cape Colony before 1860," *Journal of African History* 29 (1998): 273.80. Deschamps Chapeaux, *El negro en la economía habanera*, 170.

81. *El Diario de la Habana*, 6 February 1828, Newspaper Collection, Bibloteca Nacional José Martí, Havana, Cuba.

82. Deborah K. McGregor, *From Midwives to Medicine: The Birth of American Gynecology* (New Brunswick: Rutgers University Press, 1998), 38; Moitt, *Women and Slavery in the French Antilles*, 62; John Tate Lanning,. *The Royal Protomedicato: The Regulations of the Medical Professions in the Spanish Empire*, edited by John Jay TePaske (Durham: Duke University Press, 1985), 303–306; Lebsock, *Free Women of Petersburg*, 169.

83. Mexico City appears as the main exception, listing twenty-four midwives in its 1811–1812 census. Steven Palmer, *From Popular Medicine to Medical Populism: Doctors, Healers, and Public Power in Costa Rica, 1800–1940* (Durham: Duke University Press, 2003), 140; Luz Maria Hernández Sáenz and George M. Foster, "Curers and Their Cures in Colonial New Spain and Guatemala," in *Mesoamerican Healers*, edited by Brad R. Huber and Alan R. Sandstrom (Austin: University of Texas Press, 2001), 38; Lanning and TePaske, *The Royal Protomedicato*, 298.

84. *El Diario de la Habana*, 6 February 1828. For a detailed discussion of race, honor, and midwifery in Cuba, see Michele B. Reid, "Tensions of Race, Gender and Midwifery in Colonial Cuba," in *Africans to Colonial Spanish America*, edited by Sherwin Bryant and Ben Vinson III (Chicago: University of Illinois Press, forthcoming December 2011).

85. "Academia de Parteras," *El Diario de la Habana*, 28 February 1828.

86. *El Diario de la Habana*, 11 August, 1828; *El Diario de la Habana*, 1 December, 1833, quoted in Deschamps Chapeaux, *El negro en la economía habanera*, 173.

87. "Formado para acuerdo de la Inspectora sobre la necesidad y consecuencia de que las que aspiran a ser examinadas de comadronas reunían los necesarios conocimientos," Archivo Nacional de Cuba, Havana, Instrucción Pública (hereafter ANC-IP), Leg. 40, Exp. 2115; *El Diario de la Habana*, 26 December 1829.

88. Manzano, *Autobiography of a Runaway Slave*, 53.

89. Francisco de Paula Aremey to Cuba Captain General, Havana, 24 October 1859, ANC-GSC, Leg. 1268, Exp. 49818.

90. Ben Vinson III and Matthew Restall, "Black Soldiers, Native Soldiers: Meanings and Military Service in the Spanish American Colonies," in *Beyond Black and Red: African-Native Relations in Colonial Latin America*, edited by Matthew Restall (Albuquerque: University of New Mexico Press, 2005), 23; Vinson, *Bearing Arms for His Majesty*, 16; Herbert Klein, "Colored Militia of Cuba," *Caribbean Studies* 6:2 (June 1966): 18.

91. Johnson, *Social Transformation of Eighteenth-Century Cuba*, 66.

92. Ibid., 43, 44.

93. Ibid.; Allan J. Kuethe, *Cuba, 1753–1815: Crown, Military and Society* (Knoxville: University of Tennessee Press, 1986), 37–45.

94. Marchena Fernandez, *Oficiales y Soldados*, 33, 81–82; Kuethe, *Cuba*, 142,

95. Kuethe, *Cuba*, 46–48; Lyle N. McAlister, *The "Fuero Militar" in New Spain, 1764–1800* (Gainesville: University of Florida Press, 1957), 6–11, 45–51.

96. Landers, *Atlantic Creoles in the Age of Revolution*, 140.

97. Klein, "Colored Militia," 18.

98. Ibid., 20;

99. Johnson, *Social Transformation of Eighteenth-Century Cuba*, 66–67.

100. Deschamps Chapeaux, *El negro en la economía habanera*, 69; Deschamps Chapeaux, *Los batallones de pardos y morenos libres*, 59.

101. Allan J. Kuethe, "The Status of the Free Pardo in the Disciplined Militia of New Granada," *Journal of Negro History* 56.2 (April 1971): 110; Klein, "Colored Militia," 22; Matt D. Childs, "The Aponte Rebellion of 1812 and the Transformation of Cuban Society: Race, Slavery, and Freedom in the Atlantic World" (PhD diss., University of Texas at Austin, 2001), 232; *Justo Sentimiento de pardos y morenos españoles libres de la Habana* (Oficina Filantrópica de don J.M. de Oro, Havana, 1823), ANC-CM, Leg. 60, No. 2.

102. *Justo Sentimiento*, ANC-CM, Leg. 60, No. 2.

103. Ben Vinson III, "Race and Badge: Free-Colored Soldiers in the Colonial Mexican Militia," *The Americas* 56.2 (April 2000): 491; Christon I. Archer, "Pardos, Indians, and the Army of New Spain: Inter-Relationships and Conflicts, 1780–1810," *Journal of Latin American Studies* 62 (November 1974): 235.

104. Archer, "Pardos, Indians, and the Army of New Spain," 234.

105. Francisco Arango y Parreño, *De la factoría a la Colonia* (Havana: Publicaciones de la Secretaría de Educación, 1936), 88–91.

106. Félix Varela, "Memoria que demuestra la necesidad de extinguir la esclavitud de los negros en la Isla de Cuba, atendiendo a los intereses de sus propietarios, por el presbítero don Félix Varela," in Saco, *Historia de la esclavitud*, 4: 12; Hugh Thomas, *Cuba: The Pursuit of Freedom* (London: Pan Books, 1971), 62.

107. Saco, *Historia de la esclavitud*, 4: 350–352.

108. Childs, *The 1812 Aponte Rebellion*, 1–3; Howard, *Changing History*, 73–75, 78. For a detailed discussion of the Aponte conspiracy, see Childs, *The 1812 Aponte Rebellion*; and José Luciano Franco, *La conspiración de Aponte* (Havana: Publicaciones del Archivo Nacional, 1963).

109. Miguel Tacón, Cuba Captain General to Juan Batista Velasquez, Captain Pedaneo, Havana, 12–13 July 1835, ANC-CM, Leg. 11, Exp. 1.

110. Deschamps Chapeaux, *El negro en la economía habanera*, 43–44.

111. Rafael Duharte Jiménez, *Rebeldía esclava en el Caribe* (Xalapa, Mexico: Gobierno del Estado de Veracruz, 1992), 56; Laird W. Bergad, *The Comparative Histories of Slavery in Brazil, Cuba, and the United States* (Cambridge: Cambridge University Press, 2007), 209.

112. "Insurrection of Slaves in Cuba," *Daily National Intelligencer*, 5 August 1835.

113. Circular from Miguel Tacón, Havana, 3 January 1835, and circular from Mariano Ricafort, Havana, 20 July 1832, Real Órdenes y Cédulas, Leg. 133, Exp. 220.

114. "Insurrection in Cuba," *Mississippi Free Trader and Natchez Daily Gazette*, 15 April 1843.

115. Saco, *Colección de papeles científicos*, 1: 216–217.

116. Vinson, "Free Colored Voices," 176; Childs, "The Aponte Rebellion of 1812," 232.

117. Saco, *Historia de la esclavitud*, 4: 350–352.

2 / Spectacles of Power

1. Gabriel de la Concepción Valdés, *Poesias completas de Placido* (Paris: C. Denné Schmitz, 1856), 380. The quote contains the opening and closing stanzas to Plácido's final poem, "A Plea to God."

2. "The following letter contains some details of the last Havana executions, the consequence of the late conspiracy of the blacks to conquer Cuba from the whites," *Dover Gazette & Strafford Advertiser*, 19 October 1844, Nineteenth Century U.S. Newspapers Database, Pullen Library, Georgia State University (hereafter NCUS-GSU) .3. *Aurora*, 29 June 1844, "Copia de artículos publicados en periódico *Aurora* de Matanzas dando cuenta de la entrada en papila y ejecución de los reos Gabriel de la Concepción Valdés (Plácido) y otros," ANC-AP, Leg., 42, Exp. 5, p. 4.

4. "Diligencias obradas por la introducción de un libreto titulado "El Negro Feliz" que fue descrubierto abordo de la valandra *Flor de Mayo* procedente de la isla de Nassau en provediencia, Remedios, 20 May 1837," ANC-AP, Leg. 38, Exp. 31; Francisco Arango to King of Spain, Havana, 30 August 1830, AGI-Indiferente 2828, folio 16; David Patrick Geggus, "Slavery, War and Revolution in the Greater Caribbean," in David Gaspar and David Geggus, *Turbulent Time: The French Revolution and the Greater Caribbean* (Bloomington: Indiana, 1997), 7–8. For a discussion of major slave rebellions in the Caribbean, South America, and the circum-Caribbean United States, see the following. For the circum-Caribbean United States, seeEdward A. Pearson, ed., *Designs against Charleston: The Trial Record of the Denmark Vesey Slave Conspiracy of 1822* (Chapel Hill: University of North Carolina Press, 1999). For Guyana, see Douglas R. Egerton, *"He shall go out free": The Lives of Denmark Vesey* (Madison: Madison House, 1999); Albert Thrasher, *On to New Orleans!: Louisiana's Heroic 1811 Slave Revolt: A Brief History and Documents Relating to the Rising of Slaves in January 1811 in the Territory of New Orleans* (New Orleans: Cypress Press, 1995); James Sidbury, *Ploughshares into Swords: Race, Rebellion, and Identity in Gabriel's Virginia, 1730–1810* (Cambridge: Cambridge University Press, 1997), 119; Kenneth S. Greenberg, ed., *Nat Turner: Rebellion in History and Memory* (Oxford: Oxford University Press, 2003). For the Caribbean and South America, see Franco, *La conspiración de Aponte*, 53; Geggus, "Slavery, War and Revolution in the Greater Caribbean," 7–8; Eugene D. Genovese, *From Rebellion to Revolution: Afro-American Slave Revolts in the Making of the Modern* World (Baton Rouge: Louisiana State University Press, 1979), 43; Emilia Viotti da Costa, *Crowns of Glory, Tears of Blood: The Demerara Slave Rebellion of 1823* (Oxford: Oxford University Press, 1994), 243; Michael Craton, *Resistance to Slavery in the British West Indies* (Ithaca: Cornell University Press, 1982), 314–315; João José Reis, *Slave Rebellion in Brazil: The Muslim Uprising of 1835 in Bahia* (Baltimore: Johns Hopkins University Press, 1993); Guillermo A. Baralt, *Esclavos rebeldes: Conspiraciones y sublevaciones de esclavos en Puerto Rico (1795–1873)* (Río González, Puerto Rico: Ediciones Huracán, 1982), 99; Manuel Barcia Paz, *Con el látigo de la ira: Legislación, represión y control en las plantaciones cubanas, 1790–1870* (Havana: Ciencias Sociales, 2000).

5. Kiple, *Blacks in Colonial Cuba*, 84, 90.

6. Klein, *The Atlantic Slave Trade*, 63; Michael Crowder, *The Story of Nigeria* (London: Faber and Faber, 1973), 77; Toyin Falola, "The Yoruba Wars of the Nineteenth Century," in *Yoruba Historiography*, edited by Toyin Falola (Madison: University of Wisconsin Press, 1992), 140.

7. For a discussion of the Yoruba in Cuba, see Rafeal L. López Valdés, "Notas para el studio etno-histórico de los esclavos lucumí de Cuba," *Anales del Caribe* 6 (1986): 54–74; Julia Cuervo Hewitt, "Yoruba Presence in Contemporary Cuban Narrative" (Ph.D. diss., Vanderbilt University, 1981), 19; Alejandro de la Fuente, "Esclavos africanos en la Habana: Zonas de procedencia y denominaciones étnicas, 1570–1699," *Revista Española de Antropología Americana* 20 (1990): 135–160; Michele Reid, "Yoruba in Cuba: Origins, Identities, and Transformations," in *The Yoruba Diaspora in the Atlantic World*, edited by Toyin Falola and Matt Childs (Bloomington: Indiana University Press, 2005), 111–129.

8. John George F. Wurdemann, *Notes on Cuba* (Boston: James Munroe, 1844), 257–262 in Pérez, *Slaves, Sugar, and Colonial Society*, 107.

9. Fernando Ortiz, *Hampa afro-cubana*, 246–248; Paquette, *Sugar Is Made with Blood*, 67.

10. Howard, *Changing History*, 73–75, 78. For a detailed discussion of the Aponte conspiracy, see Childs, *The 1812 Aponte Rebellion*; and Franco, *La conspiración de Aponte*.

11. Alexander, *Transatlantic Sketches*, 1: 350–359.

12. *Dover Gazette & Strafford Advertiser*, 19 October 1844.

13. Miguel Tacón, Cuba Captain General, to Juan Batista Velasquez, Captain Pedaneo, Havana, 12–13 July 1835, ANC-CM, Leg. 11, Exp. 1ñ. Deschamps Chapeaux, *El negro en la economía habanera*, 43–44.

14. Juan Bautista Velásquez to Miguel Tacón, Cuba Captain General, Havana, 15 July 1835, ANC-CM, Leg. 11, Exp. 1, folio 177; Deschamps Chapeaux, *Los batallones pardos y morenos libres*, 83–84; Barcia Paz, *La resistencia esclava en las plantaciones cubanas*, 33.

15. "Insurrection of Slaves in Cuba," *Daily National Intelligencer*, 5 August 1835.

16. Deschamps Chapeaux, *Los batallones pardos y morenos libres*, 83–84; Sartorius, "My Vassals," 5; Alain Yacou, "La insurgencia negra en la isla de Cuba en la primera mitad del siglo XIX," *Revista de Indias* 53.197 (1993): 49.

17. Juan Bautista Velásquez to Miguel Tacón, Cuba Captain General, Havana, 15 July 1835, ANC-CM, Leg. 11, Exp. 1, folio 177; Deschamps Chapeaux, *Los batallones pardos y morenos libres*, 83–84; Barcia Paz, *La resistencia esclava en las plantaciones cubanas*, 33.

18. Ibid.; Childs, "The Aponte Rebellion of 1812," 45; Alexander, *Transatlantic Sketches*, 1: 350–59.

19. Louis A. Pérez, Jr., *Cuba: Between Reform and Revolution* (New York: Oxford University Press, 1995), 410; Robin Blackburn, *The Overthrow of Colonial Slavery, 1776–1848* (London: Verso, 1988), 339, 387–388.

20. Pérez, *Cuba*, 410; Blackburn, *The Overthrow of Colonial Slavery*, 387–388.

21. Childs, *The 1812 Aponte Rebellion*, 1–3; Howard, *Changing History*, 73–75, 78

22. See note 4, this chapter, for a list of works.

23. The 1841 census has been acknowledged as flawed by contemporary officials and twentieth-century scholars. It is likely that colonial authorities inflated the slave

numbers to create fear among Cuban planters and persuade them to remain loyal to the crown.

24. Quoted in Jonathan Curry Machado, "Catalysts in the Crucible," 123.

25. Ibid.

26. "Further Particulars of the Insurrection in Cuba," *New York Herald*, 18 April 1843, NCUS-GSU.

27. "A Negro Insurrection in Cuba," *Pennsylvania Inquirer and National Gazette*, 13 April 1843, NCUS-GSU; "The Insurrection in Cuba," *Pennsylvania Inquirer and National Gazette*, 18 April 1843, NCUS-GSU; "Insurrection in Cuba," *Mississippi Free Trader and Natchez Daily Gazette*, 15 April 1843, NCUS-GSU.

28. "An Insurrection in Cuba—Important," *Pennsylvania Inquirer and National Gazette*, 6 June 1843, NCUS-GSU; Arthur P. Whitaker, "Antonio de Ulloa," *Hispanic American Historical Review* 15.2 (May 1935): 189.

29. "Another Slave Insurrection in the Island of Cuba," *Emancipator and Free American*, 15 June 1843, NCUS-GSU.

30. Paquette, *Sugar Is Made with Blood*, 210; "Highly Important from Cuba," *New York Herald*, 7 January1844, NCUS-GSU.

31. "Slave Revolt in Cuba," *Cleveland Herald*, 1 December 1843, NCUS-GSU; *New York Herald*, 7 January 1844, NCUS-GSU.

32. Paquette, *Sugar Is Made with Blood*, 209, 210; Leopoldo O'Donnell to Secretario de Estado and Despacho de la Gobernación de Ultramar, Havana, 8 November 1843, AGI-AHNU, Leg. 8, Exp. 21, folio 1–2.

33. AGI-AHNU, Leg. 8, Exp. 21, folio 1–2.

34. *New York Herald*, 7 January 1844, NCUS-GSU.

35. Cuba, *Colección de los fallos*, No. 38; Leopoldo O'Donnell, Cuba Captain General to Secretario del Estado y del Despacho de la Gobernación de Ultramar, Havana, 1 December 1843, AGI-AHNU, Leg. 8, Exp. 14, No. 2, folios 1–2; Paquette, *Sugar Is Made with Blood*, 209, 210, 214–215. It should be noted that for revealing the rebellion, Polina received her freedom and 500 pesos.

36. Leopoldo O'Donnell, Cuba Captain General to Secretario del Estado y del Despacho de la Gobernación de Ultramar, Havana, 31 January 1844, AGI-AHNU, Leg. 8, Exp. 14, No. 7, folio 1; *New York Herald*, 7 January 1844, NCUS-GSU.

37. Paquette, *Sugar Is Made with Blood*, 217.38. 31 January 1844, AGI-AHNU, Leg. 8, Exp. 14, No. 7, folio 1.

39. Paquette, *Sugar Is Made with Blood*, 219–220; Richard Kimball, "Letters from Cuba," *Knickerbocker* 26 (October 1845): 542–543.40. Leopoldo O'Donnell to Secretario de Estado y del Despacho de la Gobernación de Ultramar, Havana, 30 March 1844, AHN-UGC, Leg. 4620, Exp. 33, folio 1.

41. Paquette, *Sugar Is Made with Blood*, 110.

42. Deschamps Chapeaux, *El negro en la economía habanera*, 65, 157.

43. Cuba, *Colección de los fallos*, No. 12.

44. Ibid.

45. Kimball, *Cuba, and the Cubans*, 86; Kimball, "Letters from Cuba," 542–543.

46. Henry A. Murray, *Lands of the Slave and the Free: or, Cuba, the United States, and Canada* (London: John W. Parker and Son, 1855), 1: 301.

47. Thomas Rodney to U.S. Secretary of State, Matanzas, April 1844, National

Archives, Washington, D.C., U.S. Dept. of State Consular Dispatches, Matanzas, Cuba (hereafter NA-CD).

48. Paquette, *Sugar Is Made with Blood*, 223.

49. David William Foster and Daniel Altamiranda, eds, *From Romanticism to Modernismo in Latin America* (New York: Routledge, 1997), 133 n. 12.

50. Larry R. Jensen, *Children of Colonial Despotism: Press, Politics, and Culture in Cuba, 1790–1840* (Tampa: University Press of Florida, 1988), 135 n. 46; Paquette, *Sugar Is Made with Blood*, 3, 156, 223, 229.

51. Cuba, *Colección de los fallos*, Nos. 7, 17, 14.

52. Villaverde to del Monte, Havana, 9 September 1844, in Cirilo Villaverde, *Homenaje de Cirilo Villaverde* (Havana: UNESCO, 1964), 71; Lazo, *Writing to Cuba*, 11.

53. Lazo, *Writing to Cuba*, 10; Paquette, *Sugar Is Made with Blood*, 223–224; Brigida Pastor, "Symbiosis between Slavery and Feminism in Gertrudis Gómez de Avellaneda's 'Sab'" *Bulletin of Latin American Research* 16.2 (1997): 189.

54. Lazo, *Writing to Cuba*, 63.

55. Jensen, *Children of Colonial Despotism*, 113; Paquette, *Sugar Is Made with Blood*, 262–263.

56. Lazo, *Writing to Cuba*, 3, 11–12, 63,

57. Ibid., 64, 74; Gerald E. Poyo, *With All, and for the Good of All: The Emergence of Popular Nationalism in the Cuban Communities of the United States, 1848–1898* (Durham: Duke University Press, 1989), 6; William Cullen Bryant, *Letters of a Traveller: Or, Notes of Things Seen in Europe and America* (London: Richard Bentley, 1850), 399.

58. Lazo, *Writing to Cuba*, 92, 175.

59. Ibid., 141, 148.

60. Ibid., 77, 142, 175.

61. Murray, *Lands of the Slave and the Free*, 1: 301.

62. Mollier, French Consul in Cuba to O'Donnell, Havana, 25 February 1844, AGI-AHN, Leg. 8, Exp. 14, No. 14, folio 1; "We have received by express the Paris papers," *Times*, 11 April 1844, Times Digital Archive, Woodruff Library, Emory University (hereafter TDA-Emory).

63. Thomas M. Rodney to U.S. Secretary of State, Matanzas, 13 April 1844, NA-CD.

64. "From Cuba," *Daily Atlas*, 11 May 1844, NCUS-Emory.

65. Pérez, *Cuba: Between Reform and Revolution*, 410; Blackburn, *The Overthrow of Colonial Slavery*, 339, 387–388.

66. Thomas Rodney to U.S. Secretary of State, April 1844, National Archives, Washington, D.C., U.S. Dept. of State Consular Dispatches, Matanzas, Cuba, 1820–1889 (hereafter NADC-DSCD); *New Orleans Times-Picayune*, 20 April 1844, NA-LANC.

67. Paquette, *Sugar Is Made with Blood*, 220, 236.

68. Kimball, "Letters from Cuba," 543.

69. Curry Machado, "Catalysts in the Crucible," 124; Paquette, *Sugar Is Made with Blood*, 226.

70. "Slavery in Cuba," *Times*, 24 April 1844, TDA-Emory.

71. Thomas M. Rodney to U.S. Secretary of State, Matanzas, 13 April 1844, NA-CD; *Spectator*, 25 April 1844, AGI-AHN, Leg. 5064, Exp. 28, No. 3, folio 3.

72. Paquette, *Sugar Is Made with Blood*, 228.

73. Thomas Rodney to U.S. Secretary of State, 1 January 1844, NA-CD.

74. Cuba, *Colección de los fallos*, No. 12.

75. Ibid., No. 1. Italicized terms such as *carabalí*, *lucumí*, and *gangá* are ethnic designations that emerged during the Atlantic slave trade, and are frequently used in conjunction with the names of former slaves. They refer to cultural, linguistic, or geographic groupings, or ports of origin in West Africa. In Spanish America, *carabalí* typically referred to individuals who arrived from ports along the Bight of Biafra, located in the eastern bay of the Gulf of Guinea. The term *lucumí* was typically used to identify those of Yoruba heritage in colonial Spanish America. Although the origin of those designated as *gangá* remains unclear, several scholars have situated this group near the Ivory Coast. See Paul E. Lovejoy, "Ethnic Designations of the Slave Trade and the Reconstruction of the History of Trans-Atlantic Slavery," in *Trans-Atlantic Dimensions of Ethnicity in the African Diaspora*, edited by Paul E. Lovejoy and David V. Trotman (London: Continuum, 2004), 17Joseph C. Dorsey, "It Hurt Very Much at the Time: Patriarchy, Rape Culture, and the Slave Body-Semiotic," in *The Culture of Gender and Sexuality in the Caribbean*, edited by Linden Lewis (Gainesville: University of Press of Florida, 2003), 319 n 25.76. Cuba, *Colección de los fallos*, No. 10.

77. Paquette, *Sugar Is Made with Blood*, 229. The total of 78 executions were enumerated as one slave woman, one white man, 38 males slaves, and 38 free men of color.

78. Cuba, *Colección de los fallos*, No. 11.79. Ibid., No. 23.

80. Ibid., No. 14.

81. Paquette, *Sugar Is Made with Blood*, 229.

82. Cuba, *Colección de los fallos*, Nos. 1 and 2.

83. Ibid., No. 24; Deschamps Chapeaux, *El negro en la economía habanera*, 106, 108.

84. Cuba, *Colección de los fallos*, Nos. 37, 45, and 71. The Military Commission instituted group expulsions as follows: 15 in session 37, 24 in session 71, and 28 in session 45.

85. Paquette, *Sugar Is Made with Blood*, 229.

86. Anslo Cabalino to Ministro de Gobernación del Reino, Madrid, 13 July 1847, Archivo Histórico Nacional, Madrid, Ultramar, Gobierno, Cuba (hereafter AHN-UGC), Leg. 4627, Exp. 9, No. 1; Felipe Valdés García to Presidente del Consejo de Ministros, 31 March 1854, Madrid, AHN-UGC, Leg. 4641, Exp. 2.

87. Cuba, *Colección de los fallos*, No. 24.

88. Ibid., No. 1.

89. Ibid. No. 11.

90. Ibid., Nos. 1, 11, and 24.

91. Ibid., No. 24.

92. Ibid., Nos. 2 and 5.

93. Pérez, *Cuba*, 410; Blackburn, *The Overthrow of Colonial Slavery*, 339, 387–388.

94. Paquette, *Sugar Is Made with Blood*, 229. The total 1,835 sentences of imprisonment are divided as follows: 1,286 free people of color, 543 slaves, and 6 whites.

95. Cuba, *Colección de los fallos*, No. 16.

96. Paquette, *Sugar Is Made with Blood*, 229. The Military Commission listed 1,292 sentences of imprisonment: 543 slaves, 743 free people of color, and 6 whites.

97. Cuba, *Colección de los fallos*, No. 11.

98. Ibid., No. 26.

99. Ibid., No. 69.

100. Manzano to Rosa Alfonzo, 5 October 1844 in José Luciano Franco, ed., *Obras: Juan Francisco Manzano* (Havana: Instituto del Cubano Libro, 1972), 91, 94.

101. Deschamps Chapeaux, *El negro en la economía habanera*, 144–147.

102. Kimball, "Letters from Cuba," 543.

103. Cuba, *Colección de los fallos*, Nos. 37, 71; Fulgencio Salas, El Brigadier Gobierno, to Captain General of Cuba, Matanzas, 6 June 1844, "Relación de los individuos rematados a presido y deportados a perpetuidad de esta isla y la de Puerto Rico de los que se acompañan duplicados testimonios de condena marcados con los mismos puertos al margen de cada nombre," ANC-AP, Leg. 42, Exp. 3.

104. Cuba, *Colección de los fallos*, No. 71.

105. "Sentencia pronunciada por la Sección de la Comisión militar establecida en la ciudad de Matanzas para conocer de la causa de conspiración de la gente de color," 12 September 1844, Matanzas, ANC-AP, Leg. 42, No. 18.

106. Cuba, *Colección de los fallos*, No. 71; Paquette, *Sugar Is Made with Blood*, 229, 248. The Military Commission in Matanzas listed sentences for 1,836 individuals, divided among 1,232 *libres de color*, 590 slaves, and 14 whites. The *libres de color* are broken down as follows: 78 executed (48.7% *libres de color*), 1,165 imprisoned (52.9% *libres de color*), 435 banished (99.5% *libres de color*), 31 sentenced to workhouses and lighter punishments (58% *libres de color*). For a complete breakdown by race and legal status, see Paquette, *Sugar Is Made with Blood*, 229.

107. María del Francito Flores to Military Commission, Havana, 12 December 1844, ANC-CM, Leg. 57, Exp. 1, pieza 3.

108. Severino Flores to Military Commission, Havana, 12 December 1844, ANC-CM, Leg. 57, Exp. 1, pieza 3.

109. María de los Ángeles Pedroso to Brigadier Presidente de la Sección de la Comisión Militar, Matanzas, 28 August 1844, ANC-CM, Leg. 79, Exp. 9.

110. Leopoldo O'Donnell to Secretario de Estado y del Despacho de la Gobernación de Ultramar, Havana, 22 February 1844, AHN-UGC, Leg. 4618, Exp. 11, folio 1.

111. Leopoldo O'Donnell to Ministro de Estado, Havana, 15 June 1844, ANC-AP, Leg. 42, Exp. 3.

112. Sidbury, *Ploughshares into Swords*, 123.

113. *Daily Picayune*, April 20, 1844, NA-LANC.

114. "Cuba," *Emancipator and Weekly Chronicle*, 1 May 1844, NCUS-Emory.

115. "Havana Full Particulars of the Insurrections in Cuba—That Island and Hayti Compared—The Results," *New York Herald*, 10 May 1844, NCUS-GSU.

116. *Times*, 24 April 1844, TDA-Emory.

117. "State of Things in Cuba," *Liberator*, 9 February 1844, NCUS-Emory.

118. *Spectator*, 25 April 1844, AGI-AHN, Leg. 5064, Exp. 28, No. 3, folio 3.

119. "Cuba," *Emancipator and Weekly Chronicle*, May 15, 1844, NCUS-Emory.

120. "Havana Awful State of Affairs in Cuba—Condition of the Markets—Drought and the Crops—What Is to Be Done?" *New York Herald*, 3 May 1844, NCUS-Emory, 3 May 1844.

121. *Times*, April 24, 1844, TDA-Emory.

122. "From Cuba," *Daily Atlas*, 11 May 1844, NCUS-Emory; *Times*, 11 April 1844, TDA-Emory; Mollier, French Consul in Cuba to O'Donnell, Havana, 25 February

1844, AGI-AHN, Leg. 8, Exp. 14, No. 14, folio 1; "Late from Cuba," *New York Herald*, 24 May 1844, NCUS-GSU; *New York Herald*, -NCUS-Emory, 3 May 1844, NCUS-Emory.

123. Ultramar to Conde de Marasol, Puerto Rico Captain General, Madrid, 15 October 1844, AGI-AHN, Leg. 5064, Exp. 28, Nos. 1–2.

124. *Aurora*, 27 June 1844, ANC-AP, Leg. 42, Exp. 5, pp. 2–3.

125. Real Junta de Fomento de Agricultura y Comercio de la Isla de Cuba to La Reina de España, Havana, 2 April 1844, AGI-AHN, Leg. 16, Exp. 9, No. 3, folio 2.

126. Ibid., folios 7–8.

127. *Aurora*, 29 June 1844, ANC-AP, Leg. 42, Exp. 5, pp. 7–8.

128. Da Costa, *Crowns of Glory, Tears of Blood*, 243.

129. Craton, *Resistance to Slavery in the British West Indies*, 314–315.

130. Thomas M. Rodney to U.S. Secretary of State, Matanzas, 13 April 1844, NA-CD.

131. Paquette, *Sugar Is Made with Blood*, 232.

3 / Calculated Expulsions

1. Cuba, *Colección de los fallos*, No. 1.

2. Leopoldo O'Donnell to Ultramar,30 March 1844, Havana, "Sobre salida de la Isla de Cuba de los negros y mulatos libres y sobre que puedan pasar a Fernando Poó los que voluntariamente lo soliciten," AHN-UGC, Leg. 4620, Exp. 33, folio 4.

3. Paquette, *Sugar Is Made with Blood*, 104–105.

4. A total of 1,232 free people of color were convicted in Matanzas. Ibid., 229.

5. Pedro Pascual de Oliver, Ministro de España en México to Primer Secretario del Despacho de Estado, Mexico, 20 June 1844, Archivo Histórico Nacional, Madrid, Estado (hereafter AHN-Estado), Leg. 8039, Exp. 10, doc. 4; Ángelo Cabalino to Ministro de la Gobernación del Reino, Madrid, 13 July 1847, AHN-UGC, Leg. 4627, Exp. 9.

6. Paquette, *Sugar Is Made with Blood*, 229. The breakdown for the 3,066 individuals sentenced by the Military Commission in Matanzas is as follows: free blacks, 2,187; slaves, 783; whites, 96 (82 of the whites were acquitted); Leopoldo O'Donnell to Ultramar, Havana,30 March 1844, "Sobre salida de la Isla de Cuba de los negros y mulatos libres y sobre que puedan pasar a Fernando Poó los que voluntariamente lo soliciten," AHN-UGC, Leg. 4620, Exp. 33, p. 3. It should also be noted that although several white planters were charged with conspiracy, none in the available Military Commission records for Matanzas were formally sentenced to banishment.

7. Cuba, *Colección de los fallos*, No. 6.

8. Ibid., No. 9; "Cuaderno de costas no. 23 de la causa de conspiración de negros," 15 December 1844, ANC, Copia de la sesión 23 de la Sentencia pronunciada por la Sección de la Comisión militar establecida en la ciudad de Matanzas para conocer de la causa de conspiración de la gente de color," Matanzas, 12 September 1844, ANC-AP, Leg. 42, Exp. 18.

9. Ruth B. Barr and Modeste Hargis, "The Voluntary Exile of Free Negroes of Pensacola," *Florida Historical Quarterly* 17.1 (July 1938): 1; *New Orleans Times-Picayune*, 20 April 1844.

10. Cuba, *Colección de los fallos*, No. 1.

11. Anslo Cabalino to Ministro de Gobernación del Reino, Madrid, 13 July 1847, AHN-UGC, Leg. 4627, Exp. 9, No. 1.

12. Felipe Valdés García to Presidente del Consejo de Ministros, 31 March 1854, Madrid, AHN-UGC, Leg. 4641, Exp. 2.

13. Sir J. Browing, *Some Account of the State of Prisons in Spain and Portugal* (London: Bensley, 1822), 2–3, 5.

14. Ibid., 16, 18.

15. Ruth Pike, "Penal Servitude in the Spanish Empire: Presidio Labor in the Eighteenth Century," *Hispanic American Historical Review* 58.1 (February 1978): 22, 27. Other major Spanish prisons in Morocco were located in Oran and Melilla.

16. Ángelo Cabalino to Ministro de la Gobernación del Reino, Madrid, 13 July 1847, AHN-UGC, Leg. 4627, Exp. 9.

17. Felipe Valdés García to Presidente del Consejo de Ministros, Madrid, 31 March 1854, AHN-UGC, Leg. 4641, Exp. 1No. 2; Ministro de Estado, Ultramar, to Ministerio de la Guerra, Madrid, 13 December 1854, AHN-UGC, Leg. 4641, Exp.1No. 5.

18. Circular, 20 July 1832, Havana, ANC-ROC, Leg. 133, Exp. 220.

19. Circular, 22 December 1842, Havana, ANC-AP, Leg. 140, Exp. 36.

20. Leopoldo O'Donnell, Havana, 13 May 1844, ANC-ROC, Leg. 133, Exp. 220; Leopoldo O'Donnell, Havana, 13 May 1844, ANC-ROC, Leg. 133, Exp. 220.

21. Ira Berlin, *Slaves without Masters: The Free Negro in the Antebellum South* (New York: Pantheon Books, 1978), 92, 96; Donald Everett, "Emigres and Militamen: Free Persons of Color in New Orleans, 1803–1815," *Journal of Negro History* 38.4 (October 1953): 384–385.

22. Walter C. Rucker, "'I Will Gather All Nations': Resistance, Culture, and Pan-African Collaboration in Denmark Vesey's South Carolina," *Journal of Negro History* (2001): 142–143.

23. Turnbull, *Travels in the West*, 69.

24. David O. Whitten, *Andrew Durnford: A Black Sugar Planter in Antebellum Louisiana* (Natchitoches, La.: Northwestern State University Press, 1981), 36–37.

25. Lacy K. Ford, *Deliver Us from Evil: The Slavery Question in the Old South* (New York: Oxford University Press, 2009), 279; Kevin C. Julius, *The Abolitionist Decade, 1829–1838: A Year-by-Year History of Early Events in the Antislavery Movement* (Jefferson, N.C.: McFarland, 2004), 163.

26. Antonio Lorenzo Valdés to Alcalde, Remedios, 20 May 1837, ANC-AP, Leg. 38, Exp. 31.

27. "Matanzas, Sept. 20, 1837. A Caution to Travelers in General," *Colored American*, 21 October 1837. NCUS-Emory.

28. Turnbull, *Travels in the West*, 71.

29. Ultramar to Cuba Captain General, Madrid, 1 September 1856, ANC-ROC, Leg. 195, Exp. 9.

30. Leopoldo O'Donnell, Havana, 13 May 1844, ANC-ROC, Leg. 133, Exp. 220; José María Zamora y Coronada, *Biblioteca de legislación ultramarina en forma de diccionario alfabético* (Madrid: Imprenta de J Martin Alegría, 1845), 3: 139–141; Paquette, *Sugar Is Made with Blood*, 273–274.

31. Carlota Molina to Cuba Captain General, Kingston, Jamaica, 10 January 1844, ANC-AP, Leg. 140, Exp. 36.

32. Ibid.

33. Circular, Havana, 22 December 1842, ANC-AP, Leg. 140, Exp. 36.

34. Carlota Molina to Cuba Captain General, Kingston, Jamaica, 10 January 1844, ANC-AP, Leg. 140, Exp. 36.

35. Reid, "Tensions of Race, Gender and Midwifery in Colonial Cuba," 8.

36. Circular by Leopoldo O'Donnell, Havana, 31 May 1844, ANC-ROC, Leg. 133, Exp. 220.

37. Leopoldo O'Donnell, 13 May 1844, Havana, ANC-ROC, Leg. 133, Exp. 220.

38. Ernesto Sagás and Orlando Inoa, eds., *The Dominican People: A Documentary History* (Princeton, N.J.: Markus Wiener, 2003), 60–61.

39. ANC-AP, Leg. 140, Exp. 11; ANC-AP, Leg. 140, Exp. 35.

40. ANC-AP, Leg. 140, Exp. 3; ANC-AP, Leg. 140, Exp. 34.

41. "Solicitudes de negros extranjeros para que no se les deporte," 1844, ANC-AP, Leg. 141, Exp. 6.

42. Juan Arregui to Cuba Captain General, Havana, 4 May 1844, ANC-AP, Leg. 140, Exp. 17.

43. Kuethe, "The Status of the Free Pardo," 110; Klein, "The Colored Militia of Cuba," 22. For a detailed discussion of the black participation in the Spanish military, see chapter 1.

44. Ben Vinson III, "Free-Colored Voices: Issues of Representation and Racial Identity in the Colonial Mexican Militia," *Journal of Negro History* 80.4 (Fall 1995): 172.

45. For a detailed discussion of these revolts, see Childs, *The 1812 Aponte Rebellion*; Franco, *La conspiración de Aponte*; Miguel Tacón, Cuba Captain General to Juan Batista Velasquez, Captain Pedaneo, Havana, 12–13 July 1835, ANC-CM, Leg. 11, Exp. 1; Deschamps Chapeaux, *Los batallones pardos y morenos libres*, 83–84; Sartorius,"My Vassals," 3.

46. José Ramón Ortega to Captain General of Cuba, Havana, 19 May 1844, ANC-AP, Leg. 139, Exp. 13.

47. "Solicitudes de negros extranjeros para que no se les deporte," 1844, ANC-AP, Leg. 141, Exp. 6.

48. Ibid., Leg. 140, Exp. 38.

49. Eusebia Josefa Courbille to Cuba Captain General, Havana, 6 May 1844, ANC-AP, Leg. 140, Exp. 6.

50. Saco, *Colección de papeles científicos* 1: 216–217.

51. Paquette, *Sugar Is Made with Blood*, 105.

52. "Solicitudes de negros extranjeros para que no se les deporte," 1844, ANC-AP, Leg. 140, Exp. 18.

53. Ibid., ANC-AP, Leg. 140, Exp. 11.

54. Antonio Merlin to Cuba Captain General, Havana, 17 May 1844, ANC-AP, Leg. 140, Exp. 19.

55. Eusebia Josefa Courbille to Cuba Captain General, Havana, 6 May 1844, ANC-AP, Leg. 140, Exp. 6.

56. José González to Cuba Captain General, Havana, 29 April 1844, ANC-AP, Leg. 140, Exp. 20.

57. Twinam, *Public Lives, Private Secrets*, 33.

58. Blackburn, *The Overthrow of Colonial Slavery*, 451–457.

59. Circular, 20 July 1832, Havana, ANC-ROC, Leg. 133, Exp. 220; Circular, Havana, 22 December 1842, ANC-AP, Leg. 140, Exp. 36; Leopoldo O'Donnell, Havana,

13 May 1844, ANC-ROC, Leg. 133, Exp. 220; Leopoldo O'Donnell, Havana, 13 May 1844, ANC-ROC, Leg. 133, Exp. 220.

60. Soledad Vargas to Spanish Consul in Jamaica, Santiago de Cuba, 31 October 1851, "Documentación relacionado con la solicitud hecha por Doña Soledad Vargas para que se permitirse regresar a Cuba a su esposo José María de la Peña." Archivo Nacional de Cuba, Havana, Gobierno General (hereafter ANC-GG), Leg. 525, Exp. 27015.

61. Ibid.; Leopoldo O'Donnell, Havana, 13 May 1844, ANC-ROC, Leg. 133, Exp. 220.

62. "Solicitudes de negros extranjeros para que no se les deporte," 1844, ANC-AP, Leg. 140, No. 38; Landers, *Atlantic Creoles in the Age of Revolution*, 229–230, 249–250.

63. Leopoldo O'Donnell, Cuba Captain General, to Pedro Pascual de Oliver, Ministro de España in Mexico, to Primer Secretario del Despacho de Estado, Havana, 8 July 1844, in Javier Malagón Barceló, et al., *Relaciones diplomáticas hispano-mexicanas (1839–1898): Documentos procedentes del Archivo de la Embajada de España en México*, 4 vols. (Mexico City: El Colegio de Mexico, 1949–1966), 3 (1966): 71.

64. Pedro Pascual de Oliver, Ministro de España in México, to Señor Primer Secretario del Despacho de Estado, Mexico, 27 July 1844, AHN-Estado, Leg. 8039, Exp. 10, doc. 1.; O'Donnell to Ministro de Estado, Havana, 15 June 1844, ANC-AP, Leg. 42, Exp. 3, 1844; Deschamps Chapeaux, *El negro en la economía habanera*, 25–26; Paquette, *Sugar Is Made with Blood*, 228.

65. The figure 152,838 is taken from the 1841 census, the last census prior to the repression of La Escalera. Kiple, *Blacks in Colonial Cuba*, 84–86, 88–90.

66. Document 271, Anexo II, Havana, 8 July 1844, in *Relaciones diplomáticas hispano-mexicanas*, 3: 71.

67. Ibid.

68. Deschamps Chapeaux, *El negro en la economía habanera*, 25–26; Ángel Calderón de la Barca, Spanish Consul in the United States to O'Donnell, Washington, D.C., 31 December 1844, ANC-AP, Leg. 140, Exp. 39.

69. O'Donnell to Ministro de Estado, Havana, 15 June 1844, ANC-AP, Leg. 42, Exp. 3.

70. Leopoldo O'Donnell to Ultramar,Havana, 30 March 1844, "Sobre salida de la Isla de Cuba de los negros y mulatos libres y sobre que puedan pasar a Fernando Poó los que voluntariamente lo soliciten," AHN-UGC, Leg. 4620, Exp. 33, folio 4.

71. O'Donnell to Ministro de Estado, Havana, 15 June 1844, ANC-AP, Leg. 42, Exp. 3.

72. Cuba, *Colección de los fallos*; Deschamps Chapeaux, *El negro en la economía habanera*, 25–26. This figure is derived from the 433 free people of color who received sentences of banishment made by the Military Commission, the roughly 100 sent to overseas prisons, and the estimated 739 coerced emigrants.

73. Deschamps Chapeaux, *El negro en la economía habanera*, 25–26.

74. Pedro Pascual de Oliver, Ministro de España en México to José María de Bocanegro, Ministro de Relaciones Exteriores y Gobernación, Mexico, 26 May 1844 AHN-Estado, Leg. 8039, Exp. 10, doc. 2.

75. Ibid.; José María de Bocanegro, Ministro de Relaciones Exteriores y Gobernación to Pedro Pascual de Oliver, Ministro de España en México, Mexico, 27 May 1844, AHN-Estado, Leg. 8039, Exp. 10, doc. 3; Pedro Pascual de Oliver, Ministro de España en México to Primer Secretario del Despacho de Estado, Mexico, 27 May 1844, AHN-Estado, Leg. 8039, Exp. 10, doc. 1.

76. Document 272, Anexo Único, México, 19 June 1844, in *Relaciones diplomáticas hispano-mexicanas*, 3: 73.

77. Pedro Pascual de Oliver, Ministro de España en México to Primer Secretario del Despacho de Estado, Mexico, 20 June 1844, AHN-Estado, Leg. 8039, Exp. 10, doc. 4.

78. Document 291, Anexo I, Mexico, 22 August, 1844, in *Relaciones diplomáticas hispano-mexicanas*, 3: 100.

79. Document 279, Mexico, 26 August 1844, in *Relaciones diplomáticas hispano-mexicanas*, 3: 81.

80. Document 271, Anexo II, Havana 8 July 1844, in *Relaciones diplomáticas hispano-mexicanas*, 3: 71.

81. Document 291, Anexo II, Havana, 9 September 1844, in *Relaciones diplomáticas hispano-mexicanas*, 3: 101.

82. Ramón María Narváez, Primer Secretario del Despacho de Estado, to Pedro Pascual de Oliver, Ministro de España en México, Madrid, 2 October 1844, AHN-Estado, Leg. 8039, Exp. 10, doc. 5; Document 271, Anexo III, "Real Orden del Primer Secretario del Despacho de Estado al Ministro de España en México, Pedro Pascual de Oliver, acusando recibido de sus despachos 403 y 420 y recomendando vigile la conducta de los negros que lleguen a México, Madrid, 2 Septiembre 1844," in *Relaciones diplomáticas hispano-mexicanas*, 3: 72.

83. Document 278, Mexico, 22 August 1844, in *Relaciones diplomáticas hispano-mexicanas*, 3: 80; Document 280, Madrid, 23 August 1844, in *Relaciones diplomáticas hispano-mexicanas*, 3: 84.

84. Document 291, Anexo IV, Mexico, 27 September 1844, in *Relaciones diplomáticas hispano-mexicanas*, 3: 102–103.

85. Document 292, Mexico, 27 October 1844, in *Relaciones diplomáticas hispano-mexicanas*, 3: 105.

86. Pedro Pascual de Oliver, Ministro de España en México, to Ramón María Narváez, Primer Secretario del Despacho de Estado, Mexico, 24 October 1844, AHN-Estado, Leg. 8039, Exp. 10, doc. 8.

87. Document 291, Anexo VI, Mexico, 17 October 1844, in *Relaciones diplomáticas hispano-mexicanas*, 3: 103.

88. José Moreno to Ministro de Gracia y Justicia, Campeche, Mexico, 26 June 1846, ANC-ROC, Leg. 159, Exp. 106.

89. 15 April 1844, Veracruz, Movimiento Marítimo, Vol. 14, folio 6, Archivo General de la Nación, Mexico City, Mexico.

90. O'Donnell to Ministerio de Marina, Havana, 22 April 1846, ANC-AP, Leg. 141, Exp. 15; José Moreno to Ministro de Gracia y Justicia, Campeche, Mexico 26 June 1846, ANC-ROC, Leg. 159, Exp. 106.

91. O'Donnell to Ministerio de Marina, Havana, 22 April 1846, ANC-AP, Leg. 141, Exp. 15.

92. Secretario de Estado y del Despacho de la Gobierna de Ultramar to Ministro de Gracia y Justicia, Madrid, 24 November 1846, ANC-AP, Leg. 141, Exp. 15.

93. Ibid.

94. "Sobre la salida de Cuba los morenos libres Lino Lamoneda y Claudio Brindis de Salas que se introdujeron clandestinamente," Havana, 22 November 1850, ANC-AP, Leg. 44, Exp. 19.

95. José Muriel, el Coronel 2nd Jefe de S.M., Gobernación, to Capitán General

Superentiende Delegada De Hacienda, Havana, 25 July 1857, 31 July 1857, 17 September 1857, 4 November 1857, 20 October 1857, "Expediente sobre interesar el moreno José de los Ángeles Inocencio, residente en Veracruz, se le permite regresar a esta Isla de donde se le expulsó por los sucesos políticos del año de 1844," ANC-AP, Leg. 50, Exp. 17.

96. O'Donnell to Telestono G. De Escalante, Consulado de España en Veracruz, Havana, 5 November 1844, AHN-Estado, Leg. 8039, Exp. 10, doc. 9.

97. Ibid.

98. Spanish Consul in Vera Cruz to Cuba Captain General, Havana 22 November 1844, ANC-AP, Leg. 140, No. 39.

99. Leopoldo O'Donnell, Captain General of Cuba, to Primer Secretario de Estado y del Despacho, Havana, 22 November 1844, AHN-Estado, Leg. 8039, Exp. 10, doc. 6.

100. Royal Order from Francisco Martínez de la Rosa, Primer Secretario del Despacho de Estado, to Pedro Pascual de Oliver, Ministro de España in Mexico, Madrid, 4 January 1845, AHN-Estado, Leg. 8039, Exp. 10, doc. 11.

101. Salvador Bermúdez de Castro, Ministro de España in Mexico, to Primer Secretario de Despacho de Estado, Mexico, 20 February 1846, in *Relaciones diplomáticas hispano-mexicanas*, 3: 259.

102. J. M. de Castillo y Lanzas, Ministro de Relaciones Exteriores de México, to the Governor of Yucatán, Mexico, 19 January 1846 in *Relaciones diplomáticas hispano-mexicanas*, 3: 263.

103. Leopoldo O'Donnell to Secretario de Estado y del Despacho de la Gobernador de Ultramar, Havana, 30 November 1844, AHN-UGC, Leg. 4619, Exp. 5, letter no. 214; Francisco Martínez de la Rosa, Primer Secretario del Despacho de Estado, to Leopoldo O'Donnell, Madrid, 4 January 1845, AHN-Estado, Leg. 8039, Exp. 10, No. 12.

104. AHN-UGC, Leg. 4619, Exp. 5, letter no. 214.

105. Deschamps Chapeaux, *El negro en la economía habanera*, 25–26.

106. Angel Calderon de la Barca, Spanish Consul in U.S., to O'Donnell, Washington, D.C., 31 December 1844, ANC-AP, Leg. 140, Exp. 39.

107. Poyo, *With All, and for the Good of All*, 2.

108. Lazo, *Writing to Cuba:* 65, 91. See chapter 2 for details on Cuban exile writers, political positions, and newspapers established between in the mid-1840s to the mid-1850s.

109. Poyo, *With All, and for the Good of All*, 8–10.

110. Angel Calderon de la Barca, Spanish Consul in U.S., to O'Donnell, Washington, D.C, 18 February 1845, 21 February 1845, ANC-AP, Leg. 140, Exp. 39.

111. Ibid.

112. Richard S. Newman, *The Transformation of American Abolitionism: Fighting Slavery in the Early Republic* (Chapel Hill: University of North Carolina Press, 2002), 18, 24.113. Christopher Phillips, *Freedom's Port: The African American Community of Baltimore, 1790–1860* (Urbana: University of Illinois Press, 1997), 191–192.

114. Angel Calderon de la Barca, Spanish Consul in U.S., to O'Donnell, Washington, D.C., 21 February 1845, ANC-AP, Leg. 140, Exp. 39.

115. Ibid., 18 February 1845, ANC-AP, Leg. 140, Exp. 39.

116. Ibid.

117. Ibid.

118. Ibid.

119. Ibid., 22 April 1845, ANC-AP, Leg. 140, Exp. 39.

120. Ibid., 5 June 1845, ANC-AP, Leg. 140, Exp. 39.

121. O'Donnell to Calderon de la Barca, Spanish Consul in U.S.- Washington, D.C., New York City, 8 April 1847, AHN-UGC, Leg. 4628, Exp. 5, No. 3, folios1–2.

122. O'Donnell to Secretario de Estado y del Despacho de la Gobernación del Reina, Havana, 29 April 1847, AHN-UGC, Leg. 4628, Exp. 5, No. 2, folios 1, 4.

123. O'Donnell to Calderon de la Barca, Spanish Consul in U.S.- Washington, D.C., New York City, 8 April 1847, AHN-UGC, Leg. 4628, Exp. 5, No. 3, folios.1–2; Lazo, *Writing to Cuba*, 65, 141–142.

124. O'Donnell to Secretario de Estado y del Despacho de la Gobernación del Reina, Havana, 29 April 1847, AHN-UGC, Leg. 4628, Exp. 5, No. 2, folios 1, 4.

125. Ultramar to O'Donnell, Madrid, 28 June 1847, AHN-UGC, Leg. 4628, Exp. 5, No.9, folio 2.

126. Navarro, Ministro de la Gobernación de la Reina to Ultramar, Madrid, 14 November 1847, AHN-UGC, Leg. 4628, Exp. 5, No. 2, folios 11, 12; O'Donnell to Secretario de Estado y del Despacho de la Gobernación del Reino, Havana, 20 November 1847, AHN-UGC, Leg. 4628, Exp. 5, No.16, folios1–2.

127. Poyo, *With All, and for the Good of All*, 10.

128. Schmidt-Nowara, *Empire and Antislavery*, 35; "The Spanish Revolution," *New York Times*, 21 August 1854.

129. Joan Casanovas, *Bread, or Bullets!: Urban Labor and Spanish Colonialism in Cuba, 1850–1898* (Pittsburgh: University of Pittsburgh Press, 1998), 45, 64, 66.

130. Martínez-Fernández, *Fighting Slavery in the Caribbean*, 133; Estorch, *Apuntes para la historia*, 29, 34.

131. Casanovas, *Bread, or Bullets!*, 63–64, 67–69.

132. Royal Order, "Concediendo amnistía general a todos los que tomaron parte en conspiraciones en la Isla de Cuba," Madrid, 22 May 1854, ANC-AP, Leg. 122, Exp. 48.

133. Royal Order, Madrid, 12 December 1857, ANC-AP, Leg. 50, Exp. 23.

134. Ibid., Articles 2 and 4.

135. Ibid., Article 3.

136. Pedro de la Guardia to Captain General of Cuba, Veracruz, 20 August 1857; José del Carmen Arrisola to Cuba Captain General, Veracruz, 20 August 1857; Francisca Santa Cruz to Captain General of Cuba, Veracruz, 21 August 1857, "Documentos que se refieren a la solicitud de Pedro de la Guardia, José del Carmen Arrisola y Francisca Santa Cruz para que se les permita regresar a la isla comprendidos en la amnistía por delitos políticos," ANC-AP, Leg. 50, Exp. 21.

137. Jefe de Gobierno de Policía to Pablo de Urrutia, Spanish Consul in Veracruz, 9 November 1857, Havana, "Documentos que se refieren a la solicitud de Pedro de la Guardia, José del Carmen Arrisola, y Francisca Santa Cruz para que se les permita regresar a la isla comprendidos en la amnistía por delitos políticos," ANC-AP, Leg. 50, Exp. 21.

138. José Claudio Pieda to Senor Fiscal, Real Carcel de Havana , 28 September 1861, ANC-AP, Leg. 122, Exp. 72; Fiscal of the King to the Senior Fiscal, Havana, 6 October 1861, ANC-AP, Leg. 122, Exp. 72.

4 / Acts of Excess and Insubordination

1. Leopoldo O'Donnell to Secretario de Estado y del Despacho de la Gobernador

de Ultramar, Havana, 30 November 1844, 31 January 1845; 14 February 1845; 2 and 12 March 1845; 5 and 18 April 1845; 9, 21, and 31 May 1845; 31 July 1845; 10 and 31 August 1845; 10 and 28 September 1845; 11 and 31 October 1845; 4, 10, and 30 November 1845; and 10 December 1845, AHN-UGC, Leg. 4619, Exp. 5; correspondence from 30 April 1845 reports damage to the sugar harvest by a hurricane; correspondence from 30 June and 10 July 1845 reports on accidental fires in Matanzas.

2. Paquette, *Sugar Is Made with Blood*, 232, 273–274.

3. Teniente Gobernador de Puerto Príncipe, to Captain General of Cuba, Puerto Príncipe, 4 November 1845, "Expediente en que el Señor Teniente Gobernador de Puerto Príncipe ocurre a esta Real Audiencia exponiendo la necesidad de reprimir ejecutivamente las frecuentes faltas y excesos de las gentes de color y solicita se sierva autorizarle para imponer hasta cuatro jueces de obras públicas sin procedimiento escrito," ANC-AP, Leg. 43, Exp. 5, folio 3.

4. Pilar Poveda to Cuba Captain General, Havana, 27 August 1845, Archivo Nacional de Cuba, Instrucción Pública (hereafter ANC-IP), Leg. 40, Exp. 2114.

5. José María Pacheco to Gobierno Superior Civil, Havana, 20 April 1848; Felipe de Loira, Tenencia de Gobierno Político y Militar, to Gobierno Superior Civil, San Antonio, Archivo Nacional de Cuba, Gobierno General, Licencias (hereafter ANC-GG-L), Leg. 1245, Exp. 49330 and Exp. 49332.

6. Manuel Roque, Sección de Artes, to Cuba Captain General, Havana, 3 September 1852, Archivo Nacional de Cuba, Gobierno Superior Civil (hereafter ANC-GSC), Leg. 1055, Exp. 37514; Manuel Roque, Sección de Artes, to Cuba Captain General, Havana, 11 March 1852, ANC-GSC, Leg. 1055, Exp. 37516.

7. Paquette, *Sugar Is Made with Blood*, 236.

8. Leopoldo O'Donnell to Secretario del Estado y del Despacho de la Gobernación de Ultramar, Havana, 20 April 1844, AHN-UGC, Leg. 4618, Exp. 14, folios 4–5.

9. For Brazil, see Reis, *Slave Rebellion in Brazil*, 223; for Cuba, see Childs, *The 1812 Aponte Rebellion*, 147, 178; for Jamaica, see Michael Craton, *Testing the Chains: Resistance to Slavery in the British West Indies* (Ithaca: Cornell University Press, 1982); for New Orleans, see Albert Thrasher, *On to New Orleans! Louisiana's Heroic 1811 Slave Revolt* (Monterey, Cal.: Cypress Press, 1996); for Puerto Rico, see Guillermo A. Baralt, *Slave Revolts in Puerto Rico: Slave Conspiracies and Unrest in Puerto Rico 1795–1873* (Princeton, N.J.: Markus Wiener, 2008); for Virginia, see Sidbury, *Ploughshares into Swords*, 123–130, and Mary Kemp Davis, "What Happened in This Place?: In Search of the Female Slave in the Nat Turner Slave Insurrection," in Kenneth S. Greenberg,. ed., *Nat Turner: A Slave Rebellion in History and Memory* (Oxford: Oxford University Press, 2003), 161.

10. Pérez, Jr., *Cuba: Between Reform and Revolution*, 78–78; Bergad, Iglesias García, and Barcia, *The Cuban Slave Market*, 27, 31, 55.

11. Cirilo Villaverde, *Cecilia Valdés* (Havana: Editorial Letras Cubanas, 1981), 71; Lazo, *Writing to Cuba*, 10–11.

12. Leopoldo O'Donnell to Ministro de Estado, Havana, 15 June 1844, ANC-AP, Leg. 42, Exp. 3.

13. Dolores Ruiz to Cuba Captain General, 4 September 1848, Havana, ANC-GSC, Leg. 1449, No. 56824; Jane McManus, *Cuba's Islands of Dreams: Voices from the Isle of Pines and Youth* (Gainesville: University of Florida Press, 2000), 4.

14. Félix Erenchun, *Anales de la isla de Cuba: Diccionario administrativo,*

económico, estadístico y legislativo, Año 1855 (Havana: Imprenta de la Antilla, 1859), 3: 1480.

15. Ibid., 3: 2254–2255.

16. Royal Order of Carlos III to José de la Concha, Captain General of Cuba, 2 April 1855, Havana, ANC-GSC, Leg. 1153, No. 44259.

17. Erenchun, *Anales de la isla de Cuba*, 3: 1480.

18. "Cedula de libres de color," ANC-GSC, Leg. 1268, No. 49827; Erenchun, *Anales de la isla de Cuba*, 3: 2254–2255.

19. "Cedula de libres de color," ANC-GSC, Leg. 1268, No. 49827. According to the report, authorities had issued a total of 51,610 *cédulas de seguridad*.

20. Erenchun, *Anales de la isla de Cuba*, 3: 1480.

21. Ibid., 3: 2253–2256.

22. Estimate calculated by projecting a steady annual population increase between the 1851 and 1862 censuses. See Kiple, *Blacks in Colonial Cuba*, 92–93; Casanovas, *Bread, or Bullets!*, 51.

23. Leopoldo O'Donnell to Secretario del Estado y del Despacho de la Gobernación de Ultramar, Havana, 20 April 1844, AHN-UGC, Leg. 4618, Exp. 14, folio 4.

24. Minutes of the Royal Order to the Captain General of Cuba, Madrid, 29 July 1844, AHN-UGC, Leg. 4618, Exp. 14, folios 1–2; Orovio and González, *Racismo e inmigración en Cuba*, 109.

25. General Regulations, Articles 2 and 7; Estate Regulations, Article 5 and 6. Zamora, *Biblioteca de legislación*, 3: 139–141; Paquette, *Sugar Is Made with Blood*, 273–274.

26. Paquette, *Sugar Is Made with Blood*, 273–274.

27. *Anales de las reales juntas de fomento y sociedad económica de la Habana, julio a diciembre, 1849* (Havana: Imprenta del Gobierno y Capitania general por S.M., 1849), I28. José María Pacheco to Gobierno Superior Civil, Havana, 20 April, 1848; Felipe de Loira, Tenencia de Gobierno Político y Militar to Gobierno Superior Civil, San Antonio, ANC-GG-L, Leg. 1245, Exp. 49330, Exp. 49332.

29. José Lamarra to Gobierno Superior Civil, Havana, 1 April 1848, ANC-GG-L, ANC, Leg. 1245, Exp. 49316.

30. Ramón Campos to Gobierno Superior Civil, Havana, 18 June 1848, 28 June 1848, 3 July 1848, ANC-GG-L, Leg. 1245, Exp. 49303.

31. José Isidoro Hernández to Gobierno Superior Civil, Havana, 20 May 1848, ANC-GG-L, Leg. 1245, Exp. 49332.

32. Casanovas, *Bread, or Bullets!*, 58–59.

33. General Regulations, Articles 2 and 7; Estate Regulations, Article 5 and 6. Zamora, *Biblioteca de legislación*, 3: 139–141; Paquette, *Sugar Is Made with Blood*, 273–274.

34. Casanovas, *Bread, or Bullets!*, 59.

35. Manuel Roque, Sección de Artes, to Cuba Captain General, Havana, 3 September 1852, ANC-GSC, Leg. 1055, Exp. 37514.

36. Gefetura Principal de Policía to Cuba Captain General, Havana, 30 November 1851, ANC-GSC, Leg. 1055, Exp. 37496.

37. Manuel Roque, Sección de Artes, to Cuba Captain General, Havana, 11 March 1852, ANC-GSC, Leg. 1055, Exp. 37516.

38. Kiple, *Blacks in Colonial Cuba*, 91, 94.

39. *Anales de las Reales Juntas*, I: 46–47.

40. Casanovas, *Bread or Bullets!*, 49, 66–67.

41. General Regulations, Articles 2 and 7; Estate Regulations, Article 5 and 6. Zamora, *Biblioteca de legislación*, 3:139–141; Paquette, *Sugar Is Made with Blood*, 273–274.

42. Juan García Feblita, Havana, 24 January 1845, ANC-GSC, Leg. 1448, Exp. 56802.

43. Leopoldo O'Donnell, Havana, 31 May 1844, Circular, "Prohíbo que por ningún motivo o causa sea cual fuese la que se a le que tenga entrada en esta Isla aunque sea procedente de ella o haya mediado corta ausencia, individuos alguno de color clase de libres o emancipados," ANC-ROC, Leg. 133, Exp. 220.

44. Zamora, *Biblioteca de legislación*, 3:139–141; Paquette, *Sugar Is Made with Blood*, 273–274.

45. Reid, "Tensions of Race, Gender and Midwifery in Colonial Cuba," 14–17.

46. Cuba, *Colección de los fallos*, Nos. 15, 2.

47. Ibid.; Deschamps Chapeaux, *El negro en la economía habanera*, 180–182.

48. Pilar Poveda to Cuba Captain General, Havana, 27 August 1845, ANC-IP, Leg. 40, Exp. 2114.

49. Inspección de Estudios de las islas de Cuba y Puerto Rico to Francisco Alonso Frudz, Presidente de la Sección 3a, Havana, 20 September 1845, ANC-IP, Leg. 40, Exp. 2115.

50. "Reglamento para la clase de parteras establecida en el hospital de caridad de San Francisco de Paula de esta Ciudad, bajo los auspicio de la Real Sociedad Patriótica y dirigida por el Don D. Domingo Rosain," Havana, 1845, ANC-IP, Leg. 40, Exp. 2115.

51. "Real Orden remitiendo a informa la solicitud de Doña Francisca Calderón pidiendo ejercer el oficio de partera," Havana, 5 January 1857, ANC-ROC, Leg. 196, Exp. 10.

52. Jacobo de la Pezuela, *Diccionario geográfico, estadístico, histórico de la isla de Cuba* (Madrid: Imprenta del establecimiento de Mellado, 1863), 3: 357, 360, 363, 371; 4: 30.

53. "Matricula General de Comercio en el año 1869–70," Havana, ANC-GG, Leg. 478, Exp. 23542.

54. ANC-GG, Leg. 478, Exp. 23542, 1869–70.

55. In Cuba, these organizations evolved over the colonial era from *cofradías de negros* (black brotherhoods) to *cabildos de nación*, and finally to *sociedades de color* (societies of color). Carmen Victoria Montejo Arrechea, *Sociedades de instrucción y recreo de pardo y morenos que existieron en Cuba colonial: Periódo 1878–1898* (Veracruz: Instituto Veracruzano de Cultura, 1993), 15; Klein, *African Slavery in Latin America and the Caribbean*, 233; Matthew Restall, *The Black Middle: Africans, Maya, and Spaniards in Colonial Yucatán* (Palo Alto: Stanford University Press, 2009), 237.

56. Deschamps Chapeaux, *El negro en la economía habanera*, 31–33; Montejo Arrechea, *Sociedades de instrucción y recreo*, 17.

57. Deschamps Chapeaux, *El negro en la economía habanera*, 43–44; Paquette, *Sugar Is Made with Blood*, 120.

58. Ivor L. Miller and Bassey E. Bassey, *Voice of the Leopard: African Secret Societies and Cuba* (Jackson: University Press of Mississippi, 2009), 83–84; Deschamps Chapeaux, *El negro en la economía habanera*, 22; Gloria García, *Conspiraciones y revueltas: La actividad política de los negros en Cuba (1790–1845)* (Santiago de Cuba: Editorial Oriente, 2003), 104– 108.

59. "An Insurrection in Cuba—Important," *Pennsylvania Inquirer and National Gazette*, 6 June 1843; "Another Slave Insurrection in the Island of Cuba," *Emancipator and Free American*, 15 June 1843.

60. Finch, "Insurgency at the Crossroads," 341.

61. Cuba, *Colección de los fallos*, No. 27.

62. Ibid., Nos. 1, 27.

63. Paquette, *Sugar Is Made with Blood*, 228, 74.

64. Quoted in Deschamps Chapeaux, *El negro en la economía habanera*, 44.

65. Bergad, *The Comparative Histories of Slavery in Brazil, Cuba, and the United States*, 275, 277; Saco, *Supresión del trafico de esclavos en Cuba*, 50.

66. Howard, *Changing History*, 96.

67. Cabildo Nuestra Señora de Monserate, Havana, 27 October 1848, ANC-GSC, Leg. 1677, No. 83984; Cabildo San Pedro Nolasco, Havana, 5 July 1862, ANC-GSC Leg. 1677, No. 83997; Cabildo Santo Cristo de Buen Viaje, Havana, 8 August 1864, ANC-GSC, Leg. 1677, No. 84,001; Cabildo Satísima Trinidad, Havana, 13 December 1866, ANC-GSC, Leg. 1677, No. 83985.68. Casanovas, *Bread or Bullets!*, 63, 69.69. Expediente solicitud del pardo libre José de la Paz Zequeira para establecer una sociedad de socorros mutuos en el barrio de Monserrate, 1857, Havana, ANC-GSC, Leg. 406, No. 15914.

70. José Maria Armenteros and Vencelad Manresa to Gobernador y Capitán General, 30 January 1860, Havana, ANC-GSC, Leg. 410, No. 16102.

71. Expediente que se refiere a la solicitud hecha por Antonio Bonilla y otros, para establecer un cabildo de nación bajo la advocación de Nuestra Señora de Regla, 1859, ANC-GSC, Leg. 1677, No. 83983.

72. Archivo Histórico Nacional, Madrid, Ultramar, Fomento (hereafter AHN-UF), Libro 1, Leg. 30, Exp. 1–40.

73. Kiple, *Blacks in Colonial Cuba*, 92–93, 95–96. The 1846 and 1861 censuses listed increase in the free population of color from 149,226 to 232,493 (+83,267 or 35.8%) and slaves from 323,759 to 370,553 (+46,794 or 12.6%).

74. "Consulte sobre no permitir cabildos de negros criollos," 1864, Archivo Nacional de Cuba, Consejo de la Administración de la Isla de Cuba (hereafter ANC-CA), Leg. 8, No. 562.

75. El Consejo de Administración de Cuba, Zambrana to Consejero Presente El Conde O'Reilly, 6 September 1864, Havana, ANC-CA, Leg. 8, No. 562.

76. "Expediente en que Antonio Veites y Zayas solicita establecer un cabildo de negros gangá," Havana, 1869, ANC-GSC, Leg. 1677, No. 83981.

77. Casanovas, *Bread or Bullets!*, 93.

78. "Antecedentes al No. 22 de la causa de conspiración de negros," 23 May 1853, Havana, ANC-AP, Leg. 48, No. 22; "Sentencia de la causa por conspiración conocida por la de la Vuelta de Abajo," 7 April 1853, Havana, ANC-AP 48, Leg. 18

5 / The Rise and Fall of the Militia of Color

1. Cuba, *Colección de los fallos*, No. 6.

2. Deschamps Chapeaux, *El negro en la economía habanera*, 65, 67, 74–75.

3. Paquette, *Sugar Is Made with Blood*, 228; Klein, "The Colored Militia of Cuba," 22–23; Justo Zaragoza, *Las insurrecciones en Cuba*, 2 vols. (Madrid: Imprenta de Miguel G. Hernández, 1872–1873), 1: 536; Zamora, *Biblioteca de legislación*, 4: 285.

4. Kuethe, *Cuba*, 123–26; Paquette, *Sugar Is Made with Blood*, 251; Johnson, *Social Transformation of Eighteenth-Century Cuba*, 184.

5. Arango, *De la factoría a la Colonia*, 88–91; Vinson, "Race and Badge," 491; Archer, "Pardos, Indians, and the Army of New Spain," 235.

6. Klein, "The Colored Militia of Cuba," 23.

7. Deschamps Chapeaux, *Los batallones pardos y morenos libres*, 83–84; Deschamps Chapeaux, *El negro en la economía habanera*, 22.

8. Vicente Vázquez Queipo, *Informe fiscal sobre fomento de la población blanca en la isla de Cuba y emancipación progresiva de la esclava con una breve reseña de las reformas y modificaciones que para conseguirlo convendría establecer en la legislación y constitución coloniales presentado a la superintendencia general delegada de Real Hacienda en diciembre de 1844 por el Fiscal de la misma* (Madrid: Imprenta de J. M. Alegria, 1845), 12.

9. Captain General Juan de la Pezuela to La Gaceta Havana, 4 August 1859, ANC-GSC, Leg. 1267, Exp. 49801, folios 30–31.

10. Ursula Viviana to Gobierno Político, 11 October 1859, Havana, ANC-GSC, Leg. 1268, No. 49806, folio 257.

11. Johnson, *Social Transformation of Eighteenth-Century Cuba*, 184.

12. Ibid., 121–122, 147.

13. Ibid., 123; Kuethe, *Cuba*, 139–140.

14. Kuethe, *Cuba*, 140.

15. Johnson, *Social Transformation of Eighteenth-Century Cuba*, 128–129,130,138, 146–147; Kuethe, *Cuba*, 163.

16. Francisco de Arango y Parreño, "Discurso sobre la agricultura de la Habana y medios de fomentarla" in *Obras* (Havana: Howson y Heinen, 1888), 1: 97.

17. Johnson, *Social Transformation of Eighteenth-Century Cuba*, 147.

18. Kuethe, *Cuba*, 164–165. For a detailed discussion of military privileges, see chapter 1.

19. Kuethe, *Cuba*, 140, 141, 144–145.

20. Arango, "Discurso sobre la agricultura," *Obras* 1: 97.

21. "Representación dirigida por el Real Consulado de la Habana al ministro de hacienda en 10 de Julio 1799," reprinted in Saco, *Historia de la esclavitud*, 5: 136–137.

22. Childs, *The 1812 Aponte Rebellion*, 91.

23. Johnson, *Social Transformation of Eighteenth-Century Cuba*, 127–128.

24. Landers, *Atlantic Creoles in the Age of Revolution*, 143.

25. Paquette, *Sugar Is Made with Blood*, 124–125.

26. Deschamps Chapeaux, *Los batallones pardos y morenos libres*, 73–76.

27. Spain, Córtes (1810–1813), *Diario de las Sesiones de las Córtes generales y extraordinarias, dieron principio el 24 de septiembre de 1810, y terminaron el 20 de septiembre de 1813* (Madrid, 1870), 1: 331.

28. James F. King, "The Colored Castes and American Representation in the Córtes of Cadiz," *Hispanic American Historical Review* 33.1 (February 1953): 33, 42–44.

29. James E. Rodríguez O., *The Independence of Spanish America* (Cambridge: Cambridge University Press, 1998), 87; King, "The Colored Castes and American Representation,"41; Adolfo de Castro, ed., *Córtes de Cadiz: Complementos de las sesiones verificadas en la isla de Le6n y en Cádiz* (Madrid, 1913), 1: 177–178; Marie Laure

Rieu-Millán, *Los diputados americanos en las Córtes de Cádiz: Igualdad o independencia* (Madrid: Consejo superior de Investigaciones Científicas, 1990), 168–169.

30. Manuel Chust, *La cuestión nacional americana en las Córtes de Cádiz (1810–1814)* (Valencia: Centro Francisco Tomás y Valiente, UNED Alzira-Valencia, Fundación Instituto Historia Social, 1999), 108–111.

31. Ibid.

32. Rieu-Millán, *Los diputados americanos en las Córtes de Cádiz*, 169; Childs, *The 1812 Aponte Rebellion*, 159.

33. King, "The Colored Castes and American Representation," 33.

34. Ibid., 33, 44.

35. Ibid., 47, 52–53; Jon Cowans, ed., *Modern Spain: A Documentary History* (Philadelphia: University of Pennsylvania Press, 2003), 26–27.

36. Rodríguez O., *The Independence of Spanish America*, 86; King, "The Colored Castes and American Representation," 53.

37. King, "The Colored Castes and American Representation," 54.

38. Rodríguez O., *The Independence of Spanish America*, 91.

39. Quoted in Childs, *The 1812 Aponte Rebellion*, 1–4, 191–192; Paquette, *Sugar Is Made with Blood*, 123–124.

40. Deschamps Chapeaux, *El negro en la economía habanera*, 70.

41. Ibid., 123–125.

42. Justo Sentimiento-ANC-CM, Leg. 60, No. 2.

43. Marco Rodriguez to Captain General of Cuba, Havana, 12 July 1830, AGI-Cuba, Leg. 2114, No. 7.

44. Kuethe, *Cuba*, 123, 126, 170, 172; Klein, "The Colored Militia of Cuba," 24–25.

45. Kuethe, *Cuba*, 176.

46. Childs, *The 1812 Aponte Rebellion*, 89.

47. For a discussion of *fuero militar* privileges, see chapter 1.

48. Childs, *The 1812 Aponte Rebellion*, 91–92.

49. Paquette, *Sugar Is Made with Blood*, 126.

50. Varela, "Memoria que demuestra la necesidad de extinguir la esclavitud," 4: 12; Thomas, *Cuba: The Pursuit of Freedom*, 62.

51. Deschamps Chapeaux, *El negro en la economía habanera*, 21.

52. Miguel Tacón, Cuba Captain General to Juan Batista Velasquez, Captain Pedaneo, Havana, 12–13 July 1835, ANC-CM, Leg. 11, Exp. 1.

53. Howard, *Changing History*, 79.

54. Miguel Tacón, Cuba Captain General to Juan Batista Velasquez, Captain Pedaneo, Havana, 12–13 July 1835, ANC-CM, Leg. 11, Exp. 1.

55. Deschamps Chapeaux, *Los batallones pardos y morenos libres*, 83–84; Deschamps Chapeaux, *El negro en la economía habanera*, 22–23.

56. Pedro Deschamps Chapeaux, "Margarito Blanco, 'Ocongo de Ultan'," *Boletín del Instituto de Historia y del Archivo Nacional* (Havana) 65 (July-December 1964): 98, 102, 104.

57. Quoted in Deschamps Chapeaux, *El negro en la economía habanera*, 23.

58. Paquette, *Sugar Is Made with Blood*, 123; Klein, "The Colored Militia of Cuba," 22–23.

59. Simo Jerodes to Cuba Captain General, Santo Domingo, 6 May 1844, ANC-GG, Leg. 286, No. 13907; Deschamps Chapeaux, *El negro en la economía habanera*, 108.

60. Leopoldo O'Donnell to Ministro de Estado, Havana, 15 June 1844, ANC-AP, Leg. 42, Exp. 3, folios. 1–2; Zamora, *Biblioteca de legislación*, 4: 285.

61. Vinson, *Bearing Arms for His Majesty*, 212.

62. Mónico de Flores, Francisco Abrante, Marcelino Gamarra, et al., *Justo sentimiento de pardos y morenos españoles libres de la Habana* (Havana: Oficina Filantrópica de Don J. M. de Oro, 1823), p. 5, ANC-CM, Leg. 60, No. 2.

63. Kuethe, *Cuba*, 174; Johnson, *Social Transformation of Eighteenth-Century Cuba*, 60.

64. Spain, Superintendencia General, *Informe fiscal sobre fomento de la población blanca*, 80.

65. Casanovas, *Bread, or Bullets!*," 67; Klein, "The Colored Militia of Cuba," 25.

66. Juan de la Pezuela, Captain General of Cuba, to Secretaria Militar, Havana, 24 May 1854, in Estorch, *Apuntes para la historia*, Document 16, 160.

67. Spain, Superintendencia General, *Informe fiscal sobre fomento de la población blanca*, 80; Klein, "The Colored Militia of Cuba," 25.

68. James M. Phillippo, *The United States and Cuba* (London: Pewtress, 1857), 418.

69. Casanovas, *Bread, or Bullets!*, 69, Cárlos de Sedano y Cruzat, *Cuba desde 1850 a 1873: Colección de informes, memorias, proyectos y antecedentes sobre el gobierno de la isla de Cuba relativos al citado período* (Madrid: Imprenta Nacional, 1873), 178; Estorch, *Apuntes para la historia*, Document 16, 160.

70. Captain General of Cuba to El Brigador Jefe, Joaquín Morales de Brada, Delegada de Hacienda, Havana, 22 October 1855, "Expediente sobre la reforma de la milicia de color," ANC-GSC, Leg. 1371, Exp. 53440, folios 1–2.

71. Amelia Matilda Murray, *Letters from the United States, Cuba, and Canada* (London: G. P. Putnam, 1856), 243, 263.

72. Estorch, *Apuntes para la historia*, 33–35.

73. Klein, "The Colored Militia of Cuba," 24.

74. Captain General of Cuba to El Brigador Jefe, "Expediente sobre la reforma de la milicia de color," folio 3.

75. "Estado del contingente que debe dar la jurisdicción de la Habana a las secciones de Milicias de Color," Havana, 7 July 1859, ANC-GSC, Leg. 1267, Exp. 49801, folio7.

76. Cuba Captain General to La Gaceta, Havana, 4 August 1859, ANC-GSC, Leg. 1267, Exp. 49801, folios 30–31.

77. *Pardos* increased from 196 to 300. *Morenos* increased from 136 to 703. See table 2, "Estado del contingente que debe dar la jurisdicción de la Habana a las secciones de Milicias de Color," Havana, 7 July 1859, ANC-GSC 1267/49801, folio18.

78. Leon G. Campbell, "Black Power in Colonial Peru: The 1779 Tax Rebellion of Lambayeque," *Phylon* 33.2 (1972): 143.

79. Peter Blanchard, *Under the Flags of Freedom: Slave Soldiers and the Wars of Independence in Spanish South America* (Pittsburgh: University of Pittsburgh Press, 2008), 68–70.

80. Cuba Captain General to La Gaceta, Havana, 4 August 1859, ANC-GSC, Leg. 1267, Exp. 49801, folios 30–31.

81. Campbell, "Black Power in Colonial Peru," 143.

82. ANC-GSC, Leg. 1267, Exp. 49801, folios 30–31.

83. Leopoldo O'Donnell, *Reglamento para las milicias disciplinadas de color de la Isla de Cuba* (Madrid, 1858), ANC-GSC, Leg. 1189, Exp. 46571.

84. Cuba Captain General to La Gaceta, Havana, 4 August 1859, ANC-GSC, Leg. 1267, Exp. 49801, folios 30–31.

85. Marcelino Lamadrón to Sr. Alcalde de primera, Matanzas, 25 August 1859, ANC-GSC, Leg. 1268, Exp. 49804, folios 1–5; Margarita Chacón to Cuba Captain General, Havana, 20 August 1859, ANC-GSC, Leg. 1267, Exp. 49800, folio 1; "Documentos justificaciones de las exenciones verificados en el sorteo para el reemplazo de milicias de la sistema verificado el primero de septiembre," Santa Clara, 27 August 1859, ANC-GSC 1267, Exp. 49799, folio 64; Juan Amierra y Díaz, Teniente de Gobierno de Cienfuegos to Gobierno Superior Civil, Cienfuegos, 20 August 1859, "Cuaderno de las exclusiones y exenciones del servicio de Milicia de Color," ANC-GSC, 1267, Exp. 49798, folios 12–16.

86. O'Donnell, Reglamento para las milicias disciplinadas, ANC-GSC, Leg. 1189, Exp. 4657187. Marcelino Lamadrón to Sr. Alcalde de primera, Matanzas, 25 August 1859, ANC-GSC, Leg. 1268, Exp. 49804, folios 1–5.

88. Santiago Ramos to Cuba Captain General, Havana, 5 November 1860, ANC, GSC, Leg. 1268, Exp. 49810.

89. Florencio Quesada to Captain General Gobierno Superior Civil, Havana, 27 October 1859, ANC-GSC, Leg. 1268, Exp. 49820.

90. Commandant's report; Teniente Coronel, Blanes to Gobernador, Matanzas, 16–17 August 1859, ANC-GSC, Leg. 1268, Exp. 49805, folios 17–19.

91. Emilio Navarro to Cuba Captain General, Havana, 6 October 1860, ANC-GSC, Leg. 1268, Exp. 49849.

92. Ana Consnegra to Gobernador Político, Havana, 26 September 1859, ANC-GSC, Leg. 1267, Exp. 49802.

93. Lorenza Reyes to Gobernador Político, Havana, 22 October 1859, ANC-GSC, Leg. 1268, Exp. 49813.

94. Report; Teniente Coronel, Blanes to Gobernador, Matanzas, 16–17 August 1859, "Oficina abierto el juicio de excepciones para alistamiento de las mismas milicias," ANC-GSC, Leg. 1268, No. 49805, Exp. 19; Juan Amierra y Diaz, Teniente de Gobierno de Cienfuegos to Gobierno Superior Civil, Cienfuegos, 20 August 1859, "Cuaderno de las exclusiones y exenciones del servicio de Milicia de Color," ANC-GSC, 1267, Exp. 49798, folios 12–16; "Documentos justificaciones de las exenciones verificados en el sorteo para el reemplazo de milicias de la sistema verificado el primero de septiembre," Santa Clara, 31 August 1859, ANC-GSC, Leg. 1267, Exp. 49799, folio116; Santa Clara, 30 August 1859, ANC-GSC 1267, Exp. 49799, folio 77.

95. Felipe José Bernal to Cuba Captain General, Havana, 3 October 1859, ANC-GSC, 1268, Exp. 49834; Juan Amierra y Diaz, Teniente de Gobierno de Cienfuegos to Gobierno Superior Civil, Cienfuegos, 20 August 1859, "Cuaderno de las exclusiones y exenciones del servicio de Milicia de Color," ANC-GSC, Leg. 1267, Exp. 49798, folios 12–16; José Isidoro Valdés to Gobierno Político de Havana, Havana, 26 October 1860, ANC-GSC, Leg. 1268, Exp. 49821.

96. O'Donnell, *Reglamento para las milicias disciplinadas de color*, ANC-GSC, Leg. 1189, Exp. 46571, folios15–16.

97. Cayetano Fantini to Someruelos and report to the King, Havana, 9 September 1802, Archivo General de Indias, Papeles de Cuba, Leg. 1578, quoted in Kuethe, *Cuba*, 145.

98. José de los Ángeles Acosta to Gobernador Político, Havana, 21 September 1859, ANC-GSC, Leg. 1268, Exp. 49806, folio 237; Ciriaco García to Presidente del

Ayuntamiento, Havana 12 September 1859, ANC-GSC, Leg. 1268, Exp. 49811; Report, Teniente Coronel, Blanes to Gobernador, Matanzas 16–17 August 1859, ANC-GSC, Leg. 1268, Exp. 49805, folio 19; Francisco Pérez de Alejos to Cuba Captain General, Santa Clara, 27 August 1859, "Documentos justificaciones de las escenciones verificados en el sorteo para el reemplazo de milicias de la sistema verificado el primero de septiembre," ANC-GSC, Leg. 1267, Exp. 49799, folio 64.

99. Santa Clara, 20 August 1859, ANC-GSC, Leg. 1267, Exp. 49799, folios. 58, 99–101.

100. Regino Ordar to Ayuntamiento, Havana, 5 October 1859, ANC-GSC, Leg. 1268, Exp. 49827.

101. General Subgobernador del Cuerpo to Primera Comandancia de Batallón de Honrados Bomberos de la Havana, 23 September 1859, ANC-GSC, Leg. 1267, Exp. 49802.

102. José Antonio Peña to Cuba Captain General, Havana, 1 October 1859, ANC-GSC, Leg. 1268, Exp. 49809.

103. ANC-GSC, Leg. 1189, Exp. 46571, folio 9.

104. Secundino de la Hoz to Cuba Captain General, Havana, 8 November 1860, ANC-GSC, Leg. 1268, Exp. 49840.

105. José de la Rosa Valdés to Cuba Captain General, Havana, 27 October 1860, ANC-GSC, Leg. 1268, Exp. 49839.

106. Magdeleno García to Cuba Captain General, Havana, 17 October 1859, ANC-GSC, Leg. 1268, Exp. 49832.

107. José Marcos Mora to Gobernador Militar, Havana, 24 October 1859, Havana, ANC-GSC, Leg. 1268, Exp. 49822.

108. Medical Certificate for Juan Rodríguez, Havana, 25 March 1861, ANC-GSC, Leg. 1268, Exp. 49857.

109. Pedro Pablo de Rojas to Gobernador, Havana, 22 October 1859, ANC-GSC, Leg. 1268, Exp. 49816.

110. Francisco Javier Pita to Cuba Captain General, Havana, 27 October 1859, ANC-GSC, Leg. 1268, Exp. 49843.

111. Enlistment Committee to Cuba Captain Gen, 20 September 1859, Havana, ANC-GSC, Leg.. 1267, Exp. 49802, folios 164–165, 177–183. Out of the 538 individuals enumerated in the report, there were a total of 147 desertions (27.3%): 10 *pardos* and 137 *morenos*.

112. Dana, *To Cuba and Back*, 246.

113. Pezuela, *Diccionario geográfico, estadístico, histórico de Cuba*, 2: 276; Estado del contingente que debe dar la jurisdicción de la Habana a las secciones de Milicias de Color," Havana, 7 July 1859, ANC-GSC-1267/49801, folio 7.

114. Klein, "The Colored Militia of Cuba," 25.

115. Frederick Hardman, *The Spanish Campaign in Morocco* (Edinburgh: William Blackwood and Sons, 1860), 310; "Documento acerca del proyecto de Don Martín de Arredondo y Oléa de formar un batallón de voluntarios de pardos y morenos libres que pasasen a tomar parte en la guerra de Afrecha, recaudación de recursos al efecto y ofrecimientos de servicios," Havana, 24 February 1860, ANC-AP, Leg. 53, Exp. 1, folios. 4–5;

116. Virgil de Quiñones, Consejero Presente to La Sección de Gobierno, Havana, 21 September 1865, ANC-CA, Leg. 9, Exp. 740.

117. Virgil de Quiñones, Consejero Presente to La Sección de Gobierno, Havana, 11 September 1865, ANC-CA, Leg. 9, Exp. 740.

118. Havana, 11 and 21 September 1865, ANC-CA, Leg. 9, Exp. 740.

6 / Balancing Acts

1. Leopoldo O'Donnell to Secretario del Estado y del Despacho de la Gobernación de Ultramar, Havana, 20 April 1844, AHN-UGC, Leg. 4618, Exp. 14, folio 4.

2. Leopoldo O'Donnell, Havana, 13 May 1844, ANC-ROC, Leg. 133, Exp. 220; Leopoldo O'Donnell, Havana, 13 May 1844, ANC-ROC, Leg. 133, Exp. 220; Leopoldo O'Donnell to Ministro de Estado, Havana, 15 June 1844, ANC-AP, Leg. 42, Exp. 3. For a detailed discussion, see chapter 4.

3. Paquette, *Sugar Is Made with Blood*, 229. The Military Commission listed a total of 78 executions, which included one slave woman, one white man, 38 male slaves, and 38 free men of color; and 1,292 individuals sentenced to imprisonment, including 543 slaves, 743 free people of color, and 6 whites.

4. The 1841 census lists 436,495 slaves and 152,838 free people of color, and the 1846 census enumerates 323,759 slaves and 149,226 free people of color. Kiple, *Blacks in Colonial Cuba,* 88–90; Spain, Superintendencia General Delegada de Real Hacienda, 1841, *Informe fiscal sobre fomento de la población blanca en la isla de cuba y emancipación progresiva de la esclava con una breve reseña de las reformas y modificaciones que para conseguirlo convendría establecer en la legislación y constitución coloniales* (Madrid, 1845), 6.

5. Torres-Cuevas, Ibarra Cuesta, and García Rodríguez, eds., *Félix Varela,* 2: 115–116.

6. McCadden and McCadden, *Félix Varela*, 45–46; Julio Hernández García, "La presencia de las Islas Canarias en la Cuba decimonónica: análisis y valoración cuantitativa (1834–1912)," in *Memorias del Primer Congreso sobre la emigración española hacia el área del caribe desde finales siglo xix* (Santo Domingo: Ediciones Fundación García Arévalo, 2002), 70; Torres-Cuevas, Ibarra Cuesta, and García Rodríguez, eds., *Félix Varela*, 115–116.

7. Francisco Arango to King of Spain, 30 August 1830, Havana, AGI-Indiferente, Leg. 2828, folio 4.

8. Saco, *La supresión del trafico de esclavos*, 27.

9. Hernández García, "La presencia de las Islas Canarias en la Cuba decimonónica," 69–72.

10. Duvon C. Corbitt, "Immigration in Cuba," *Hispanic American Historical Review* 22 (May 1942): 294.

11. Naranjo Orovio and García González, *Racismo e inmigración*, 99.

12. James J. Parsons, "The Migration of Canary Islanders to the Americas: An Unbroken Current since Columbus," *The Americas* 39.4 (April 1983): 470.

13. Ibid., 469; Naranjo Orovio and García González, *Racismo e inmigración*, 103–104.

14. Turnbull, *Travels in the West*, 135, 144, 261. Turnbull listed the official returns as 8,061, with the following breakdown: 3,769 (46.8%) from Spain, 2,690 (33.4%) from the Canary Islands, 1,004 (12.5%) from the United States, 347 (4.3%) from Mexico and other parts of America, 170 (2.1%) from France, and 81 (about 1%) from England and other parts of Europe.

15. Corbitt, "Immigration in Cuba," 294.

16. Ultramar to Intendente de Ejército de la Habana and Presidente de la Junta de Fomento de Agricultura y Comercio, Madrid, 8 March 1841, AGI-AHN, Leg. 91, Exp. 3, No. 3, folio 1.

17. Ayuntamiento to Ultramar, Santiago de Cuba, 14 May 1841, AGI-AHN, Leg. 91, Exp. 3, No. 15, folio 3.

18. Antonio Magín Plá to Ultramar, Lugo, 31 March 1841, AGI-AHN, Leg. 91, Exp. 3, No. 23, folio 2; Gobierno Político to Secretario de Estado y del Despacho de la Gobernación de la Península, Pontevedra, 21 March 1841, AGI-AHN, Ultramar, Leg. 91, Exp. 3, No. 25, folio 1.

19. Antonio Magín Plá to Ultramar, Lugo, 31 March 1841, AGI-AHN, Leg. 91, Exp. 3, No. 23, folio 2.

20. Ultramar to Ministro de la Gobernación de la Península, Madrid, 3 March 1841, AGI-AHN, Leg. 91, Exp. 3, No. 4, folio 1; recommended locations in Spain were La Coruña, Lugo, and Pontevedra.

21. Naranjo Orovio and García González, *Racismo e inmigración en Cuba*, 114.

22. Paquette, *Sugar Is Made with Blood*, 95.23. Naranjo Orovio and García González, *Racismo e inmigración en Cuba*, 107–109, 115

24. Julio Hernández García, "La planificación de la emigración canaria a Cuba y Puerto Rico, siglo XIX," in *Coloquio de Historia Canario-Americana* II (Seville: Ediciones del Excmo, Cabildo de Gran Canaria, 1979), 1: 211.

25. Turnbull, *Travels in the West*, 261.

26. Kiple, *Blacks in Colonial Cuba*, 88–90; Spain, Superintendencia General Delegada de Real Hacienda, 1841, *Informe fiscal sobre fomento de la población blanca en la isla de cuba y emancipación progresiva de la esclava con una breve reseña de las reformas y modificaciones que para conseguirlo convendría establecer en la legislación y constitución coloniales* (Madrid: Imprenta. de J. M. Alegria, 1845), 6.

27. Bergad, Iglesias García, and Barcia, *The Cuban Slave Market*, 29.28. Kiple, *Blacks in Colonial Cuba*, 88–90.

29. Parsons, "The Migration of Canary Islanders to the Americas," 469; Schmidt-Nowara, *Empire and Antislavery*, 105; Gallenga, *The Pearl of the Antilles*, 109; Pérez, *Cuba: Between Reform and Revolution*, 115–116.

30. Spain, Superintendencia General, *Informe fiscal sobre fomento de la población blanca*, 37.

31. Naranjo Orovio and García González, *Racismo e inmigración en Cuba*, 117–118.32. Hernández García, "La planificación de la emigración canaria a Cuba y Puerto Rico, siglo XIX," 211– 212.

33. Juan Francisco Martin Ruiz, *El N.W. de Gran Canaria: Un estudio de demografía histórica (1485–1860)* (Las Palmas: Excma, Mancomunidad de Cabildos de Las Palmas, 1978), 128, 130.

34. Parsons, "The Migration of Canary Islanders to the Americas," 469.

35. Casanovas, *Bread, or Bullets!*, 51. The data lists a total of 55,487 immigrants a follows: 27,264 Peninsular Spaniards, 19,759 Canary Islanders, 8,464 other foreign-born Europeans.

36. Kiple, *Blacks in Colonial Cuba*, 88–90, 92–93; Spain, Superintendencia General Delegada de Real Hacienda, 1841. *Informe fiscal sobre fomento de la población blanca en la isla de cuba y emancipación progresiva de la esclava con una breve reseña de las reformas y modificaciones que para conseguirlo convendría establecer en la legislación*

y constitución colonials (Madrid, 1845), 6; Cuba, Comisión de estadística, Cuadro estadístico de la siempre fiel isla de Cuba, 1846 (Havana, 1847), inserts 1–2.

37. Hernández García, "La planificación de la emigración canaria a Cuba y Puerto Rico, siglo XIX," 212–213.

38. Hernández García, "La presencia de las Islas Canarias en la Cuba decimonónica," 73.

39. Parsons, "The Migration of Canary Islanders to the Americas," 473.

40. Ibid., 470; Martin Ruiz, *El N.W. de Gran Canaria*, 131.

41. Parsons, "The Migration of Canary Islanders to the Americas," 470; Naranjo Orovio and García González, *Racismo e inmigración en Cuba*, 115;Eugene Pégot-Ogier, *The Fortunate Isles: The Archipelago of the Canaries*, translated by Frances Locock (London: Richard Bentley, 1871), 1: 246.

42. Royal Order, "Concediendo amnistía general a todos los que tomaron parte en conspiraciones en la Isla de Cuba," Madrid, 22 May 1854, ANC-AP, Leg. 122, Exp. 48.

43. 22 September 1852, Mexico, Pasaportes, Caja 45, folio 328, Archivo General de la Nación, Mexico City, Mexico.

44. Casanovas, *Bread, or Bullets!*, 51.

45. Joseph C. Dorsey, "Identity, Rebellion, and Social Justice among Chinese Contract Workers in Nineteenth-Century Cuba," *Latin American Perspectives* 31.3 (May 2004), 22.

46. Evelyn Hu-DeHart, "Chinese Coolie Labor in Cuba in the Nineteenth Century: Free Labor or Neoslavery," *Contributions in Black Studies* 12.1 (1994): 38; Paul Estrade, "Los colonos yucatecos como substituyes de los esclavos negros," in *Cuba, La perla de las Antillas*, edited by Consuelo Naranjo Orovio and Tomás Mallo Gutiérrez (Madrid: Doce Calles, 1994), 94, 96.

47. Walton Look Lai, *Indentured Labor, Caribbean Sugar: Chinese and Indian Migrants to the British West Indies, 1838–1918* (Baltimore: Johns Hopkins University Press, 1993), 39–40.

48. Denise Helly, *The Cuba Commission Report: A Hidden History of the Chinese in Cuba* (Baltimore: Johns Hopkins University Press, 1993), 20; Lai, *Indentured Labor, Caribbean Sugar*, 19–20.

49. Edward Bartlett Rugemer, *The Problem of Emancipation: The Caribbean Roots of the American Civil War* (Baton Rouge: Louisiana State University Press, 2008), 261.

50. Persia Crawford Campbell, *Chinese Coolie Emigration to Countries within the British Empire* (London: P. S. King & Son, 1923), 87–88.

51. Lai, *Indentured Labor, Caribbean Sugar*, 10; Rugemer, *The Problem of Emancipation*, 261.

52. Lisa Yun, *The Coolie Speaks: Chinese Indentured Laborers and African Slaves of Cuba* (Philadelphia: Temple University Press, 2008), 6, 14, 15, 17.

53. Helly, *The Cuba Commission Report*, 14.

54. Terry Rugeley, "Preface: The Caste War," *The Americas* 53.4 (April 1997), vii.

55. Nelson Reed, *The Caste War of Yucatán: Revised Edition* (Stanford: Stanford University Press, 2002), 142.

56. Schmidt-Nowara, *Empire and Antislavery*, 104.

57. Estrade, "Los colonos yucatecos como substituyes de los esclavos negros," 94, 96; Stanley L. Engerman, "Servants to Slaves to Servants: Contract Labour and European Expansion," in *Colonialism and Migration; Indentured Labour before and after*

Slavery, edited by P. C. Emmer (Boston: Martinus Nijhoff, 1986), 272; Javier Rodríguez Piña, *Guerra de castas: La venta de indias mayas a Cuba, 1848–1861* (Mexico City: Consejo Nacional Para La Cultura y Las Artes, 1990), 101, 102, 103; Corbitt, "Immigration in Cuba," 301–302.

58. Corbitt, *A Study of the Chinese in Cuba*, 5; Junta de Fomento de Agricultura y Comercio to Ultramar, Havana, 31 July 1848, AHN-UF, Leg. 23, 2nd pieza, Exp. 7, No. 4, folio 2.

59. Quoted in Juan Pérez de la Riva, *Los culíes chinos en Cuba (1847–1880)* (Havana: Editorial de Ciencias Sociales, 2000), 62.

60. Ramón de la Sagra, *Historia física, económico-política, intelectual y moral de la isla de Cuba* (Paris: Imprenta de Simon Raçon, 1861), 150–151.

61. Juan Pérez de la Riva, "Documentos para la historia de las gentes sin historia: El tráfico de culíes chinos," *Revista de la Biblioteca Nacional* (Havana) 6.2 (April-June, 1964): 85; Pérez de la Riva, *Los culíes chinos en Cuba*, 60.

62. Reed, *The Caste War of Yucatán*, 142, 222.

63. Piña, *Guerra de castas*, 103.

64. Tomich, "The Wealth of Empire," 1, 19.

65. Henry A. Murria, *Lands of the Slave and the Free: or, Cuba, the United States, and Canada* (London: John W. Parker and Son, 1855), 1: 311.

66. Amelia Matilda Murray, *Letters from the United States, Cuba, and Canada* (New York: G. P. Putnam, 1856), 247.

67. Gallenga, *The Pearl of the Antilles*, 109, 247.

68. Reed, *The Caste War of Yucatán*, 142.

69. Dorsey, "Identity, Rebellion, and Social Justice," 19.

70. Evelyn Hu-DeHart, "Chinese Coolie Labor in Cuba in the Nineteenth Century," *Journal of Chinese Overseas* 1.2 (November 2005): 170; Benjamin Narvaez, "Chinese Coolies in Cuba and Peru: Race, Labor, and Immigration, 1839–1886" (Ph.D. diss., University of Texas at Austin, 2010), 60.

71. Watt Stewart, *Chinese Bondage in Peru: A History of the Chinese Coolie in Peru, 1849–1874* (Durham: Duke University Press, 1951), 8.

72. Yun, *The Coolie Speaks*, 25.

73. Quoted from Moon Ho Jung, *Coolies and Cane* (Baltimore: Johns Hopkins University Press, 2006), 166.

74. Martinez-Alier, *Marriage, Class and Colour in Nineteenth-Century Cuba*, 76–77.

75. Jung, *Coolies and Cane*, 166–167.

76. Hu-DeHart, "Chinese Coolie Labor in Cuba in the Nineteenth Century," 48.

77. Martinez-Alier, *Marriage, Class and Colour in Nineteenth-Century Cuba*, 77.

78. Dorsey, "Identity, Rebellion, and Social Justice," 20–21, 24–25.

79. Yun, *The Coolie Speaks*, 26.

80. Richard Henry Dana, *Two Years before the Mast and Other Voyages* (New York: Literary Classics of the United States, 2005), 501.

81. Helly, *The Cuba Commission Report*, 48.

82. Ibid., 83.

83. Gallenga, *The Pearl of the Antilles*, 109; Murray, *Letters from the United States, Cuba, and Canada*, 247.

84. Sagra, *Historia física, económico-política, intelectual y moral de la isla de Cuba*, 150.

85. *Diaro de la Marina*, Havana, 3 January 1858, 2, University of Florida, Gainesville, Florida, Smathers Library, Latin American Collection, January 1–June 30, 1857; reel no. 0023; Dorsey, "Identity, Rebellion, and Social Justice," 19.

86. Yun, *The Coolie Speaks*, 17; Reed, *The Caste War of Yucatán*, 142; Dorsey, "Identity, Rebellion, and Social Justice," 22.

87. Rosanne Adderley, *"New Negroes from Africa": Slave Trade Abolition and Free African Settlement in the Nineteenth-Century Caribbean* (Bloomington: Indiana University Press, 2006), 45.

88. Martínez-Fernández, *Fighting Slavery in the Caribbean*, 42, 47, 51; Adderley, *"New Negroes from Africa,"* 95.

89. Paquette, *Sugar Is Made with Blood*, 274.

90. "Autorizando la salida de negros para Africa," 4 January 1845, Madrid, ANC, Leg. 139, Exp. 152.

91. Juan Pérez de la Riva, *Documentos para la historia de las gentes sin historia* (Havana: Biblioteca Nacional, 1969), 30–33.

92. Paquette, *Sugar Is Made with Blood*, 134; Martínez-Fernández, *Fighting Slavery in the Caribbean*, 51.93. Royal Order, "Concediendo amnistía general a todos los que tomaron parte en conspiraciones en la Isla de Cuba," Madrid, 22 May 1854, ANC-AP, Leg. 122, Exp. 48.

94. Ignacio María Zangroniz to Ultramar, Havana, 23 December 1853, AHN-UGC, Leg. 4642, Exp. 13, No. 2, folios 1–3.

95. Ultramar to Cuba Captain General, Madrid, 16 March 1854, AHN-UGC, Leg. 4642, Exp. 13, No. 1, folios 2–3; Solimar Otero, *Afro-Cuban Diasporas in the Atlantic World* (Rochester: University of Rochester Press, 2010), 40–48.

96. Ramon Mandillo to Ultramar, Santa Cruz de Tenerife, 24 April 1857, AGI-AHN, Leg. 90, Exp. 14, No. 7, folios 1–4.

97. Pérez de la Riva, "Documentos para la historia de las gentes sin historia," 85; Pérez de la Riva, *Los culíes chinos en Cuba (1847–1880)*, 60; Dirección General de Administración to Ministro de la Gobernación, Santa Cruz de Tenerife, 25 April 1857, AGI-AHN, Leg. 90, Exp. 14, No. 6, folio 1.

98. Ministro de la Gobernación to Ultramar, Madrid, 7 June 1857, AGI-AHN, Leg. 90, Exp. 14, No. 4, folio 1.

99. Ruiz Lacasa y Compañía to Ultramar, Madrid, 16 January 1859, AGI-AHN, Leg. 90, Exp. 14, No. 13, folios 1–7.

100. Ruiz Lacasa y Compañía, "Reglamento para llevar a cabo el proyecto de inmigración africana en la Isla de Cuba," and "Empresa de colonización africana de la Isla de Cuba, autorizada por S.M. la Reina de España," AGI-AHN, Leg. 90, Exp. 14, No. 13, folios 8–14.

101. José Suárez Argudin, "Proyecto, o representación respetuosa sobre inmigración," AGI-AHN, Leg. 90, Exp. 14, No. 3, folio 7, p. 3; José de la Concha, Cuba Captain General to Ministro de Estado, Havana, April—July 1855, AHN-UGC, Leg. 4643, Exp. 7, Nos. 7, 12, 20–24.

102. José Suárez Argudin, "Extracto de las razones en que se funde el vivo empeño de los habitantes de Cuba de ver introducida en su suelo la inmigración africana y de las que se ofrecen así mismo para que por ningún motivo justo y razonable pueda ser impugnada; y se publica con el objeto de que agregado al proyecto que acaba de imprimirse en la Habana, referente á este importante fin, pueda contribuir de algún

modo á su favorable resolución," Havana, 1 May 1856, AGI-AHN, Leg. 90, Exp. 14, No. 3, folio 14, p. 3.

103. Ibid., folio 11, p. 12; folio 8, p.5; folio 12, p. 13.

104. José Suárez Argudin, Luciano Fernández Perdones, and Manuel Basilio de Cunha Reis to Ultramar, Madrid, 9 July 1861, AGI-AHN, AGI, Seville, Leg. 90, Exp. 14, No. 23, folios 1–3; Manuel Basilio de Cunha Reis and Luciano Fernández Perdones to Cuba Captain General, Havana, 3 March 1860, AGI-AHN, Leg. 90, Exp. 14, No. 17, folios 1–9.

105. Director de Política del Estado to Ministro de la Guerra y de Ultramar, Palacio, Madrid, 19 June 1861, AGI-AHN, Leg. 90, Exp. 14, No. 21, folios 1–3.

106. Ministerio de Ultramar, Junta informativa de Ultramar. *Extracto de las contestaciones dadas al interrogatorio sobre la manera de reglamentar el trabajo de la población de color y asiática, y los medios de facilitar la inmigración que son más conveniente en las mismas provincias* (Madrid: Imprenta de la Biblioteca Económica, 1869), AGI-AHN, Leg. 288, Exp. 16, No. 1, folio 4, p. 4.

107. Ibid., folio 21, pp. 37, 40.

108. Ministerio de Ultramar, Junta Informativa de Ultramar, AGI-AHN, Leg. 288, Exp. 16, No. 1, folio 51, p. 45.

109. Ibid., folio 82, p. 160.

110. Ibid. and folio 81, p. 158.

111. Kiple, *Blacks in Colonial Cuba*, 96–97; the 1861 census listed Cuba's total population of 1,396,530 as follows: 793,474 whites, 370, 553 slaves, and 232, 493 free people of color.

112. Phillippo, *The United States and Cuba*, 429.

113. Samuel Hazard, *Cuba with Pen and Pencil* (Hartford and Chicago: Pitkin and Parker, 1871), 88.

114. Casanovas, *Bread or Bullets!*, 51; Scott, *Slave Emancipation in Cuba*, 7;

115. Kiple, *Blacks in Colonial Cuba*, 92–97.

116. Casanovas, *Bread or Bullets!*, 48–49, 54–55, 62.117. Antonio Chuffat Latour, *Apunte histórico de los chinos en Cuba* (Havana: Molina, 1927), 18; Narvaez, "Chinese Coolies in Cuba and Peru," 448.

118. Pérez de la Riva, *Los culies chinos en Cuba*, 245.

119. Howard, *Changing History*, 98.

120. José María Armenteros and Vencelad Manresa to Cuba Captain General, 30 January 1860, Havana, ANC, Gobierno Superior Civil, Leg. 410, No. 16102.

121. Casanovas, *Bread or Bullets!*, 69–70; Howard, *Changing History*, 98.

122. Ramón de la Sagra, "Estados anexos a la memoria sobre el estado de la instrucción elemental en la Isla de Cuba," AGI-Indiferente 1533, Exp. 7, Nos. 1–11, Cuba, 1861, 275–343; Schmidt-Nowara, *Empire and Antislavery*, 128; Howard, *Changing History*, 105–106; Rafael María de Labra y Cadrana, *La abolición de la esclavitud en el orden económico* (Madrid: Imprenta de J. Noguera, 1873), 232–233.

123. Deschamps Chapeaux, *El negro en la economía habanera*, 131.

124. Yun, *The Coolie Speaks*, 189.

125. Deschamps Chapeaux, *El negro en el periodismo*, 50, 103.

126. "Cédula de inscripción que en cumplimiento de la Real orden de 2 de diciembre de 1859," Archivo Nacional de Cuba, Miscelánea, Leg. 3782, Exp. AN.

127. Schmidt-Nowara, *Empire and Antislavery*, 100.

128. Alejandro Ávila Fernández and Ángel Huerta Martínez, *La formación de maestros de primeras letras en Sevilla y Cuba durante el siglo XIX* (Seville: Instituto de Ciencias de la Educación Universidad de Sevilla, 1995), 33, 36.

129. Huerta Martínez, *La enseñanza primaria en Cuba en el siglo XIX (1812–1868)* (Seville: Diputación Provincial de Sevilla, 1992), 170–171.

130. Helg, *Our Rightful Share*, 37.

131. José Antonio Saco, *Colección póstuma de papeles científicos, históricos, políticos y de otros ramos sobre la isla de Cuba* (Havana: Imprenta del Avisador Comercial, 1881), 444–445, 450.

132. Scott, *Slave Emancipation in Cuba*, 101–102; Casanovas, *Bread, or Bullets!*, 51.

133. Casanovas, *Bread, or Bullets!*, 51; Schmidt-Nowara, *Empire and Antislavery*, 138.

Conclusion

1. Hazard, *Cuba with Pen and Pencil*, 195; Henry Latham, *Black and White: A Journal of a Three Months' Tour in the United States* (London: Macmillan, 1867), 200.

2. Hazard, *Cuba with Pen and Pencil*, 35, 167–169.

3. ANC-AP, Leg. 140, Exp. 17; Leg. 140, Exp. 38; ANC-AP, Leg. 139, Exp. 13.

4. ANC-IP, Leg. 40, Exp. 2114.

5. ANC-GSC, Leg. 1268, Exp. 49804, folios 1–5; ANC-GSC 1267, Exp. 49799, folio 77.

6. ANC-ROC, Leg. 159, Exp. 106; AHN-UGC, Leg. 4627, Exp. 9.

7. ANC-AP, Leg. 140, Exp. 39; AHN-Estado, Leg. 8039, Exp. 10, doc. 9.

8. Schmidt-Nowara, *Empire and Antislavery*, 126–127.

9. Arturo Morales Carrión, *Puerto Rico: A Political and Cultural History* (New York: W. W. Norton, 1983), 110–112.

10. Schmidt-Nowara, *Empire and Antislavery*, 127.

11. Howard, *Changing History*, 144–146.

12. Schmidt-Nowara, *Empire and Antislavery*, 127.

13. Ferrer, *Insurgent Cuba*, 8.

Bibliography

Archival Sources

Cuba

ANC: Archivo Nacional de Cuba, Havana
ANC- AP: Archivo Nacional de Cuba, Asuntos Políticos
ANC-CA: Archivo Nacional de Cuba, Consejo de la Administración de la Isla de Cuba
ANC-CM: Archivo Nacional de Cuba, Comisión Militar
ANC-GG: Archivo Nacional de Cuba, Gobierno General
ANC-GG-L: Archivo Nacional de Cuba, Gobierno General, Licencias
ANC-GSC: Archivo Nacional de Cuba, Gobierno Superior Civil
ANC-IP: Archivo Nacional de Cuba, Instrucción Pública
ANC-ROC: Archivo Nacional de Cuba, Real Órdenes y Cédulas
Aurora. Matanzas, Cuba.
Biblioteca Nacional José Martí, Havana
Diario de la Habana, Havana, Cuba.

Mexico

Archivo General de la Nación, Mexico City
Movimiento Marítimo, Pasaportes

Spain

AGI: Archivo General de Indias, Seville
AGI-AHNU: AGI Digital Collection, Archivo Histórico Nacional, Ultramar
AGI-Indiferente: Archivo General de Indias, Indiferente

AHN: Archivo Histórico Nacional, Madrid
AHN-Estado: Archivo Histórico Nacional, Madrid, Estado
AHN-UF: Archivo Histórico Nacional, Madrid, Ultramar, Fomento
AHN-UGC: Archivo Histórico Nacional, Madrid, Ultramar, Gobierno, Cuba
The Spectator, Jamaica

Florida

Smathers Library, University of Florida, Latin American Collection

Georgia

NCUS-Emory: Nineteenth Century U.S. Newspapers Database, Woodruff Library, Emory University
NCUS-GSU: Nineteenth Century U.S. Newspapers Database, Pullen Library, Georgia State University
TDA-Emory: Times Digital Archive, Woodruff Library, Emory University
The Cleveland Herald. Cleveland
The Colored American. New York
The Daily Atlas, Boston
Daily National Intelligencer, Washington, D.C.
Dover Gazette & Strafford Advertiser, Dover, New Hampshire
Emancipator and Free American, New York
Emancipator and Weekly Chronicle, Boston
The Liberator, Boston
Mississippi Free Trader and Natchez Daily Gazette, Natchez
The New York Herald, New York
New York Spectator, New York
The North American and Daily Advertiser, Philadelphia, 1844
Pennsylvania Inquirer and National Gazette, Philadelphia
The Times, London

Illinois

AC: Edward E. Ayer Collection
GC: General Collections, Non-Circulating
NL: Newberry Library, Chicago

Massachusetts

CC: Cuban Collection
EC: Escoto Collection
HL: Houghton Library, Harvard University

Texas

BLAC: Nettie Lee Benson Latin American Collection, University of Texas at Austin

PCL: Perry-Castañeda Library, University of Texas at Austin
RBM: Rare Books and Manuscripts
USNM: U.S. Newspaper Micofilm Collection

Washington, D.C.

NA-CD: U.S. Department of State Consular Dispatches, Matanzas, Cuba, 1820–1889
NADC-DSCD: National Archives, Washington, D.C., U.S. Dept. of State Consular Dispatches, Matanzas, Cuba, 1820–1889
NA-LANC: Latin American Newspaper Collection, National Archives and Records Administration, Washington, D.C.
NARA : National Archives and Records Administration, Washington, D.C.
Diario de la Habana. Havana
The New Orleans Times-Picayune. New Orleans

Printed Primary Sources

Arango y Parreño, Francisco. *De la factoría a la Colonia*. Havana: Publicaciones de la Secretaría de Educación, 1936.
———. *Obras*. 2 vols. Havana: Howson y Heinen, 1888.
Bryant, William Cullen. *Letters of a Traveller: or, Notes of Things Seen in Europe and America*. London: Richard Bentley, 1850.
Castro, Adolfo de, ed., *Córtes de Cadiz: Complementos de las sesiones verificadas en la isla de Le6n y en Cádiz*. 2 vols. Madrid, 1913.
Dana, Jr., Richard Henry. *To Cuba and Back: A Vacation Voyage*. Boston: Ticknor and Fields, 1859.
———. *Two Years before the Mast and Other Voyages*. New York: Literary Classics of the United States, 2005.
Erenchun, Félix. *Anales de la isla de Cuba: Diccionario administrativo, económico, estadístico y legislativo*, 1855. 16 vols. Havana: Imprenta de la Antilla, 1859.
Estorch, M. *Apuntes para la historia sobre la administración del Marques de la Pezuela*. Madrid: Imprenta por Manuel Galiano, 1856.
Flores, Mónico de, Francisco Abrante, Marcelino Gamarra, et al. *Justo sentimiento de pardos y morenos españoles libres de la Habana*. Havana: Oficina Filantrópica de Don J. M. de Oro, 1823.
Franco, José Luciano, ed. *Obras: Juan Francisco Manzano*. Havana: Instituto del Cubano Libro, 1972.
Gallenga, Antonio. *The Pearl of the Antilles*. London: Chapman and Hall, 1873; rept. New York: Negro Universities Press, 1970.
Gonzáles del Valle, Ambrosio. *Manuel de obstetricia*. Havana: Imprenta y Liberia de A. Graupera, 1854.
Hardman, Frederick. *The Spanish Campaign in Morocco*. Edinburgh: William Blackwood and Sons, 1860.
Hazard, Samuel. *Cuba with Pen and Pencil*. Hartford and Chicago: Pitkin and Parker, 1871.

Huber, B. *Apercu Statistique de L'Ile de Cuba, précédé de quelques lettres sur la Havane.* Paris, 1826.

Kimball, Richard Burleigh. "Letters from Cuba." *Knickerbocker* 26 (October 1845): 544–554.

———. *Cuba, and the Cubans; comprising a history of the Island of Cuba, its present social, political and domestic condition; also, its relation to England and the United States. By the author of "Letters from Cuba" with an appendix, containing important statistics, and a reply to Senñor Saco on Annexation, etc.* New York: Samuel Hueston, 1850.

Labra y Cadrana, Rafael María de. *La abolición de la esclavitud en el orden económico.* Madrid: Imprenta de J. Noguera, 1873.

Latham, Henry. *Black and White. A Journal of a Three Months' Tour in the United States.* London: Macmillan, 1867.

Madden, Richard. *Address on Slavery Presented to the General Anti-Slavery Convention.* London: Johnston and Barrett, 1840.

Manzano, Juan Francisco. *Autobiography of a Runaway Slave.* Detroit: Wayne State University Press, 1996.

———. *Poems by a Slave in the Island of Cuba, Recently Liberated.* Translated from the Spanish by R. R. Madden. London: T. Ward, 1840.

Murray, Amelia Matilda. *Letters from the United States, Cuba, and Canada.* New York: G. P. Putnam, 1856.

Murray, Charles Augustus. *Travels in North American during the Years 1834, 1835, & 1836: Including a summer residence with the Pawnee tribe of Indians in the remote prairies of the Missouri and a visit to Cuba and the Azore Island.* 2 vols. London: Richard. Bentley, 1835.

Murray, Henry A. *Lands of the Slave and the Free: or, Cuba, the United States, and Canada.* 2 vols. London: John W. Parker and Son, 1855.

Norman, Benjamin Moore. *Rambles by Land and Water, or, Notes of Travel in Cuba and Mexico: Including a canoe voyage up the river Panuco, and researches among the ruins of Tamaulipas.* New York: Paine & Burgess, 1845.

Pégot-Ogier, *The Fortunate Isles: The Archipelago of the Canaries.* Translated by Frances Locock. 2 vols. London: Richard Bentley, 1871.

Pérez, Jr., Louis A., ed., *Slaves, Sugar, and Colonial Society: Travel Accounts of Cuba, 1801–1899.* Wilmington: Scholarly Resources, 1992.

Pezuela, Jacobo de la. *Diccionario geográfico, estadístico, histórico de Cuba.* 4 vols. Madrid: Imprenta del establecimiento de Mellado, 1863.

Phillippo, James M. *The United States and Cuba.* London: Pewtress,1857.

Saco, José Antonio. *Colección de papeles científicos, históricos, políticos, y de otros ramos sobre la isla de Cuba.* 3 vols. Havana: Ministerio de Educación, 1960.

———. *Colección póstuma de papeles científicos, históricos, políticos y de otros ramos sobre la isla de Cuba.* Havana: Imprenta del Avisador Comercial, 1881.

———. *Historia de la esclavitud desde los tiempos más remotos hasta nuestros días.* 6 vols. Havana: Editorial "Alfa," 1937.

———. *La historia de la esclavitud de la raza africana en el Nuevo mundo y el especial en los países américo-hispanos.* 4 vols. Havana: Cultural S.A., 1938.

———. *La supresión del trafico de esclavos en Cuba.* Paris: Imprenta de Panckoucke, 1845.

Sagra, Ramón de la. *Historia económico-política y estadística de la isla de Cuba o sea de sus progresos en la población, la agricultura, el comercio y rentas.* Havana: Imprenta de las Viudas de Arazoza y Solér, 1831.

———. *Historia física, económico-política, intelectual y moral de la isla de Cuba.* Paris: Imprenta de Simon Raçon, 1861.

Sedano y Cruzat, Cárlos de. *Cuba desde 1850 a 1873: Colección de informes, memorias, proyectos y antecedentes sobre el gobierno de la isla de Cuba relativos al citado período.* Madrid: Imprenta Nacional, 1873.

Sociedad Económica de Amigos del País. *Anales de las Reales Juntas de Fomento y Sociedad Económica de la Habana.* 4 vols. Havana: Imprenta del Gobierno y Capitanía General, 1849.

Suárez Argudin, José. *Projecto, o representación respetuosa sobre inmigración africana.* Havana: Imprenta de Spencer y Compañía, 1856.

Torres-Cuevas, Eduardo Jorge Ibarra Cuesta, and Mercedes García Rodríguez, eds. *Félix Varela: El que nos enseñó primero en pensar.* 3 vols. Havana: Imagen Contemporánea, 1997.

Turnbull, David. *Travels in the West.* London: Longman, Orme, Brown, Green, and Longmans, 1840.

Valdés, Gabriel de la Concepción. *Poesias completas de Placido.* Paris: C. Denné Schmitz, 1856.

Wurdemann, John G. F. *Notes on Cuba.* Boston: James Munroe, 1844. Reprinted in Robert M. Goldwin, ed., *Physician Travelers.* New York: Arno Press and the New York Times, 1971.

Zamora y Coronada, José María. *Biblioteca de legislación ultramarina en forma de diccionario alfabético,* 7 vols. Madrid: Imprenta de Alegría y Charlain, 1844 1849.

Zaragoza, Justo. *Las insurrecciones en Cuba.* 7 vols. Madrid: Imprenta de Miguel G. Hernández, 1872–1873.

Government Documents

Cuba. Comisión Militar Ejecutiva y Permanente. *Colección de los fallos pronunciados por una sección de la Comisión militar establecida en la ciudad de Matanzas para conocer de la causa de conspiración de la gente de color.* Matanzas, Cuba: Imprenta del gobierno por S. M. y la Real marina, 1844.

Cuba. Comisión de estadística. *Cuadro estadístico de la siempre fiel isla de Cuba, 1846.* Havana: Imprenta del Gobierno, 1847.

Cuba. *Reglamento para las milicias de infantería y caballería de la isla de Cuba aprobado por S.M. en real cédula de 19 de enero de 1769.* Havana, 1849.

Malagón Barceló, Javier, et al. *Relaciones diplomáticas hispano-mexicanas*

(1839–1898): Documentos procedentes del Archivo de la Embajada de España en Mexico. 4 vols. Mexico City: El Colegio de Mexico, 1949–1966.

O'Donnell, Leopoldo. *Reglamento para las milicias disciplinadas de color de la Isla de Cuba.* Madrid, 1858.

Spain. *Diario de las Sesiones de las Córtes generales y extraordinarias.* 5 vols. Madrid, 1870.

Spain. *Reglamento para las milicias de infantería y caballería de la isla de Cuba aprobado por S.M. en real cédula de 19 de enero de 1769.* Havana, 1827.

Spain. Córtes (1810–1813).*Diario de las Sesiones de las Córtes generales y extraordinarias, dieron principio el 24 de septiembre de 1810, y terminaron el 20 de septiembre de 1813.* 9 vols. Madrid, 1870–1874.

Spain. Cortes. *Documentos de que hasta ahora se componen el expediente que principaran las cortes extraordinaria sobre el trafico y esclavitud de los negros.* Madrid, 1814.

Spain. Ministerio de Ultramar. *Cuba desde 1850 a 1873: Colección de informes, memorias, proyectos y antecedentes.* Madrid: Imprenta Nacional, 1873.

Spain. Ministerio de Ultramar. *Junta informativa de Ultramar; Extracto de las contestaciones dadas al interrogatorio sobre la manera de reglamentar el trabajo de la población de color y asiática, y los medios de facilitar la inmigración que son más conveniente en las mismas provincias.* Madrid: Imprenta de la Biblioteca Económica, 1869.

Vázquez Queipo, Vicente. *Informe fiscal sobre fomento de la población blanca en la isla de Cuba y emancipación progresiva de la esclava con una breve reseña de las reformas y modificaciones que para conseguirlo convendría establecer en la legislación y constitución coloniales presentado a la superintendencia general delegada de Real Hacienda en diciembre de 1844 por el Fiscal de la misma.* Madrid: Imprenta de J. M. Alegria, 1845.

Secondary Sources

Acevedo, Roberto P. De, and Benito Alonso y Artigas, "Nuevas noticias y documentos acerca del poeta Plácido." *El País,* 25 January 1941.

Adderley, Rosanne. *"New Negroes from Africa": Slave Trade Abolition and Free African Settlement in the Nineteenth-Century Caribbean.* Bloomington: Indiana University Press, 2006.

Andrews, George Reid. *The Afro-Argentines of Buenos Aires, 1800–1900.* Madison: University of Wisconsin Press, 1980.

———. *Afro-Latin America, 1800–2000.* New York: Oxford University Press, 2004.

Archer, Christon I. "Pardos, Indians, and the Army of New Spain: Inter-Relationships and Conflicts, 1780–1810." *Journal of Latin American Studies* 6.2 (November 1974): 231–255.

Armitage, David, and Michael J. Braddick, eds. *The British Atlantic World, 1500–1800.* New York: Palgrave Macmillan: 2002.

Ávila Fernández, Alejandro, and Ángel Huerta Martínez, *La Formación de*

Maestros de Primeras Letras en Sevilla y Cuba durante el siglo XIX. Sevilla: Instituto de Ciencias de la Educación Universidad de Sevilla, 1995.

Baralt, Guillermo A. *Slave Revolts in Puerto Rico: Slave Conspiracies and Unrest in Puerto Rico, 1795–1873.* Princeton, N.J.: Markus Wiener, 2008.

Barcia Paz, Manuel. *Con el látigo de la ira: legislación, represión y control en las plantaciones cubanas, 1790–1870.* Havana: Ciencias Sociales, 2000.

———. "Fighting with the Enemy's Weapons: The Usage of the Colonial Legal Framework by Nineteenth-Century Cuban Slaves." *Atlantic Studies*3.2 (October 2006): 159–188.

———. *La resistencia esclava en las plantaciones cubanas, 1790–1870.* Pinar del Rio, Cuba: Ediciones Vitral, 1998.

Barr, Ruth B., and Modeste Hargis. "The Voluntary Exile of Free Negroes of Pensacola." *Florida Historical Quarterly* 17.1 (July 1938): 1–15.

Baur, John E. "International Repercussions of the Haitian Revolution." *The Americas* 26.4 (April 1970): 394–418.

Blanchard, Peter. *Under the Flags of Freedom: Slave Soldiers and the Wars of Independence in Spanish South America.* Pittsburgh: University of Pittsburgh Press, 2008.

Buckley, Roger Norman. *Slaves in Red Coats: The British West India Regiments, 1795–1815.* New Haven: Yale University Press, 1979.

Bergad, Laird W. *The Comparative Histories of Slavery in Brazil, Cuba, and the United States.* New York: Cambridge University Press, 2007.

Bergad, Laird W., Fe Iglesias García, and María del Carmen Barcia. *The Cuban Slave Market, 1790–1880.* New York: Cambridge University Press, 1995.

Berlin, Ira. *Slaves without Masters: The Free Negro in the Antebellum South.* New York: New Press, 1974.

Blackburn, Robin. *The Overthrow of Colonial Slavery, 1776–1848.* London: Verso, 1988.

Brasseaux, Carl A., and Glenn R. Conrad, eds. *The Road to Louisiana: The Saint Domingue Refugees 1792–1809.* Lafayette: University of Southwestern Louisiana, 1992.

Bryan, Patrick E. *The Haitian Revolution and After.* N.p., 1979.

Campbell, Leon G. "Black Power in Colonial Peru: The 1779 Tax Rebellion of Lambayeque." *Phylon* 33.2 (1972): 31–57.

Campbell, Mavis C. *The Dynamics of Change in a Slave Society: A Sociopolitical History of the Free Coloreds of Jamaica, 1800–1865.* London: Associated University Presses, 1976.

Campbell, Persia Crawford. *Chinese Coolie Emigration to Countries within the British Empire.* London: P.S. King & Son, 1923.

Carbonell, Walterio. "Plácido, ¿Conspirador?" *Revolución y cultura* 2 (February 1987): 53–57.

Carroll, Patrick J. *Blacks in Colonial Veracruz: Race, Ethnicity, and Regional Development.* Austin: University of Texas Press, 2001.

Casanovas, Joan. *Bread or Bullets!: Urban Labor and Spanish Colonialism in Cuba, 1850–1898*. Pittsburgh: University of Pittsburgh Press, 1998.

Castellanos, Jorge. *Plácido, poeta social y político*. Miami: Ediciones Universal 1984.

Chambers, Sarah C. *From Subjects to Citizens: Honor, Gender, and Politics in Arequipa, Peru, 1780–1854*. University Park: Penn State University Press, 1999.

Childs, Matt D. *The 1812 Aponte Rebellion in Cuba and the Struggle against Atlantic Slavery*. Chapel Hill: University of North Carolina Press, 2006.

———."The Aponte Rebellion of 1812 and the Transformation of Cuban Society: Race, Slavery, and Freedom in the Atlantic World." Ph.D. diss. University of Texas at Austin, 2001.

———. "Sewing" Civilization: Cuban Female Education in the Context of Africanization, 1800–1860." *Americas* 54.1 (July 1997): 83–107.

Chuffat Latour, Antonio. *Apunte histórico de los chinos en Cuba*. Havana: Molina, 1927.

Chust, Manuel. *La cuestión nacional americana en las Cortes de Cádiz (1810–1814)*. Valencia: Centro Francisco Tomás y Valiente, UNED Alzira-Valencia, Fundación Instituto Historia Social, 1999.

Cohen, David W., and Jack P. Greene, eds. *Neither Slave nor Free: The Freedman of African Descent in the Slave Societies of the New World*. Baltimore: Johns Hopkins University Press, 1972.

Cope, Douglas R. *The Limits of Racial Domination: Plebian Society in Colonial Mexico, 1660–1720*. Madison: University of Wisconsin Press, 1994.

Corbitt, Duvon C. "Immigration in Cuba." *Hispanic American Historical Review* 22 (May 1942): 280–308.

Corwin, Arthur. *Spain and the Abolition of Slavery in Cuba, 1817–1886*. Austin: University of Texas Press, 1967.

Costa, Emilia Viotti da. *Crowns of Glory, Tears of Blood: The Demerara Slave Rebellion of 1823*. Oxford: Oxford University Press, 1994.

Cowans, Jon, ed. *Modern Spain: A Documentary History*. Philadelphia: University of Pennsylvania Press, 2003.

Cox, Edward C. *Free Coloreds in the Slave Societies of St. Kitts and Grenada, 1743–1833*. Knoxville: University of Tennessee Press, 1984.

Craton, Michael. *Testing the Chains: Resistance to Slavery in the British West Indies*. Ithaca: Cornell University Press, 1982.

Cué Fernández, Daisy. "Plácido y la conspiración de la Escalera. *Santiago* 42 (June 1981): 145–206.

Cuervo Hewitt, Julia. "Yoruba Presence in Contemporary Cuban Narrative." Ph.D. diss. Vanderbilt University, 1981.

Curtin, Phillip D. *The Rise and Fall of the Plantation Complex: Essays in Atlantic History*. New York: Cambridge University Press, 1993.

De la Fuente, Alejandro. "Esclavos africanos en la Habana: Zonas de procedencia y denominaciones étnicas, 1570–1699." *Revista Española de Antropología Americana* 20 (1990): 135–160.

———. *Havana and the Atlantic in the Sixteenth Century.* Chapel Hill: University of North Carolina Press, 2008.

———. "Slaves and the Creation of Legal Rights in Cuba: *Coartación* and *Papel.*" *Hispanic American Historical Review* 87.4 (2007): 659–692.

Deacon, Harriet. "Midwives and Medical Men in the Cape Colony before 1860." *Journal of African History* 29 (1998): 271–291.

Deschamps Chapeaux, Pedro. *Los batallones pardos y morenos libres.* Havana: Instituto Cubano del Libro, 1976.

———. *Los cimarrones urbanos.* Havana: Editorial de Ciencias Sociales, 1983.

———. *Contribución a la historia de la gente sin historia.* Havana: Editorial de Ciencias Sociales, 1974.

———. "Historia de la gente sin historia: testamentaria de pardos y morenos libres en la Habana del siglo XIX." *Revista de la Biblioteca José Martí* 63 (May-August 1971): 45–54.

———. "Margarito Blanco, 'Ocongo de Ultan'." *Boletín del Instituto de Historia y del Archivo Nacional* (Havana) 65 (July-December 1964): 97–109.

———. *El Negro en el periodismo en el siglo XIX*: E*nsayo bibliográfico.* Havana: Ediciones Revolución, 1963.

———. *El negro en la economía habanera del siglo XIX.* Havana: UNEAC, 1971.

Dessens, Nathalie. *From Saint-Domingue to New Orleans: Migration and Influences.* Gainesville: University of Florida Press, 2007.

Díaz, María Elena. *The Virgin, the King, and the Royal Slaves of El Cobre: Negotiating Freedom in Colonial Cuba, 1670–1780.* Stanford: Stanford University Press, 2000.

Dominguez, Jorge I. *Insurrection or Loyalty: The Breakdown of the Spanish American Empire.* Cambridge: Harvard University Press, 1980.

Dorsey, Joseph C. "Identity, Rebellion, and Social Justice among Chinese Contract Workers in Nineteenth-Century Cuba." *Latin American Perspectives* 31.3 (May 2004): 18–47.

———. "It Hurt Very Much at the Time: Patriarchy, Rape Culture, and the Slave Body-Semiotic." In *The Culture of Gender and Sexuality in the Caribbean*, edited by Linden Lewis, 294–322 (Gainesville: University of Press of Florida, 2003).

———. *Slave Traffic in the Age of Abolition: Puerto Rico, West Africa, and the Non-Hispanic Caribbean, 1815–1859.* Gainesville: University Press of Florida, 2003.

Du Bois, W.E.B. *The Souls of Black Folk.* [1903] New York: Bantam, 1989.

Dubois, Laurent. *A Colony of Citizens: Revolution and Slave Emancipation in the French Caribbean, 1787–1804.* Chapel Hill: University of North Carolina Press, 2004.

Duvan C. Corbitt. *A Study of the Chinese in Cuba, 1847–1947*. Wilmore, Ky.: Asbury College, 1971.

Duharte Jiménez, Rafael. *El negro en la sociedad colonial*. Santiago de Cuba: Editoral Oriente, 1988.

———. *Rebeldía esclava en el Caribe*. Xalapa, Mexico: Gobierno del Estado de Veracruz, 1992.

Egerton, Douglas R. *"He shall go out free": The Lives of Denmark Vesey*. Madison, Wisc.: Madison House, 1999.

Elisabeth, Léo. "The French Antilles." In *Neither Slave nor Free: The Freedman of African Descent in the Slave Societies of the New World*, edited by David W. Cohen and Jack P. Greene, 134–171. Baltimore: Johns Hopkins University Press, 1972.

Eltis, David. *The Rise of Africans in the Americas*. Cambridge: Cambridge University Press, 2000.

———. "The Nineteenth-Century TransAtlantic Slave Trade: An Annual Time Series of Imports into the Americas Broken Down by Region." *Hispanic American Historical Review* 67.1 (1987): 109–138.

Engerman, Stanley L. "Servants to Slaves to Servants: Contract Labour and European Expansion." In *Colonialism and Migration; Indentured Labour before and after Slavery*, edited by P. C. Emmer, 263–294. Boston: Martinus Nijhoff, 1986.

Engerman, Stanley L., and Eugene D. Genovese, eds. *Race and Slavery in the Western Hemisphere: Quantitative Studies*. Princeton: Princeton University Press, 1975.

Estrade, Paul. "Los colonos yucatecos como substituyes de los esclavos negros." In *Cuba, La perla de las Antillas*, edited by Consuelo Naranjo Orovio and Tomás Mallo Gutiérrez, 93–108. Madrid: Doce Calles, 1994.

Everett, Donald E. "Emigres and Miltiamen: Free Persons of Color in New Orleans, 1803–1815." *Journal of Negro History* 38.4 (October 1953): 377–402.

Ewald, Janet J. "Crossers of the Sea: Slaves, Freedmen, and Other Migrants in the Northwestern Indian Ocean, c. 1750–1914." 105.1 (February 2000): 69–91.

Falola, Toyin, ed. *Yoruba Historiography*. Madison: University of Wisconsin Press, 1992.

Fernández Robaina, Tomás. *El Negro en Cuba, 1902–1958: Apuntes para historia de la lucha contra la discriminación racial*. Havana: Editorial de Ciencias Sociales, 1990.

Ferrer, Ada. *Insurgent Cuba: Race, Nation, and Revolution, 1868–1898*. Chapel Hill: University of North Carolina Press, 1999.

Fick, Carolyn E. *The Making of Haiti: The Saint Domingue Revolution from Below*. Knoxville: University of Tennessee Press, 1990.

Finch, Aisha K. "Insurgency at the Crossroads: Cuban Slaves and the Conspiracy of La Escalera, 1841–44." Ph.D. diss. New York University, 2007.

Fischer, Sibylle. *Modernity Disavowed: Haiti and the Cultures of Slavery in the Age of Revolution.* Durham: Duke University Press, 2004.

Foner, Philip. *Antonio Maceo: The "Bronze Titan" of Cuba's Struggle for Independence.* New York: *Monthly Review Press,* 1977.

———. *A History of Cuba and Its Relationships with the United States.* 2 vols. New York: 1962–1963.

Ford, Lacy K. *Deliver Us from Evil: The Slavery Question in the Old South.* New York: Oxford University Press, 2009.

Foster, David William, and Daniel Altamiranda, eds. *From Romanticism to Modernismo in Latin America.* New York: Routledge, 1997.

Foucault, Michel. *Discipline and Punish: The Birth of the Prison.* New York: Vintage, 1979.

Fradera, Josep M. "Quiembra imperial y reorganización policía en las Antillas españolas, 1818–1868." *Recerques* 9 (1997): 289–318.

Franco, José Luciano. *La conspiración de Aponte.* Havana: Consejo Nacional de Cultura, Publicaciones del Archivo Nacional, 1963.

———. Las rebeldías negras." In *Tres ensayos: Alejandro Serguéievich Pushkin. Los pintores impresionistas franceses. Las rebeldías negras,* 87–101. Havana: Ayon, 1951.

———. "Introducción al proceso de la Escalera." *Boletín del Archivo Nacional* 67 (January-December 1974): 54–63.

García, Enildo. *Plácido: Poeta mulato de la emancipación, 1809–1844.*New York: Senda Nueva de Ediciones, 1986

Gaspar, David Barry. *Bondmen and Rebels: A Study of Master-Slave Relations in Antigua with Implications for Colonial British America.* Baltimore: Johns Hopkins University Press 1985.

———. "From 'The Sense of Their Slavery': Slave Women and Resistance in Antigua, 1632–1783." In *More than Chattel: Black Women and Slavery in the Americas,* edited by David Barry Gaspar and Darlene Clark Hine, 218–238. Bloomington: Indiana University Press, 1996.

Geggus, David P. "Slave and Free Colored Women in Saint Domingue." In *More than Chattel: Black Women and Slavery in the Americas,* edited by David Barry Gaspar and Darlene Clark Hine, 259–278. Bloomington: Indiana University Press, 1996.

———. "Slavery, War and Revolution in the Greater Caribbean." In *Turbulent Time: The French Revolution and the Greater Caribbean,* edited by David Barry Gaspar and Darlene Clark Hine, 1–50. Bloomington: Indiana University Press, 1997.

Genovese, Eugene D. *From Rebellion to Revolution: Afro-American Slave Revolts in the Making of the Modern* World. Baton Rouge: Louisiana State University Press, 1979.

Gilroy, Paul. *The Black Atlantic: Modernity and Double Consciousness.* Cambridge: Harvard University Press, 1993.

Gomariz, José. "Francisco de Arango y Parreno: El discurso esclavista de la ilustración cubana." *Cuban Studies* 25 (2004): 45–61.

González del Valle, Francisco. *La conspiración de la Escalera: I. José de la Luz y Caballero*. Havana: El Siglo XX 1925.

Greenberg, Kenneth S., ed. *Nat Turner: A Slave Rebellion in History and Memory*. Oxford: Oxford University Press, 2003.

Griñan Peralta, Leonardo. "La defensa de los esclavos." In *Ensayos y conferencias*. Santiago de Cuba: Editora del Consejo Nacional de Universidades, Universidad de Oriente, 1964.

Guerra y Sánchez, Ramiro. *Manual de historia de Cuba*. Havana: Editorial de Ciencias Sociales, 1971.

Guerra y Sánchez, Ramiro, et al., eds. *Historia de la nación cubana*. 10 vols. Havana: Editorial Historia de la Nación Cubana, 1952.

Hall, Gwendolyn Midlo. *Social Control in Slave Plantation Societies: A Comparison of St. Domingue and Cuba*. Baltimore: Johns Hopkins University Press, 1971.

Hall, Neville A. T. *Slave Society in the Danish West Indies: St. Thomas, St. John, and St. Croix*. Baltimore: Johns Hopkins University Press, 1992.

Handler, Jerome S. *The Unappropriated People: Freedmen in the Slave Society of Barbados*. Baltimore: Johns Hopkins University Press, 1974.

Hanger, Kimberly S. *Bounded Lives, Bounded Places: Free Black Society in Colonial New Orleans, 1769–1803*. Durham: Duke University Press, 1997.

Hart, Richard. *The Slaves Who Abolished Slavery*. 2 vols. Kingston, Jamaica: Institute of Social and Economic Research, University of the West Indies, 1985.

Helg, Aline. "The Limits of Equality: Free People of Colour and Slaves during the First Independence of Cartegena, Colombia, 1810–15." *Slavery and Abolition* 20.2 (August 1999): 1–30.

———. *Our Rightful Share: The Afro-Cuban Struggle for Equality, 1886–1912*. Chapel Hill: University of North Carolina Press, 1995.

———. "Race and Black Mobilization in Colonial and Early Independent Cuba: A Comparative Perspective." *Ethnohistory* 44.1 (Winter 1997): 53–74.

Helly, Denise. *The Cuba Commission Report: A Hidden History of the Chinese in Cuba*. Baltimore: Johns Hopkins University Press, 1993.

Henderson, James D. "Mariana Grajales: Black Progenitress of Cuban Independence." *Journal of Negro History* 63.2 (April 1978), 135–148.

Herminio Portell Vilá, *Historia de Cuba en sus relaciones con los Estados Unidos y España*. Havana, 1938.

Hernández García, Julio. "La planificación de la emigración canaria a Cuba y Puerto Rico, siglo XIX." In *Coloquio de Historia Canario-Americana II*, I: 201–238. Seville: Ediciones del Excmo, Cabildo de Gran Canaria, 1979.

———. "La presencia de las Islas Canarias en la Cuba decimonónica: Análisis y valoración cuantitativa (1834–1912)." In *Memorias del Primer Congreso sobre la emigración española hacia el área del caribe desde finales siglo xix*, 69–81. Santo Domingo: Ediciones Fundación García Arévalo, 2002.

Hernández Sáenz, Luz María, and George M. Foster, "Curers and Their Cures in Colonial New Spain and Guatemala." In *Mesoamerican Healers*, edited by Brad R. Huber and Alan R. Sandstrom, 19–46. Austin: University of Texas Press, 2001.

Hoberman, Louisa Schell, and Susan Midgen Socolo, eds. *Cities and Society in Colonial Latin America*. Albuquerque: University of New Mexico Press, 1986.

Hoetink, Harmannus. *Slavery and Race Relations in the Americas*. New York: Harper & Row, 1973.

Holloway, Thomas H. "A Healthy Terror": Police Repression of Capoeiras in Nineteenth-Century Rio de Janeiro." *Hispanic American Historical Review* 69.4 (November 1989): 637–676.

Thomas, Hugh. *Cuba: The Pursuit of Freedom*. New York: Harper & Row, 1971.

Howard, Philip A. *Changing History: Afro-Cuban Cabildos and Societies of Color in the Nineteenth Century*. Baton Rouge: Louisiana State University Press, 1998.

Hu-DeHart, Evelyn. "Chinese Coolie Labor in Cuba in the Nineteenth Century." *Journal of Chinese Overseas* 1.2 (November 2005): 169–183.

———. "Chinese Coolie Labor in Cuba in the Nineteenth Century: Free Labor or Neoslavery." *Contributions in Black Studies* 12.1 (1994): 38–54.

Huerta Martínez, Huerta. *La enseñanza primaria en Cuba en el siglo XIX (1812–1868)*. Seville: Diputación Provincial de Sevilla, 1992.

Hunefeldt, Christine. *Paying the Price of Freedom: Family and Labor among Lima's Slaves, 1800–1854*. Berkeley: University of California Press, 1995.

Ingersoll, Thomas N. *Mammon and Manon in Early New Orleans: The First Slave Society in the Deep South, 1718–1819*. Knoxville: University of Tennessee Press, 1999.

Jennings, Evelyn Powell. "War as the 'Forcing House of Change': State Slavery in Late-Eighteenth-Century Cuba." *William and Mary Quarterly*, third series, 62.3, "*The Atlantic Economy in an Era of Revolutions*" (July 2005): 411–440.

Johnson, Sherry. *Social Transformation of Eighteenth-Century Cuba*. Gainesville: University of Florida Press, 2001.

Johnson, Whittington B. *Race Relations in the Bahamas, 1784–1834: The Nonviolent Transformation from a Slave to a Free Society*. Fayetteville: University of Arkansas Press, 2000.

Julius, Kevin C. *The Abolitionist Decade, 1829–1838: A Year-by-Year History of Early Events in the Antislavery Movement*. Jefferson, N.C.: McFarland, 2004.

Jung, Moon Ho. *Coolies and Cane*. Baltimore: Johns Hopkins University Press, 2006.

Karasch, Mary C. *Slave Life in Rio de Janeiro*, 1808–1850. Princeton: Princeton University Press, 1987.

Kimmel, Michael, and Michael Messner, eds. *Men's Lives*. Boston: Allyn & Bacon, 1995.

King, James F. "The Colored Castes and American Representation in the Cortes of Cadiz." *Hispanic American Historical Review* 33.1 (February 1953): 33–64.

King, Stewart R. *Blue Coat or Powdered Wig: Free People of Color in Pre-Revolutionary Saint Domingue*. Athens: University of Georgia Press, 2001.

Kinsbruner, Jay. *Not of Pure Blood: The Free People of Color and Racial Prejudice in Nineteenth-Century Puerto Rico*. Durham: Duke University Press, 1996.

Kiple, Kenneth F. *Blacks in Colonial Cuba, 1774–1899*. Gainesville: University Press of Florida, 1976.

Klein, Herbert S. *African Slavery in Latin America and the Caribbean*. New York, Oxford University Press, 1986.

———. "The Colored Militia of Cuba: 1568 to 1868." *Caribbean Studies* 6.2 (June 1966): 17–27.

———. *Slavery in the Americas: A Comparative Study of Virginia and Cuba*. Chicago: University of Chicago Press, 1967.

Knight, Franklin W. "Cuba." In *Neither Slave nor Free: The Freedman of African Descent in the Slave Societies of the New World*, edited by David W. Cohen and Jack P. Green, 279–308. Baltimore: Johns Hopkins University Press, 1972.

———. "The Free Colored Population in Cuba during the Nineteenth Century'." In *Sugar without Slavery: Diversity in Caribbean Economy and Society since the 17th Century*, edited by Verene A. Shepard, 224–247. Gainesville: University Press of Florida, 2002.

———. "The Haitian Revolution." *American Historical Review* 105.1 (February 2000): 103–115.

———. *Slave Society in Cuba during the Nineteenth Century*. Madison: University of Wisconsin Press, 1970.

Kraay, Hendrik. *Race, State, and Armed Forces in Independence-era Brazil: Bahia, 1790's–1840's*. Stanford: Stanford University Press, 2001.

Kuethe, Allan J. *Cuba, 1753–1815: Crown, Military and Society*. Knoxville: University of Tennessee Press, 1986.

———. "The Development of the Cuban Military as a Sociopolitico Elite, 1763–83." *Hispanic American Historical Review* 6.4 (November 1981): 695–704.

———. *Military Reform and Society in New Granada, 1773–1808*. Gainesville: University Press of Florida, 1978.

———. "The Status of the Free Pardo in the Disciplined Militia of New Granada." *Journal of Negro History* 56.2 (April 1971): 105–117.

Lai, Walton Look. *Indentured Labor, Caribbean Sugar: Chinese and Indian Migrants to the British West Indies, 1838–1918*. Baltimore: Johns Hopkins University Press, 1993.

Landers, Jane. *Atlantic Creoles in the Age of Revolution*. Cambridge: Harvard University Press, 2010.

———. *Black Society in Spanish Florida*. Urbana: University of Illinois Press, 1999.

Lanning, John Tate. *The Royal Protomedicato: The Regulations of the Medical Professions in the Spanish Empire*. Edited by John Jay TePaske. Durham: Duke University Press, 1985.

Lazo, Rodrigo. *Writing to Cuba: Filibustering and Cuban Exiles in the United States*. Chapel Hill: University of North Carolina Press, 2005.

Lebsock, Suzanne. *The Free Women of Petersburg: Status and Culture in a Southern Town, 1784–1860*New York: Norton, 1984.

Lockhart, James. *Spanish Peru, 1532–1560: A Colonial Society*. Madison: University of Wisconsin Press, 1994.

López Valdés, Rafeal L. "Notas para el studio etno-histórico de los esclavos lucumí de Cuba." *Anales del Caribe* 6 (1986): 54–74.

Lovejoy, Paul E. "Ethnic Designations of the Slave Trade and the Reconstruction of the History of Trans-Atlantic Slavery." In *Trans-Atlantic Dimensions of Ethnicity in the African Diaspora*, edited by Paul E. Lovejoy and David V. Trotman, 9–41. London: Continuum, 2004.

Marchena Fernandez, Juan. *Oficiales y Soldados* en el ejército de América Sevilla: Escuela de Estudios Hispano-Americanos, C.S.I.C., 1983.

Marland, Hilary. *Medicine and Society in Wakefield and Huddersfield, 1780–1870*. Cambridge: Cambridge University Press, 1987.

Márquez, José de J. *Plácido y los conspiradores de 1844*. Havana: Imp. La Constancia, 1894.

Martin Ruiz, Juan Francisco. *El N.W. de Gran Canaria: Un estudio de demografía histórica (1485–1860)*. Las Palmas: Excma, Mancomunidad de Cabildos de Las Palmas, 1978.

Martínez-Alier, Verena. *Marriage, Class and Colour in Nineteenth-Century Cuba: A Study of Racial Attitudes and Sexual Values in a Slave Society*. Ann Arbor: University of Michigan Press, 1989.

Martínez-Fernández, Luis. *Fighting Slavery in the Caribbean: The Life and Times of a British Family in Nineteenth-Century Havana*. Armonk, N.Y.: M. E. Sharpe, 1998.

Matos Rodríguez, Félix V. *Women and Urban Change in San Juan Puerto Rico, 1820–1868*. Gainesville: University Press of Florida, 1999.

McAlister, Lyle N. *The "Fuero Militar" in New Spain, 1764–1800*, Gainesville: University of Florida Press, 1957.

McCadden, Jospeh J. "The New York-to-Cuba Axis of Father Varela." *The Americas* 20.4 (April 1964): 376–392.

McCadden, Joseph, and Hellen M. McCadden. *Félix Varela: Torch Bearer from Cuba*. San Juan: Ramallo Bros., 1984.

McGregor, Deborah K. *From Midwives to Medicine: The Birth of American Gynecology*. New Brunswick: Rutgers University Press, 1998.

McManus, Jane. *Cuba's Islands of Dreams: Voices from the Isle of Pines and Youth*. Gainesville: University of Florida Press, 2000,

Miller, Ivor L., and Bassey E. Bassey. *Voice of the Leopard: African Secret Societies and Cuba*. Jackson: University Press of Mississippi, 2009.

Mirabal, Nancy. "De Aquí, De allá: Race, Empire and Nation in the Making of Cuban Migrant Communities in New York and Tampa, 1823–1924." Ph.D. diss. University of Michigan, 2001.

Moitt, Bernard. *Women and Slavery in the French Antilles, 1635–1848*. Bloomington: Indiana University Press, 2001.

Montejo Arrechea, Carmen Victoria. *Sociedades de Instrucción y Recreo de pardo y morenos que existieron en Cuba colonial: Periódo 1878–1898*. Veracruz: Instituto Veracruzano de Cultura, 1993.

Montes, Jordi Maluquer de. *Nación e inmigración: Los españoles en Cuba*. Oviedo, Spain: Ediciones Jucar, 1992.

Morales Carrión, Arturo. *Puerto Rico: A Political and Cultural History*. New York: W. W. Norton, 1983.

Morales y Morales, Vidal. *Iniciadores y primeros mártires de la revolución cubana*. Havana: Avisador Comercial, 1901.

Morgan, Zachary. "Legislating the Lash: Race and the Conflicting Modernities of Enlistment and Corporal Punishment in the Brazilian Military during the Empire." *Journal of Colonialism and Colonial History* 5.2 (Fall 2004)1–47.

Muriel, Josefina. *Conventos de monjas en la Nueva España*. Guerro, Mexico: Editorial JUS, 1995.

Murray, David. *Odious Commerce: Britain, Spain, and the Abolition of the Cuban Slave Trade*. Cambridge: Cambridge University Press, 1980.

Naranjo Orovio, Consuelo, and Armando García González. *Racismo e inmigración en Cuba en el siglo XIX*. Madrid: Ediciones Doce Calles, S.I., 1996.

Narvaez, Benjamin. "Chinese Coolies in Cuba and Peru: Race, Labor, and Immigration, 1839–1886." PhD. diss. University of Texas at Austin, 2010.

Newman, Richard S. *The Transformation of American Abolitionism: Fighting Slavery in the Early Republic*. Chapel Hill: University of North Carolina Press, 2002.

Nwankwo, Ifeoma Kiddoe. *Black Cosmoplitanism: Racial Consciousness and Transnational Identity in the Nineteenth-Century Americas*. Philadelphia: University of Pennsylvania Press, 2005.

Olwell, Robert. "'Loose, Idle and Disorderly': Slave Women in the Eighteen-Century Charleston Marketplace." In *More than Chattel*, edited by David Barry Gaspar and Darlene Clark Hine, 97–110. Bloomington: Indiana University Press, 1996.

Otero, Solimar. *Afro-Cuban Diasporas in the Atlantic World*. Rochester: University of Rochester Press, 2010.

Ortiz, Teresa. "From Hegemony to Subordination: Midwives in Early Modern Spain." In *The Art of Midwifery: Early Modern Midwives in Europe*, edited by Hilary Marland, 95–114. London: Routledge, 1993.

Ortiz Fernández, Fernando. "Los cabildos afro-cubanos." *Revista Bimestre Cubana* 16 (January-February 1921): 9–15.

———. *Hampa afro-cubana: Los negros esclavos; Estudio sociológico y de derecho público.* Havana: Revista Bimestre Cubana, 1916.

Palmer, Steven. *From Popular Medicine to Medical Populism: Doctors, Healers, and Public Power in Costa Rica, 1800–1940.* Durham: Duke University Press, 2003.

Paquette, Robert L. *Sugar Is Made with Blood: The Conspiracy of La Escalera and the Conflict between Empires over Slavery in Cuba.* Middleton: Wesleyan University Press, 1988.

Parcero Torre, Celia María. *La pérdida de la Habana y las reformas borbónicas en Cuba, 1760–1773.* Spain: Junta de Castilla y León, 1998.

Parsons, James J. "The Migration of Canary Islanders to the Americas: An Unbroken Current since Columbus." *The Americas* 39.4 (April 1983): 447–481.

Pastor, Brigida. "Symbiosis between Slavery and Feminism in Gertrudis Gómez de Avellaneda's "Sab"? *Bulletin of Latin American Research* 16.2 (1997): 187–196.

Peard, Julyan G. *Race, Place, and Medicine: The Idea of the Tropics in Nineteenth-Century Brazilian Medicine.* Durham: Duke University Press, 1999.

Pearson, Edward A., ed. *Designs against Charleston: The Trial Record of the Denmark Vesey Slave Conspiracy of 1822.* Chapel Hill: University of North Carolina Press, 1999.

Pérez, Jr., Louis A. *Cuba: Between Reform and Revolution.* New York: Oxford University Press, 1995.

Pérez de la Riva, Juan. *Los culíes chinos en Cuba (1847–1880).* Havana: Editorial de Ciencias Sociales, 2000.

———. *Documentos para la historia de las gentes sin historia.* Havana: Biblioteca Nacional, 1969.

———. "Documentos para la historia de las gentes sin historia: el tráfico de culíes chinos." *Revista de la Biblioteca Nacional, Havana* 6 (April-June 1964): 85–90.

———. *La Isla de Cuba en el siglo xix vista por los extranjeros.* Havana: Editorial de Ciencias Sociales, 1981.

Pérez Murillo, María Dolores. *Aspectos demográficos y sociales de la isla de Cuba en la primera mitad del siglo xix.* Cádiz: Servicio de Publicaciones Universidad de Cádiz, 1988.

Phillips, Christopher. *Freedom's Port: The African American Community of Baltimore, 1790–1860.* Urbana: University of Illinois Press, 1997.

Pike, Ruth. "Penal Servitude in the Spanish Empire: Presidio Labor in the Eighteenth Century." *Hispanic American Historical Review* 58.1 (February 1978): 21–40.

Powers, Jr., Bernard E. *Black Charlestonians: A Social History, 1822–1885.* Fayetteville, Arkansas: University of Arkansas Press, 1994.

Poyo, Gerald E. *With All, and for the Good of All: The Emergence of Popular Nationalism in the Cuban Communities of the United States, 1848–1898*. Durham: Duke University Press, 1989.

Prados-Torreira, Teresa. *Mambisas: Rebel Women in Nineteenth-Century Cuba*. Gainesville: University Press of Florida, 2005.

Putney, Martha S., *Black Sailors: Afro-American Seamen and Whalemen prior to the Civil War*. Westport, Conn.: Greenwood, 1987.

Ramsey, Matthew. *Professional and Popular Medicine in France, 1770–1830: The Social World of Medical Practice*. Cambridge: Cambridge University Press, 1988.

Reed, Nelson. *The Caste War of Yucatán: Revised Edition*. Stanford: Stanford University Press, 2002.

Reid, Michele. "Yoruba in Cuba: Origins, Identities, and Transformations." In *The Yoruba Diaspora in the Atlantic World*, edited by Toyin Falola and Matt Childs, 111–129. Bloomington: Indiana University Press, 2005.

Reid-Vazquez, Michele. "Tensions of Race, Gender and Midwifery in Colonial Cuba." In *Africans to Colonial Spanish America*, edited by Sherwin Bryant, Rachel O'Toole, and Ben Vinson III. Chicago: University of Illinois Press, forthcoming 2012.

Reis, João José. *Slave Rebellion in Brazil: The Muslim Uprising of 1835 in Bahia*. Baltimore: Johns Hopkins University Press, 1993.

Restall, Matthew. *The Black Middle: Africans, Maya, and Spaniards in Colonial Yucatán*. Palo Alto: Stanford University Press, 2009.

Rieu-Millán, Marie Laure. *Los diputados americanos en las Cortes de Cádiz: Igualdad o independencia*. Madrid: Consejo superior de Investigaciones Científicas,1990.Rodríguez O, Jaime E. *The Independence of Spanish America*. Cambridge: Cambridge University Press, 1998.

Rodríguez O., James E. *The Independence of Spanish America*. Cambridge: Cambridge University Press, 1998.

Rodríguez Piña, Javier. *Guerra de castas: La venta de indias mayas a Cuba, 1848–1861*. Mexico City: Conseo Nacional Para La Cultura y Las Artes, 1990, 63.

Rucker, Walter C. "I Will Gather All Nations": Resistance, Culture, and Pan-African Collaboration in Denmark Vesey's South Carolina." *Journal of Negro History* (2001): 132–147.

Rugeley, Terry. "Preface: The Caste War." *The Americas* 53.4 (April 1997): vi–xiii.

———. "Rural Political Violence and the Origins of the Caste War." *The Americas* 53.4 (April 1997): 469–496.

Rugemer, Edward Bartlett. *The Problem of Emancipation: The Caribbean Roots of the American Civil War*. Baton Rouge: Louisiana State University Press, 2008.

Russell-Wood, A.J. R. "Colonial Brazil." In *Neither Slave nor Free: The Freedman of African Descent in the Slave Societies of the New World*, edited by David W. Cohen and Jack P. Greene, 84–133. Baltimore: Johns Hopkins University Press, 1972.

Sagás, Ernesto, and Orlando Inoa, eds. *The Dominican People: A Documentary History*. Princeton, N.J.: Markus Wiener, 2003.

Sarracino, Rodolfo. "Inglaterra y las rebeliones esclavas cubanas: 1841–1851." *Revista de la Biblioteca* Nacional José Martí 28 (May-August 1986): 37–83.

Sartorius, David. My Vassals: Free-Colored Militias in Cuba and the Ends of Spanish Empire." *Journal of Colonialism and Colonial History* 5.2 (2004): 1–25.

Schmidt-Nowara, Christopher. *Empire and Antislavery: Spain, Cuba, and Puerto Rico, 1833–1874*. Pittsburgh: University of Pittsburgh Press, 1999.

Scott, Julius S. "The Common Wind: Currents of Afro-American Communication in the Era of the Haitian Revolution." Ph.D. diss., Duke University, 1986.

Scott, Rebecca J. *Degrees of Freedom: Louisiana and Cuba after Slavery*. Cambridge: Belknap Press of Harvard University Press, 2005.

———. *Slave Emancipation in Cuba: The Transition to Free Labor, 1860–1899*. Princeton: Princeton University Press, 1985.

Scott, Rebecca J., and J. M. Hébrard. "Les papiers de la liberté: Une mère africaine et ses enfants à l'époque de la révolution haïtienne." *Genèses* 66 (2007): 4–29.

Sidbury, James. *Ploughshares into Swords: Race, Rebellion, and Identity in Gabriel's Virginia, 1730–1810*. Cambridge: Cambridge University Press, 1997.

Sio, Arnold. "Marginality and Free Coloured Identity in Caribbean Slave Society." In *Caribbean Slave Society and Economy*, edited by Hilary Beckles and Verene Shepherd, 140–159. Kingston, Jamaica: Ian Randle, 1991.

Socolow, Susan M. "Economic Roles of the Free Women of Color of Cap Français" in *More than Chattel*, edited by David Barry Gaspar and Darlene Clark Hine, 279–297. Bloomington: Indiana University Press, 1996.

Soeiro, Susan. "The Social Composition of the Colonial Nunnery: A Case Study of the Convent of Santa Clara do Desterro Salvador, Bahia, 1677–1800." Occasional Papers, No. 6. New York: New York University, 1973.

Sterns, Peter N. *1848: The Revolutionary Tide in Europe*. New York: W. W. Norton, 1974.

Stewart, Watt. *Chinese Bondage in Peru: A History of the Chinese Coolie in Peru, 1849–174*. Durham: Duke University Press, 1951.

Stinchcombe, Arthur. *Sugar Island Slavery in the Age of Enlightenment: The Political Economy of the Caribbean World*. Princeton: Princeton University Press, 1995.

Sweet, James. "Manumission in Rio de Janeiro, 1749–54: An African Perspective." *Slavery and Abolition* 24.1 (April 2003): 54–70.

Thomas, Hugh. *Cuba: The Pursuit of Freedom*. New York: Harper & Row, 1971.

Thornton, John. *Africa and the Africans in the Making of the Atlantic World, 1400–1800*. Cambridge: Cambridge University Press, 1998.

Thrasher, Albert. *On to New Orleans!: Louisiana's Heroic 1811 Slave Revolt. A*

Brief History and Documents Relating to the Rising of Slaves in January 1811 in the Territory of New Orleans. New Orleans: Cypress Press, 1995.

Tierno Galván, Enrique. *Actas de las Cortes de Cadiz.* 2 vols. Madrid: Taurus, 1964.

Tomich, Dale. "The Wealth of Empire: Francisco Arango y Parreño, Political Economy, and the Second Slavery in Cuba." *Comparative Studies in Society and History* 45.1 (January 2003): 4–28.

Torres-Cuevas, Eduardo, Jorge Ibarra Cuesta, and Mercedes García Rodríguez, eds. *Félix Varela: El que nos enseñó primero en pensar.* Havana: Imagen Contemporánea, 1997.

Twinam, Ann. *Public Lives, Private Secrets: Gender, Honor, Sexuality, and Illegitimacy in Colonial Spanish America.* Stanford: Stanford University Press, 1999.

Valle, A. del. *Historical Document from the Conspiracy of the Grand Legion of Aguila Negra.* Havana, 1930.Villaverde, Cirilo. *Cecilia Valdés.* 2 vols. Havana: Editorial Letras Cubanas, 1981.

Vinson III, Ben. *Bearing Arms for His Majesty: The Free-Colored Militia in Colonial Mexico.* Stanford: Stanford University Press, 2001.

———. "Free-Colored Voices: Issues of Representation and Racial Identity in the Colonial Mexican Militia." *Journal of Negro History* 80.4 (Fall 1995): 170–182.

———. "Race and Badge: Free-Colored Soldiers in the Colonial Mexican Militia." *The Americas* 56.2 (April 2000): 471–496.

Vinson III, Ben, and Matthew Restall. "Black Soldiers, Native Soldiers: Meanings and Military Service in the Spanish American Colonies." In *Beyond Black and Red: African-Native Relations in Colonial Latin America*, edited by Matthew Restall, 15–52. Albuquerque: University of New Mexico Press, 2005.

Voelz, Peter. *Slave and Soldier: The Military Impact of Blacks in the Colonial Americas.* New York: Garland, 1993.

Walker, Daniel E. *No More, No More: Slavery and Cultural Resistance in Havana and New Orleans.* Minneapolis: University of Minnesota Press, 2004.

Whitten, David O. *Andrew Durnford: A Black Sugar Planter in Antebellum Louisiana.* Natchitoches, La.: Northwestern State University Press, 1981.

Whitaker, Arthur P. "Antonio de Ulloa." *Hispanic American Historical Review* 15.2 (May 1935): 155–194.

Wood, James A. "The Burden of Citizenship: Artisans, Elections, and the Fuero Militar in Santiago de Chile, 1822–1851." *The Americas* 58.3 (January 2002): 443–469.

Woodman, Harold D. "Comment." In *Race and Slavery in the Western Hemisphere: Quantitative Studies*, edited by Stanley L. Engerman and Eugene D. Genovese, 451–454. Princeton: Princeton University Press, 1975.

Woodward, Rachel. "It's a Man's Life!': Soldiers, Masculinity and the Countryside." *Gender, Place and Culture* 5.3 (1 November 1998): 277–300.

Wright, Winthrop R. *Café con leche: Race, Class, and National Image in Venezuela.* Austin: University of Texas Press, 1990.

Ximeno, Dolores María de. "Aquellos tiempos, Memorias de Lola María." *Revista Bimestre Cubana* 24 (November-December 1929): 97–131.

Ximeno, José Manuel de. "Un pobre histrión (Plácido)." In *Primer Congreso Nacional de Historia*, 371-377. 2 vols. Havana: Sección de artes gráficas, C.S.T. del Institúto cívico militar, 1943.

Yun, Lisa. *The Coolie Speaks: Chinese Indentured Laborers and African Slaves of Cuba.* Philadelphia: Temple University Press, 2008.

Index

Early American Places

On Slavery's Border: Missouri's Small Slaveholding Households, 1815–1865
by Diane Mutti Burke

Sounds America: National Identity and the Music Culture of the Lower Mississippi River Valley, 1800–1860
by Ann Ostendorf

The Year of the Lash: Free People of Color in Cuba and the Nineteenth-Century Atlantic World
by Michele Reid-Vazquez